AF605982

The Social Construction of Russia's Resurgence

The Social Construction of Russia's Resurgence

Aspirations, Identity, and Security Interests

ANNE L. CLUNAN

The Johns Hopkins University Press

Baltimore

Printed in the United States of America on acid-free paper
9 8 7 6 5 4 3 2 1

The Johns Hopkins University Press
2715 North Charles Street
Baltimore, Maryland 21218-4363
www.press.jhu.edu

Library of Congress Cataloging-in-Publication Data
Clunan, Anne L., 1968–
The social construction of Russia's resurgence : aspirations, identity, and security interests / Anne L. Clunan.
p. cm.
Includes bibliographical references and index.
ISBN 978-0-8018-9157-1 (hardcover : alk. paper)
1. Russia (Federation)—Foreign relations. 2. National security—Russia (Federation) I. Title.
JZ1616.C58 2009
355′.033047—dc22 2008033833

A catalog record for this book is available from the British Library.

Special discounts are available for bulk purchases of this book. For more information, please contact Special Sales at 410-516-6936 or specialsales@press.jhu.edu.

The Johns Hopkins University Press uses environmentally friendly book materials, including recycled text paper that is composed of at least 30 percent post-consumer waste, whenever possible. All of our book papers are acid-free, and our jackets and covers are printed on paper with recycled content.

For

my parents, Dorothy and Jim,

for the windows you've flung wide

so that I might sail through them and explore the world,

and

for Ernie,

for the aspirations you always cherished for me

Contents

Figures and Tables

Figures

Tables

Acknowledgments

The inspiration for this book came from my first exposure to foreign policy makers twenty years ago—begun while I was working at the Soviet desk of the U.S. Department of State during my undergraduate years, and afterwards in my work in the former Soviet Union and the newly post-communist countries of the former Soviet bloc. It was clear to me then that the dominant theoretical argument that I studied in university—that material power drove how countries behaved with each other—did not match up with what I witnessed among practitioners. It seemed, in contrast, that the government and political officials with whom I interacted were moved by forces other than material power and that ideas and identity had much to do with how they defined what their country was about and what it should do.

As it turned out, this question—of what shapes a country's national interests and its behavior—was sparking what would become a major debate in the field of international relations theory and would lead to the development of a new theoretical approach, that of constructivism. This book began as a continuation of that debate, with the modest intention of challenging the dominant explanations of what motivates states and of improving on some prominent constructivist work on the subject.

That initial effort subsequently morphed into a more ambitious investigation of the interactions linking international relations theory, identity, and social psychology. This book is the result. It investigates the role of human aspirations and human reason in shaping how policymakers perceive, interpret, and construct the world around them. It combines insights from international relations and social identity theories to help us understand how Russian elites, relying on collective historical aspirations, define Russia's proper place in the twenty-first century.

The present book owes a great deal to my conversations with Jeffrey Knopf, who has been an unfailing friend and colleague, the person who showed me that I was onto a study of aspirations and their effect on identity and national interests. He went above and beyond the call of duty and friendship in commenting on more iterations of the entire manuscript than he cares to remember. Many of the improvements are owed to him, while all faults remain my responsibility.

I would like to thank my family and my friends, particularly my parents, who have provided the support, labor, and love that have seen me through this project. A special thanks goes to Kari Johnstone for her unflagging help in reading and commenting on the dissertation and to Rosemarie Purcell and Izumi Wakugawa for their research assistance and friendship. Thanks also to Cecelia Lynch, Beth Kier, and Wayne Sandholtz for their comments on various versions of the manuscript. My love to Alan, who lifted me up in the final stages of the project and helped bring it—and me—home.

Most of all, I would like to thank Ernie Haas. Not only did he introduce me to the realm of international relations theory, he also opened up new ways of thinking about the world to me. His guidance, patience, friendship, outstanding pedagogy, and occasional none-too-gentle prodding allowed me to explore new worlds—and to develop the mark I would like to leave on this one. I owe him a debt of gratitude that cannot be repaid. His intellectual mentorship is sorely missed, by me and by all those who knew him.

Note on Transliteration of Russian

In general I have adhered to the Library of Congress standard for the transliteration of Russian. In some cases I have deviated from this standard. As a rule, when the surname begins with a soft vowel (я, ю, E), I have used *Ya, Yu, Ye*. In the case of some well-known politicians, I have used the spelling of the name that is commonly used in the Western media. So, for example, I have used *Yeltsin* instead of *El'tsin*. In cases where a Russian has published in a West European language, I have used the publication's spelling of his or her name when citing that particular work (e.g., Baranovsky) but have retained the standard transliteration (Baranovskii) when referring to the author in the text.

The Social Construction of Russia's Resurgence

ONE

Introduction

Identity and Interests in World Politics

What do states want? It is a truism of international politics that national interests—what states want—drive foreign policy. But how are national interests formed? How do they develop, change, reproduce, or decline over time? How stable are they? This book addresses these questions with reference to post-Soviet Russia. Russian foreign policy after the collapse of the Soviet Union in 1991 is an especially useful and important case for studying the formation of national identity and national interests. This may be as close to a natural experiment as history ever offers.

The Russian state that emerged was both old and new. It was newly sovereign and thus had to define from scratch *Russian* as opposed to *Soviet* national interests and a Russian role in the post–Cold War world. However, Russia had been the center of both the tsarist and Soviet empires, and memories of past national greatness would hardly disappear just because the Soviet Union no longer existed. Russian politicians faced a difficult choice: hold on to past international grandeur and historical aspirations or let them go. This set the stage for a potentially stark contest over national identity. Would Russia dedicate itself to regaining past glory and revert to viewing the West as its enemy? Or would Russia embrace a vision of itself as a blank slate and allow present-day realities—reduced economic and military power, the effects of globalization, the spread of democracy in the former Soviet bloc—to lead it to adopt a different view of its role and interests?

The definition of Russia's national interests and the process of constructing its identity mattered, for the outcome would have great consequences for world politics. Would efforts to construct Russia's resurgence create a more or less secure and stable world? When political elites aspire to maintain or regain a country's past greatness, it is likely to produce national interests with a stake in challenging other countries for international status. A revanchist definition of Russia's identity and interests would likely lead to a new Cold War and revive nuclear dangers, given that Russia retained a large nuclear arsenal. Conversely, a decision to cooperate closely with other states and accept existing norms of Western-dominated international society could make Russia an important contributor to the management of global problems ranging from terrorism to the supply of energy to the prevention of nuclear proliferation. The choice between the two extremes—a decision by Russia to pursue "soft balancing" against the United States or a move to become a status quo or revisionist power—would also have important real-world consequences, particularly for the countries on Russia's periphery.[1]

Russian political elites have debated these questions intensely since Russia became an independent republic. However, the outcome of these debates could not have been easily predicted and was hardly predetermined.[2] There have been major swings in Russia's relationship with the West under both its post-Soviet leaders, presidents Boris Yeltsin and Vladimir Putin. Western policymakers and scholars have had a difficult time understanding and predicting whether or not Russia will be friendly and cooperative.[3] Russia is powerful enough that its choices affect how conflict-ridden or cooperative the global security environment will be, as its 2008 war with Georgia demonstrated, so understanding the sources of its national interests is important for both Western and Russian policymakers.

In post-Soviet Russia, the parallel processes of forming a national identity and developing security interests have involved a domestic debate about two central questions: What is Russia? and What does Russia do? Both questions entail a comparison of what Russia *was* and *did* in the past. The first question involves asking whether or not the geographic, political, and cultural boundaries of Russia are those of the Soviet Union and, if not, what they should be. The second involves asking what the domestic and international roles of the Russian state are. Is Russia a protector of all Slavic peoples? Are non-Slavs equal members of the Russian body politic? Is Russia a melting pot of European and Asian cultures whose role is to mediate cultural conflict between these two global regions? Is Russia a geographical giant that must act independently on the global stage, or is it a democratic European country that should seek entry into Western political and economic organizations?

These questions make clear that the definition of the national interests of any state, not just Russia, is bound up with the formation of its national identity. Getting at the root of a state's national interests means unearthing what its elites identify as the country's political purpose and international status. That identification is itself shaped by the legitimacy of the past. It is this identification that turns ideas and objects into national interests, which in turn define a state's foreign policy orientations. By examining Russia's elite debates about Russia's post-Soviet development, we can deepen our understanding of how Russians define their state's national identity and interests and identify where they see potential or actual threats to them.

This book offers a new approach—"aspirational constructivism"—that addresses these questions. Aspirational constructivism is rooted within the constructivist tradition of international relations scholarship, and it develops the core constructivist insight that social institutions, including national identities, arise out of the ongoing interaction of both societal structures and human agents. In line with the constructivist emphasis on how collectively held ideas create social structures and shape people's interests, this book focuses on how collectively held ideas, in this case national identities, create national interests.

Aspirational constructivism is different from other constructivist scholarship, however, in that it incorporates important insights from social psychology, particularly the work of social identity theorists, to provide microfoundations for the establishment of collective identities such as national identity. While theorists have long drawn on cognitive psychology in the study of world politics, aspirational constructivism introduces to international relations theory a body of social psychological work that has not yet been explored by international relations theorists.[4] At the root of social identity theory is the need for positive distinctiveness—self-esteem—and the psychological motivations it creates for people to create social groups and collective or "we" identities. People often establish this sense of positive distinctiveness with reference to their own history and experiences and use it to create aspirations regarding their future. These aspirations play a central role in shaping which historical legacies are incorporated into national identities and national interests and which are discarded. The purpose of this book is to develop this new aspirational constructivist approach, using the case of post-Soviet Russia to illustrate its empirical applicability.

Alternative Explanations of Identity and Interests

The questions of how national interests are formed and change became the subject of an important and wide-ranging debate in the field of international relations in the 1990s. The debate took place primarily between social constructivists and rationalists.

Many rationalist scholars in the realist tradition tend to treat such questions as unproblematic and do not make them the focus of their empirical research programs. For rationalists, the primary logic driving political choices and behavior is the consequences of action in a particular situation.[5] They assume that states all have a stable set of core tasks that amount to the national interest. These usually include providing for national security by accumulating power and wealth. Prevailing conditions—usually material factors such as geography, the military balance, or levels of economic interdependence—dictate whether states will have a national interest in pursuing power and wealth through cooperation or conflict.

In this rationalist vein, realist accounts of national interests and foreign policy suggest that the ideas and preferences entailed in national identities are governed by the material constraints elites face in a given situation. Changes in the material situation—the distribution of available military and economic resources—should produce corresponding changes in the definitions of the national interest. According to one such account of Soviet foreign policy, "ideas and preferences allegedly changed in tandem with elite perceptions of material constraints."[6] In defensive realist accounts, such changes should occur according to a rationalist learning through weakness—Soviet, or Russian, foreign policy becomes more accommodationist as the country weakens.[7] Such explanations are problematic, as Soviet foreign policy went far beyond a rational response to weakness in offering the revolutionary and highly cooperative agenda of New Thinking; moreover, Russian foreign policy moved away from accommodation and hardened throughout the 1990s even as Russia continued to weaken economically and militarily.[8] This hardening began in

1993, much earlier than the global rise in oil prices beginning in 1999 that strengthened Russia's economic standing.

Other realist explanations predicting a more offensive posture suggest that when the international distribution of power is changing—as occurred with the collapse of the Soviet Union in 1991 and the relative increase in U.S. power thereafter—wars are most likely to break out among great powers. It is in periods when material or political power recedes that state leaders are most likely to view preventive aggression as necessary to safeguard their national security.[9] These theories would expect Russian policy elites rationally to develop national interests in aggression against neighboring states and in preparation for war with the United States as a last-ditch effort to shore up the sources of their physical security and political influence. Such revanchist predictions were in fact made as the Cold War was coming to a close.[10]

Yet the historical record suggests that Russia reacted in ways contrary to these predictions and indeed, unilaterally ceded power and influence over the former Soviet satellites and republics during the course of the late 1980s and early 1990s. And while Russia hardened its foreign policy in the 1990s, it did not do so in accordance with offensive realist expectations. Rather than lashing out in an effort to hold on to power and security, Russia peacefully ceded influence and control over its outer and inner empires—far more retrenchment than was necessary. The peaceful end to the Cold War has been one of the hardest events for realists to explain.

These rationalist approaches rely on a situational stimulus-response model of national interests, with the stimulus arising from the distribution of material power. They lack a nuanced explanation of what, aside from military capabilities and offensive intentions, produces perceptions of threat. They assume that the national interest amounts to national security and survival and that the response to threats to national security will take the form of increases in military capabilities, new military alliances, or even preventive war. In rationalist accounts, national interests are derived from the material situation in which states find themselves. Explanations are situational and "presentist."

Constructivists, in contrast, believe that interests are more ambiguous and problematic. They argue that definitions of the national interest are shaped not only by material factors but also by identity, norms, and other social and cultural factors. In some accounts, existing social identities generate social structures that govern what choices and actions are appropriate in given circumstances.[11] In others, social norms shape what actions are deemed possible, given the potential consequences of social ostracism or social mobility.[12] Actors react to the current distribution of identities, norms, and practices in the international community. In other constructivist accounts, existing social norms determine what kinds of arguments can be made and which claims will be persuasive. In this account, actors react to the best arguments being conveyed, given the standards of judgment prevailing at the present time.[13] Ironically, similar to rationalist approaches, these constructivist accounts all tend to focus on present situations. They also offer situational explanations, where the prevailing set of ideational conditions shapes the outcome, whether that outcome is an actor's behavior or interests.

Despite the efforts of some scholars, the most prominent constructivist work on identity—that of Alexander Wendt—has focused on international structural factors, ignoring the role that internal forces play in shaping a state's identity, including but not restricted to historical aspirations and domestic politics.[14] Structural constructivist approaches that focus on the international system as the source of national interests tend to treat the state itself as a blank slate with no meaningful preexisting identity or historical past.[15] Wendt adopts Sheldon Stryker's structural reinterpretation of the symbolic interactionist theory proposed by George Herbert Mead in 1934, which argues that reflected appraisals—the views and behaviors of important others—are the key source of the self's identity.[16] Identity is the product of how an other views the self, with the self taking on the identity of itself projected by the other. Identity in this view rests on an other-image rather than a self-image; national identity is based on how a state is identified by another state or, in accounts such as Finnemore's, on its conformity with prevailing international norms, not on how a state views itself in the context of its own historical experience.[17] Such accounts take no account of the *content* of the self, which has been the focus of much social psychological research since George Herbert Mead wrote in 1934 on social identity.

Other situational constructivist accounts, such as Ted Hopf's, that draw on cognitive psychology argue that identities are social cognitive structures. As a result, they also give a highly structural account of how identity shapes behavior. Such accounts leave no room for agency and identity choice; they contain no account of how particular identities come to dominate at different points in time and how they change. Yet empirical evidence indicates that identity choice occurs frequently and that identities do change.[18] While Hopf's richly detailed study of Russian popular identity attends to the role of history and thus goes well beyond Wendt's approach, it still offers limited insight into whether and how identities develop and change.[19] Hopf deliberately adopts a radically inductive approach based on the study of two single years to arrive at Russian national identity for each year. He concedes that he is not able to apply his approach to other places and points in time, making his approach highly situation-dependent. More fundamentally, his focus on social cognitive structures tends toward the deterministic position found in some psychological approaches that such cognitive structures, including schema, analogies, and scripts, determine how individuals process information, arrive at their interests, and behave.[20] Once such structures are in place, in this view, there is no expectation that individuals can change them and no explanation of how such change comes about; indeed, according to Hopf, human behavior in the presence of such structures becomes the "unthinking, unintentional, automatic, everyday reproduction of the Self and Other."[21]

At the other end of structural approaches to national interests from such "presentist," situational approaches are essentialist works on strategic culture and national identity that locate identities and interests purely in culture or shared history. In these works, identities and interests are completely reduced to a country's history, and their origins are lost in the mists of time. Rather than explanation based on the present situation, here explanation is solely based on "objective" and "primordial" historical ties such as geography, culture, language, and ethnicity that lead directly to fixed identities. Approaches such as those of Samuel Huntington, Colin Gray, and Richard Pipes assume that shared historical ties create a fixed national identity and set of interests that is embraced by all of a state's elites.[22] These studies overlook the possibility of international influences or changing identities and entirely eliminate politics and agency from the study of identity.

Aspirational constructivism eschews the determinism and primordialism of such approaches. National identities are neither simply the result of historical traditions and customs nor the emotional power of "ancient" group ties.[23] Instead they are subject to change by political elites, who use reason, not just historical aspirations, to define national identities and national interests. Aspirational constructivism thus lies between approaches that base their explanations entirely on the present situation and those that rely entirely on the past. It takes history, in the form of historical memory, as a serious force shaping the aspirations of political elites. But it also takes into account human agency and the present situation that political elites face to explain how the combination of political elite perceptions of the past and present shape current national identity and national interests. In aspirational constructivism, identity formation is a *process* shaped by past and present and by human reason—it is not fixed for all time, and it can be reduced monocausally neither to historical traditions and culture nor to present conditions.

Aspirational Constructivism: The Roles of History and Reason in Identity Formation

Although the philosophical underpinnings of this book fall within constructivism, it takes issue with this previous constructivist work and offers instead a new aspirational constructivist approach to studying the way national interests take shape. The first wave of constructivist research established convincingly that social and cultural context matters, making it no longer necessary to argue for the usefulness of a constructivist approach in opposition to rationalist alternatives. With this acceptance, it is now time to move ahead and work out some of the details and problems of constructivist theory. In particular, constructivists need to develop a better understanding of how a state's identity forms, how identity is related to its national interests, and how all this can complement rationalist theories.[24]

The aspirational constructivist approach developed here supports the constructivist proposition that a country's interests are shaped by its prevailing national identity.[25] However, this book takes issue with the situational nature of prominent structural constructivist explanations, particularly Alexander Wendt's strong structural constructivism.[26] Aspirational constructivism draws on recent work in social psychology—work new to international relations theory—to offer a synthesis that underscores the role of historical aspirations and human reason in constructivist explanations of identity and interests.[27] It focuses on the *sources* of competing national identities and interests and the *mechanisms* through which political actors select among them. In doing so, this book incorporates history and human reason into a theory of identity selection and provides a framework for assessing the impact of history and reason across cases and time. It attempts to generate a truly constructivist theory of national identity and interests, one that incorporates the interaction of historical ideational structures and reasoning human agents. It does so by focusing on the question of why and how, in the presence of multiple possible national identities, only some become epistemically powerful enough to act as a dominant national identity and thereby define a country's national interest.

In the pages to come, I use aspirational constructivism to address three questions: What are the sources of Russian national identity? Why do multiple identities come into contention? Why does one come to dominate and act as Russia's national identity and define its interests? The first question requires considering both the motivations Russians (and all humans) have for constructing social identities and the content of those identities. Here, social identity theory's concern for self-esteem is brought to bear on motivation, while constructivism's attention to value rationality and ideas is used to address the question of content. When answering why Russian policy elites introduced multiple candidate identities into the political discourse, the analysis focuses on how Russian policy elites were motivated to employ "identity management strategies" in the form of candidate national identities as the Soviet Union unraveled. In addressing why Russian political elites settled on one of them as the dominant identity, the theory outlines a correspondence process of legitimacy-testing—incorporating aspirations and history and efficacy tests—that explains which national self-image, of the multiple candidate identities on offer to post-Soviet Russian policy elites, was "selected" as the dominant identity.

Aspirational constructivism suggests that a logic of aspiration plays a central role in the creation of national identities and national interests.[28] Underlying aspirations is the human need for self-esteem. Collective self-esteem is affected by internally generated conceptions of the collective self, by its own behavior and by the conditions and actors the collective self faces in the external environment. In order to maintain or enhance self-esteem, people seek to change themselves or the world around them.[29] Aspirations derive from the need to maintain positive self-esteem or improve negative self-esteem. In reference to national identities, political elites seek to enhance or maintain collective self-esteem. Political elite historical memories of what the state's purpose and status were in the past affect collective self-esteem and generate aspirations for its present and future.

These historical aspirations shape whether a candidate national identity—what is referred to throughout this book as a *national self-image*—is perceived as legitimate and whether that candidate will come to define a state's interest in security affairs. National self-images consist of two pillars: beliefs about a state's appropriate system of governance and mission—what is referred to here as its *political purpose*—and ideas about a state's *international status*—its international rank, rights, and obligations. Such ideas entail historical judgments about the state's prior domestic and international experiences.

The Argument

The aspirational constructivist argument put forward here can be summarized in the following fashion. Members of the political elite develop aspirations based on common historical memories. Motivated by value rationality and the need for collective self-esteem, they introduce competing national self-images into the political discourse. National self-images are sets of ideas about the country's political purpose and international status. These self-images deploy an identity management strategy—choosing from among mobility, creativity, and competition—to enhance national self-esteem.[30] Members of the political elite propagate national self-images in an effort to define "the" national identity and interest.

Domestic political elites then argue publicly about the practicality and historical legitimacy of the purpose and status portrayed in contending national self-images. This selection process consists of correspondence tests of legitimacy: a process of history- and efficacy-testing in which political elites vet self-images for their correspondence to aspirations and circumstances. To test a national self-image for historical "fitness" or "correctness," political elites assess it in light of historical aspirations—dominant memories of the high and low points in their country's past. Political elites also use their reason to evaluate whether national self-images, in addition to being historically appropriate, are "realistic," that is, effective or *practical* guides for the state, given the prevailing international and domestic conditions the country faces and its historical aspirations. Perceptions of external factors, such as the behavior of other states or international crises, and the perceived success or failure of persons and policies associated with particular national self-images affect whether political elites will view a particular national self-image as a practical guide for the state's interests and as conforming to their historical aspirations.

As the state accrues more of a past as time passes, that history becomes the source of new aspirations and new interpretations of previous events. The self-image (and its attendant identity management strategy) that best corresponds with historical aspirations and practicality should come to dominate how political elites define the national interest. If historical aspirations and the practicality of a national self-image conflict with each other, the national interests the self-image espouses are likely to be moderated to make them more practicable. However, aspirational constructivism expects historical aspirations to weigh more in the development of identity and interests if history tests and efficacy tests produce conflicting results. Social psychologists expect that lack of conformity between the self's "identity prototype" and objective conditions to produce behaviors either to change those conditions or to change the self in order to bring self back into conformity with the identity prototype.[31]

The core assumptions of this book are that national identities reflect aspirations that, when fulfilled, enhance national self-esteem. Additionally, these aspirations stem from comparison with the historical self, and with others. These assumptions in turn generate several key expectations regarding how identities and interests form. Aspirations motivate elites to develop new bases for national self-esteem through the invention of national self-images and to pursue identity management strategies (discussed in chapters 2 and 4) in order to fulfill them. Whether the national self-images and the identity management strategies they entail come to represent the dominant "national interest" depends on whether they pass two correspondence tests of legitimacy—a history test and an efficacy test. Historical memories of past international grandeur, victimization, or failure matter most in shaping aspirations and, consequently, in determining domestic actors' convergence around a national self-image and its attendant national interest. For example, Larson and Shevchenko highlight how in an effort to enhance Soviet self-esteem, Gorbachev offered a radical new identity for the USSR in which it would lead a new moral international political order, one that would ensure the Soviet Union's long-held aspiration to great power status. Such an identity led to a sharp shift from a national interest premised on the inevitability of East-West conflict to one of cooperation in order to combat global scourges.[32] These arguments are more fully developed in the next chapter.

Historical Aspirations and Identity Formation

This book begins with the premise, drawn from social psychology, that identity is largely a product of people's efforts to enhance their self-esteem and their understanding of themselves and the world—the self and self-in-context, in social psychology terms.[33] This book also draws from prospect theory the insight that humans base their behavior on their aspirations. A core source of conceptions of the collective self is historical memory. Commonly held memories of the past self generate aspirations for what the self should (and should not) be and do in the future. Such aspirations are most likely to be apparent when states are undergoing major political, social, or economic transformations, though they are present even in normal times. Kahneman and Tversky, in developing prospect theory, demonstrated that people are more strongly motivated by aspirations to regain what they had in the past and subsequently lost rather than by aspirations to acquire what they have never possessed.[34]

In their efforts to enhance national self-esteem, political elites compete over what is desirable and usable in their country's *history,* a force whose impact has been underappreciated in the leading structural constructivist account of identity.[35] This is not to suggest that other constructivists have not considered historical memories and traditions; indeed, a rich body of work has done so.[36] However, this work has not theorized about the role that such historical memories may play more generally in the development and selection of national identities. Aspirational constructivism develops such a theory, drawing on insights from social psychology new to international relations theorists to investigate how self-esteem and historical memories of a state's past create aspirations for its future. These aspirations serve as a baseline against which national identities and interests are developed. The role of history is considered alongside the role of current situations—the focus of situational constructivist and rationalist accounts—in explaining how national identities are created and how they shape interests.

History does not only serve to generate aspirations based on a state's past. History directly enters into the creation of national interest, influencing how political elites define the situation their state faces in ways the situational approaches outlined above cannot explain. National identities and national interests are therefore historically contingent, as human agents continuously produce and modify them through public debate over their legitimacy. While there may be periods when identities and interests are more coherent and stable than others, even in times of stability and calm, the nation is always reinventing itself.[37]

With its assumption that national identities and other social institutions are always subject to alteration by human beings, this book does not accept the determinism found in some cognitive psychology sources that historical memories *determine* which identities get adopted or what interests are formed. Such work on human cognition suggests that schemas and scripts, such as historical analogies, form cognitive structures that can decisively determine how decisionmakers define their interests in a given situation.[38] In this view, U.S. decisionmakers in 1965 viewed the situation in Vietnam as analogous to the conditions prevailing in Europe prior to World War II. Therefore, the disastrous consequences of the appeasement policy manifested in the 1938 Munich Pact made appeasement in Vietnam an unthinkable policy choice for key decisionmakers, as it would have equally catastrophic results. As a result the United States favored an increased commitment to defeat communist forces rather than withdrawal.

Rather than determining interests and behavior, as such accounts suggest, in aspirational constructivism historical aspirations form a key benchmark that political elites use for vetting national self-images. History provides aspirations and a measure against which human agents judge present-day self-images, but in contrast to deterministic cognitive psychological approaches, historical aspirations do not *determine* what identities get adopted or what interests are formed. Instead, people rely on metacognitive abilities to reflect on whether aspirations, schemas, analogies and the like are right, given their interactions with the world around them and their own experiences.[39]

Reason and Agency in Identity Formation

In addition to taking history and aspirations seriously, this book follows John Gerard Ruggie in accepting that "constructivism is about human consciousness and its role in human life."[40] Political elites compete with one another to have their preferred national self-image become *the* national identity and define the state's interests. In doing so, they are motivated by the desire to enhance national self-esteem, which entails using *value* rationality to uphold or create a legitimate social order that institutionalizes values, norms, beliefs, and procedures that give them a positive self-image of their country.[41] Taking a page from the work of social psychologist Albert Bandura, this book emphasizes that humans are not cybernetic information processing machines governed by cognitive structures. Instead they are agents: "Agency . . . involves not only the deliberative ability to make choices and action plans, but also the ability to construct appropriate courses of action and to motivate and regulate their execution. . . . People are not only agents of action. They are also self-examiners of their own functioning. . . . The metacognitive ability to reflect upon oneself and the adequacy of one's thoughts and actions is the most distinctly human core property of agency."[42] Much structural constructivist scholarship underplays the role of human reason and overemphasizes the role of structural conditions in explaining political outcomes.[43]

In contrast to such accounts, this book assumes that humans use their reason to assess whether competing national identities, and the interests they espouse, are legitimate.[44] To be legitimate, candidate identities must be perceived to be effective and historically appropriate. Political elites are not merely acting out structural or cognitive scripts when they approve of a self-image; they also make reasoned judgments about the practicality and historical appropriateness of such an image in light of current opportunities, constraints, and the behavior of those advocating the image and those others depicted in the image.[45] Actors are able to learn and alter their understanding of reality and their identity by testing the correspondence between what is historically desirable and what is realistic.[46] Humans use their metacognitive ability to evaluate the fit of their aspirations, their experiences, and their environment and to adjust their perceptions of legitimate national identities, attitudes toward others, and behavior accordingly.[47] This process of trying to change the environment and the self as a result of cognition and metacognition is central to much work on identity in social psychology.[48]

The attention here to efficacy-testing—metacognitive assessments of existing conditions and behavior—should be familiar to scholars who emphasize the importance of a state's present situation to explain its identity or interests.[49] These scholars expect political elites to base their interests on the conditions they currently face.[50] Rational elites will engage in simple learning, adapting to the constraints and opportunities imposed by the situation they are in. As scholars who employ situational theories suggest, political elites assess the appropriateness of a national self-image in the light of prevailing international social norms, its consequences, and the types of arguments likely to persuade them.[51] Political elites do indeed engage in such situational learning, but it is not the sole factor shaping what national self-images come to define national interests.

Political elites also employ a logic of aspirations. An important baseline for vetting a self-image is its correspondence with the best or worst parts of the past self that political elites seek to reclaim or reproduce or reject, not merely the appropriateness of the self-image in light of contemporary international norms or its foreseeable consequences given current material conditions. In this view, agency is not limitless: legitimacy is conditioned by historical aspirations, which may derive from a previously dominant identity as well as by perceptions of current conditions. Both aspirations and current conditions influence actors' views regarding the historical legitimacy and the practicality and efficacy—the "realism"—of competing national self-images.[52] One of the results of this project will be a better understanding of the conditions under which such reinvention occurs according to aspirational versus situational logic.

Identity and Interests in Post-Soviet Russia

This book examines the usefulness of aspirational constructivism by applying it to the case of foreign policy in post-Soviet Russia. It focuses on two traditional national security concerns: relations with Europe and nuclear arms control. This book finds that Russia's national interests in European security and strategic arms control have not been defined on the basis of conventional cost-benefit assessments, perceptions of material threat, or the identities projected onto Russia by other countries. Aspirations to regain the international great power status that Russians believe their country enjoyed during the tsarist and Soviet past were critical to the creation of its present national identity and national security interests. Indeed, history and status far outweighed political purpose and practicality in determining Russia's post-Soviet identity. As early as 1993, Russia's elites converged around a status-driven statist national self-image that generated diffuse national interests in social, rather than material, competition for global status, primarily with the United States. Looking through the lens of this national self-image produced a dynamic whereby cooperative actions by the United States were discounted while U.S. moves perceived as efforts to diminish Russia's status were highlighted.

However, human reason, through the procedure of correspondence tests of legitimacy, has played a constraining role in shaping Russia's national security interests. Moderates among the elite used efficacy tests to persuade others of Russia's weakness in an attempt to reduce the competitive orientation of Russia's national identity of global great power. However, they failed to supplant the weight of historical aspirations that solidified Russia's past great power status as the core of Russian national identity and interests. The rise of Vladimir Putin to the presidency did not bring a radical shift in Russia's definition of its national identity or national interests; rather, Putin reflected and entrenched the elite consensus that Russia's identity was that of a global great power and that state strength and modernity are the core methods to attain its interests. Dire predictions of aggressive and risky Russian behavior, whether based on offensive realism or prospect theory, were not fulfilled, suggesting an important role for human reason in limiting the power of history and aspirations in creating national identity and interests.

The core expectations of this book are (1) that the psychological need for national self-esteem and value rationality drive political elites to develop new national self-images and to promote these self-images through identity management strategies; (2) that these national self-images and identity management strategies generate national interests and behavioral orientations regarding ingroups and outgroups identified in the national self-images; and (3) that political elites "select" a national self-image to become the national identity and define national self-interests if that self-image is perceived to correspond to shared historical aspirations and to be capable of effective enactment under current conditions.

While the primary focus of this book is theoretical, the choice of Russia as an empirical focus is significant. The better that other states can understand the forces shaping Russia's self-defined identity and interests, the better that they will be able to forecast the direction Russia's policy is likely to take—and the better that their position will be to influence that policy in a more cooperative direction. The need for such understanding is all the more evident in light of Russia's reassertiveness in the Putin era.

Case Selection: Why Post-Soviet Russia?

This book is an attempt to build a new theory of national identity and interest formation. In theory-building exercises, the emphasis is less on definitive tests of the theory-in-progress than on establishing its logical and empirical plausibility. The empirical study of post-Soviet Russia in the chapters to come therefore represents a "plausibility probe" of aspirational constructivism. Plausibility probes are especially appropriate when building theories as opposed to evaluating established ones.[53] In such cases, Harold Eckstein recommended using plausibility probes as "attempts to determine whether potential validity may reasonably be considered great enough to warrant the pains and costs of testing."[54]

To assess the plausibility of the argument that historical aspirations play a role in shaping national identity and interests and its alternatives, it is also useful to analyze cases of major institutional change or "critical junctures," as these represent as close to an "unstructured" or ahistorical moment as social scientists are likely to encounter.[55] Post-Soviet Russia is such a case, as its rebirth offers one of the rare instances in which a clear "critical juncture" occurred domestically and internationally.

During such moments, prior social and political structures have weakened such that the range and process of political choice, including what the state's identity and national interests are, are at their most open. The collapse of communism in 1989 and the implosion of the Soviet Union in 1991 created a "historical juncture where new cultural complexes make possible new and reorganized strategies of action."[56] It is at such moments that social scientists expect countries to be able to move off of their past trajectories and onto new ones.[57] Domestically, Russia in 1991 faced a situation in which Soviet political, social, and economic institutions were in utter disarray. All institutions, including national identity, were open to question. Borders, internal and external, and identities—who does and does not count as a "Russian"—were thrown into doubt with the collapse of the USSR. Internationally, the structure of the international system was rapidly changing. In terms of the international distribution of power, Russia was a smaller, albeit still huge, country with fewer of the internal resources and external satellites that had made the Soviet Union a superpower. The international social structure—the Cold War system—had collapsed with the demise of Soviet ideology, and international society was no longer divided into two ideological camps. At the end of the Cold War, the opportunity to create a new world order was apparent to all.

In the view of many analysts and policymakers, the end of the Cold War and the Belovezhsky Accords of December 8, 1991, among the Russian, Ukrainian, and Belarussian leadership dissolving the Soviet Union created a "clean slate" for Russian-U.S. relations.[58] Analysts and advisors from the West began pouring into the former communist countries, advocating the wholesale scrapping of political, economic, and social systems throughout the region, on the assumption that these countries were starting from a *tabula rasa*. Many governments in the region, including Russia, accepted this premise. The Russian government had to create and to staff a foreign ministry from scratch. The ideological, social, political, economic, and foreign affairs institutions of the old Soviet Union were all in question. For the first time in seventy years, the United States faced a different actor in Moscow, and 1991 therefore represents as close to a critical juncture in Russia's foreign relations as history is likely to grant social scientists.

During an international critical juncture such as the end of the Cold War, Wendt's "culture of anarchy" is fluid. History and past identities are least likely to matter.[59] Old patterns of interaction and old appraisals have been thrown into question. States, including former enemies, should have the fewest predispositions to behave in any particular fashion. With the implosion of the Soviet Union, the Hobbesian culture of anarchy typical of the Cold War no longer reigned. Russia and the United States were not structurally bound to start off their interactions in a hostile manner.

Indeed, Russia's initial post–Cold War behavior toward the West was quite friendly. Old Cold War institutions and structures were less likely to steer Russia's appraisal of foreign states, and new identities were more likely to develop from "scratch." This extraordinary period allows analysts to attempt to evaluate Wendt's thesis about the importance of first contact in establishing a state's identity.[60] While almost no point in constructivist analysis allows for truly "first contact" (Wendt's hypothetical meeting between Earth people and aliens aside), the establishment of new states and their interaction with outsiders is the best historical approximation we can hope to find.

For realism, critical junctures are periods of change that alter the distribution of power. A critical juncture such as the end of the Cold War is a crucial test of the realist logic of consequences. The dire consequences of the sudden shift in the distribution of power away from Russia and therefore Russia's interests in holding on to that power through conflict (in offensive realist views) or through retreat and accommodation (in defensive realist views) are clearest at such times of dramatic change.

The post–Cold War period also provides an important case for aspirational constructivism and its emphasis on history. The literature on critical junctures expects preexisting social institutions, including identities, to matter least at such moments. In this view, at such moments people are most able to cast aside historical legacies and re-forge identities and national self-interest along new lines, as little constrained by the past as possible.[61] In contrast, aspirational constructivism argues that Russia's past self matters to the process of identity at all times, but *especially* in times of change. Such moments therefore are important to study, if we hope to determine the effect of historical aspirations on agents who are trying to create a new national interest.

During such periods, deciding whether to discard or salvage the past is at the heart of any political effort to create new institutions. Should historical aspirations and correspondence tests of legitimacy play no or little role in winnowing competing national self-images of the new Russia and shaping the resulting institutionalization of a new Russian national identity, then aspirational constructivism would have little plausibility. Should the case studies suggest otherwise, this would add support to the recent literature in comparative politics that suggests institutional transformation takes on a "layered" or "syncretic" character, with new institutions being grafted onto older institutions or older institutions being modified and extended rather than discarded.[62] If historical aspirations are demonstrated to exert significant influence on the definition of Russia's post-Soviet national identity and to constrain the definition of its interests, this book will have demonstrated the need to incorporate—in a theoretically systematic fashion—temporality, historical memory, and aspirations into our explanations of how states arrive at their national interests. This book therefore takes Russia from the 1991 collapse of the Soviet Union to the 2004 reelection of Russia's second president, Vladimir Putin, as its empirical focus.

Conclusion

This book seeks to construct an aspirational constructivist theory that emphasizes the mutual effect of historical structures and human agency on the formation of national identity and interest. It examines the plausibility of such an approach through an application to post-Soviet Russia. To understand Russian interests in and orientations toward the outside world, the domestic identity debates that informed them during the post-Soviet period are the empirical subject of analysis.

This book's primary objective, however, is to develop a more complete aspirational constructivist account of the process through which identities are formed and generate interests. National identities are the product of debates among political elites over what their state's appropriate international status and political purpose are in light of its history, on the one hand, and its external and domestic circumstances, on the other. Human agents play a crucial role in explaining why some national self-images are "selected" to become *the* dominant national identity and define the national interest while others are not. The ultimate choice of national self-image arises both from aspirations derived from of a state's own past and from the practicality of a self-image given the state's present environment and relations with other states. How political elites imagine the present and future against their own past is necessary to understand their historical aspirations and their assessments of what is practical. These aspirations and assessments in turn shape a state's national identity and national interests. In contrast, structural constructivist accounts of identity and interests focus on the present social structures states face and underplay the important role that historical aspirations play in shaping identities and interests.

This book tries to overcome these limitations by incorporating social *and* psychological sources of identity and the roles of history and human reason into an aspirational theory of national identity formation. It emphasizes that identity and interest formation is a *process* to be analyzed rather than a discrete outcome that can be explained by the structures an actor faces.[63] It brings history and reason into constructivist accounts of identity formation. It also provides a constructivist account of the sources and processes through which ideas spread, one that has implications for strategic culture, domestic politics, and ideational diffusion. Finally, it develops a framework that can be used to analyze other cases of national interest formation under a variety of historical conditions.

In doing so, aspirational constructivism moves the scholarly debate on national interests forward in four ways. First, it adds a new, alternative logic—the logic of aspirations—to prevailing explanations that focus on the material or social consequences of behavior or the persuasiveness of contemporary arguments. It shifts the focus to human agents, and how their aspirations and their reason create and affect identity, interests, and behavior.[64] Second, it contrasts the importance of the "shadow of the past"—a historicized view of reality that places actors within their own history—with the ahistorical and situational nature of much structural constructivism and rationalism that relates interests and choice to current circumstances and current expectations of the future. Third, because of its emphasis on historical legitimacy *and* assessment of current conditions, it offers the potential of bridging constructivist and rationalist accounts of international politics. Finally, in its emphasis on aspirations and the role of international status in the creation of national identities, it has the potential to engage with realism on the causes and consequences of national prestige. Elaborating this aspirational constructivist framework is the task of the remainder of this book.

TWO

Aspirational Constructivism

A Theory of Identity and Interests

Aspirational constructivism is centrally concerned with how national identities are formed and how these shape what political elites view as the national interest. It draws on the constructivist and social psychological literature to address three questions: What are the sources of national identity? Why do multiple identities come into contention? Why does one identity come to dominate and act as "the" national identity and define national interests? In doing so, it addresses some weaknesses in prior constructivist efforts to incorporate sociological (Wendt) and psychological (Hopf) insights as well as some shortcomings of social psychological approaches to explain how identities develop and how and why humans choose among alternative national identities.[1] These questions challenge the notion that national identities are "primordial" and amount to unchanging cultural, social, or cognitive structures buried in the mists of time or neurobiology, while the answers highlight the forces that shape the content, adoption, and durability of a particular national identity.[2] Answering them provides the organizing framework for this chapter.

The first question, regarding the sources of national identity, requires considering both the motivations humans have for constructing social identities and the content of those identities. The answer to this question draws on social identity theory's focus on the psychological need for self-esteem and its production of aspirations and constructivism's emphasis on value rationality and ideas. When answering why people introduce multiple national self-images into the political discourse, the explanation focuses on the value rationality of elites and their efforts to employ "identity management strategies" to propose self-images that enhance collective self-esteem. The answer to the third question of identity selection looks to the correspondence process of legitimacy-testing—incorporating aspirations and historical memory and efficacy tests. These concepts, and how they function, are developed in the sections to come.

What Are the Sources of National Identity and National Interests? Self-Esteem, Aspirations, and Ideas

Underlying the aspirational constructivist argument is the core motive of self-esteem at the heart of much of social psychology.[3] At the center of the social psychological literature on identity is the notion that individuals have a self-concept, or self, that is constituted by personal and social identities.[4] Self-esteem is the overall positive evaluation of the personal and social self.[5] Self-esteem has two dimensions: value-based self-esteem (or self-worth, the need to feel valuable and worthy) and efficacy-based self-esteem (or self-efficacy, the need to feel competent and effective).[6] In this study, I focus on a social self—the national self. Therefore, the emphasis here is on the need for collective self-esteem—the self-esteem of one's social group—rather than personal self-esteem.[7]

Individuals have psychological motives to identify with social groups that enhance their value- and efficacy-based self-esteem. The need for self-esteem is fulfilled when one feels a part of a social collective, what social identity theorists call a "social category," that one values positively and views as distinctive.[8] Membership in a social category, such as nationality, "is represented in the individual member's mind as a social identity that both describes and prescribes one's attributes as member of that group—that is, what one should think and feel, and how one should behave. . . . Social identities are not only descriptive and prescriptive; they are also evaluative."[9] The self-evaluation entailed in social identities produces motives to adopt behavioral strategies—identity management strategies—to achieve or maintain positive views of the collective self.[10] These strategies include mobility, creativity, and competition. Humans use identity management strategies to establish and maintain the distinctiveness, positive nature, and effectiveness of their group—the group's collective self-esteem.[11] A group identity that fulfills these needs is most likely to "become an integral part of the individual's sense of self and the basis for a secure and stable self-concept."[12] Underpinning much of this psychological research is the assumption that perceived positive status is a necessary component of self-esteem.[13] Recognizing the importance of perceptions of status leads us to consider the roles of historical memory and aspirations.

Human Agency, Historical Memory, and Aspirations

One of the core propositions of aspirational constructivism is that historical memory and the aspirations it generates are a critical determinant of what identities are accepted as self-defining. This acceptance requires a degree of human agency that is often missing in structural constructivism. Structural constructivist work on identity as applied to international relations has suggested that the present situation, either in the form of other countries' behavior or social cognitive structures, is the source of the self's national identity. The present external environment acts automatically to produce an identity for the self, with almost no action or agency on the part of the self. Structural constructivist accounts based on George Herbert Mead's symbolic interactionism, such as Alexander Wendt's, explain identity as the product of how an other images the self, with the self taking on the image of itself broadcast by the other.[14] Wendt draws on Sheldon Stryker's structural reinterpretation of Mead's work to argue that the origins of identity are explained by a process of "alter-casting" or reflected appraisals: the behavior that an other (an alter-ego) currently exhibits toward the self (ego) determines the self's identity.[15] Other constructivist accounts, such as Ted Hopf's, which draw on individual cognitive psychology, give a deterministic account of how identity shapes behavior. Hopf's account rests on the existing social cognitive structures that are automatically accepted by humans to produce their identities.[16] Such approaches leave little room for agency and identity choice and include no account of how particular identities come to dominate at different points in time.[17]

Agency and Self-Definition

However, current research in social psychology suggests that the views of others and existing social structures do not automatically determine a group's self-esteem. In contrast to Wendt's theory, the self consists of core elements that constitute an identity prototype separate from others' portrayal of the self.[18] Research drawing on Amos Tversky's work finds that the most important point of comparison is likely to be the self, rather than others.[19] This suggests that the core causal mechanism at the root of Wendt's theory of identity formation is not an automatic psychological process. In addition, and in contrast to Hopf's approach, this literature also finds that such externally defined identities only matter if they are *accepted* as self-defining, requiring at least some agency on the part of actors and rejecting the notion of automaticity.

As Penelope Oakes notes, "A sociological categorization (such as race, ethnicity, gender, etc.) only gains psychological significance once it has been accepted as self-defining."[20] For social identity theorists, the question of how social categories become self-defining (which they term the process of identification) is their core research puzzle. In this view, people use social categories, including national identity, as part of a more general process of sense-making—categories help structure people's causal understanding of the environment around them and help them make sense of that environment.[21] Part of this sense-making is making sense of the self and developing a "self-definition in a social context."[22] Social identities, such as national identities, are one outcome of this process of sense-making, "the aspect of the self-concept that is defined in terms of psychological affiliation with social groups."[23] Interaction between the perceiver's preexisting sense of the self and the environment is key here. Social identity theorists developed this interactionist perspective in explicit opposition to social cognition research in which "the agency and judgment of the social perceiver had been summarily excluded from consideration."[24]

Social identity theorists attempt to find a middle ground between cybernetic psychological approaches that focus on the individual as an "information-processing machine" and those that treat individual behavior as determined by social or cognitive structures. Oakes emphasizes that "*identity is an interactive product of person and social context,* not an element of personality or a cognitive structure in the head, and certainly not an automatic effect of 'the simple designation of group boundaries.'" This reflects the turn in social identity theory away from cognitivism and a conception of identity as a cognitive structure and toward a view of identity as a process.[25] Other work in developmental psychology has more fully laid out the ontological basis for a psychology that incorporates human agency and its role in the creation of social identities. These approaches are similar in their ontological foundations to that of social constructivism in international relations theory and to philosopher John Searle's discussion of agency and "collective intentionality."[26]

In constructivist terms, this suggests that the intersubjective understandings that create social reality must be subjectively accepted in order to define a person's social identity. One's personal construction of social reality must incorporate the socially constructed identities that a person encounters if they are to shape a person's attitudes and behavior. Here I propose that a key factor shaping whether agents will accept a candidate national identity as self-defining is their historical memory, which establishes their aspirations. The other factor is the candidate national identity's perceived legitimacy, a subject covered in the section on correspondence tests of legitimacy.[27]

History and Aspirations

Psychologists have long looked at the impact of history in shaping aspirations. This location of the self in historical memory can be traced back to John Locke, who identified the self with memory in 1690.[28] Psychologists from William James onward have suggested that history provides the benchmark against which the present situation and the self is judged.[29] Temporal comparisons are grounded in people's need to maintain a sense of self-continuity even though they experience change.[30] Tajfel and Forgas emphasize that social identity creation is much more than the purely cognitive classification of groups into ingroups and outgroups in light of the present situation; instead it is an affective process shaped by one's past.[31] In his temporal theory of comparison, Albert writes that "to the extent that a person has a strong sense of self-identity based on comparisons within his own history, contemporary comparisons with others will be less needed." This strong sense of self is most likely to exist with larger and more depersonalized identities, such as national identity.[32] Of particular relevance here is Albert's supposition that people are more likely to engage in a process of temporal comparison if the affective quality of the present is negative rather than positive—a hypothesis that has been confirmed in subsequent research.[33] As Stets and Burke note, identity creation occurs within a previously constructed society with preexisting identities, each with "more or less power, prestige, status and so on" attached to them. Comparison with these preexisting identities shapes but does not determine the development of new candidate identities.[34]

Building from this literature, I argue that historical memory is critical to establishing the variance in prestige, power, and status attached to these identities and to the acceptance or rejection of them as self-defining. All this suggests that the present situation does not determine the self's identity. This is especially the case if the present situation produces negative self-esteem; in such circumstances, people are more likely to focus on their past for their sense of self. This literature suggests that the past self can serve as the key identity standard, particularly in times of change, and the past becomes the benchmark against which the self attempts to verify its present identity.[35]

The role of the historical self in these literatures dovetails nicely with the role of reference points in prospect theory. Kahneman and Tversky, in their development of prospect theory, relate historical memory to the creation of aspirations for the present and future.[36] They focus on how the status quo ante sets an individual's perception of whether the present situation is one in which she has lost or gained.[37] In this formulation, contrary to Wendt's, it is comparisons to one's self that are the primary influence on identity dominance, rather than the appraisals of others.[38] The self's past position anchors how it evaluates its present situation. The past therefore sets up the self's aspirations for what it seeks in the present and future and establishes the baseline for judgments of self-worth and self-efficacy. Aspirational constructivism draws on this research to argue that the historical self is therefore likely to be a key source of aspirations that serve as the central standard for the comparison of competing national self-images and decisions regarding which one comes to dominate its competitors. The other key sources of national identities are ideas—ideas about the collective national self.

National Self-Images: Ideas of the Collective Self

In social identity theory, "groups derive from how people categorize the world and are therefore imagined in the sense that people believe themselves to be members of the groups that have been socially constructed."[39] This literature applies to the study of abstract groups such as "nations" as well; indeed, Henri Tajfel, one of the originators of social identity theory, noted that his definition of a group was the same as Rupert Emerson's definition of a nation: "a body of people who feel they are a nation."[40]

Such a view of the collective self fits neatly with constructivism's emphasis on the social construction of reality. For social identity theory, social groups are coterminous with social or collective identities. This sets the stage for the definition of one form of collective identity, national identity, which will be used in this work.

A national identity is a type of collective identity that constitutes a particular set of actors as a state.[41] Collective identity is a set of ideas that are generally accepted by any group of actors as defining what their collectivity is and the general rules under which it operates. The constituent elements of collective identity "serve as the 'givens' of a political community, even if they are not, and especially if 'they' are not, understood as such. . . . [They] appear not as claims about the world but as 'common sense.'"[42] These ideas include notions of the proper boundaries (whether physical or conceptual) that distinguish the group from outsiders, the appropriate nature and structure of relations within the group and with outsiders, and the principles, values, and symbols that guide the group. These ideas both constitute the collectivity as a group and regulate its behavior. As such, collective identity consists of notions of the group's internal *purpose* and its *status* vis-à-vis others. For states, national identity consists of ideas about the country's political purpose and international status.

National identity, like other collective identities, is not a static or fixed concept, unchanging for all time.[43] In the case of national identities, politicians, intellectuals, and media representatives continuously instantiate and recreate the country's collective ideas, values, and symbols, but to borrow from Marx, they do not do so in circumstances of their own choosing.[44] These members of the political elite repeatedly interpret and reinvent the country's identity in light of past experience and new events.[45] In contrast to those, such as Hopf, who argue that national identities are fixed cognitive structures from which interests automatically flow, identities are subject to modification and alteration as political elites seek to incorporate current events and experiences that may not initially "fit" with an identity and its prescriptions.[46] Structuralist accounts omit the power of agents to engage in politics and persuasion and alter social structures, including identities. For Wendt, identities create a culture of anarchy that then perpetuates itself by reinforcing and reproducing the identities and behaviors that originally created the culture.[47] As previously noted, though, agency is required to accept an identity as self-defining. Human agents are capable of changing their identities to align better with new experiences and information and changing notions of appropriateness.[48] It is this ongoing interpretation in the light of old and new circumstances that makes identity dynamic.[49] Later in this chapter, I draw on social identity theory to explain how historical aspirations and perceptions of legitimacy shape this interpretation.

In the remainder of this work, candidate national identities—ones that have not come to dominate their competitors—are referred to as national self-images. The term *national identity* is reserved for a dominant national self-image—one that has succeeded in dominating the political discourse. The rest of this chapter develops the concept of national self-images and the mechanism through which they can become a national identity.

National Self-Images and National Identity

National self-images are candidate national identities at play in political debate at any given time. Like national identities, national self-images consist of ideas regarding a state's international status and its political purpose. They entail prescriptions regarding what the country should be and do, in other words the country's substantive national interests and its interests in behaving in particular ways in its external relations.[50] In this, national self-images are a set of prescriptive as well as descriptive and evaluative ideas. Different ideas of the state's status and purpose make up competing national self-images. National self-images differ from national identity in that they are the temporally discrete conceptions of what the collectivity ought to be and how it ought to behave, and there are usually several national self-images in competition in the political arena at any one time.[51]

If one national self-image succeeds in dominating public discourse over time, it becomes institutionalized not only in the form of domestic laws, regulations, and symbolic and governmental structures but also as stable expectations of rights, privileges, jurisdictions, obligations, and norms of behavior in relations with other states and among domestic societal actors. The ideas it entails about the state's international status and political purpose become national interests—values to be upheld, defended, and projected. Other national self-images will continue to exist and be debated in the political discourse, but unless they displace the dominant national self-image in appearing to offer historically appropriate and practical means to fulfill aspirations, and thus enhance collective self-esteem, they are unlikely to be salient for the majority and therefore unlikely to shape national interests.[52]

A national identity has been established when a particular national self-image consistently dominates the political discourse for an extended period of time. Five years is tentatively set as the minimum length of time required for a national self-image to dominate and begin to become institutionalized as a collective identity. While this timeframe is arbitrary, it improves on other work that suggests that identities can be discovered in one year and which leaves the dynamic development of identity unexplored.[53] Keeping the timeframe limited is important, as the politics of identity formation can be lost when overly broad swaths or narrow slices of history are studied. It is important to focus on the process by which particular identities become epistemically infirm and others become established. I leave the periodicity of identity change and formation as an empirical issue yet to be uncovered. The issue of the timing and pace of identity change is unresolved in the literature, with some arguing that identities change very slowly, if at all, and others arguing that identities can change quite quickly and episodically.[54] Even if the latter position is the most supportable, some elements of the past identity are likely be "stickier" than others and may, through a process of bricolage and reinterpretation, become part of the new identity.[55] Social identities, like social institutions, can collapse quite suddenly, but that does not imply that others immediately take their place or replace all their content.[56]

Even once a national self-image becomes a national identity, it does not become a given but rather a moving target.[57] Its elements may be more or less stable over time.[58] As Burke notes, "It is subject to constant change, revision, editing, and updating as a function of variations in situations and situational demands."[59] It may be most likely to change or collapse during what Sewell calls "initial ruptures," during which unpredictable events create "a surprising break with routine practice."[60] Searle argues that institutional facts such as collective identities collapse suddenly because they are sustained by habit rather than rational calculations of gain. Once the habit becomes widely enough questioned, the institution ceases to exist, "as when people lose confidence in their currency or cease to recognize their government as a government."[61]

Some elements of national identity are likely to be more continuous over time than others, while new elements may be added and older ones transformed.[62] Social psychologists recognize that a person's identity—or self-concept—has an aspect that varies with the situation and "a more lasting, relatively stable and durable self-conception that one carries across relationships, situations, and contexts."[63] One of the core insights derived from prospect theory and social psychology is that a group's view of its status vis-à-vis other groups is likely to be more inertial than other elements of group identity and to serve as the reference point against which a group frames its interests.[64] This is particularly true in times of change.[65] A state's past international status may well be a more durable part of identity even in conditions where a group experiences significant changes in its social environment. However, elites are likely to subject even these elements to legitimacy-testing in times of change. The process of correspondence-testing developed below provides a framework for understanding how a durable part of a past identity is altered and modified to match current understandings of legitimacy.

International Status and Political Purpose National identities and interests rest on two pillars, political purpose and international status.[66] These pillars consist of sets of ideas, one referring primarily to the internal features and mission of a state and the other to its external position, rights, and obligations. Political purpose encompasses beliefs about the appropriate system of political and economic governance for one's country and whether this system is also universally appropriate. Political purpose includes ideas about what values, principles, traits, and symbols characterize the country and what values and principles should govern relations between countries. It also involves ideas about what the country's national mission is, if there is one. The United States might have a political purpose of "promoting political and economic freedom at home and abroad." The Russian Federation might have a political purpose of "becoming a Western country" or "protecting all Slavs" or "restoring the Soviet empire."

The second pillar on which national identity rests is international status. International status includes questions of rank, of the positioning of one's country in an imagined international hierarchy of political, military, social, and economic power. Such ranking involves evaluations of the material power possessed by oneself and all other parties. Status includes immaterial factors as well. For example, citizens of the United States often claim that their country is the "leader of the free world." International status involves ideas about the proper position, respect, deference, rights, and obligations that one's country should be accorded, based on the groups one believes it belongs to, not only the amount of material power it does or does not have.

Political purpose tells a state which ingroups it should belong to (see chapter 4). These include groups defined by material attributes such as power and wealth and groups defined by political and economic governance, cultural affinity, or tradition. Examples of the former are "ranks of the great powers" or the "developed nations," and examples of the latter include being a "civilized country," a "market economy," a member of the "Islamic nation," "Big Brother to all Slavs," or "the leader of the free world." This is not to say that political purpose determines which groups a state actually is a member of but rather those it aspires to join. As such, purpose also indicates whether a country is a status-seeker or a status-maintainer with regard to a particular issue or ingroup. A country that seeks to join the group of advanced industrial countries or the group of "civilized countries" is a status-seeker, whereas a state that recognizes itself as being an advanced industrial country or a civilized country is a status-maintainer. Ideas about international status are therefore interdependent with political purpose. They are kept separate to impose analytic order on the discourse of identity. The indicators used to measure these elements of identity are discussed in the appendix.

The need for national self-esteem and the prevalence of historical aspirations make national self-images—these sets of ideas about a country's political purpose and international status—fundamental variables in the process of national identity formation. Knowing what the sources of national identities are does not explain why many identities can appear to contend for dominance.

Why Do Multiple National Self-Images Come into Contention? Value Rationality and the Search for National Self-Esteem

A central reason that multiple identities contend with one another for dominance in public discourse is that policymakers and opinion makers are self-consciously engaged in creating and legitimating what "ought to be," not merely judging or accepting what "is." They are value-rational—

driven by their values, ideas, and beliefs—to undertake actions that instantiate them.[67] Political elites are not merely passive reproducers of social structures; they also seek to shape the world around them. Political elites, more than other members of society, are actively engaged in a legitimation project of asserting a particular set of ideas to empower their values, norms, and beliefs and shape the state's policy course—to create a valid social order, in Max Weber's terms.[68] Weber distinguished between legitimacy of social orders at the individual level and at the group level. When norms, values, beliefs, practices, and procedures are legitimate at the group level, Weber calls this "validity," while at the individual level he refers to the same belief as "legitimacy." A social order that is collectively accepted is a valid social order.[69] The main actors in this story are the members of the political elite who put forward national self-images that capture their vision of a valid social order—a vision, which in their view, enhances national self-esteem—and the other political elites, whom they attempt to persuade.[70]

Ian Lustick captures the role of political elites in this legitimation process:

> Political and ideological entrepreneurship . . . [is] seen as the transmission belt carrying ideas with hegemonic potential forward into the political arena. . . . This kind of politics is practiced by imaginative leaders who are not risk averse, by intellectuals, and the organizations they build or control. . . . The inventors and promoters of hegemonic projects are people who understand the decisive importance of "reclothing political questions in cultural forms." By shaping the cognitions and values of elites and masses these entrepreneurs seek to (re)define . . . the allowable boundaries and the appropriate stakes of political competition.[71]

These political elites are psychologically motivated to find positive meaning in their societal situation; a key method of establishing meaning is to create and defend a collective identity based on one's values, beliefs, norms, and practices and make it the foundation of social order.[72] It is for these reasons that they introduce national self-images into the political discourse.

National self-images are not merely political platforms put forward by political parties; indeed, members of competing political groups may accept them. Self-images are more akin to Max Weber's "world images," which offer a frame of political reality and seek to lay "the tracks along which action is pushed by the dynamic interest."[73] As such, they can—if they are accepted as legitimate—act as filters on events, ideas, and symbols associated with what a person's country is or should be and the environment that it does or should inhabit.[74]

National Self-Esteem and Identity Management Strategies

Advocates of national self-images implicitly employ identity management strategies designed to enhance national self-esteem. Inherent in national self-images are prescriptions and comparators—such as political-economic system, rank, international roles, or mission—that are designed to make members of the nation feel positive and distinctive—in other words, to enhance self-esteem. Social psychologists have identified a number of identity management strategies.[75] Implicit in all of these strategies is the assumption that social groups compare themselves on the dimension of social status—with the recognition that the factors constituting social status are socially constructed.[76] Each strategy seeks to overcome a group's perceived negative social status: "An unsatisfactory status position leads to engagement in strategies to cope with and overcome [it]. Likewise, . . . people tend to defend a satisfactory status position and maintain a positive in-group evaluation."[77] These strategies fall into three categories: mobility, competition, and creativity.[78]

Mobility includes mobility (leaving one group and joining another) and assimilation (one group dissolves into another, taking on the second group's distinguishing characteristics). The strategy is "to leave a negatively laden group in order to seek a membership in another, more satisfactory group."[79] For example, a national self-image of Russia as a Western liberal democracy entails a strategy of assimilation into the West.

Competition involves "social action intended to change the existing situation" and includes "social competition" over status and "realistic competition" (variously referred to in the social identity theory literature as "realistic," "instrumental," or "objective" competition) over resources.[80] Social competition entails competing for a positive evaluation of the in-group according to existing ranking criteria—trying to gain a higher status level for one's group or to reverse the status relationship between one's group and a specific other group. A national self-image that is premised on Russia's rightful status as a global great power might include a strategy of seeking social recognition of Russia's rights and privileges through rhetorical assertion and diplomacy, rather than the exercise of material power. "Realistic" competition entails attempting to gain allocations of resources that favor the group.[81] A national self-image premised on a neomercantilist view of the global economy might entail a strategy of realistic competition for resources, market share, and foreign direct investment.

Social creativity strategies aim to redefine the attractiveness of existing group attributes or create new ones; they involve "contesting the validity and legitimacy of existing criteria for status allocations."[82] Creativity incorporates strategies that entail changing the dimensions of comparison between groups, including comparing oneself on a new dimension.[83] For example, in the USSR, Secretary General Mikhail Gorbachev used such a strategy to alter the Soviet Union's status in the world by proposing a new identity—encapsulated in the New Thinking—in which the USSR would be a revolutionary leader of world politics, creating a new, moral world order.[84] Creativity can also mean a strategy of comparing the self to different, subordinate others rather than to a superior group—such a strategy might entail comparing Russia to the former Soviet republics or other "inferior" countries. Creativity can mean turning a perceived positive element of identity of the other into a negative, whereby Western economic achievements become a sign of "heartless capitalism" or the like. Creativity also can entail a strategy of comparing the self to the other along a different dimension—emphasizing the cultural achievements of Russia or its uniqueness as an amalgamation of many civilizations rather than comparing Russia to the West on economic lines.

These strategies, and the motivations underpinning them, help explain the presence of multiple candidate national identities at any given time. Different strategies, reflected in different national self-images, can be employed at the same time, as they are not structurally determined.[85] (Chapter 4 develops the identity management strategies used by post-Soviet Russian elites.) They also help explain why identities change. Different strategies highlight different dimensions of identity that their proponents believe provide self-esteem and meaning. A full account of the development or change in national identity must explain why one of the many national self-images comes to dominate the others and define national interests. This requires understanding why members of the political elite accept a national self-image and its identity management strategy as self-defining.

Why Does One Identity Come to Dominate Its Competitors? Correspondence Tests of Legitimacy

Social identity theorists suggest that whether an identity becomes dominant depends on the extent to which the identity is perceived to fit the environmental stimuli under consideration and the perceiver's readiness to use that particular identity.[86] Social identity theory allows us to consider how the self and human agency figure into the construction of national identities and assess the importance of fit and readiness in explaining why a candidate national identity is able to dominate other constructions of the national self.[87] Social identity theory holds that whether an identity becomes dominant (or "salient," in the terminology of social identity theory) is a function of the perceived permeability of group boundaries, and the perceived legitimacy and stability of the social status implied by the identity.[88] What social identity theory does not account for is what factors shape the perceptions of permeability, legitimacy, and stability of social status—in other words, what factors shape the perceived fit between a candidate identity and "reality" and the perceiver's readiness to accept that identity as her own.[89] Aspirational constructivism fills this gap by focusing on the role that aspirations and correspondence tests of legitimacy play in shaping fit and readiness.

To explain why one identity comes to dominate others, we need to examine the role that aspirations, historical memory, and reason all play in making some candidate national identities appear illegitimate, impossible, or impractical and others seem legitimate, natural, and feasible. The sets of ideas contained in national self-images are persuasive to various degrees. Their persuasiveness rests in part on their content—the particular ideas they entail—and the extent to which these ideas correspond to aspirations derived from intersubjective memories of the country's past and elite perceptions of current conditions. The content of a particular national self-image privileges some historical memories over others and prescribes what the state can and should aspire to by historical right. The persuasiveness of the self-image is related to the congruence between its depiction of the state's history and commonly held historical aspirations. But self-images are also more likely to persuade to the extent that they make current events more easily interpretable and proffer a practicable and effective roadmap forward. The more persuasive a national self-image is, the more likely it is to dominate the political discourse and shape elite perceptions of national interests. In other words, the "fit" between historical aspirations and the practical applicability of national self-images should matter in convincing people of their "rightness" and "naturalness"—in other words, of their legitimacy.

The process by which members of the political elite select a national self-image as dominant entails the application of what I call history and efficacy tests, which are conditioned by historical aspirations. When referring to all three elements of this process (aspirations, history tests, and efficacy tests), I use the terms *correspondence tests of legitimacy* or *correspondence process of legitimacy-testing*. Political elites apply two correspondence tests to a national self-image over time: a history test of the appropriateness of the image's portrayal of usable and important elements derived from the country's past, and an efficacy test of the image's practicality. Three factors determine whether a national self-image meets the tests of being both historically appropriate and effective: intersubjective or commonly held historical aspirations; the success or failure of policies and personages associated with particular self-images; and perceptions of other states' behavior. This correspondence process of legitimacy-testing synthesizes social psychological arguments regarding people's self-worth and self-efficacy, rationalist assumptions about the current utility of particular choices and constructivist assumptions about the importance of normative appropriateness. Rather than insisting either on a rationalist "logic of consequences" or a constructivist "logic of appropriateness," aspirational constructivism argues that both matter in elite perceptions and in the choices they make.[90]

Central to correspondence-testing is the meaning actors attach to alternative identities and to the current status quo.[91] Such meaning is based on three factors: historical memories that give meaning to the alternatives and shape aspirations derived from the status quo ante; perceptions of those proposing and enacting candidate identities; and perceptions of foreign countries. Some self-images may promote a political purpose that is viewed as historically inappropriate or impractical. In the United States, a self-image promoting a centralized, unitary state rather than decentralized, federated rule would be considered illegitimate and incredible, as would a self-image that negated private property or individual liberties. In other self-images, it might be the depiction of international status that is seen as ineffective or inappropriate. In Germany, for example, a self-image promoting Germany's status as an expansionist military superpower would be historically illegitimate in light of the Nazi era and impractical given the constitutional limitations on the use of the military. Such self-images might exist among the political elite, but they will be marginal. Instead, self-images emphasizing a break from the Nazi past would be viewed as legitimate.[92]

Figure 2.1 outlines how correspondence-testing on the part of elites leads both to the winnowing out of illegitimate and ineffective national self-images and the reinforcement of some images over others. To become dominant, a national self-image must be socially plausible in that its prescriptions for enhancing national self-esteem are viewed as feasible under current conditions (perceived to be capable of enactment or effective) while also being historically legitimate.

Political elites are likely to converge on a particular national self-image if its depiction of the state's political purpose and international status passes tests of historical legitimacy (a history test) and practical applicability (an efficacy test). One benchmark political elites use to assess national self-images are aspirations derived from the state's history. The other factors shaping these assessments are the current domestic and international conditions the state faces. I next address historical aspirations, history tests, and efficacy tests in turn.

Historical Aspirations

History shapes individuals' readiness to accept an identity.[93] Historical aspirations derived from the country's past international status and political purpose set standards that shape how individuals verify the fit of a proposed identity and its attendant identity management strategy and affect whether it appears "natural."[94] Under different conditions, historical aspirations derived from a country's past international status and purpose, the two pillars of national identity, will have varying effects on the

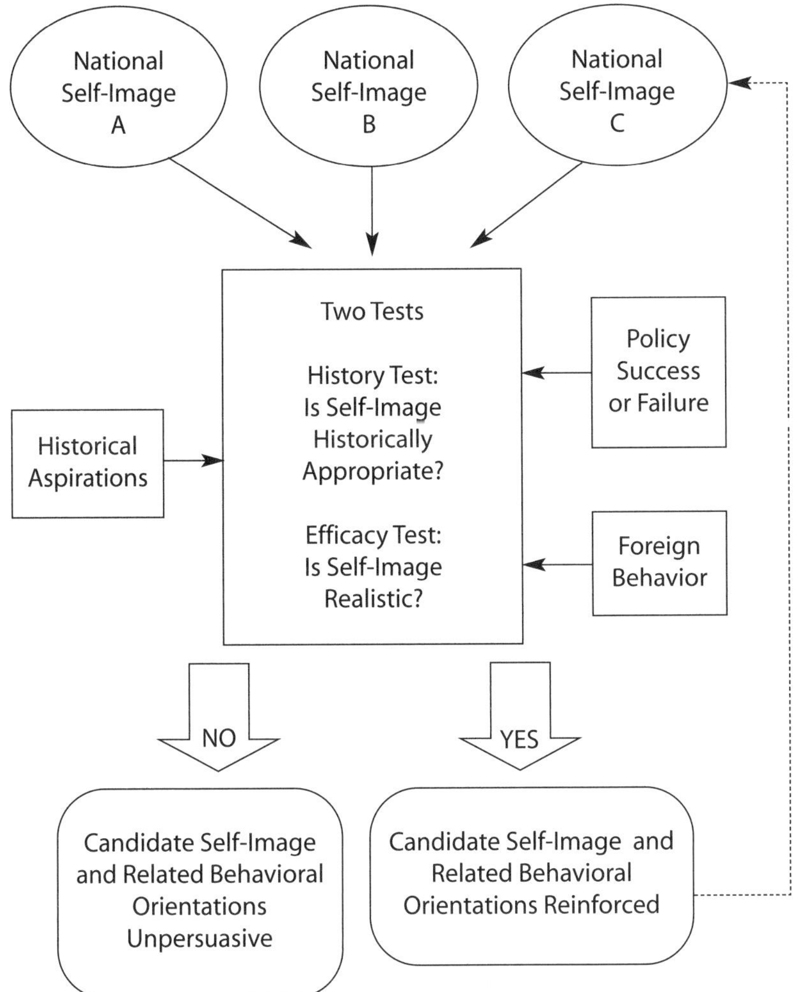

FIGURE 2.1. Correspondence Testing: How a National Self-Image Becomes Dominant

selection of a present-day national self-image. Historical aspirations matter both in times of institutional stability and flux, but they are likely to exert more influence in times of change.[95]

A past international status or political purpose that is positively remembered is likely to serve as an aspiration around which an elite consensus can converge. Conversely, bad memories of the state's past international status or political purpose—for example as an expansionist fascist state, an agent or object of colonialism, repression, subjugation, or teleological imperialism—might prompt a desire to change or avoid that status ("never again will we be that oppressor/victim"). As a result, the legitimacy of a national self-image with respect to historical aspirations is likely to dominate the practical assessment of actual status. In times of institutional flux, commonly held historical aspirations are likely to become the primary baseline for assessing the propriety and practicality of competing national self-images.[96] In times of institutional stability, a dominant national self-image is likely to be largely unquestioned; it may be tinkered with to bring it into accord with historical aspirations and current conditions, but it is unlikely to undergo radical revision.

In the case of Russia, if Russia's past international status or political purpose is viewed positively, it will likely create aspirations among present-day political elites to reclaim or maintain it. In such cases, national self-images that promote status or purpose restoration are more likely to be accepted than those that downplay or reject them. A past status or purpose that is negatively perceived should produce aspirations to replace it with a positive one. In these circumstances, national self-images that favor a new status should be preferred over those promoting the old one.

History Tests or Correspondence of Historical Legitimacy

History-testing is the process of comparing contending national identities against historical aspirations. History tests are likely to matter a great deal in shaping the national identity and national interest during periods of institutional fluidity, given the human propensity for temporal comparison during such periods.[97] In history tests, the perceived legitimacy and stability of the status implied by a candidate identity is judged against the common historical memories of the high and low points of the country's past.[98] For example, an identity of Russia as a Western liberal democracy rests on an identity management strategy of mobility: Russia would seek to join the West and assimilate to its standards of liberal democracy. Implicit in this identity is a rejection of Russia's past. History tests focus on the perceived legitimacy of the status implied by assimilation—changing oneself to become part of a "superior" social group, the West, and thereby accepting Russia's past non-Western status as inferior. The legitimacy of that inferior past status likely would be judged in the light of common historical memories of Russia's past status as a superpower on a par with the West and a champion of an alternative way of development.

Efficacy Tests or Correspondence of Effective Legitimacy

The legitimacy of competing national self-images is not only determined by historical aspirations and history tests. Political elites also engage in correspondence tests of the realism and practicality—efficacy tests—of a particular national self-image, given current conditions. External conditions and policy outcomes play a significant role in efficacy-testing and thereby in the politics of selecting a national self-image.[99] Perceptions of the behavior of other states and international conditions feed into political elites' correspondence-testing, as do perceived successes and failures of policies and persons associated with particular self-images. These enter into domestic political competition as political elites use them to raise or lower the intersubjective credibility and legitimacy of a particular self-image.

There is an established psychological basis for efficacy tests as well as history tests. Social psychologists studying identity argue that individuals judge whether the proposed identity can be enacted—what they call the process of self-verification, or verification of the "self-in-context." Humans need to feel that their identities can actually be performed in order to feel that they are valuable and effective agents, the elements of positive self-esteem.[100] This need for self-esteem motivates people to match "perceptions of the environment or the 'actual' performance of the self" with the prototypical meanings of a given identity.[101] In attempting to verify an identity, individuals assess whether those proposing the identity and those group members who would have to enact it have the necessary skills and performance level to achieve its enactment. Those who are perceived to perform well are valued and accorded status, respect, and esteem.[102] They are also seen as effective: "When individuals reflect on their behavior and observe that they have been successful at maintaining a match between situational meanings and identity standards, efficacy-based self-esteem results from such 'successful' behavior."[103]

Efficacy-testing incorporates this process of self-reflection and self-verification: elites test the realism and practicality of the ideas and practices of a candidate national identity in light of current conditions. Central to the notion of efficacy tests is that national self-images put forth a set of expectations regarding values, norms, behaviors, and practices for national enhancement. These expectations are then assessed in light of ongoing events. It is not only the socially appropriate manner in which an argument is presented that shapes its persuasiveness, as some constructivists claim, but also the extent to which its substance is deemed to be reasonable in light of current conditions.[104] Current policies and perceptions of other countries associated with national self-images affect their legitimacy. As Jeffrey Legro notes, "Ideational prescriptions carry a set of social expectations of what should or should not result from group action. These expectations become salient vis-à-vis events. . . . Collective ideas contain not only a notion of appropriate action, but also a portrayal of which consequences are a success . . . or a failure."[105]

Perceptions of the success or failure of political policies and the personas associated with national self-images influence their chances of dominating the political discourse, as successful proponents and policy outcomes make the national self-images associated with them appear more effective in the eyes of political elites. Political elites will regard failures as indicators of the impraticable nature of some national self-images and use their flaws as reasons to seek alternatives.[106] In contrast, an event that is perceived to be a policy success flowing from a national self-image gives "its advocates persuasion power: they not only criticize, but offer a socially salient solution."[107]

Efficacy-testing takes three forms. The first consists of verifying consistency: whether the actual enactment of an identity and its attendant identity management strategy can be done in a way that comports with the intrinsic values, norms, and practices entailed in the identity under current conditions.[108] Elites assess the behavior of persons associated with particular national self-images against their professed ideals to see if they match. Second, efficacy tests can also focus on capacity: whether the persons and groups charged with enacting the identity have the requisite skills to do so and whether their enactment reaffirms the positive skills and practices that the self possessed in the past.[109] Elite perceptions of policy outcomes associated with national self-images are key sources of information about whether those self-images will be seen as effective.

Finally, efficacy tests also evaluate the overall plausibility of a national self-image, whether the proposed identity is perceived to be capable of enactment in whole or in part under current conditions and in light of the behavior of other states. Here elite perceptions of external actors and their behavior are particularly important. Successful enactment of a national self-image premised on the strategy of social mobility, for example, may be conditioned by whether group boundaries are perceived to be permeable enough to permit mobility.

Take for example a national self-image of Russia as a Western liberal democracy. Those proposing it argue that Russia can leave its past behind and assimilate into the West. Efficacy tests of this strategy would focus on whether in fact the group boundary between Russia and the West was perceived to be permeable or not, whether liberal democratic policies enacted domestically and implemented in foreign policy were perceived to succeed or fail, and whether those proposing the identity actually behaved like liberal democrats in their policies and practices. If those proposing the identity do not act according to their own principles, this undermines value-based self-esteem. If their policies are perceived to fail, then this undermines efficacy-based self-esteem. And if the boundary between the West and Russia is perceived as impermeable and Western countries are perceived to behave in ways suggesting that Russia is not Western, then the identity management strategy of mobility is unlikely to appear feasible. However, if the reverse is true, then a Western liberal democratic identity premised on an identity management strategy of mobility is likely to be perceived as effective. Whether it is seen as legitimate is an analytically separate matter, one that rests on the content of historical aspirations and history-testing.

The Relationship between the National Self and Foreign Others in Correspondence-Testing

Not all external actors or behaviors have an equal likelihood of influencing internal debates about national self-image. The candidate self-images themselves single out certain countries and policy issues as central, thus focusing attention on specific actors and behaviors. A realist might expect all great powers to matter in the definition of another great power's national interests, as they can threaten it, particularly those that are geographically proximate.[110] In this view, Russia should be gravely concerned about China as well as the United States. In contrast, aspirational constructivism suggests that national self-images are more selective, potentially ignoring some states, even great powers, and focusing on others. The national mission and international status inherent in national self-images make the current behavior of those states important variables in the selection of one national self-image over another. In this view, the United States and China are not necessarily equally significant for Russians.

The nature of a country's relationship with foreign countries serves to reinforce or undermine the legitimacy of different national self-images by affecting whether these images are viewed as historically legitimate and effective. This is particularly true where a national self-image is modeled on a foreign country. The behavior of that country will significantly affect the success of the candidate national self-image associated with it. Suppose a national self-image sets up country A as a meanie and country B as a nice guy. If country A behaves well and B becomes mean, then that national self-image will not be viewed as effective. If, on the other hand, A is mean and B is nice, then the national self-image and its proponents will be strengthened in their efforts to make their values take root as the national identity.

To summarize, a national self-image must pass two legitimacy tests in the eyes of a country's political elites for it to become persuasive and politically dominant: a history test and a efficacy test. The history test involves asking: Is the candidate national self-image congruent with historical aspirations? Does it aspire to what is good and successful from the past and deemphasize the bad and unsuccessful? Are the foreign ingroups it designates congruent with its historical aspirations?

The efficacy test involves a different set of questions: Is the candidate national self-image effective and practical? Are its policies perceived to succeed or fail? Do foreign countries of significance behave as the self-image predicts? If a particular self-image undermines aspirations of status or purpose (the history test), or if it is connected with damaging political programs (the efficacy test), then political elites are unlikely to view it as persuasive and it is not likely to dominate the political discourse, become the national identity, and define the national interest. Likewise, if a particular self-image is associated with a foreign state or group of states, and that foreign state is seen as undermining the country's desired international status or political purpose, then that self-image is unlikely to dominate. On the positive side, if a particular self-image reinforces historical aspirations or is associated with successful political programs and the positive behavior of foreign countries, then that self-image is likely to serve as a basis for national interests.

National identity formation is a historically contingent process that is subject to human reasoning; the dominance of a self-image depends on political elite evaluations of past national identity and of present domestic and international political circumstances. Elite perceptions of success or failure of domestic policies, external actions, and international events help to confirm or undermine the historical legitimacy and practicality of a self-image. However, external action does not automatically determine domestic reaction, as in the realist and structural constructivist explanations of the sources of a state's interests or its identity; elites understand external action in terms of a state's own past, which affects whether an act is interpreted as hostile or friendly, cooperative or confrontational, and whether the act itself is salient or ignored. Empirical work in social psychology indicates that not all groups connect their self-esteem to outgroups.[111] Instead, a group's "significant other" may be itself over time or an ideal image of itself.[112]

The Creation of National Identity and National Interests

Once a majority of political elites are persuaded of the correspondence among a national self-image, historical aspirations, and reality, that self-image becomes dominant and defines national interests. Should its dominance persist, it becomes a national identity on which a collectively valid social order can be built. The substantive and behavioral aspects of the national interest are dictated by a core set of ideas about a state's international status and political purpose that goes largely uncontested. Political elites will continue to test the practicality and historical appropriateness of the identity and interests in light of external and internal events; this is how stable national identities are altered and modified. Figure 2.2 illustrates how a candidate national self-image, once it has become dominant, is changed, reinforced, or rejected as a result of the process of history- and efficacy-testing.

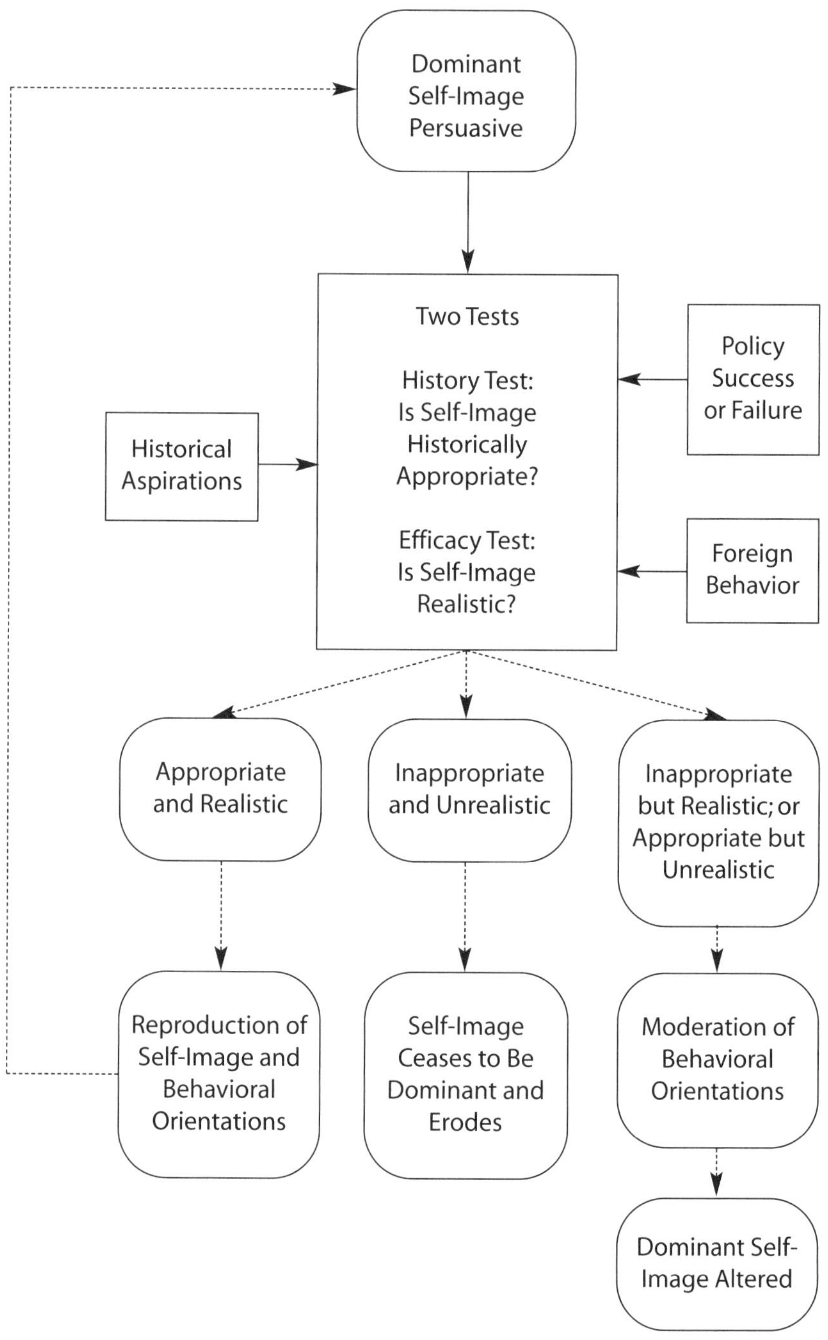

FIGURE 2.2. Altering, Reproducing, or Eroding a Dominant National Self-Image

National Self-Images, National Interests, and Behavioral Orientations

National self-images entail identity management strategies and comparisons that generate national interests in particular behaviors toward other countries. Aspirational constructivism expects that political elites will develop behavioral orientations toward cooperation, competition, or confrontation with another state based on the content of the dominant national self-image—particularly the countries that it constructs as ingroups and outgroups, as well as the dimension on which that in-/outgroup construction is based—and what type of identity management strategy it entails. Identity management strategies entail certain interests and behaviors with regard to foreign countries that are the focus of comparison for the group.

Identity Management Strategies and Behavioral Orientations

As noted earlier, social identity theory identifies three broad strategies that people employ to attain and defend their sense of self: strategies of mobility, competition, and creativity. Strategies of mobility are unlikely to produce confrontational or conflictual behavioral orientations toward the group that one is seeking to join. Mobility strategies are premised on the notion that a desired group (or other) is valued and superior, and therefore that the self should become more like it. Mobility strategies therefore are likely to produce cooperative and potentially friendly behavioral orientations toward the valued group. Whether orientations are friendly depends on whether the valued dimension of the group is its political purpose. If the self seeks to take on and assimilate the political purpose of the group, then it is likely to favor friendship with it.

Competition strategies, in contrast, entail competitive and potentially hostile orientations. "Realistic" competition is likely to produce conflict over resources, while social competition produces conflict over whatever dimension of status the self feels is unfavorable, for example, one's place in a international social hierarchy of prestige. In both strategies, if the national self-image also entails a political purpose at odds with the other's, then competition is likely to produce confrontational and hostile—in addition to merely competitive—orientations. If the national self-image contains a political purpose whose values are perceived to be similar to that of the other, competition should remain competitive but not hostile.

The behavioral orientations associated with social creativity strategies cannot be deduced before the fact; they depend on the content of the national self-image. In some cases, such as Gorbachev's New Thinking, the proposed identity may involve reconceptualizing world politics as a cooperative affair, requiring partnership among powerful nations. This would produce highly cooperative foreign policy orientations toward the West.[113] One might argue that the Bolsheviks, in their advocacy of international socialist revolution, employed a social creativity strategy designed to enshrine the Soviet Union's identity as the leader of a new world order—but one premised on hostile conflict with capitalist countries. The behavioral orientations arising from social creativity strategies therefore need to be inductively determined.

The Construction of Comparison Groups and Behavioral Orientations

Other factors affecting the behavioral orientations toward foreign countries are the ingroups and outgroups that national self-images construct and, in particular, the dimensions along which that identification occurs. Ingroups and outgroups, as social identity theorists have noted, are social constructions that can be created on almost any basis, ranging from eye color to musical preferences to ethnicity.[114] For our purposes, construction of ingroups and outgroups in national self-images can range from perceptions of similarity and dissimilarity along value dimensions (particularly political purpose) as well as material and status dimensions.

The international behavioral results of the construction of such ingroups and outgroups are often misrepresented, suggesting that the construction of an outgroup disposes the self to be hostile and competitive with that group, while the construction an ingroup produces friendly and cooperative behavior toward group members. Jonathan Mercer applies social identity theory, as developed by Muzafer Sherif, to international relations in order to critique Alexander Wendt's thesis on the potential for the development of benign collective identities.[115] However, Sherif's findings of vicious behavioral competition among young boys on the basis of arbitrary categorization are quite different than the results social identity theorists, beginning with Henri Tajfel and John C. Turner, have produced since Sherif's studies in the 1950s and 1960s. Their empirical research emphasizes that the mere designation of ingroups and outgroups does not necessarily produce the ingroup and outgroup rivalry and conflict that Sherif emphasized.[116] Instead, as Marilynn Brewer has most prominently investigated, the creation of ingroups and outgroups creates favoritism toward the ingroup and fosters ingroup collective action and ingroup trust, but not necessarily discrimination, or worse, toward the outgroup.[117] These findings are also more nuanced than the earlier studies, as they recognize that people often identify themselves with multiple, overlapping groups. The behavioral orientations associated with the construction of ingroups and outgroups in post-Soviet Russia is fully developed in chapter 4; here, the basic theoretical expectations, drawn from recent work by social identity theorists, are outlined and integrated with the aspirational constructivist concern with the two elements of national identity: political purpose and international status.

The primary behavioral expectation that social identity theorists have identified regarding the self's construction of ingroups and outgroups concerns self's behavior toward the ingroup. The self's identification of an ingroup is expected to produce orientations toward favoring the ingroup, and is a necessary (but not sufficient) condition for collective action with the group.[118] The other condition shaping whether the self will in fact cooperate with the group is "subjectively apprehended features of social reality."[119] In addition, even if the self views itself as belonging to a particular group, it still has the desire to retain its own positive distinctiveness within that group, what Marilynn Brewer calls "optimal distinctiveness." This results in the self enhancing those features of itself that make it distinctive from others and at the same time seeking to make itself more like the ingroup.[120] The construction of outgroups can, but does not necessarily, produce competitive or confrontational orientations in the self toward the outgroup. Social identity theory expects that such orientations are most likely to arise only when the self perceives a threat to its identity or its physical survival from the outgroup.[121]

Moreover, people often categorize themselves as belonging to more than one social group, and this creates the potential for cross-cutting or reinforcing behavioral orientations. Cross-cutting group memberships include cases in which the self identifies others as an outgroup on one dimension but an ingroup on another dimension. Reinforcing group memberships exist when the self sees itself as an ingroup member on two or more dimensions—or, conversely, sees others as an outgroup on two or more dimensions.[122] In cases where people feel that they belong to multiple cross-cutting groups, social identity theory expects people to try and reconcile the differences among the groups, with the behavioral consequence of being more tolerant and reducing actions that would hurt one of the identities.[123] Cross-cutting group memberships are expected to produce pressures for the self to moderate its views and compromise with partial outgroup members. "Cross-cutting memberships also make the distinction between ingroups and outgroups less pronounced" for the self.[124] On the other hand, if the self constructs others as a double outgroup, it is more likely to display favoritism toward double ingroup and partial ingroup members and more bias toward double outgroup members.[125]

Aspirational constructivism suggests that a key dimension of identity on which a national self-image compares the self with outgroups is political purpose, with significant consequences for a national self-image's depiction of Russia's national interests toward ingroups and outgroups on that dimension. Generally speaking, comparisons highlighting political purpose produce friendly or hostile orientations. If a national self-image constructs an ingroup according to similar political purpose, this should produce a friendly orientation toward members of that ingroup and those accepting the self's purpose. Hostile orientations should develop toward those with purposes that are dissimilar or that are seen to undermine the self's political purpose. The political purpose entailed in national self-images and the legitimacy of the ingroups and outgroups they construct are therefore critical variables in understanding a country's national interests and behavioral orientations.

Aspirational Constructivism's Core Expectations regarding Identity and Interests

The foregoing discussion develops the theoretical foundations upon which aspirational constructivism rests and sets the stage of summarizing its core expectations with regard to the creation of national identities and national interests. This section briefly sketches these theoretical expectations; successive chapters elaborate on them and explore their plausibility.

The first core expectation derives from aspirational constructivism's emphasis on value rationality and self-esteem as motivating forces in the creation of national identity and the definition of national interests. The psychological need for self-esteem should produce efforts to maintain or enhance one's country's positive distinctiveness, especially in times of change. This need, combined with political elites' pursuit of their values, should result in political elites' promulgation of national self-images. It should also lead to political elites' use of identity management strategies in their effort to have their preferred self-image become the dominant identity and define the national interest. This expectation is developed in chapter 3, which considers the development of Russian national self-images, and chapter 4, which covers the identity management strategies deployed by Russian elites.

The second aspirational constructivist proposition is that these efforts to offer new bases for national self-esteem and a valid social order—the construction of national self-images and the adoption of identity management strategies—generate national interests in cooperation, competition, or confrontation with foreign countries identified as members of ingroups, partial ingroups, and outgroups. The self should be oriented toward cooperation with ingroup members and partial ingroup members. Any existing competition with ingroup and partial ingroup members should remain bounded within a disposition toward cooperation. In contrast, the self should be oriented toward competition with outgroup members. Confrontational orientations are most likely to develop with respect to double outgroup members, particularly where there is dissimilarity in the self and the other's political purposes. Interests in competition and confrontation are likely to arise when the self feels that its identity is threatened, either through lack of recognition of its status as a group member by other group members, or when a national self-image constructs an other as an outgroup inherently threatening to the self. This proposition is more fully elaborated in chapter 4.

The third and final core aspirational constructivist expectation concerns how one national self-image comes to be epistemically dominant and act as the national identity and shape national interests. The expectation is that national self-images and the identity management strategies associated with them are most likely to enhance national self-esteem if political elites perceive them to be both historically appropriate and capable of effective enactment under current conditions, and that elites conduct correspondence tests of the historical and effective legitimacy of self-images. In sum, a national self-image that passes both history and efficacy tests should dominate competitors. National self-images that are congruent with shared historical aspirations should appear more legitimate to political elites; conversely, political elites should find illegitimate ones that downplay or reject shared historical aspirations. National self-images that are perceived to enact their vision of the social order under current conditions—what social psychologists term verification of "the self-in-context"—are most likely to dominate those that appear incapable of fulfillment or harmful. The policy outcomes and persons affiliated with a national self-image should be critical to elite perceptions of the self-image's effective legitimacy. Finally, if the historical and effective legitimacy of a national self-image are at odds, then historical legitimacy is likely to matter more than effective legitimacy in elite assessments of the overall legitimacy of the self-image because of their perception of the linkage between national self-esteem and historical aspirations. Chapter 5 develops this expectation and applies it to Russian identity politics and foreign policy debates from 1991 to 2004.

Conclusion

Knowing how states, particularly important states such as Russia, come to define their national interests is a necessary step in understanding whether they will seek cooperation or conflict in their external relations. The purpose of this study is to improve constructivist accounts of this process through theory building. The remainder of this work evaluates whether the proposed logic of aspirations can plausibility be considered an improvement over existing situational accounts through an application to post-Soviet Russia. The next five chapters each take up a portion of this theory building and plausibility probe. Chapters 3 through 5 develop and evaluate the core aspirational constructivist expectations regarding the creation of national identity and interests. Chapters 6 and 7 then examine whether national identity debates affected Russian interests on concrete issues of vital national security: Russia's interests in European security and nuclear arms control.

THREE

Russian National Self-Images in the 1990s

With the implosion of the Soviet Union in December 1991, Russian political elites were faced with the question of whether the new Russia would cast off the legacy of the Soviet and tsarist past or carry that legacy forward in whole or in part. The question of Russia's identity—what sort of state Russia would be and what it wanted—pervaded the political discourse. Should Russia seek to "return to Europe," as many of its postcommunist neighbors sought to do? Should it rebuild the Soviet Union? Should Russia be a liberal market democracy or a post-authoritarian regime attempting to modernize along Chinese lines?

The aspirational constructivist approach outlined in the previous chapters expects, especially in times of change such as those Russian political elites were experiencing, that the basic need for collective self-esteem would motivate them to maintain or enhance that self-esteem. The collapse of the Soviet Union in 1991 caused massive disruption to the prevailing Soviet identity and produced for many a sense of loss. According to aspirational constructivism, this period of identity crisis should motivate Russian political elites to find new bases of collective self-esteem in ways that promote their particular values and yield multiple ideas of the post-Soviet national self. The present chapter and the next develop this core aspirational constructivist expectation. The post-Soviet period offers ample evidence of Russian political elites' search for a new basis for national self-esteem. Multiple national self-images came into being during the 1990–1993 period, the timeframe for the empirical focus of this chapter. First among them was a Western national self-image, liberal internationalism.

When Russia appeared as an independent entity in 1991, the new political leadership led by Boris Yeltsin, Egor Gaidar, and Andrei Kozyrev resoundingly embraced a Western and liberal internationalist self-image of Russia. This national self-image was not the only one available to political elites, however. This chapter maps the geography of the political discourse in post-Soviet Russia and the national self-images that competed with liberal internationalism. It proceeds with an inductive investigation of the historical aspirations Russian political elites shared in the immediate years following the demise of the Soviet Union that shaped their collective understanding of national self-esteem and the basis for judging competing national self-images. It then analyzes the different bases for national self-esteem that Russian political elites developed through the construction of national self-images and provides a typology of national self-images. The content of the national self-images are constructed using the ideal types developed in the appendix and yield a map of elite national self-images that remained in contention in post-Soviet Russia.

Aspirations and Russia's Images of Its Past

At the core of aspirational constructivism is the argument that aspirations derived from shared historical memories serve as benchmarks against which national self-images are evaluated. These aspirations can be found in elite debates and survey data about Russia's course in the twilight of the Soviet Union and the early beginnings of post-Soviet Russia. To establish what these historical aspirations are, elite narratives regarding Russia's past and the appropriate models to adopt and elite survey responses from 1990 through 1993 were analyzed to construct the discursive topography described in this chapter. This data suggests that shared memories of the Russian and Soviet past produced common aspirations with regard to Russia's international status, but not regarding its future political purpose.

The majority of Russians regretted the collapse of the Soviet Union and the independence of the Soviet republics from Soviet/Russian rule, setting them up to view their current position as one of loss and to aspire to regain what had been lost.[1] This regret was higher among the mass public than among the elite; 69 percent of respondents in a survey of the general public expressed regret in 1992 that the USSR was no more.[2] In 1993, 56 percent of elites believed that the breakup of the USSR was avoidable and the result of "irresponsible" or "criminal" actions.[3] This sense of regret remained as the post-Soviet period lengthened, with approximately 65 to 75 percent of political elites regretting the Soviet collapse in 2001. Mass public regret also continued, peaking in 1999 at 85 percent and decreasing to 76 percent in December 2001.[4] The common aspirations suggested by this sense of loss were restoring Russia's status as a great power and recreating in whole or part Russia's role as the guiding force among the former Soviet republics. However, there was not broadly shared regret among political elites over the loss of the Soviet political and economic system or its ideology and foreign policy interests.[5]

The most commonly held historical aspirations among political elites concerned Russia's status as a great power—a status premised on Russia's modernity.[6] Russia's quest for great power status has a long historical pedigree. Shared memories of Russia's past status as a great power—whether global, European, or Eurasian—created a core aspiration among most political elites to retain or regain that status. The USSR's status as a great power had not been discredited. Almost all political elites viewed Russia's past status as a great power positively and as a core facet of Russian identity.[7] In the spring of 1993, 95 percent of political elites aspired for Russia to be a major international power. Of that number, 59 percent thought Russia should be one of the five great powers or a superpower; 30 percent thought it should be one of the most advanced countries in the world, while 6 percent favored Russia's status as the leading great power in the former Soviet Union (see table 3.1).[8]

When asked in 1993 "At what should Russian foreign policy be directed above all?" 57 percent favored preserving Russia's great power status, but only through nonviolent means, while another 4 percent favored regaining Russia's status as a military superpower. Thirty-six percent saw "striving to fit in on an equal basis with others in the global community, including the EC and NATO" as the most important foreign policy goal, one which would effectively place Russia on par with the most important Western powers.[9] Only a minority of political elites placed little value on Russia's past great power status.[10] A mere 4 percent said that Russia should simply seek to be one of the world's many sovereign countries.[11] Even a majority of those who favored rejecting Russia's past mode of development and adopting Western modes desired to hold on to Russia's great power status.[12] For nationalists and self-proclaimed great power "patriots," restoration of Soviet-style superpower status and Russia's im-

TABLE 3.1. *Preferences of Russian Political Elites regarding International Status, June 1993*

Speaking of Russia's role in the world, what role do you think she should try to occupy under present conditions?				
One of the five great powers	One of the 10 to 15 most developed countries in the world	The leading great power within the territory of the former USSR	Superpower status	One of the many sovereign [*ravnopravnie*] countries of the world
55%	30%	6%	4%	4%

What should Russia's foreign policy above all be directed toward?			
Preservation of Russia's status as a great power, but through nonviolent means, active rivalry with other countries	Striving to fully fit in on an equal basis with others in the global community, including in the EC and NATO	To regain Russia's status as a military superpower, on a par with the U.S.	Other
57%	36%	4%	3%

Source: VTsIOM, *Vneshniaia Politika Rossii—1993: Analiz Politikov i Ekspertov. Sotsiologicheskoe Issledovanie Vzgliadov i Predstavlenii po Problemam Vneshnei Politiki Uchastnikov Vneshnepoliticheskogo Protsessa v Rossii, Iiun 1993 g* (Moscow: VTsIOM and SINUS Moscow with funding from the Friedrich Ebert Stiftung, 1993), 22.

perial past greatness was their primary goal.[13] But in May 1993 only 5 to 7 percent of political elites shared this aspiration.[14]

Other shared memories did not produce such universally shared aspirations with regard to newly independent Russia's political purpose. Memories of the negative policy consequences of Soviet ideological messianism produced a substantially, though not universally shared aspiration to avoid an identity and foreign policy premised on ideology and especially ideologically driven confrontation with the outside world. For most Russian political elites, the USSR's reliance on nuclear weapons, a militarized economy, and ideological confrontation with the West as the source of its superpower status had been discredited. Memories of both the Afghan war and the economic *defitsity* (shortages) of the *perestroika* period symbolized the failure of the Soviet militarized economic model. Ninety percent of foreign policy elites in 1993 did not want to return to the pre-*perestroika* Soviet system.[15]

Many rejected the Soviet Union's ideologically driven national identity and national interests.[16] Indicative of this rejection is political elites' shared memory of Soviet *sverkhderzhava* (superpower) status as connoting the ideological and military confrontation between communism and capitalism, a struggle that had been thoroughly discredited.[17] As noted above, only 4 percent of political elites favored restoration of "military superpower status on par with the U.S."[18] The illegitimacy of the USSR's political purpose was also indirectly reflected in the welcoming of the demise of the Warsaw Pact on the part of political elites. More than half of elites in 1993 accepted this as "the movement of the peoples [of the Warsaw Pact countries] towards freedom." Only a quarter regretted the Warsaw Pact's demise.[19] These views hardly reflect the urge for revanchism that offensive realists feared in the 1990s.[20]

The common negative memory of an ideologically driven past was also used as a benchmark against which to measure both Gorbachev's New Thinking and Yeltsin's new policy of democratic reform.[21] As Igor Malashenko put it in 1991, the Soviet experience taught the futility of "restoring the hopelessly discredited totalitarian ideology or merely borrowing the Western system of liberal democracy."[22] Past ideological messianism and efforts to lead an ideologically driven world order were negatively perceived as undermining Russia's ability to thrive internationally, and other ideologically driven identities were viewed with wariness.[23]

However, despite the rejection of the ideologically driven past, elites shared common memories of Russia's past as a distinct civilization that not only was premised on ideology but also arose out of Russia's history as a multicultural authoritarian empire as well as Russia's cultural traditions. Shared memories regarding the successes and failures of distinctly Russian and Soviet development produced common aspirations to be a modern and economically advanced country. These shared memories did not, however, yield shared aspirations as to how to achieve such a status or agreement on whether Russia's traditional uniqueness was positive or negative. Common memories of Russia's distinctive, non-Western traditions and efforts to pursue non-Western paths of development therefore produced conflicting aspirations. Some members of the elite viewed this Russian uniqueness as the basis for Russia's future development. Others saw it as the reason for Russia's past failure to achieve the desired level of political and economic development and a reason to embrace a Western path. On this question of what political purpose should provide the basis for new Russia's national identity, "the elite [was] divided, the way society [was] divided."[24] As later chapters show, this lack of agreement persisted throughout the post-Soviet period.

For those who positively memorialized Russia's history as a civilizing force for backward peoples, the assimilation of a multitude of peoples into a multinational Eurasian empire capable of harmonizing East and West lent Russia a distinctive, if not unique, path of development that ruled out full assimilation into the West. Forty-five percent of political elites in spring 1993 generally accepted this notion that Russia should follow "a special Russian path" rather than copy "the experience and achievements of Western civilization."[25] Democrat Vladimir Razuvaev doubted in 1991 that a "Russian-European identity" could be created for Russia.[26] His reasons were the different historical, cultural, and religious experiences of Russia and Europe. He emphasized that Russia and the Soviet Union at present and throughout recorded history were "composed not only of members of the Orthodox Church or even not only of Christians. . . . It is indisputable that Russian culture was influenced not only by the Orthodox Church but Islam as well."[27] In this view, Russian civilization is historically different from European civilization and makes the one-way adoption of European culture impossible. In social identity theory terms, these features are a central part of national self-esteem for these Russian elites; they distinguish Russia in positive ways, making it special and unique.

For Razuvaev and many others, the tsarist and Soviet past ruled out an aspiration to "join Europe," as Russia neither can nor should be purely European or Western. Instead it would have to follow a distinct or special Russian path. Many others shared this historical aspiration and suggested that "our country is bound to retain certain cultural, social and political characteristics setting it apart from the United States and other Western countries and serving as a possible source of friction." For them, Russia's aspiration "lies in making a synthesis of Russia's centuries-old ideological and political traditions, primarily general democratic ones, and the non-totalitarian part of the country's post-revolutionary heritage."[28]

This recollection underscores that many Russian elites saw much that was positive in Russia's history. For them these positive points of Russian history should serve as the guideposts for Russia's future, rather than some non-historical, "unnatural" cultural borrowing. For those with reformist leanings, this insistence on Russian distinctiveness did not rule out trying to use "global standards and norms" in addition to "Russian ways" to solve internal problems. In 1993, a quarter of those who thought Russia should follow a special path also advocated the use of global standards and norms.[29] But such use would not result in Russian becoming fully Western. Nationalists, communists, and great power "patriots" also emphasized Russia's historical past as a culturally unique civilization destined to be distinct from the West, but in contrast to the majority of Russian political elites, they also believed that Russia had a mission to lead the rest of the world in confronting it.[30] They rejected relying on global standards in favor of Soviet and Russian traditions.[31] Aspirations to emulate the West, in their view, represented a "betrayal" of "the whole of our history."[32]

On the other hand, almost equal numbers of political elites in the 1991–1993 period viewed Russian history as demonstrating that Russia's uniqueness had prevented Russia from attaining its place as a modern, civilized country.[33] The past, in this view, taught that democracy and private property were imperatives for development and that "any society which fails to meet them understandably finds itself on the sidelines of world development."[34] Instead of aspiring to a unique Russian path, Russia should adopt Western values and institutions, not just its technologies.[35] In 1993, 52 percent of political elites held this general attitude that Russia should solve its problems through application of "global [Western] standards and norms."[36] In this view, Russia's past demonstrated that there was no "need to chart an independent non-Western course in economic and political development; [Russians] did not need to 're-invent the wheel' when it had already been created by others."[37] However, when questioned about the nature of Russia's transition to a market economy, twice as many political elites favored a special Russian path as did a Western path.[38] This fundamental disagreement about the sources of Russian self-esteem, according to aspirational constructivism, shape the politics of national identity and Russia's national interests.

In sum, the collapse of the Soviet Union left Russian political elites with a shared aspiration to restore Russia's status as a great power on par with the leading countries in the West and an aversion to an ideologically driven foreign policy but little else. This status aspiration is based in part on a sense of the loss of that greatness in the wake of Gorbachev's reforms, the August 1991 attempted putsch, and the dissolution of the Soviet Union on December 8, 1991, by the leaders of the Russian, Belarussian, and Ukrainian republics but also on positive memories of Russia's distinctive history as a multinational empire shaping world affairs. Such an aspiration should shape political elites' acceptance or rejection of the competing national self-images and the attendant identity management strategies that were put into play in as the Soviet Union was unraveling.

Ideal-Type Russian National Self-Images in the 1990s

Five main national self-images—Western, statist, national restorationist, neocommunist, and Slavophile—were in play in the Russian political discourse during the 1990s.[39] Each national self-image was constructed by examining indicators of elite preferences regarding Russia's political purpose (derived from elite views on the proper form of political-economic system, territorial boundaries, membership criteria, and national mission) and Russia's international status (indicated by elite views of its appropriate roles, rank, and nature of international relations). The content of these images was uncovered through an inductive qualitative analysis of post-1991 elite discourse, political party platforms, and political movement manifestos related to these indicators (further elaboration of methodology is available in the appendix).

Two of the self-images, statism and Western, bring together politically significant sub-types. The statist national self-image incorporates statist developmentalism, which emphasizes economic development, and Eurasian statism, which underscores Russia's positive distinctiveness as a Eurasian country. The Western national self-image has two sub-types: a liberal internationalist self-image, which emphasizes idealism and cosmopolitan interaction and deemphasizes Russia's great power status, and the democratic developmentalist self-image, which stresses utilitarian interaction and assumes Russia's great power status.

Preferences regarding Russia's form of political economy are measured on the opposition of public versus private control of the country's political and socioeconomic spheres and are coded as liberal democracy, social democracy, statist democracy, liberal statism, social statism, and total statism. Views regarding Russia's proper territorial boundaries are either status quo or revisionist, with revisionism including desires to enlarge or shrink present borders. Membership in the body politic is coded on a civic-statist-ethnic scale. National mission is coded on a scale constructed of the missions of autonomy, inclusion into some larger grouping, and expansion, with separate scales for territorial, cultural, economic, and political-ideological mission.

Proper international roles are a function of which ingroups members of the elite believe their country is or should be a member of and are coded inductively, as regional, global, geographic, cultural, economic, political, and so on. The indicator of rank is coded as super, great, medium, or small power; within an ingroup, perceived rank is coded as positive or negative, with negative meaning that Russia does not occupy the rank within the group that it deserves. Finally, the indicator of the nature of international relations refers to elite ideas and folk theorems about the fundamental principles governing interstate relations, which are coded as idealism, interactionism, and materialism. Idealism focuses on ideological similarity and dissimilarity in political ideology and values to explain cooperation and conflict. Interactionism expects interaction to yield more beneficial relations either for utilitarian reasons regarding the coincidence of individual and collective interest or for cosmopolitan reasons of the convergence of individual and collective values. Materialism incorporates views that reify race, culture, religion, economics, and power as material and "primordial" sources of cooperation and conflict. Table 3.2 displays the content of each of the five main national self-images according to these ideal types.

Western National Self-Images

Like the statist self-image, the Western one is an umbrella for two closely related but distinct sub-types: democratic developmentalism and liberal internationalism. Both emphasize Russia's adoption of a Western political purpose. The creation of markets and democracy in Russia are viewed as the means of ensuring Russia's national mission of joining the West and its international status as a Western great power. Membership in the body politic is based on citizenship, not on bloodlines or ethnic identification and loyalty. Russia's 1954 borders (excluding Crimea) are legitimate, and

TABLE 3.2. *Russian National Self-Images: Desired Political Purpose and International Status*

	National Restorationism	Neocommunism	Slavophilism	Statism	Western
			Political Purpose		
Political Economy	Total or social statism	Social statism	Statist democracy	Liberal statism, statist or social democracy	Liberal or social democracy
Borders	Revisionist	Revisionist	Revisionist	Status quo	Status quo
Membership	Ethnic	Statist	Ethnic	Statist	Civic
National Mission	Expansion: Cultural, economic, political, territorial (FSU)	Expansion: Economic, political (FSU) Autonomy: Territorial and cultural	Expansion: Cultural, political, territorial (Slavdom) Autonomy: Cultural Inclusion: Economic (West)	Inclusion: Political-Economic (West) Expansion: Political-Economic (FSU) Autonomy: Political	Inclusion: Cultural, political, economic (West)
			International Status		
Roles	Global Regional (FSU) Anti-Western Eastern Slav Modern	Global Regional (FSU) Modern	Moral Regional ("Russian Lands," Slavdom) Modern	Global Regional (FSU, Eurasia) Advanced industrial Modern	Global Regional (Asia, Europe) Western Modern
Rank	Great power Regional hegemon	Great power Regional hegemon	Great power Regional hegemon	Great power Regional hegemon	Great power Western
Nature of IR	Confrontation: Marxist/ Geocultural Materialism	Competition: Idealism Marxist/ Materialist	Conflict: Geocultural Materialism	Competition and Cooperation: Political, economic, and cultural materialism; utilitarian and some cosmopolitan interactionism	Competition and Cooperation: Economic materialism and utilitarian interactionism; idealism and cosmopolitan interactionism

close integration with or restoration of the Soviet Union is undesirable, as it will slow Russia's modernization along Western lines. Relations with the former Soviet republics should be based on free economic or trade zones. A market economy that is either a liberal or social democracy is advocated. In these self-images, political purpose is a key source of international status, so it takes precedence over international status. Russia's in-groups are the West writ large, market democracies, the G-7, WTO, the United States, and the European great powers. Russia's national mission is to be included in Western political and economic organizations. The Westernizer position is found in newspapers and magazines such as *Kommersant, Kommersant Vlast', Ekspert, Nezavisimaia Gazeta,* and *Novaia Izvestiia.*

Democratic Developmentalism

What divides the two Western self-images is the different conceptions they have of Russia's proper international status and the nature of international relations. In democratic developmentalism, Russia is a global and European great power. The nature of interstate relations is based on a combination of materialism and utilitarian interactionism. Democratic developmentalists draw on a combination of dependency theory, *realpolitik,* and liberal institutionalism, and their view of world affairs is most similar to neoliberal institutionalism in American IR theory. There are two intertwined realms of international relations: the political and the economic. Democracy and liberal multilateral institutions reduce interstate conflict among countries. However, conflicts among states in the core of the world economy will still occur, because states pursue their selfish interests. But since foreign and economic policy are intertwined, trade wars do not become military conflicts. War, however, will continue to be a threat outside of the core, so military defense is necessary. In democratic developmentalism, Russia's status is that of a global great power with geographically given national interests in Asia and the South, though the priority is the West.

Proponents of democratic developmentalism include Grigorii Yavlinskii and Aleksei Arbatov, former Yabloko parliamentarians; Boris Nemtsov, former deputy prime minister; Sergei Kirienko, formerly prime minister and member of the Security Council; and scholars Andrei Kortunov (after 1993), Dmitrii Trenin, and Lilia Shevtsova.

Liberal Internationalism

The liberal-internationalist national self-image draws heavily on cosmopolitan interactionism and liberal idealism. Russia's political purpose is to become a liberal market democracy and to transform international relations along cosmopolitan liberal lines. In contrast to democratic developmentalism, the emphasis is less on markets and power and more on democracy and universal values. Liberal internationalism downplays the utilitarian pursuit of self-interest and Russia's national interests outside of the West. The key assumption drawn from liberal idealism is that a shared belief in democracy creates peace. The key cosmopolitan-interactionist assumption is that rising interdependence requires increased institutionalized cooperation to handle an increasingly broader common fate.

The central premise is that Russia's democratic future can only be secured through integration into and cooperation with the West. Unlike the democratic-developmentalist self-image, Russia's proper status is that of a Western state, with little regard for global rank or greatness. Liberal internationalism deemphasizes Russia's great power status. Correspondingly, Russia should seek political inclusion into all Western and global institutions, including military alliances. Russia should also promote human rights and democracy abroad. The main proponents of liberal internationalism include Andrei Kozyrev (from 1990–93), former foreign minister; Galina Starovoitova and Sergei Kovalev, former parliamentarians and human rights activists; Anatolii Chubais, Gennadii Burbulis, and Egor Gaidar, former deputy prime ministers; and scholar Andrei Zagorskii.

Statist National Self-Images

Statism is a broad umbrella under which two similar national self-images are clustered. They are statist developmentalism and Eurasian statism. Their commonalities are their agreement on the elements for Russia's international status: a strong central state, Russia's great power status and hegemonic role in the former Soviet republics, the need for integration of the former Soviet republics, and a significant state role in both politics and economics. There is much less consensus on the role of political purpose beyond a significant role for the state in domestic affairs. Its proponents may favor liberal statism and social or statist democracy. The primary criterion for citizens' membership in the Russian political community is loyalty to the state, but assimilation into Russian language and culture is expected. Both the Soviet and tsarist past offer useful lessons, and a strong version of the EU is the primary model for Soviet reintegration.

Russia's international status is premised on a strong state at home, again requiring strong centralized authority and either social or statist democracy, in the democratic versions, and social statism, in the nondemocratic forms. Return to the Soviet planned economy is ruled out, but a mixed economy is not. Russia's historical model is the Soviet and/or Russian empire, especially under Petr Stolypin (prime minister under Tsar Nicholas II) and Petr Struve (a founder of the Kadet political party), and foreign models include China, South Korea, and the Asian "dragons," as the Russians term them. The statist national self-images agree on the need for a strong and modern Russian state, a need derived from Russia's domestic history as well as its traditional role in European great power politics. For both the bases of state power are material—economic or military capability—and interactionist—diplomatic skill and political influence. Both reject idealism and ideology as the primary basis for international politics. International relations is generally based on material factors, except in Eurasian statism, where culture is a significant source of both cooperation and conflict. However, interstate interaction and cooperation can ameliorate conflict. Classical balance of power politics is an important strategy for international affairs, and Russia's role is a stabilizer of the global power balance. The main division between Eurasian statists and statist developmentalists is the degree of importance attached to economics.[40]

Statist Developmentalism

Statist developmentalists view economic and technological resources and capabilities as the key sources of state strength. For statist developmentalists, international relations are premised on economic competition. Economics is seen as the key driver of politics. In economics, international relations tends to be viewed through the prism of Marxist dependency theory, emphasizing the modern and advanced industrial core and backward periphery. Economic modernity is an essential goal and prerequisite of national power. In this image, economic backwardness is the greatest threat to Russia. It should develop its economy and industry to ensure its place among advanced industrial countries. To preserve its independent political influence, Russia should integrate into the global economy and avoid exclusion from global and regional organizations, but on its own terms (membership conferred out of deference to its great power status) and with full-fledged rights.

Statist developmentalists believe Russia should pursue economic integration only with those former Soviet republics (Ukraine, Belarus, and Kazakhstan) with an industrial and military infrastructure that would complement and strengthen the Russian economy. Eurasian statists in contrast favor political and economic integration of the entire former Soviet Union, but more for the substantial strategic depth gained through their territories and their large Russian populations than for economic reasons. Russia should seek to preserve its cultural autonomy and political independence from the West, as its role is to be one of the managers of the international system.

For statist developmentalists, the primary ingroups are the advanced industrial powers, especially the ones making up the G-7, the Western advanced industrial economies more generally, and their rising economic competitors, China, the East Asian newly industrialized countries, and India. Prominent statist developmentalists include Vladimir Putin, former president and current prime minister of Russia; Viktor Chernomyrdin, former prime minister of Russia; academic Sergei Karaganov; and businessman Arkadii Volskii.[41] The statist developmentalist national self-images lack Eurasian statism's messianic quality.

Eurasian Statism

In contrast to statist developmentalists, Eurasian statists tend to focus on military might, diplomatic skill, and cultural attractiveness over economics. Unlike statist developmentalism, Eurasian statism contains an quasi-messianic national mission that goes beyond building state power. Most commonly, Russia's Eurasian mission is to act as the bridge between East and West. In some versions, Russia is to unite the best of both civilizations, thereby ameliorating the inevitable conflict between them. In another version, Russia's geographic destiny is to be the integrator of the Slavic or Turkic or Mongol peoples, as it is the natural hegemon and patron of the Eurasian continent. At its most fundamental, Russia's Eurasian mission incorporates the idea of Russia's difference and distinctiveness from Europe, its superiority to oriental despotism, and its ability to integrate the two in a positive synthesis. Whether it takes cultural, biological, geographic, or political form, Eurasianism insists that Russia's role is unique, just as Russia itself is unique.

For Eurasian statists, Russia's natural ingroups are the former Soviet republics ("Eurasia") and the great powers, particularly the United States and China, epitomized by their veto in the United Nations Security Council and their primary position as Western and Asian powers. The West represents a partial ingroup, as Russia's Eurasianness makes it partly, but not wholly, Western. In some versions, the Eurasian ingroup incorporates the entire Eurasian landmass, with dominance over Turkey, the Middle East, Afghanistan, Persia, and the Balkans, while in others it extends only to the former Soviet and Russian empires. Economic and military reintegration should take place among the former Soviet republics (except the Baltics), following lines similar to the European Union. Eurasian statists are divided between those supporting a democratic political purpose and those downplaying or rejecting democracy. The Eurasian statist worldview is a mixture of classical realism and structural realism wherein multipolarity is viewed as second best to bipolarity, while unipolarity is anathema. Sergei Stankevich, former state chancellor for political affairs, and Evgenii Primakov, former foreign and prime minister, are the best-known centrist advocates of Eurasian statism. Other prominent Eurasianists include Vladimir Lukin, former deputy chairman of the Duma and cofounder of Yabloko; scholars Konstantin Pleshakov and Alexei Bogaturov; Iurii Skokov, a key player in Civic Union and Congress of Russian Communities (KRO); Evgenii Ambartsumov, former Yabloko parliamentarian; Evgenii Shaposhnikov, former presidential advisor and the last Soviet Minister of Defense; Sergei Kortunov, former advisor to the Security Council; Anatolii Sobchak, former mayor of St. Petersburg and patron of Vladimir Putin; and Andranik Migranian, an influential historian. Migranian, Kortunov, and Sobchak were also at times members of Yeltsin's council of advisors.

The National Restorationist National Self-Image

This self-image is a meld of orthodox communist and Russian nationalist programs. As its name suggests, history forms the primary baseline for Russia's national identity and its national mission. Restoration of the former Russian and Soviet empire is the core aspiration entailed in this self-image. It comprises a wide range of groups, often referred to as national-bolsheviks, national-socialists, national-communists, or simply nationalists. According to this messianic national self-image, Russia's borders should at a minimum be restored to those of the Soviet Union. The preferred methods of restoration are economic and political coercion, though some advocate force. Unlike the neocommunist type, membership is ethnically ascribed. Ethnic Russians are the natural and rightful leaders of Russia.[42] Other peoples must assimilate, accept secondary status, or, in the most radical versions, be expelled or even exterminated—especially "non-assimilable" Jews.[43] The political-economic system emphasizes the domination of an authoritarian state over both political and socioeconomic life. The Russian Orthodox Church should assume its rightful place as a state religious institution, restoring and guarding Russia's traditional values and spirituality.

Russia's international status is that of a global great power and a hegemon in the post-Soviet space. Russia's mission is to lead an anti-Western world order. While its proponents use much anti-Western, anti-modernist language to denounce corrupt and dehumanizing Western values, they embrace Western technology and science. Interstate relations form a zero-sum global hierarchy based on a combination of class and geocultural conflict. Russia's ingroups are the other great powers, the former Soviet republics (including the Baltics), and the Eastern Slavic peoples. Most of the "implacable opposition" in the 1993 and 1995 parliaments advocated this national self-image, as did extremist street groups such as Russkoe Natsional'noe Edinstvo, Aleksandr Barkashov's banned party of Russian national unity.

The primary political advocate of the national restorationist self-image is Communist Party of the Russian Federation (KPRF) leader Gennadii Ziuganov. The following quotation from Ziuganov captures much of the national restorationist self-image:

> By unifying the "red" ideal of social justice, which is in its own way, the earthly substantiation of a "heavenly truth"—namely, that "all are equal before God"—with the "white" ideal of nationally conceived statehood, understood as the form of existence of the centuries-old, sacred ideals of the people, Russia will at last obtain

> the social consensus of all strata and classes that it has long yearned for, as well as restore supreme state power, bequeathed to it by tens of generations of ancestors, acquired through their suffering and courage, and sanctified by the grief of the heroic history of the Fatherland![44]

Other political figures advocating a national restorationist self-image include Vladimir Zhirinovsky, leader of the Liberal Democratic Party of Russia (LDPR),[45] KPRF deputies Viktor I. Iliukhin and Albert M. Makashov; Aleksei Podberezkin, Spiritual Heritage leader; Sergei Baburin, Popular Union of Russia (ROS) leader; and Mikhail Lapshin, Agrarian Party leader.[46] In the media, the national restorationist self-image is promoted by Aleksandr Prokhanov and Iurii Bondarev and the nationalist press (*Den', Nash Sovremennik, Literaturnaia Rossiia, Sovetskaia Rossiia*).[47] The most radical (that is, pro-violence) groups advocating this self-image include fringe political movements, including Viktor Anpilov's Working Russia movement, Stanislav Terekhov's Officers' Union, and Eduard Limonov's National-Bolshevik Party.

The Neocommunist National Self-Image

This neocommunist national self-image has a less restorationist and messianic cast than the national restorationist self-image. In this view, Russia's mission is to restore the USSR but without the use of force. Restoration along the lines of a strong European Union or strong U.S.-style federation is sought. In addition, preservation of Russia's territorial and cultural autonomy is of paramount importance. Membership in the body politic is defined by loyalty to the state; while local cultures are tolerated, assimilation into the dominant Russian culture is expected for upward social mobility.[48] Ethnic Russians and Russian speakers in the former Soviet Union are therefore a priority. The favored political economic model is a strong state-led economy with a large social safety system and low democracy (social statism).

In the neocommunist national self-image, Russia's international status should be that of a great power with global responsibilities, especially to the non-Western world. Russia remains the main challenger to the West. Russia is also the hegemon in the former Soviet space, and its sphere of influence should be recognized and respected. Interstate relations are based on ideology, modes of production, and material power, producing ideological and military conflict between competing systems. This national self-image is promoted primarily by communists who are not overt Russian nationalists and who are more willing to work with reformers and democrats. Leading representatives of this national self-image are Ivan Rybkin, former secretary of the Security Council; Aman Tuleev, former minister for CIS affairs; Gennadii Seleznev, speaker of the Russian Duma from 1996 to 2003; and Egor Ligachev, former Politburo member and conservative opponent to Gorbachev.[49] Neocommunists advocate a mixed economy with private property and decreased emphasis on the military industrial complex and centralized control. They seek "the voluntary reunion of the brotherly [Soviet] peoples" in a federal union with a common military and rights to self-determination.[50] Seleznev created his own "center-left" political movement to establish his difference with Communist Party leader Gennadii Ziuganov's national restorationism.[51] Neocommunists generally favored *perestroika* and seek a reformed, reintegrated Soviet Union.

The Slavophile National Self-Image

In contrast to the national restorationist and neocommunist images, the Slavophile national self-image eschews communism as a model. Bolshevism and communism are viewed as a disruption of traditional Russian communalism. We see this in the words of Viktor Aksiuchits, leader of the Christian Democratic Movement: "The bolsheviks destroyed the foundations of the *great Russian civilization* [*velikoi russkoi tsivilizatsii*]: Orthodoxy, monarchy, statehood (Russia soldiers went to their death 'for Faith, Tsar, and Fatherland!'). . . . All that made up the originality and uniqueness of Russia was consistently annihilated by the communists. Thus international communism was the force most hostile to historical Russia."[52]

Russia's mission is to lead the Slavic or Eastern Slavic world in reviving and preserving its cultural autonomy vis-à-vis both the secular West and the non-Christian world. According to Aksiuchits, Russia's revival "can begin with the rebirth of national consciousness and historical memory."[53] Russia's role is that of a moral great power, a counterweight to the secular European great powers, and the leading power in the Eastern

Slavic lands.[54] Anti-Western sentiment laced with anti-Semitism and xenophobia are often present in the Slavophile discourse and another Slavophile, Moscow Mayor Luzhkov, is famous for his round-ups of *chernye*—literally "blacks," but meaning people from the Caucasus. Russia also should take the role of protecting Slavic brethren.[55] In an open letter to the Congress of Peoples' Deputies in April 1992, eight scholars wrote, "We are worried about the fate of the Serbs and Montenegrins—our blood brothers and reliable allies. We are linked by age-old bonds, and we shed our blood together in the two world wars of the 20th century. . . . Russia could and should act not as an accomplice in suffocating the new Yugoslavia but as its defender. Otherwise, ordinary Russian people, following national traditions, will spontaneously do this."[56]

The proper role and mission are found in the tsarist past, when "Orthodox messianism (*Moscow is the Third Rome*) was the spirit of the state system [*dushoiu gosudarstvennogo stroitel'stva byl pravoslavnyi messianizm*]."[57] Geocultural *realpolitik* tinged with Great Russian chauvinism is the method for conducting interstate relations, which are based on material power and cultural factors. Vladimir Volkov provided an example of this thinking when he suggested in 1992 that "the Foreign Ministry . . . doesn't know the Slavic world. . . . I think we just go on squandering our historical legacy. . . . [There are a lot] of opportunities of using the Slavic diaspora and the Russian diaspora in our foreign policy interests."[58]

Organic and geocultural metaphors abound in the discussion of Russia's role and fate.[59] Membership in Russia's body politic is ethnically defined, with ethnic and assimilated Russians enjoying first-class citizenship. The self-image is partly restorationist: Great Russia's borders should incorporate Ukraine, Belarus [Little and White Russia, respectively], and, in some formulations, Latvia and the northern part of Kazakhstan, where Russian-speaking majorities live.[60]

Democracy with a significant state role in the economy is advocated as a means of ameliorating the amoral individualism of Western liberalism (statist democracy).[61] Its advocates deplore "Western morality," but support the use of modern technology and institutions. Key advocates of various incarnations of this self-image are Aksiuchits, Moscow Mayor Iurii Luzhkov, and scholar Vladimir Volkov.[62] Konstantin Zatulin, a prominent parliamentarian and foreign policy critic, has advocated a Slavophile stance but also has put forth views that conform to the statist and Eurasian national self-images. The same applies to Aleksandr Tsipko, a well-known political analyst. Aleksandr Rutskoi, former vice president and head of the Derzhava (Great Power) Party, presented views that reflect a combination of the Slavophile and statist national self-images.

National Self-Images in Russian Political Space

The Venn diagram presented in figure 3.1 depicts where each of five main self-images stands in relation to each other in the context of Russian politics.[63] As figure 3.1 indicates, the political space in Russia during the 1990s was not very clear cut. If we consider these national self-images in terms of their attitudes toward the past and whether they favor creating a market-oriented democracy or advocate a complete revision of the current political-economic system, then the national restorationists, being the most restorationist, are at one extreme of the political spectrum, followed in turn by neocommunists, statists, Slavophiles, with Westerners at the other, reformist end.[64] The vectors are intended to suggest the closeness or distance of these national self-images to one another both in terms of shared concepts and political affinities. The overlap among the national self-images indicates that proponents of one national self-image share certain views and sympathies with the other image. The Slavophile national self-image does not intersect with the national restorationist or neocommunist self-image, as Slavophiles reject the Soviet past.

Conclusion

This chapter investigated the first aspirational constructivist expectation, that the need for self-esteem and value rationality motivate political elites to create new bases for national self-esteem and new social orders, particularly in times of change. The chapter found that Russian political elites agreed that Russia's international status was its primary source of national self-esteem. They shared an aspiration to retain Russia's historical status as a global great power and an aversion to an ideologically driven national mission. This chapter discovered that Russian political elites did in fact propose new visions of Russia's social order, as aspirational con-

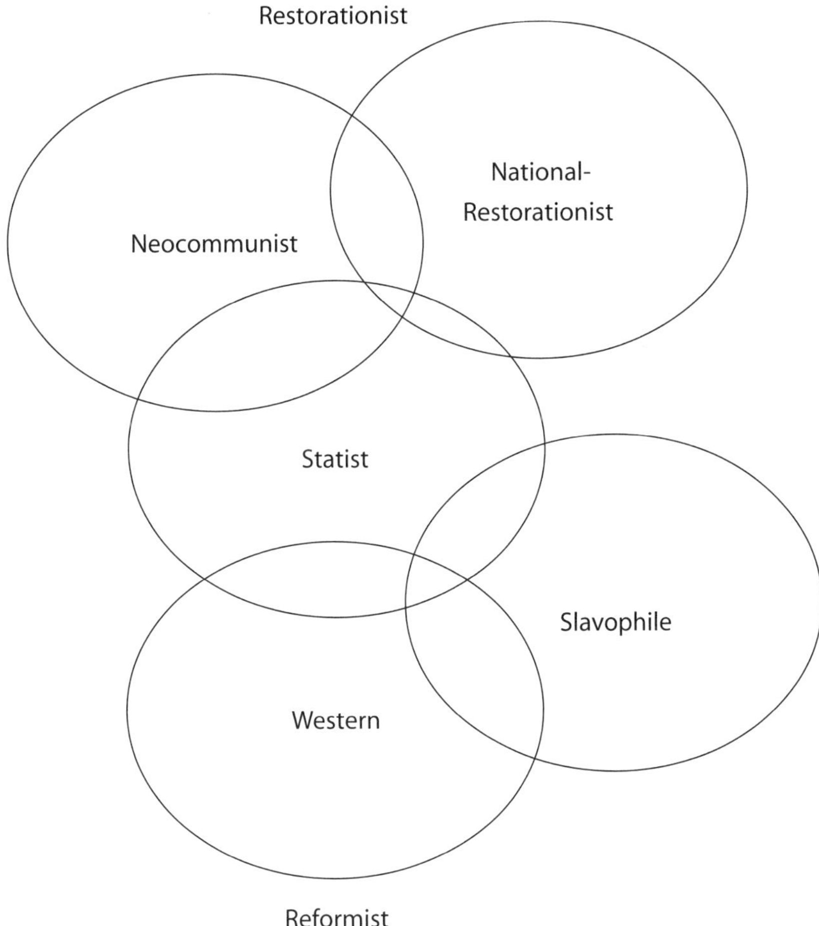

FIGURE 3.1. Russian National Self-Images in 1990s Political Space

structivism's emphasis on the motivating force of value rationality would anticipate. Post-Soviet Russian political elites were clearly split over what Russia's national identity should be in the aftermath of collapse of the Soviet Union. They evinced little agreement on Russia's political purpose or sources of national self-esteem beyond great power status. Russian political elites proposed a myriad of new types of social order for post-Soviet Russia, broadly categorized in five broad national self-images. Many have characterized this split as a renewal of the nineteenth century debate among the Russian intelligentsia between Westernizers and Slavophiles, but as the five national self-images outlined in table 3.2 and figure 3.1 highlight, Russian political elites cannot easily be divided into two coherent camps. Rather, there is an extreme of anti-Western national restorationists, an amorphous middle of advocates of some form of statism, Slavophilism and neocommunism, and proponents of Westernism who dominated the new Russian government's foreign and economic policy when the Soviet Union collapsed in December 1991.

The next chapter continues to develop the theoretical and empirical plausibility of this first aspirational constructivist expectation regarding the creation of new bases for national self-esteem and social order. Chapter 4 focuses on the identity management strategies that Russian political elites might, in theory, develop to promote their preferred self-image and then empirically explores the strategies that were actually used by proponents of the two most politically significant national self-images in post-Soviet Russia: Westernism and statism. Chapter 4 also addresses the second aspirational constructivist expectation, that elite efforts to create new identities—in the form of national self-images and identity management strategies—produce interests in cooperation, competition, and confrontation with other countries. To do so, it begins by outlining the ingroups, partial ingroups, and outgroups—and the behavioral orientations that correspond to them—that the national self-images described in the present chapter constructed.

FOUR

Russia's Foreign Policy Orientations

Ingroups, Outgroups, and Identity Management Strategies

Chapter 2 developed the three core expectations derived from aspirational constructivism: political elites, motivated by the need for collective self-esteem and their preferred values, should seek to create new bases for national self-esteem and valid social orders, especially during times of change, through the construction of national self-images and the use of identity management strategies; those efforts—in the form of national self-images and identity management strategies—should generate national interests and behavioral orientations toward ingroups and outgroups; and national self-images are most likely to come to act as the national identity and form the foundation for a valid social order if they pass both historical and effective correspondence tests of legitimacy.

Exploring the empirical applicability of the first two aspirational constructivist expectations is the subject of this chapter.[1] The previous chapter began this task in its discussion of the multiple national self-images Russian political elites proposed and the aspirations they shared in the post-Soviet period. The present chapter picks up where chapter 3 left off regarding the first expectation. It explores the identity management strategies Russian political elites adopted in order to promote the two national self-images that were the most important candidates for Russia's new identity in the post-Soviet political discourse. It details prominent Westernizers' deployment of an identity management strategy of assimilation and the strategies of social competition and social creativity put forth by statists such as Sergei Stankevich, Evgenii Primakov, and Vladimir Putin.

This chapter also illustrates the second aspirational constructivist expectation regarding the construction of national interests and behavioral orientations through the ingroups and outgroups associated with various national self-images. Designations of ingroups should produce propensities toward cooperation with those group members, while identification of outgroups are likely to create orientations toward competition and confrontation. Partial ingroups should produce conflicting orientations—a desire both to cooperate and to compete, and thus a bounded form of competition. These expectations, and how they play out in Russian discourse during the 1991–2004 period, are more fully developed below.

Russian National Self-Images and Identity Management Strategies

In studying how people manage their identities and attempt to enhance their self-esteem, social psychologists focus on the ingroups and outgroups that people construct and the strategies they employ to enhance their group's self-esteem. Applying social identity theory to the inductive categorization of national self-images in chapter 3 allows us to determine which ingroups and outgroups Russian political elites identified in the 1990s. It also lets us explore the implications these group designations have for the type of identity management strategies political elites might use to enhance Russia's position and the behavioral orientations they might be expected to develop relative to these groups. The content of the five national self-images and the identity management strategies implicit in them shed light on what national interests flow from each national self-image. Table 4.1 summarizes the ingroups, partial ingroups, and outgroups entailed in each of the five main national self-images discussed in chapter 3.

The Behavioral Consequences of Ingroups and Outgroups in Russian National Self-Images

As noted in chapter 2, social identity theory focuses on how people construct collective identities by creating ingroups and outgroups. Ingroups are based on perceived shared ties to membership in some social category, while outgroups are social categories perceived as not shared by the self.[2] Social categories related to national identity may include, but are not lim-

TABLE 4.1. *Russian National Self-Images' Depiction of Ingroups and Outgroups and Evaluation of Russia's Position*

	West/Capitalist Countries	FSU	Great Powers	South/Islamic World	East/Authoritarian Countries
Ingroup	Liberal internationalist; democratic developmentalist	All except liberal internationalist	All except liberal internationalist	—	—
Partial Ingroup	Eurasian statist; statist developmentalist; slavophile	—	—	—	Eurasian statist; statist developmentalist
Outgroup	National restorationist; neocommunist	Liberal internationalist	—	All	Liberal internationalist; democratic developmentalist; slavophile

	National Restorationism		Neocommunism		Slavophilism	Statism			Western		
	Great powers	FSU	Great powers	FSU	Slavs	Great powers	FSU	West	Great powers	West	FSU
Evaluation of position within ingroup (+/−)	–	–	–	–	–	–	–	–	–	–	+

ited to, "great power," "civilized," "Russian," "multicultural," "monocultural," "religious," "cultured," "communist," "nuclear power," "Western," "European," "Eurasian," "Eastern," and "Slavic."

The categorization of ingroups tends to produce favoritism toward ingroups and increase the potential for cooperation with ingroup members and to create negative bias toward outgroups and increase the derogation of outgroups.[3] The creation of ingroup and outgroup identities does not in and of itself produce intergroup conflict and hostility. Conflict between groups depends on the content of the group identity and the nature of the comparison between in- and outgroups. As Brewer writes, "Whether actual or imagined, the perception that an outgroup constitutes a threat to ingroup interests of survival creates a circumstance in which . . . [those identifying with the ingroup feel] fear and hostility toward the threatening group."[4]

However, people often feel part of multiple groups. When these group identities overlap, they may produce cross-cutting categorizations that can make the distinction between ingroups and outgroups less pronounced and produce less bias and even favoritism toward the partial outgroup.[5] For example, in the statist and Western national self-images, the West and the great powers are both ingroups for Russia. Statists and especially Westernizers should display preferences for special relations with the West. Statists, because they emphasize that Russia is only partly Western, construct the West as a partial ingroup. Social identity theory predicts that these cross-cutting group memberships should affect the views of Russian statists toward the West, producing less pronounced favoritism toward the West.

When group memberships reinforce each other, the opposite effect is predicted: if a country is viewed as a double outgroup member, members of the ingroup should display more bias toward them and more favoritism toward double ingroup members.[6] In the national restorationist and neocommunist national self-images, the West is a double outgroup: it is antithetical to Russia because of its cultural values, ideology, and capitalist system. Social identity theorists would therefore expect national restorationists and neocommunists to be the most hostile toward the West and to advocate confrontation with it. In contrast, for Westernizers, the West is a double ingroup, and social identity theory therefore expects them to show considerable favoritism toward Western countries.

Each Russian national self-image has multiple ingroups and outgroups, and the cross-cutting cleavages or reinforcements of those groups will shape which identity management strategies are most likely to be employed by advocates of the self-images. Below, I develop the various ingroups and outgroups entailed in each national self-image and then turn to the identity management strategies we might expect advocates of the different self-images to use.

Russian Ingroups

The West in its general and particular forms is the primary significant other for Russian political elites.[7] Some national self-images portray the West as an ingroup, while others identify it as an outgroup. The West is variously viewed as a developmental or civilizational model to emulate, as a degenerate and dehumanized foil for what Russia should not become, and as a geopolitical or geocultural rival. Within the West, Russian elites tend to focus on Western Europe as a political-economic model and the United States as a geopolitical peer in terms of status.[8]

The West is a role model in a number of Russian national self-images. As noted in the previous chapter, Western national self-images wholly endorse the generalized Western political and economic model and downplay the West as status rival, even though, following Western market economic logic, it is a competitor for markets. All statists identify the West as a desired ingroup regarding great power status, particularly the United States, and statist developmentalists, to greater or lesser extent, identify with Germany and Japan. All statists essentially accept the West as an economic role model, though the "Western" path is to be Russified (to a greater extent by Eurasian statists and to a lesser extent by statist developmentalists). Statists tend to believe that Russian history sets Russia apart from the West and that Russia will never be fully Western and will retain some uniquely Russian qualities. As such, Russia will always only be partly Western, and therefore only a partial ingroup. The West in their discourse is often identified as Russia's main competitor, either for status, cultural, or historical reasons, but it is a partial ingroup of which statists and Westernizers believe Russia should be a member. Slavophiles also view the West as a partial ingroup; it is an outgroup because of its secular humanism and corrupt decadence, but it is part of the Christian world and therefore far more similar to Russia than the alien "East."

The national restorationist and neocommunist self-images see the United States and the West more generally as Russia's primary outgroup—as Russia's rival with regard to great power status and political purpose.

Given Russia's long history of seeking to be a great power and the Soviet Union's position as the superpower peer to the United States, it is not surprising that all Russian national self-images hold that Russia belongs to the group of great powers.[9] All of these national self-images have a negative evaluation of Russia's position in the great power ingroup. In their view, Russia's rights, privileges, and obligations as a great power are not sufficiently respected by the Western great powers, particularly the United States. The Western national self-image blames Russia's negative status in the group of great powers on an internal failing: Russia's lack of Western political and economic credentials and the destructive legacy of the Soviet militarized economy and its messianic mission. The statist developmentalist self-image also focuses on internal sources of weakness and failings to account for Russia's negative status, largely resulting from the Soviet militarized economic system. However, it shares with all the other self-images the belief that the West, particularly the United States, does not accord Russia its due status.

Both the statist and Western national self-images also portray the West as an ingroup that Russia aspires to join. For statists, this aspiration is limited primarily to integration into the West's political and economic clubs and into the Western global economy. In the statist view, belonging to the Western ingroup is instrumental to achieving Russia's desired status in the great power group. For Westernizers, the aspiration is to more fully join the West and Europe, including its military alliances, and to be part of the club of Western market democracies. Russia's great power status is dependent on its transformation into a stable, prosperous democracy.

For all of the self-images except the liberal internationalist, all or part of the former Soviet Union (FSU) constitute an ingroup. The liberal internationalist national self-image sees the FSU as an outgroup, as a drag on Russia's integration into the West. The Slavophile self-image views the post-Soviet lands outside of Russia where Russian-speakers predominate to be Russian territory, while the statist, neocommunist and national restorationist self-images characterize the entire "near abroad" as Russia's rightful sphere of influence. None of these self-images have a positive evaluation of Russia's status relative to the FSU. National restorationists and neocommunists desire reestablishment of an explicit hierarchy of Russian hegemony over the other former Soviet republics through reintegration of these areas into a new Russian empire or confederation. Statists also desire Russian hegemony on the territory of the FSU but without the need for formal reintegration.

According to social psychology, such negative evaluations of Russia's position relative to ingroups contribute to negative self-esteem, which should produce motivations to improve Russia's status in these groups.

Russia's Outgroups

As noted above, the West and capitalist countries more generally are outgroups for national restorationists and neocommunists. Slavophiles view the non-Orthodox, non-Slavic West as an outgroup that threatens the autonomy of Orthodox Slav culture and lands. In the Western national self-image, authoritarian countries form an outgroup, as their purpose is inimical to the Western liberalism.

The East is the primary alternative to the Western "other" in elite discourse. However, it does not explicitly take on the shape of an outgroup in all the national self-images. Russian elites generally ignore the East. When it surfaces in discourse, they display marked ambivalence toward it, generally viewing it in terms of how it may affect Russia's position vis-à-vis the West. Rarely does the East stand on its own as a significant other in its own right. The statist national self-images point to the East as a potential economic role model in the form of the Asian "dragons" (the NICs); the neocommunist self-image looks to China's transitional model with considerable longing. All the self-images place China in the ingroup of great powers. But the East, because of its "oriental despotism," "emotionalism," and "backwardness," is still tacitly viewed as inferior to Russia.[10] The applicability of the East as a wholesale model for Russia's identity does not appear in any national self-image. On the whole, all the national self-images implicitly or explicitly view Russian or Western traditions as superior to Eastern ones.

Much of the East is perceived as an explicit outgroup in several national self-images. For Westernizers, China is an outgroup because of its communist system and political illiberalism; for Slavophiles and national restorationists, the East is an important outgroup because of its non-Slavic and non-Christian civilization, which threatens the Russian Far East. In the Western and statist self-images, China is identified as a potential military threat and great power rival and as a significant market competitor.

The South as an outgroup marks a point of almost unanimous consensus among Russian national self-images. The South in its generalized form equates with Islamic fundamentalism and is perceived as a serious threat to Russia's "weak underbelly." More specifically, Turkey represents a regional rival in the images advocating a status of great power or regional hegemon. Southern states are identified positively (Iran, Iraq, and India) only in self-images that identify the West as an outgroup. In the neocommunist and national restorationist self-images, these three countries are seen as important geopolitical allies against the United States or against the West in general. In the Western and statist self-images, the South is linked to global instability but also to Russia's status competition with the West: India is viewed as a particularly important market, as are Iran and Iraq.

It is the fear of the Islamic "other" that pervades elite discourse regarding the South, even among Eurasian statists claiming Russia's unique ability to meld Islam and Christianity. Without this blending, Islam is seen as dangerous. The South has the potential to serve as a unifying other for Russian political elites and act as the galvanizing force in shaping its foreign policy orientations, but the South's role in Russian national identity formation is secondary at best. Its role in national identity formation is eclipsed by Russian political elites' overwhelming focus on the West as *the* other.

Identity Management Strategies

Social identity theory outlines three main types of identity management strategies that people use to enhance self-esteem: mobility, competition, and creativity.[11] Social identity theory is interested in how groups with low social status, such as African Americans in the United States, are able, through identity management strategies, to create positive group identities and positive self-esteem. It is important to remember here that the primary objective of mobility, competition, and creativity strategies is to instill in the self a belief in its positive and distinctive attributes and its self-efficacy (the elements of self-esteem), not necessarily to gain positive evaluation from others. For our purposes, it is whether Russia's political elites accept the positive views entailed in the national self-images and their identity management strategies that matters, not whether other persons or other countries are in agreement that Russia conforms to those views.

A collective social mobility strategy is one of assimilation: the goal is to become more similar to the desired ingroup and eventually to merge into it.[12] For example, the desire to be a great power would lead to a strategy of becoming more and more like other great powers through the development of those characteristics seen to be indicative of great power status. Since all five national self-images posit Russia's proper status as a great power, all could employ a strategy of assimilation. Historically, Russian leaders have focused extensively on a military criterion, rather than economic, political, or diplomatic characteristics, as the key to social mobility, as a "shortcut to greatness."[13]

Assimilation is a likely strategy for Westernizers and statists. For Westernizers, their desired ingroup of the "civilized" Western world is premised on the strategy of assimilation of Western values and institutions. For statists, Russia seeks to assimilate into the group of great powers as well as into the Western international economy, requiring assimilation of some market norms and Western rationalism. Whether or not a social mobility strategy will garner support beyond the proponents of the national self-image depends on whether members of the group perceive the boundaries of the desired ingroup to be permeable or not. For those seeking great power status or Russia's place in the West, Russian political elites must view access to the group of great powers and to the West as possible. Those who reject the national self-images will attempt to persuade the rest of the political elites that assimilation is not possible through the application of history and efficacy tests portraying such a strategy as inappropriate or impractical in light of historical traditions and the behavior of the other great powers and Western countries. Advocates of assimilation will do the reverse.

Another identity management strategy that people can employ when the position of their group with respect to the desired ingroup is seen as negative and illegitimate is a strategy of social competition. The aim of social competition strategies is not to challenge or reinvent the basis on which rankings are made. Instead, the existing criteria for status allocations are accepted as correct, but negative rankings are challenged.[14] For international relations, social competition strategies are not premised on confrontation or revising the criteria for determining social status. There is no goal to create a new world order or overturn the existing one. Instead, the goal is social recognition—domestically and internationally—of the positive and distinctive features that make Russia a leading member of the existing world order—an order that is recognized as being constructed on Western terms. Social competition strategies are, per Hatch and Schultz, "motivated by self-evaluation; fed by social comparison," in contrast to "instrumental [or "realistic" or "objective"] competition strategies," which are "motivated by self-interest; fed by incompatible goals."[15]

With such a strategy, Russian political elites compete with those in the desired ingroup for positive evaluation of the self. A social competition strategy would seek to get foreign leaders to admit that Russia is a great power in their statements and to include Russia in gatherings of great powers in recognition of Russia's social status rather than because Russia would materially gain from such inclusion. The illegitimacy of Russia's negative status relative to the West is prevalent in all the national self-images except the Western. Therefore, these national self-images are most amenable to a strategy of social competition. It is important to highlight here that social competition is not reducible to a conflict of material interests between groups. Instead, the group that feels negative self-esteem is competing with other groups for prestige and social recognition, not "objective" gains and losses. Social competition is an effort to join the group through promoting recognition of the self's similarity to the group. If Russia wants to join the group of great powers, it can emphasize to domestic and foreign audiences its internal and external resources, its history of being a great power, and use its diplomatic and political skill in order to gain social recognition of its domestic and foreign achievements and great power status. Proponents of statism, neocommunism, and national restorationism are most likely to adopt this identity management strategy.

Social identity theorists characterize competition for scarce material resources as a strategy of "realistic" competition—what Hogg and Abrams call "objective" competition and Blanz, Mummendey, Mielke, and Klink have termed "instrumental" competition.[16] "Realistic" competition, according to social identity theory, by definition only takes place in zero-sum situations over indivisible material goods ("groups in competition for a goal which only one can attain").[17] Such a strategy entails struggling with competitors for material resources regardless of the impact of those resources on the group's relative prestige. As Hogg and Abrams note, "A battle over territory or bidding for a franchise, or even the arms race between the United States and the Soviet Union are all forms of objective competition (both sides have plenty to lose by lagging behind the other). However, when the aim is merely to alter the *relative* position of one's group irrespective of the objective gains or losses, this is called *social competition*. For example, the 'space race' (during the 1960s and 1970s) between the United States and the Soviet Union had as much to do with national pride and prestige as material gain."[18]

The centrality of territorial control and winner-take-all ideology in the national restorationist national self-image suggests that this self-image is most likely to rely on a strategy of "realistic" competition with Western countries. It is almost impossible to overemphasize the importance of territorial vastness in national restorationist conceptions of Russia. The notion of a huge territorial entity that developed over centuries of "organic" accretion litters elite discourse on Russia's national identity.[19] Military might is the primary source of international role and rank in the national restorationist and the neocommunist self-images. This is especially the case with national restorationism, given its construction of world politics as a zero-sum contest for global dominance between Russia and the West.

Creativity strategies involve the self taking a different perspective on its social situation. Social creativity strategies redefine the dimension causing negative self-esteem. We would expect to see, counterintuitively, devaluation of a positive pole of evaluation (economic advancement) and valuation of a negative pole (economic backwardness). For example, if Russia's economic position relative to the West is seen as the source of low collective self-esteem, it can be transformed into a positive attribute: the West embodies heartless capitalism and Russia's material backwardness reflects a more humane form of economic development. We are most likely to see such social creativity strategies in all but the Western national self-image.

Another strategy of social creativity is to find a new dimension along which to compare the self with the other. In this strategy, a new comparison dimension is created, one in which one's group holds a higher position than other groups. The Slavophile and Eurasian statist national self-images are most likely to employ such a strategy, though national restorationists and neocommunists may employ it as well. These self-images are based on a geocultural interpretation of the world in which Russia stands alongside the various world civilizations, vaguely defined by geography, culture, and religion. This notion of Russia being a unique civilization goes back to nineteenth-century Slavophiles and the original group of Eurasianists in the 1920s. For Slavophiles, Russian unity (*sobornost'*), religion, and culture are superior to Western individualism, secularism, and materialism. Russian culture not only is a source of Russian strength and uniqueness but also determines Russia's role as defender of Orthodox Christian Slavs. For Eurasian statists, it is Russia's unique amalgamation of civilizations that makes it superior to the West in bridging the divisions that separate East and West and North and South and that give it a special role in world affairs. Eurasianism varies in its definitions, but Russia is seen as creating something more than the sum of its eastern (Turkic/Islamic) and western (European/Christian) parts. This Eurasianism was reinvented in Soviet propaganda as the slogan of the USSR as a multinational nation building a new Soviet man. It appeared again under the Eurasian label in the nationalist press in 1991, where it was largely the preserve of national restorationist writers until moderate Sergei Stankevich launched Eurasian statism into elite discourse in February 1992.[20]

Each of the five national self-images in contention in the Russian political discourse is compatible with at least one identity management strategy.

National Identity Management Strategies in Post-Soviet Russia

As noted earlier, aspirational constructivism expects that political elites will deploy identity management strategies in an effort to promote their preferred national self-image and have it come to act as the basis for a new, valid social order. Such identity management strategies attempt to make their preferred national self-image persuasive by highlighting positive and distinctive elements of the self. In post-Soviet Russia, two sets of national self-images—Western and statist—were the primary contenders for defining the new order. Their advocates attempted to enhance national self-esteem and their self-image's appeal through identity management strategies that ranged from assimilation to social competition and social creativity.

Westernizers and Strategies of Assimilation

The Western national self-images in play in post-Soviet Russia included liberal internationalism, which was initially dominant in the Yeltsin administration, and democratic developmentalism, which replaced liberal internationalism as the primary Western national self-image in the Russian political discourse after the liberal internationalists were forced from office and their views ceased to be widely reflected in popular discourse. As noted in chapter 3, the two Western national self-images had much in common; their primary differences lay in the importance they attached to Russia's international great power status and in their depiction of the nature of international relations. These differences led their advocates to adopt similar methods for bringing about Russia's new identity: assimilation into the West, both through joining its clubs and through Russia's transformation into a market democracy. The differences produced divergences largely in terms of the completeness and pace of assimilation.

Liberal Internationalism and Russia's Complete Assimilation into the West

Liberal internationalists differed from democratic developmentalists in advocating that Russia's assimilation into the West should occur rapidly and without regard for Russia's historical status as a great power. They considered Russia's historical quest for great power status to be a root cause of its previous authoritarian regimes and suppression of its people. As such, they rejected efforts to uphold this status, as it would delay, even cripple, Russia's development as a Western market democracy. National self-esteem, in this view, could only be achieved by rejecting Russia's past and its great power aspirations and becoming wholly Western. Once Russia became a member of the West, its greatness would stem from its ability to be a competitive market democracy, similar to Japan or Germany.

Andrei Kozyrev laid out this strategy of assimilation in 1992.[21] National interests would be premised on "our internal transformation," not on transforming global politics or pursuing great power status. He stated Russia's national interests as joining a Western, linear path of political economic development. "We want democracy and human rights," he declared, "not a 'humane socialism,' a normal market without 'socialist' or any other reservations. This means that we, too, have finally chosen good health and prosperity. We want to return to the normal development cycle which we dropped out of for 70 years."

For liberal internationalists, the past held little of legitimate value because of Russia's autocratic traditions and the messianic and militaristic totalitarianism of Soviet rule. The nascent market democracy that was developing prior to the Bolshevik Revolution was seen as the main source of historical legitimacy, as it comported with the goal of becoming a "normal"—meaning Western—country that put the health and prosperity of its citizenry at the heart of the national interest. "Yet to be normal is probably the most difficult thing," Kozyrev argued, because "our country was fettered even before, [but] particularly in this century, by messianic ideas virtually sacrificing national interests." Communist messianism led to "expansion and reckless confrontation with the outside world" as well as the exhaustion of the economy. Russia now should reject that past and focus on its national interest of becoming a market democracy. Kozyrev and his domestic counterpart Egor Gaidar advocated a national self-image and identity management strategy that stipulated unadulterated adoption of Western institutions and values and cooperation with the West. "I think we can unhesitatingly follow the same road [as the West]," Kozyrev said. "The only way out is to return to the natural environment in which Russia should be by rights." For Russian liberal internationalists, national self-esteem could only be enhanced by adopting the positive and distinctive features of Western countries and rejecting Russian traditions because they were the source of its negative self-esteem.

Democratic Developmentalism and Gradual Assimilation into the West

Democratic developmentalists agreed with liberal internationalists that Russia's status ultimately rested on its assimilation into Western and European institutions and the internal transformation of Russia's political economy into a market democracy. However, they argued that such assimilation should be more gradual than their radical Westernizing counterparts. Most significantly, democratic developmentalists disagreed with liberal internationalists about Russia's past great power status. They believed that Russia's status as a great power need not be a hindrance to Western assimilation. Russia had legitimate national interests as a great power that, while historically based, were not forever linked to communist ideology or tsarist autocracy. This historical distinctiveness had positive elements, which did not need to be discarded.[22] As Kortunov and Volodin, proponents of democratic developmentalism, suggested, the liberal internationalist "mode of thinking can be identified as an uncritical emulation of Western models of social organization and principles of foreign policy. The [democratic developmentalist] mode regards Russia as a 'vital' European power having strategic interests in Europe and in Asia as well." In their view, Russian national interests "should creatively combine the priority of Russian geopolitical interests, on the one hand, with the consistent democratization and liberalization of the economy and polity, on the other. An open political system is equally important for Russia for the obvious reason that such a model of state-civil society relationships will create preconditions for intellectual, cultural, economic and technological potential of the society to be fully realized." In the democratic developmentalist view, "preservation of Russia's age-old geopolitical role as civilized and strong equalizer is a main resource against geopolitical chaos, for the benefit of Europe and the world."[23] Assimilation into the West therefore did not require ignoring Russia's historical distinction as a great power and should be compatible with great power status.

Statists and Strategies of Social Competition and Creativity

Statists agreed with democratic developmentalists that Russia's historical distinctiveness as a great power was important to preserve. But instead of Westernizing Russia through assimilation, those espousing statist national self-images advocated rebuilding Russia's identity and national esteem on the basis of its historical great power status and Russia's integration on that basis into the Western-dominated international polity and economy. Their strategies for doing so included demanding recognition of the counts by which Russia was rightfully a great power and through reimagining the criteria by which Russia status in the world should be judged.[24] Such reimaginings constituted social creativity strategies, while the demands for social recognition of Russia's existing great power criteria fall under social competition strategies.

Eurasian Statism and Social Creativity

As noted earlier, social creativity strategies seek to enhance self-esteem by changing the dimension on which the self and the others are compared. Instead of suggesting that Russia should only compare itself to the United States and the West in terms of military, economic, or political criteria, Eurasian statists invoked a new dimension of comparison that highlighted Russia's positive distinctiveness from the West. Advocates of the Eurasian subtype of statism, such as state chancellor and Yeltsin advisor Sergei Stankevich, clearly put forth a social creativity strategy. They emphasized the historical uniqueness of Russia as the fulcrum of four civilizations and proposed a new, transcendent role for Russia as a harmonizer of these civilizations. Stankevich succinctly captured this social creativity strategy in his depiction of Russia's unique "Eurasian" calling: "Russia's mission in the world is to initiate and maintain a multilateral dialogue of cultures, civilizations and states. Russia the conciliator, Russia the unifier, Russia the harmonizer. A merciful power, patient and open within the limits outlined by law and goodwill, but a fearsome power outside those limits. A country that takes in West and East, North and South, and that is uniquely capable—perhaps it alone has this capability—of harmoniously unifying many different elements, of achieving a historic symphony. That is how I see Russia in a new world."[25]

Statism and Social Competition

Social competition is aimed at creating a positive and distinctive identity for the self through positively differentiating it from the other on the dimension of comparison. For Russian statists, the key dimension for self-evaluation is great power status; they sought to posit a higher-status level or reverse the status relationship with the main others, the United States and the West. Those employing social competition strategies regarding status would argue that their exclusion from or lesser status in a group was unjust, that they deserve inclusion or elevation to a higher position, and that the other's elevated position should be decreased. Additionally, they emphasize that adjusting social recognition requires self-improvement (rather than competing in a zero-sum fashion for material resources), since their goals and those of the desired ingroup are not seen as mutually exclusive.[26] Russian statists, including Evgenii Primakov and Vladimir Putin, did not portray Russia and the United States or the West as having necessarily incompatible goals; rather, as both countries were great powers, they shared the same goal of preserving international order. This had significant consequences for their behavioral orientations toward the United States, a point developed below.

Russian statists predominantly employed social competition strategies, though they accepted Russia's special role in Eurasia, demanding from both domestic and international audiences social recognition of Russia's status as a great power with special rights and responsibilities and its place in Western-dominated institutions. Social competition strategies were particularly pronounced under Prime Minister Evgenii Primakov and continued under Vladimir Putin. Instead of creating a new, Eurasian dimension along which to compare Russia with the United States (the primary other), they attempted to alter Russia's negative position on the existing dimension of comparison—membership in the great power and the Western ingroups—in order to cast Russia in a more positive and distinctive light.

Primakov's social creativity strategy was to invert the relationship between the United States and Russia. Rather than conceding Russian inferiority in a unipolar world ordered by the United States, Primakov declared his doctrine of a "multipolar world" in which he put forth an image of Russia as holding the superior distinction of being a genuine status quo great power seeking to restrain its fellow great power, the United States, for its own good and return it to the right path instead of destabilizing international relations through the pursuit of ideological goals. Primakov cast the United States as the negative actor acting in a revisionist and dangerous manner, while Russia was acting responsibly and soberly, as a great power should, to uphold international order and restrain its fellow great power from going too far.[27] His creativity was to ignore the material dimensions of great power status—by which criteria the United States was superior—and to create a new dimension based on responsibility and pragmatism as the defining dimension on which Russia's status and the status of all great powers would be judged.

Vladimir Putin, a chief proponent of statist developmentalism, adopted Primakov's social creativity strategy of a multipolar world. However, he modified it to highlight Russia's "traditional" role as a *joint* stabilizer of the international system that, in Russian eyes, had placed Russia on a par with the United States during the Cold War. This theme appeared in Primakov's foreign policy as well but was especially evident in Putin's depiction after the attacks of September 11, 2001, of Russia's joint responsibility with the United States to rid the world of terrorism.[28] As Putin declared in 2002, "Russia is one of the most reliable guarantors of international stability. It is Russia's principled position that has made it possible to form a strong anti-terrorist coalition. . . . Our major goal in foreign policy is to ensure strategic stability in the world. To do this, we are participating in the creation of a new system of security, we maintain constant dialogue with the United States, and work on changing the quality of our relations with NATO."[29] In this case, the desire is to create a positive and distinctive role for Russia in which its status is equal to the United States, but using as a criterion the attributes of a truly responsible and reliable stabilizer of world politics rather than material capabilities. In contrast to the Soviet role in a "superpower condominium," this status is premised not on nuclear danger but on jointly fighting common threats from nonstate actors and thereby providing international stability for the rest of the world.[30]

In addition to promoting this social creativity strategy, Putin also adopted a social competition strategy with regard to Russia's place in the West. In Putin's statist developmentalism, Russia's place was unquestionably among the advanced industrial countries of the West, but as a country that retained its own distinct historical traditions. Putin offered a historically legitimate hybrid of Russia's greatness with a Western emphasis on international economic standards. The result was liberal statist developmentalism. Despite Putin's orientation toward the West and his pragmatism, his "idea" for Russia rested squarely on what he termed "belief in Russia's greatness." In emphasizing Russia's greatness, Putin was filling the psychological need to assert Russia's distinctiveness from other, lesser, European countries. Putin skillfully assembled "patriotism," "belief in the greatness of Russia," "statism," and "social solidarity" as "foothold[s] for the unity of Russian society" drawn from the past, together with acceptance of the "universal values" of private property and entrepreneurship drawn from the West. He argued that "the new Russian idea will come about as an alloy or an organic unification of universal general humanitarian values with traditional Russian values which have stood the test of the times, including the test of the turbulent 20th century."[31] Here we see efforts to preserve Russia's distinctive traditions while accepting elements of Western universalism and the demand of Russia's assumption of its rightful place among the group of great powers and in the West, all while being not fully Western (just as Japan and the NICs had done).

Russian National Self-Images and the Determination of National Interests

One of the central propositions of aspirational constructivism is that national self-images constitute certain countries and regions as ingroups and outgroups for the national self. As noted earlier, such group categorization leads to expectations regarding behavioral orientations toward competition and cooperation between the self and the group. National self-images rarely create ingroups or outgroups on a single dimension, and a country may appear in multiple groups. This creates overlapping or mutually reinforcing ingroups and outgroups, a dynamic that complicates the simple behavioral expectation that ingroups produce orientations toward cooperation and outgroups produce orientations toward competition.[32] The behavioral expectations associated with these sorts of groups are more complex.

The West as a Double Ingroup and Cooperative Foreign Policy Orientations

If a national self-image constructs a group as a double ingroup, in which Russia is similar to the group on both status and purpose, the expectation is that the national interest would dictate cooperation with that ingroup, even as it competes for an improved position within the group. The Western national self-images outlined in chapter 3 depict the West as a double ingroup, so we would expect advocates of these self-images to favor cooperation with the West, even when seeking a higher-status position.

Liberal internationalists constructed the West as a double ingroup, depicting Russia's international status as function of its membership in the club of market democracies. In Foreign Minister Andrei Kozyrev's words, Russia was the "missing component of the democratic pole of the Northern Hemisphere."[33] He and other liberal internationalists divided the world primarily according to type of political-economic system rather than material power, with the democratic capitalist club congregating in Western-dominated multilateral organizations. Their assumption, quickly challenged as utopian, was that once a club member, Russia would be accorded equal rank with other members. Kozyrev saw the Western democracies as "Russia's natural allies," not the post-Soviet republics, and argued that a democratic Russia would have "friendly and eventually allied relations with the civilized [meaning Western] world, including NATO, the UN, and other structures."

Prominent advocates of liberal internationalism, particularly Kozyrev, suggested that Russia, as a means to this end, end all policies implying an imperial role with respect to the former Soviet republics and satellites and accept Western policies globally. In practice, this meant cutting off subsidies to the former Soviet republics, raising their energy prices to world levels, acceding to Western conditions for aid, and prioritizing warm relations with the United States and Europe over economic profits from arms sales and losses from economic embargoes of countries out of favor with the West. Kozyrev and liberal internationalists, unlike many others, rejected calls to keep the Soviet Army unified. With regard to the former Soviet republics in general, Kozyrev represented an anti-imperial, anti-restorationist image of a Russia consolidating its own sovereign democratic identity and happy to let the other republics do likewise. In this view, as in the democratic developmentalist self-image, Russia's interests in joining the democratic club should not be held hostage to reintegration of the former Soviet republics. The central importance of membership of the democratic ingroup is clear in Kozyrev's relegation of the former Soviet republics' significance in Russian foreign policy to the effect Russia's behavior there would have on "Russia's standing in the civilized world."[34] Liberal internationalists argued that Russia had to do everything possible to avoid the appearance of imperialism, as this would both frighten Russia's newly and rightfully (in the view of liberal internationalists) sovereign neighbors and impede Russia's joining the West.

While wholeheartedly advocating cooperation with the West and the

United States, democratic developmentalists suggested that such cooperation neither precluded a self-interested policy toward the former Soviet republics nor required accepting Western policy positions on all issues.[35] As Vladimir Lukin noted, "In showing a perfectly laudable desire to overcome our imperial heritage, we occasionally tend to bear ourselves much more gently and modestly than any normal power should do when the interests of compatriots are affected."[36] Democratic developmentalists did not dispute the importance of the United States to Russia but stressed the need to influence U.S. policy, not merely track it.[37]

The West as a Double Outgroup and Confrontational Foreign Policy Orientations

In contrast to the positive and cooperative orientations toward double ingroups, double outgroups are expected to produce national interests in confrontation: a desire to compete with the outgroup in order to overturn the negative status position of the Russian ingroup and hostility based on dissimilar political purposes. The national restorationist, neocommunist and Slavophile self-images outlined in chapter 3 construct the West as a double outgroup, and we would therefore expect them to advocate hostile competition with the West, as their desired international status and political purpose are at odds with the West. While these national self-images are not the subject of this chapter, their foreign policy orientations generally are consistent with this expectation. Their advocates generally promote "realistic" competition or confrontation with the West and exhibit hostility toward the West, particularly Western behavior in areas deemed to be Russia's primary ingroup—the former Soviet republics.[38]

The West as a Partial Ingroup and Boundedly Competitive Foreign Policy Orientations

In between the cooperative and confrontational ends of the behavioral spectrum lie national self-images that construct partial ingroups, in which the group is seen as similar to Russia on one dimension but dissimilar on another. With respect to such self-images, aspirational constructivism anticipates that this cross-cutting cleavage would produce a desire for cooperation on the ingroup dimension, which moderates any interest in competition along the outgroup dimension. Russian statist national self-images fall into this category. They depict Russia as a member of the great power ingroup along with many Western countries and as a partial member of the West, but not purely Western.

This partial membership bears a bit more explanation: statism portrays Russia as combining qualities of both Western and Eastern civilizations, and in this self-image, Russia is partly Western. Russia is also depicted as a member of the modern Western group of advanced industrial countries, even though it has distinctive national characteristics that set it apart from the West. Statists also construct Russia as the most prominent member of the post-Soviet ingroup. Western countries are not part of the post-Soviet ingroup, and competition is therefore anticipated with regard to that ingroup on issues related to the FSU. So these self-images construct the Western great powers as a partial ingroup. As such, aspirational constructivism expects that statists are unlikely to advocate confrontation with the West. Instead, it expects them to develop national interests in cooperating with the West in order to integrate into it and in limiting competition with the West to that end.

For statists, Russian history and geography dictates its character as a "Eurasian" country. This character prevents Russia from being a completely Western country but also gives it a special role as the hegemon of Eurasia. This constructs the former Soviet republics and the Russian diaspora there as a natural ingroup and produces orientations to compete with outside countries trying to influence that ingroup. For many statists, as Stankevich writes, a foreign state's "attitude toward the Russian population and Russian heritage is the most important criterion for Russia in determining whether a given state is friendly." This criterion determines Russia's bilateral positions with the former Soviet republics, particularly regarding troop withdrawals, economics, and finance. It also predisposes Russian statists to favor competition with states outside of the former Soviet Union who seek to increase their standing among this ingroup.[39] The most likely points of conflict with the West therefore are likely to be over perceived threats to Russia's position in its FSU ingroup.

Russian statists view Russia as one of the handful of great powers in a multipolar world, and its responsibilities are therefore not merely regional but global. As a member of the great power ingroup, Russia therefore should cooperate with other great powers to produce international stability and compete for recognition of its position.[40] As a result, statists like Primakov favored a Gaullist mode of international relations in which Russia's position in the West was not to be questioned and its great power status relative to the United States would be asserted. Primakov's foreign policy orientation prompted Dmitrii Trenin to note that "Russian diplomacy is acquiring a French accent. Alternatively opting in and out, Moscow has managed to be anti-American on a given issue without being anti-Western."[41] While he emphasized Russia's role as a global great power and made achievement of a multipolar world a central tenet of Russian foreign policy, Primakov and his successor Vladimir Putin never moved Russian foreign policy toward confrontation, as national restorationists advocated. Instead they emphasized Russia's special status in West and the importance of its relationship with the United States.[42] A creativity strategy is apparent in statist national self-images, which devalue U.S. military preeminence and highlight Russia's positive role as the genuine *stabilizer* of the international system (in contrast to the roguish United States). For Primakov and Putin, partnership with the West remained a top priority, as the West was an important ingroup; in contrast to liberal internationalists, however, partnership was not to be the sole or main national interest, as Russia's position among the great powers, Eurasian distinctiveness, and special role in the FSU dictated social competition for recognition of its status.

For statist developmentalists like Putin, the goal of global great power status required Russia's integration into global economic and political institutions but not its subordination to the West. As Stankevich advocated, Russians should seek "integration into the world economy, without losing face and while protecting their own interests."[43] Statist developmentalists therefore advocated a national interest in cooperating with the West in order to join the global economy and maintain Russia's great power status on that dimension. Putin and other statist developmentalists sought broad cooperation and limited competition with the West, as Primakov did.

Conforming to a strategy of social competition, Putin and other statist developmentalists accepted Western economic criteria for ranking countries. In contrast to a social creativity strategy, they stressed the need for Russia to change its place in the existing ranking rather than create a new ranking system. As Putin said in his annual address to the Federal Assembly in April 2002, "The principle [*sic*] feature of the modern world is the internationalization of economy and society. And in these conditions, the best world standards become the most important criteria of success." Russian status in the global economy was determined according to Western criteria, which meant market competition. Putin highlighted the economic competition entailed in integration into the Western global economy but also rejected confrontation or hostility based on different political purposes:

> the period of confrontation has ended. We are building constructive, normal relations with all the world's nations. . . . However . . . the norm in the international community, in the world today, is also harsh competition—for markets, for investment, for political and economic influence. And in this fight, Russia needs to be strong and competitive. Today, the countries of the world compete with each other in all economic and political parameters: in the size of the tax burden, in the security level of the country and its citizens, in guarantees for protecting property rights. They compete in the attractiveness of the business climate, in the development of economic freedoms, in the quality of state institutions and the effectiveness of the legal system. The conclusion is obvious: in the world today, no one intends to be hostile towards us—no one wants this or needs it. But no one is particularly waiting for us either. No one is going to help us especially. We need to fight for a place in the "economic sun" ourselves.[44]

For statist developmentalists such as Putin, Russia's global integration required advancement in the global status hierarchy and competition for social recognition on the West's terms and therefore competition bounded by cooperation with Western powers and institutions and acceptance of Western economic values.

Conclusion

Aspirational constructivism expects political elites to use identity management strategies to promote their preferred national self-image in order for it become the basis of a new social order. It also expects these national self-images to generate behavioral orientations toward countries belonging to ingroups and outgroups. This chapter finds that advocates of the Western and statist national self-images employed such identity management strategies, whether consciously or not. As the next chapter explains, these two sets of national self-images vied for dominance in the political discourse in post-Soviet Russia throughout Russia's revolutionary decade. Both constructed Russia as at least partially a member of the West. As a result, as aspirational constructivism expects, the behavioral orientations associated with these national self-images advocated some degree of cooperation with the West.

For liberal internationalists, their strategy of complete and rapid assimilation into the West dictated a policy orientation toward conciliation and accepting the West's lead—and toward a complete rejection of Russia's past as containing any positively distinctive elements. Enhancing Russian national self-esteem could only be accomplished through Russia's complete transformation into a "normal" Western country, similar to Germany or Japan. Democratic developmentalists joined with their fellow Westernizers in using a strategy of assimilation; however, they favored a gradual process of assimilation that preserved Russia's historical distinction as a great power. They favored extensive cooperation with the West but accepted that Russian interests in preserving its historical distinctiveness would at times mean rejecting Western positions and advice.

Statists viewed Russia as largely Western but as historically distinct from the West in important ways. For Eurasian statists, such distinctiveness was Russia's special gift, enabling it to aspire to a role that transcended the great power attributes that other statists prioritized. Russia's primary ingroup was therefore the former Soviet republics, and Russia would compete with outside countries to maintain its special role there. Instead of remaking the world as a Eurasian harmonizer, Eurasian statists such as Evgenii Primakov suggested that Russia should seek recognition of its great power status through assertion of its rights and existing strengths (social competition) and by highlighting the manner in which it was a "better" great power than the United States (social creativity). Statists and statist developmentalists accepted Russia's Eurasian distinctiveness and therefore its hegemonic role in the post-Soviet ingroup but sought social recognition of Russia's status as a great power and membership in the Western global economy. They advocated a strategy of social competition in addition to social creativity. Statist developmentalists, most prominently Vladimir Putin, argued that Russia should seek its place in the Western global economy through internal transformations designed to make it more economically Western and therefore more competitive in a global marketplace. For all subtypes of statism, national interests dictated that Russia should cooperate with the West, restrain competition, and avoid confrontation.

The next chapter considers the aspirational constructivist proposition that national self-images must correspond to common notions of historical aspiration and be considered practical under current conditions in order to dominate the political discourse and act as the national identity. It evaluates how these national self-images and identity management strategies fared in the Russian political discourse as political elites assessed their legitimacy in the light of their common historical aspirations and the conditions Russia faced during the decade and a half following the collapse of the Soviet Union. It explains why liberal internationalism quickly fell from dominance and how, after ten years of vigorous debate, Russian political elites settled only partly on a statist definition of Russian national identity—the part that most conformed to shared historical aspirations regarding Russia's great power status.

FIVE

Post-Soviet Russia's "Revolutionary Decade" and the Creation of National Identity

From the dissolution of the Soviet Union in 1991 to Vladimir Putin's reelection as president in 2004, Russian debates on national identity—and Russian foreign policy—swung from warmly embracing the West and the United States to heatedly rebuking them. Russian foreign policy moved between Russia's incorporation into Western global structures and talk of a new Cold War. Western analysts struggled to understand a seemingly incoherent Russian foreign policy.[1] As Scott Parrish wrote, "It is not at all clear what the goals of Russian foreign policy . . . are—or whether Russia has a coherent foreign policy at all."[2] At the outset of this period, an initially dominant Western national self-image advocating rapid assimilation into the West fell from grace. Analysts in the West and in Russia feared a "Weimar Russia" and the dominance of revanchist national self-images advocating confrontation with the West and restoration of the Russian and Soviet empires.[3] Over the next ten years, political struggles over Russia's post-Soviet national identity—its political purpose and international status in the post–Cold War world—resulted in the delegitimization of Western and national restorationist self-images and eventual settlement on statist national self-images as the most legitimate alternative.

Aspirational Constructivism and Correspondence Tests of Legitimacy

Chapters 3 and 4 explored the aspirational constructivist expectations that political elites would develop national self-images and identity management strategies offering new bases for national self-esteem when previous identities are challenged and that these national self-images produce behavioral orientations toward cooperation, competition, and confrontation. The final aspirational constructivist proposition concerns the process or selection mechanism by which one of these candidate national identities, along with its attendant definition of the national interest, comes to dominate its competitors. It is the proposition that a correspondence process of elite legitimacy tests determines which national self-image becomes dominant. The expectation is that national self-images that pass correspondence tests of historical and effective legitimacy are most likely to dominate the political discourse and come to act as "the" national identity and define national interests.

Correspondence with Russian Historical Aspirations: Historical Legitimacy Tests

Chapter 3 highlighted how Russian political elites shared one common historical aspiration: to attain the status of a modern and distinctive great power. Aspirational constructivism anticipates that Russian national self-images that are congruent with the historical aspiration to regain this status will be more persuasive than those that are not. This should be particularly true in times of change; during such times, if historical and effective legitimacy conflict, aspirational constructivism expects historical aspirations regarding the self to matter more than the "self-in-context"—that is, effective legitimacy—in shaping identity and interests. During more stable times, aspirational constructivism expects the self-in-context to carry equal weight in determining the legitimacy of national self-images. (The plausibility of this expectation is a subject for future research, as the conditions of this study clearly reflect a period of massive change.)

With respect to post-Soviet Russia, aspirational constructivism expects Russian political elites to apply correspondence tests of historical legitimacy—history tests—to national self-images and their attendant identity management strategies and to find unpersuasive those that downplay or reject Russia's historical status as a great power. Russian political elites should be drawn to national self-images that promote Russia's positive distinctiveness and great power status.

Correspondence between Self-Images and the Self-in-Context: Effective Legitimacy Tests

The correspondence process of legitimacy-testing at the heart of aspirational constructivism focuses not just on the impact of history on identity formation but also on the self-in-context—how the self perceives its ability to enact an identity "out in the real world."[4] Here the question revolves around whether a national self-image can be "verified" or effectively enacted in current conditions—whether it can pass a "efficacy test," in aspirational constructivist terminology. Aspirational constructivism therefore expects that if Russian national self-images cannot pass efficacy tests —if they are seen as incapable of being actualized or effectively enhancing national self-esteem in the conditions Russians presently face—they should be unpersuasive to Russian political elites and not become the dominant identity.

In particular, aspirational constructivism anticipates that if Russian political elites perceive that the actions of persons and policy outcomes associated with a national self-image do not correspond to its principles and prescriptions, then the self-image is unlikely to dominate the political discourse for long. If the actions of the national self-image's advocates are contrary to its principles, then Russian political elites are likely to consider it incapable of effective enactment and impractical. If Russian political elites view policy outcomes associated with the national self-image as failures, then the self-image should likewise be considered ineffective and elites should find it unpersuasive. If the converse is true, and the policies and personages associated with a self-image are seen as successful, then that self-image should be persuasive.

Aspirational constructivism expects Russian political elites, through a correspondence process of legitimacy-testing, to end up favoring national self-images and identity management strategies that promote their historical aspirations and are deemed capable of achieving them in practical terms. The empirical plausibility of this expectation is the primary focus of this chapter. The chapter argues that liberal internationalism failed to pass both history and efficacy tests in the eyes of Russian political elites. The statist national self-image that helped dethrone it, Eurasian statism, passed history tests but was occasionally criticized for being insufficiently effective in light of current conditions. By the end of the 1990s, another statist national self-image, statist developmentalism, became the dominant national self-image, as it was broadly considered to be both historically appropriate and effective.

The remainder of the chapter assesses the plausibility of this claim, that the correspondence process of legitimacy shapes the construction of national identity and national interests, by examining the Russian political discourse regarding Russia's international status and foreign policy and political purpose and domestic reforms from 1991 to 2004. It examines elite discourse during that period to determine what role correspondence-testing played in discrediting Western liberal internationalism and the assimilation strategy of the early reformers and in consolidating the legitimacy of the statist national self-images and the identity management strategies put forward by Evgenii Primakov and Vladimir Putin. It finds that post-Soviet elite debate revolved around sources of national self-esteem and positive distinctiveness in Russia's past and the contending national self-images of Russia. Russian political elites' historical aspirations regarding Russian modernity and international status, together with their evaluations of the policy outcomes and actors associated with contending national self-images, were critical in producing the eventual dominance of statist developmentalism and a national interest in competition bounded by cooperation with the West.

The Identity Outcome of Russia's Revolutionary Post-Soviet Decade

During the political, economic, and social upheaval that marked the decade and a half of this study—Russia's "revolutionary decade"—Russian debates about foreign policy were largely debates about what Russia's post-Soviet identity should be.[5] In their struggles to define Russia's post-Soviet identity and interest, Russian political elites shared an aspiration to retain the historical great power status of tsarist and then Soviet Russia. They never settled, however, on a key element of national identity, the question of Russia's political purpose—its proper form of political economy and national mission.[6] Western, statist, and national restorationist national self-images contended for dominance.[7] This lack of agreement centered on a marked ambivalence about the extent to which one source of Russian national self-esteem—its historical status as a global great power—was commensurable with a political purpose that entailed becoming more Western rather than maintaining a "uniquely" Russian identity. As a result, what passed for Russian national identity in the 1990s and through the first Putin administration remained largely based on status-maintenance vis-à-vis the United States rather than a more rational assessment of Russia's capabilities and opportunities in a post–Cold War world.

This emphasis on a status-driven but otherwise ambivalent identity strengthened the legitimacy of the social creativity and social competition strategies of statists who proclaimed as their mission the internal strengthening of the Russian state and its right to its global great power mantle. This produced a national interest in upholding Russia's social status as a great power on a par with the United States and maintaining Russia's membership, at least in part, in the developed West. Foreign policy as a result reflected both competition and cooperation but never strayed into the realm of confrontation, as many Western analysts had feared—and as Russian national restorationists advocated. This outcome was neither preordained nor structurally given. This period produced foreign policy calculations often at odds with Russia's material and political capabilities (as the next two chapters show), and Russian foreign policy became more rather than less assertive as the Russian economy weakened and Russia's diplomatic clout faded over the 1990s.

This chapter explains this outcome in aspirational constructivist terms. Russian political elites extensively and passionately debated the question of what "national idea" best suited post-Soviet Russia. The instability in Russian national identity and national interests over this period was caused by a persistent division among Russian political elites about what the source of Russia's distinctiveness ought to be.[8] As noted in chapter 3, Russian political elites early in the process agreed that Russia's past great power status continued to be a source of national distinctiveness, and this formed their shared historical aspiration. A casualty of this shared historical aspiration was the liberal internationalist national self-image and its strategy of complete assimilation into the West. Liberal internationalism's depictions of Russia's international status were deemed early on not to correspond with aspirations to its past great power status.

Russian political elites could agree on Russia's international status, but they never arrived at a consensus on the second element of national identity: Russia's political purpose. The policies and practitioners of liberal internationalism contributed to this continued division, as they were judged to be ineffective and illegitimate under the conditions Russia faced. By 2004, Russian political elites still had not decided whether national distinctiveness and self-esteem could be attained if Russia were to transform itself in order to be accepted into the Western social order or whether such a transformation would reflect an unacceptable rejection of Russia's history of pursuing an independent model of development and building an alternative, non-Western world order.

As a result, statist national self-images that proclaimed Russia's national distinctiveness to be its historical place among the globe's great powers but also portrayed Russia as being partially Western provided the lowest common denominator on which elites could agree: Russia was a modern great power. Statists used social creativity and social competition strategies in order to assert both Russia's great power status and its modern, Western credentials. Their depictions of Russia's historical status and the need for a strong state ended up substituting for a durable agreement on Russia's political purpose and facilitated the efforts to recentralize the state in the name of "state strength" that began in the Putin era and then accelerated after 2004. Statist national interests dictated competition for social recognition of Russia's great power status while bounding that competition within a broadly cooperative orientation toward the West. This outcome, of a statist national identity and a "competitive engagement" national interest, is an important one from the perspective of Western policymakers, as it represented the victory of the status quo rather than revisionist national self-images in Russia, of ones that disposed Russian policymakers to favor limiting competition with the West.

Dynamics of Identity Politics during Russia's Revolutionary Post-Soviet Decade

During the first and crucial phase, 1991 to 1993, of Russian political elites' struggle to define a new identity and set of national interests for their country, an initially dominant Western national self-image—liberal internationalism—fell from grace, primarily because its prescription for Russia's international role did not correspond to the great power aspirations that the majority of Russian political elites accepted as historically legitimate. Even though the majority of political elites remained positively inclined toward the West and favored markets and democracy, they rejected the second-class status and negative depiction of Russia's historical distinctiveness implicit in the liberal internationalist self-image.[9] Their aspiration to global great power status and the consequent rejection of Russia's role of a follower reliant on the United States and on the West laid the foundation for the later stages of post-Soviet Russian identity politics. The policy failures attributed to liberal internationalists and the manner in which they carried out their reforms sealed the fate of their preferred self-image, as Russian political elites found them harmful and at odds with liberal internationalist principles.

As the 1990s progressed, the effective legitimacy of Westernizers and their policies was further undermined by the authoritarian manner in which the Yeltsin administration implemented reforms and the destabilizing outcomes of those reforms. From the perspective of the majority of Russian political elites, liberal internationalist Westernizers failed to pass history *and* efficacy tests, and this damaged the legitimacy of Western national self-images and prevented them from dominating the political discourse long enough to become Russia's national identity. Their perceived failures led to personnel and policy changes as well as strengthened advocates of statist and national restorationist self-images. Advocates of statism and statist developmentalism gained increasing influence, especially with regard to foreign policy, but Westernizers, particularly democratic developmentalists, remained vocal in the political discourse and influential in economic policy throughout the post-Soviet period.

Russian political elites continued to debate Russia's identity from 1994 to 1998 and failed to agree on a single national self-image whose political purpose was overwhelmingly accepted as effective and historically legitimate.[10] Consensual aspirations to great power status remained constant and provided the key benchmark of historical legitimacy against which all national self-images were judged. Throughout the post-Soviet period, the negative perception of liberal internationalism's portrayal of Russia's international status tainted moderate and radical Westernizers alike and framed political elite interpretation of the behavior of Western countries and institutions, particularly the United States, the International Monetary Fund (IMF), and the North Atlantic Treaty Organization (NATO). A range of statist, national restorationist, and Western views competed to define the national interest, with Eurasian statism serving as the lowest common denominator for most of this period.

After 1998, clear signs of Russian policy failings highlighted the policy failures of Eurasian statists and Westernizers and shifted the political discourse in favor of statist developmentalism. The triple shock of Russia's financial default in August 1998, Russia's marginalization in the 1999 Kosovo war, and the 1999 incursion of Chechen rebels in Dagestan focused elite attention on the correspondence between competing national self-images and current conditions, what social psychologists term the "self-in-context." These perceived failures solidified the appeal of the statist developmentalist national self-image, which had attracted a large number of adherents in the middle and late 1990s. This support rested on both the historical legitimacy of its advocacy of Russia's great power status and the effective legitimacy of the program for upholding that status offered by Vladimir Putin, statist developmentalism's most prominent advocate. From 1999 onward, even before Putin moved to limit opposition after 2004, his national self-image of statist developmentalism came to dominate the political discourse and define Russia's national interests. Its dominance lay in its match with elite aspirations and the perceived successes Putin was able to achieve in carrying it out, successes that owed much to the rising price of oil and the 1998 devaluation of the ruble and the consequent swelling of government coffers and increase in domestic import substitution.

Aspirations and the Historical Legitimacy of Russia's Great Power Status

The empirical record suggests that the historical legitimacy of Russia's international status as a great power significantly constrained political elite perceptions of Russia's national interest and led to early rejection of liberal internationalist proposals for assimilation into the West. Throughout the 1990s, political elites' historical aspirations interfered with efforts to develop national interests more in keeping with a rational calculation of Russia's material capabilities. Vladimir Lukin noted in 2000 that "recollections of the former might of the USSR" continued to hinder the identification of Russia's proper niche in the international system. "Unfortunately or fortunately," he said, "the shadow of Hamlet's father is still present on the world scene."[11] Throughout the 1990s and into the new millennium, Russian political elites debated whether or not the collapse of the Soviet Union in 1991 represented a historical "rupture" that had caused past identities to become obsolete.[12] The liberal internationalism of the early Yeltsin years was quickly judged illegitimate on historical grounds, as it denied Russia its proper rank as an equal member of the great power club and suggested instead that Russia was just another member of "civilized society." Those who prevailed claimed that Russia's past international status as an independent and great power was not only usable but a highly legitimate part of Russian identity—indeed, the basis for Russia's national interests.

The Historical Illegitimacy of Liberal Internationalism in Russia

The 1991–1993 period was a critical one in the discursive battle over of Russian national identity. Post-Soviet Russia began its existence with liberal internationalists dominating the new government. Many of the key politicians who occupied the senior posts in the newly minted Russian Federation's executive branch advocated a radical liberal internationalist national self-image, most prominently presidential advisor Gennadii Burbulis; Foreign Minister Andrei Kozyrev; acting prime minister Egor Gaidar; and Anatolii Chubais, head of the State Property Committee.[13] They advocated rapid assimilation into the "civilized world" of Western market democracies and opposed those who emphasized Russia's historical uniqueness, its past role as a independent pole of attraction in world politics, and its inherited great power status.[14] Despite their initial dominance, these radical Westernizers failed to lock in their liberal internationalist national self-image as the foundation for Russia's new identity and its national interests. They soon succumbed to the historical aspirations that all other political elites held.

The consensus that liberal internationalism failed to pass tests of historical legitimacy was forged in 1992 and 1993 out of the centrist and nationalist opposition to Kozyrev and Gaidar and the democratic developmentalist and statist critiques of their programs.[15] Such widespread criticism reflected the broad consensus on the historical legitimacy of Russia's past international status and the aspirations to retain it.

The early demise of liberal internationalism was not inevitable. National restorationist self-images were largely marginalized in 1991 and 1992 because of their association with the USSR and with the failed putsch against Gorbachev in August 1991. The coup attempt by Soviet hardliners served not only to further the disintegration of the Soviet Union but also briefly made critique of radical democratization and liberalization illegitimate, thereby providing a honeymoon for reformers.[16] Russian political elites were generally supportive of Yeltsin during this period. Based on a May 1993 elite survey, the All-Russia Center for the Study of Public Opinion (VTsIOM) found "support for market reform and the development of private property, [and] general support of President Yeltsin's policies." Rather it was "specific criticisms of his foreign and domestic political activities" that served as the first of the correspondence tests of legitimacy that the liberal internationalists failed to pass.[17]

Nor could the liberal internationalists' fall be easily ascribed to a failure to respond to a worsening international environment or perceptions of a hostile West, as realism and structural constructivism might expect. Russian political elites—with the exception of the conservatives and hardliners who had been marginalized by their support for the attempted August 1991 coup—did not perceive the West as a threat.[18] VTsIOM found in 1993 that most Russian foreign policy elites had positive attitudes toward the West and the United States; only 1 percent viewed the United States as "enemy number 1."[19] The same year, the Vox Populi polling agency found in its survey of 350 Russian political elites that less than one in five political elites saw the United States as a threat. Political elites identified the primary external threat as coming from the Middle East, followed by the former Soviet republics and East Asia. Significantly, these results were replicated among military officers and members of the Communist Party.[20] Moreover, three times as many elites thought that domestic rather than foreign problems were the primary threat Russia faced.[21] The overwhelming majority of elite respondents (86 percent) did not foresee an attack on Russia in the near future; of this number, over a third said there was no likelihood at all. Only one-tenth thought such an attack was likely.[22] This view continued well into the post-Soviet period.

Despite positive attitudes toward market democratic reform, Yeltsin, and the West and an unthreatening international environment, liberal internationalists were accused of betraying Russia's national interests in pursuing policies unbecoming to Russia's historical status.[23] For many political elites, the liberal internationalist manner of radical Westernization meant denying and rejecting Russia's past strengths and abandoning its history as a great power, which involved the exercise of special rights and responsibilities in the former Soviet republics and Eurasia. For them, positing a Russian identity of being purely Western meant denying Russia's historical traditions and unique role in world politics. By the spring of 1992, critics across the political spectrum had begun to attack liberal internationalist positions in foreign policy and radical market reforms on the domestic front.

The Legitimacy of Russia's Hegemonic Status in the Former Soviet Union

Policy toward the former Soviet republics emerged as one of two key tests of the historical legitimacy of liberal internationalism, the other being policy toward the West. Foreign Minister Kozyrev was criticized on all sides for being slow to realize that the former Soviet republics, as new subjects of international relations, should be the top priority of the Russian Foreign Ministry, as they formed the historical basis for Russia's status as a great power and its distinctiveness as a Eurasian, rather than Western or Eastern, power. VTsIOM found in 1993 that "on the whole, the foreign policy establishment is for the restoration of Russia's great power status via preserving her special place as a Eurasian power in the international relations system."[24] National restorationists in the Supreme Soviet and some serving military officers whipped up hysteria over the fate of the newly created Russian diaspora in the former Soviet republics.[25] Liberal internationalists, particularly Foreign Minister Kozyrev, were accused of abandoning their "compatriots" when violence broke out in March 1992 between Russian speakers and the Moldovan authorities in Transdniestria and of doing nothing to stop the anti-Russian "apartheid" being institutionalized in Estonia and Latvia.[26]

The key shift in political elite discourse away from liberal internationalism took place in April 1992, when State Chancellor Sergei Stankevich publicly broke with the Kozyrev-Gaidar line and joined national restorationists and statists in rejecting assimilation into the West as the proper national mission for Russia.[27] In so doing, Stankevich launched the decade-long debate on what the "Russian idea" or Russian national identity was.[28] Stankevich drew a firm line on Russian policy toward the FSU and criticized Kozyrev for being insufficiently "tough" on the "near abroad," a term for the former Soviet republics that heretofore had been used only in national restorationist discourse.[29]

Stankevich gave Eurasian statism its first mainstream airing in early 1992 in response to Kozyrev's attempts to defend liberal internationalism. He rejected liberal internationalism for failing to accept Russia's historical distinctiveness and role as a Eurasian great power. In contrast to liberal internationalism's emphasis on assimilation into Western structures and abandonment of the former Soviet republics, Stankevich suggested that Russia had a historic mission quite separate from the West, that of a unifier of the Eurasian landmass and stabilizer of global politics.[30] He rejected liberal internationalism's identity management strategy of assimilation into the West and argued against Kozyrev that a status for Russia comparable to Japan's was that of "the role of junior partner, which is not worth accepting."[31] Stankevich clearly and starkly set Russia's historical role of dominating the former Soviet republics as the standard for judging the legitimacy of Russia's foreign policy and for defining its interests in the former Soviet Union.[32]

Stankevich's discursive turn reflected a different identity management strategy—one of social creativity—than liberal internationalism's strategy of complete assimilation into a superior West. Rather than accept the judgment of the West's superiority and the clear implication of Russian inferiority, Stankevich redefined Russia's Eurasian identity as positive and superior to that of the West. Furthermore, he linked that superiority to Russia's historical status as a global great power and multicultural empire, the very things that liberal internationalism had deemed to be negative. It was not enough for Russia to seek democratic modernization and assimilation into the westernized global economy; its traditions demanded a more global and differentiated role and status.

After Stankevich's break with liberal internationalism, the sources of Russia's positive distinctiveness became a central axis around which the political discourse revolved. The issue was whether, in becoming more Western, Russia would lose the positive features that had distinguished it from other countries: its great power status and special role in the Eurasian heartland. Stankevich and others suggested that being like the West was not a sufficient source of national self-esteem for Russia; given its notable history, national self-esteem required distinguishing Russia in positive ways from the West.[33]

Stankevich's break with the Yeltsin administration's foreign policy was very politically significant. It marked a turn in the Russian political discourse from Western-oriented national self-images toward a more assertive advocacy of Russia's "natural" rights and roles abroad.[34] Prior to his speech, similar proclamations of Russian uniqueness and its Eurasian role had been the purview of nationalists and hardliners. Thereafter, those advocating a modified and relatively restrained version of such ideas could count a very prominent democratic ally. Many moderate voices joined Stankevich in criticizing the liberal internationalists for ignoring Russia's historical rights and responsibilities in the FSU.[35] In its effect, then, Stankevich's declaration of the historical illegitimacy of liberal internationalism shifted the center of the political discourse on Russia's international status toward statist and national restorationist self-images and their definitions of Russia's national interests. It also signaled the importance of historical aspirations in defining the legitimacy of competing national self-images. Stankevich's break with liberal internationalism prompted an eruption of public calls for a role of that emphasized Russia's historical status and its difference from the West, and a reorientation away from liberal internationalism followed.[36]

The Illegitimacy of a Status Subordinate to the West

Policy toward the West proved a second key test of liberal internationalism's historical legitimacy for Russian political elites. Overall they did not favor a "return to confrontation."[37] However, given their aspiration for international status, political elites soon found that following the West's lead was inappropriate at best and humiliating at worst.[38] The majority of political elites opposed the second-class status entailed in the liberal internationalist self-image (as distinct from opposition to the West, or the United States per se).[39] Regarded as consistent with the liberal internationalists' overtly pro-American foreign policy orientation, this second-class status led many political elites to distance themselves from pro-Western viewpoints. As moderate Sergei Karaganov stated,

> A great deal of damage has been inflicted on the country (even if in an indirect sort of way) by the actions of our ultra-liberals. Their readiness to automatically take for granted the opinions of the Western partners [while] disregarding the deep psychological trauma and a sense of injury sustained by a majority of the members of the Russian elite, even though traditionally pro-Western, over the downfall of the USSR, has led to a deepening of a split in the views on our foreign policy. Worse still is the fact that the attraction of Western civilization as such has waned, even if partially.[40]

While recognizing the continued importance of the United States to Russia, even moderates, such as Supreme Soviet member Evgenii Kozhokin, charged that "in dealing with the United States, Russia finds itself more and more often in the humiliating role of a suppliant. We may be said to be asking the Americans to help us attain prosperity in return for following in the wake of their policy. . . . What we need in the case of the United States are even, calm relations without raptures over the miracles of American democracy but also without undue mistrust or bias."[41] In its acceptance of a second-class status relative to the United States, liberal internationalism was failing on the grounds of historical aspirations to persuade Russian political elites that it sufficiently valued Russia's historical great power status and that it was capable of effective enactment of that status.

The notion of Russia's "humiliation," its illegitimate loss of its international status even though it had not been defeated in war, was a persistent theme in conservative statist, national restorationist, and neocommunist discourse. In contrast, Westernizers, especially liberal internationalists, compared post-Soviet Russia to postwar Germany and Japan, suggesting that as a defeated power it should recognize its guilt and repent in order to regain standing. In the liberal internationalist view, Russia's new status was not as a humiliated power but as a newly minted member of the democratic club that had to earn its stripes.[42]

Kozyrev, along with other liberal internationalists such as Andrei Zagorskii, attempted to fend off criticisms by arguing that national distinctiveness could be had even while assimilating into the West. They pointed to the experience of Japan and Germany in an attempt to justify their claim that the universalism of market democracy was not just compatible with but necessary for national individualism and hence Russia's uniqueness.[43] These efforts were unpersuasive to most Russian political elites, because, in their view, such second-tier status in the international system was not worth having, as it did not conform to their aspirations for great power status on a par with the status it had enjoyed in the past.[44]

Russia's status relative to the United States therefore became an important criterion in defining the historical legitimacy of national self-images. This historical status related not only to Russia's material capabilities but also to its past efforts to carve out a model of development distinct from the West's. Moderate Evgenii Kozhokin advocated Eurasian statism as the historically legitimate national identity that recognized "the Eurasian essence of Russia as a definite civilizational phenomenon."[45] This desire for an inherent and positive distinctiveness from the West, one that cast Russia as equal to the West in non-material as well as in material terms, pervaded elite discourse throughout the post-Soviet period. Such historical distinctiveness would allow Russia to be compared to the United States and the West as an equal, rather than as a pupil. Even fellow Westernizers criticized the liberal internationalist's stance on the legitimacy of Russia's past. While they believed that "there is no doubt about the wisdom of choosing in favor of the Western model of economic and political development," in their view, Russia's Soviet and tsarist history was not completely unusable.[46]

The views of Russian political elites regarding the FSU and relations with the West from 1985 to 1993 provides compelling evidence that historical aspirations weighed heavily in weakening the legitimacy of the liberal internationalist national self-image and shifting discourse toward statism and national restorationism. The major mistakes that the liberal internationalists and their New Thinking predecessors were accused of committing all related to the loss of Russia's historical status. According to VTsIOM surveys, the two major groups of elite complaints regarded the former Soviet republics ("the assumption of the USSR's collapse," "the loss of the near abroad," and "the deliberate break up of the Union") and subservience toward the United States ("concessions to the USA in the majority of foreign policy problems, and the extreme orientation toward the USA in foreign and domestic policy" and "the conclusion of unequal treaties").[47] While neither anti-Western or anti-American, "the majority of members of the elite [wanted] Russia and the USA to be *equal* partners [*ravnopravnie partneri*] in the future."[48] Most political elites regretted the USSR's collapse, for which Boris Yeltsin and the liberal internationalists in his administration were widely blamed.[49]

Russian political elites themselves emphasized the importance of the past in forging the "patriotic consensus" on the legitimacy of Russia's historical status as a great power. Observers and participants from across the political spectrum ascribed the dominance of great power thinking among political elites to the "trauma" of having lost their past status, which led to a national "inferiority complex."[50] In the words of national restorationist Valentin Rasputin, "Every people must have a national and state idea. For Russians it is to free themselves from the inferiority complex that has been thrust upon them, recognize their worth and uniqueness, and interpret that worth not as national arrogance but as qualitative spiritual development. For Russia, [the national idea] is the preservation of its statehood and the return of its former glory and honor."[51] In arguing for Western understanding, liberals and moderates wrote of the need on the part of the Russian elites for "psychological adaptation" to their changed position on the world scene.[52]

Effective Legitimacy and Enactment of National Self-Images in Post-Soviet Russia

In addition to correspondence between elite historical aspirations and national self-images, aspirational constructivism expects the legitimacy of a national self-image to be shaped by the correspondence between its prescribed outcomes and principles, on the one hand, and the perceptions of its actual enactment in current conditions, on the other—in other words, verification of the self-in-context. In this process of efficacy-testing, two factors affect legitimacy: the match between behavior of those advocating a particular self-image and its principles and the perceived effects of domestic and foreign policy outcomes associated with a self-image. This section first covers the correspondence between a national self-image's declared principles and the behavior of its acolytes before turning to the correspondence between prescriptions and policy outcomes.

Mismatch between Principles and Deeds: Liberal Reform by Diktat

Aside from its correspondence with Russian historical aspirations, Russian liberal internationalist behavior was judged according to the democratic and market principles it espoused, and it was found wanting. To its critics in parliament, the manner in which the Yeltsin administration sought to push through rapid political and economic change undermined the democratic and market credentials of the liberal internationalists. As early as 1992, such criticism began to erode the effective legitimacy of the liberal internationalist self-image. Russian political elites began to question the ability of a liberal internationalist identity to be enacted and verified under Russian conditions, as liberal internationalists did not appear to be acting in accordance with their democratic principles.

Members of the first Russian legislature—the Supreme Soviet and Congress of People's Deputies, elected in 1990—had in October 1991 granted the Yeltsin team a year of rule by decree in order to implement radical economic reforms. When negative results began to surface in 1992, they demanded a more gradual and gentle process of economic reform. The nature and pace of economic reforms was central in the open struggle for control over the nature of Russia's transformation between the radically reformist members of the presidential administration and the more conservative parliamentarians. This power struggle in turn sharpened the division between the radical Westernizers and the rest of the elites over the legitimacy of Russia's liberal internationalist course.

Yeltsin often acted in an autocratic fashion, appointing himself prime minister and others to cabinet positions and even changing the official name of the country, all without consulting the elected legislature (Yeltin's autocratic ways and habit of referring to himself with the royal we earned him the widely used moniker "Tsar Boris"). The administration was using "bolshevik" tactics, avoiding compromise, attempting reform through diktat, and refusing to share power with the legislature, which put the lie, in the eyes of many Russian political elites, to the liberal internationalists' claim that Western-style democracy was realistically possible in Russia.[53] In May 1993, 87 percent of Russian political elites believed that interactions between Yeltsin's government and the legislature were destabilizing the country.[54] Yeltsin's style prompted disappointed or offended former allies to unite with his main ideological opponents, the national restorationists.[55]

The result was a bloody constitutional crisis. Yeltsin had demanded a new constitution that made permanent his temporary powers of legislation-by-decree, which the parliament refused to approve. Throughout 1993, the executive and legislative branches battled over the constitutional basis for Russia's future governance and control of Russia's post-Soviet development. The leaders of the parliament voted to impeach Yeltsin in the late summer of 1993; Yeltsin, in turn, dissolved the parliament, in direct contravention of the existing constitution, and called new elections.

In October 1993, this confrontation turned violent. Opposition parliamentarians refused to step down and, with their armed supporters, occupied the parliament building. Yeltsin ordered the army to attack and occupy the parliament. In the ensuing fighting, over one hundred people were reportedly killed and over five hundred were injured.[56] Elections to a new parliamentary body, consisting of the Federal Assembly and the Duma, were held in December at Yeltsin's initiative, in which voters also approved his version of the new constitution, endowing the Russian president with extraordinary powers and significantly weakening the power of the legislature. Yeltsin had triumphed, but the October confrontation and the subsequent super-presidentialist constitution did little to convince Russian political elites that liberal internationalism had much to do with Russian reality.[57]

The 1993 elections brought national restorationists to dominance in the new parliament, and they acted to block Yeltsin's reform agenda. As in the previous parliament, political parties advocating liberal internationalism and democratic developmentalism were minorities. Parties that represented moderate and conservative statist views and that had been created at Yeltsin's command formed the main counterbalance to the national restorationists. As a result of the dominance of the "red-brown" coalition of communist and nationalist parties in the parliament, Yeltsin's administration often enacted economic and political reforms by presidential diktat rather than seek adoption by legislation. Such behavior continued to make many question the applicability of Western national self-images to Russian political conditions.[58]

From late 1993 onward, many political elites did not view the political system as genuinely democratic. The illegitimacy of Yeltsin's tactics had the effect of tarnishing the image of liberal internationalism and liberal democracy for both elites and the public. Politics was seen on all sides as a war between ideologies. Westernizers, in this and later periods, framed the struggle with the Supreme Soviet and later the Duma as a zero-sum war between privileged Soviet-era elites and new Russian democrats in which no compromise was possible. For the radical democrats espousing liberal internationalism, building the political system was a day-to-day battle with ideological opponents in which democratic principles and the rule of law were sacrificed to ensure the continuation of their reforms.[59] The executive-legislative struggle for power served to polarize the political discourse and prevent consensus on domestic reform and more broadly on Russia's political purpose, a polarization that would continue into the new millennium.

Questions about the legitimacy of liberal democratic reform as practiced in Russia continued throughout the Yeltsin years. The 1996 presidential election season saw Yeltsin, critically ill with heart disease and immensely unpopular because of the catastrophic first Chechen war and no improvement in the average standard of living, face off against his Communist Party nemesis, Gennadii Ziuganov. With his popularity hovering close to zero, Yeltsin appointed Anatolii Chubais as chairman of his reelection team. Chubais was a liberal internationalist tightly linked to the early shock therapy and privatization reforms. In 1995, in a bid to raise cash for the ailing state and secure support for Yeltsin among the owners of many of Russia's television and print media outlets, he organized the corrupt sale of national assets to these media "oligarchs" in what became known as "loans-for-shares" privatization.[60] In addition, as happened periodically throughout the 1990s, Yeltsin's administration obtained financial assistance from the World Bank and the IMF. For many, the agreement of the IMF in particular to loan Russia $10 billion in 1996 was seen as overt U.S. and Western intervention in Russian politics to ensure that Western-style market reforms would continue.[61] It became conventional wisdom that Yeltsin and the liberal reformers were leading Russia into unseemly dependence on the West and relying on nondemocratic and nonmarket means of implementing their reforms.[62]

Policy Outcomes and Correspondence Tests of Effective Legitimacy

While Russian political elites broadly favored constructive relations with the West, an end to imperialistic foreign policy, and market and democratic reforms, they looked with disfavor on the actual implementation and outcomes of liberal internationalist foreign and domestic policies.[63]

Liberal Internationalist Foreign Policy In foreign policy, in addition to viewing Kozyrev's policy as historically illegitimate, Russian political elites viewed it as idealistic and harmful. They charged the radical Westernizers of the early post-Soviet period with not being realistic enough and with "blindly following the West's lead" when this did not coincide with Russia's interests.[64] Political elites argued that liberal internationalism was incorrectly focused on the United States exclusively.[65] Democrats argued that while the West was important, the Yeltsin administration had to put the former Soviet republics first, not only for security reasons but also to prevent the Russian military from dominating policy in the Commonwealth of Independent States (CIS), which would destabilize democracy within Russia and prevent Russia's integration into the West.[66] Even the liberal internationalists themselves cautiously criticized their colleagues in official positions for their overblown expectations of Western assistance, noting that the West wanted to prevent weapons proliferation from the former Soviet republics without valuing Russia "as such."[67] Most political elites thought that it was not friendly concern and an altruistic desire to help that made the world take interest in Russia, but rather nuclear weapons and political instability in the region.[68] Russia therefore did not need to follow the West's lead, merely to look after its own interests.

Liberal internationalists were accused of lacking the diplomatic skill and experience and the overarching framework on which to base Russia's international identity and interests—key factors in assessing the effective legitimacy of the liberal internationalist national self-image.[69] Russian elites sharply criticized them for pursuing an ideologically driven foreign policy, rather than one pragmatically focused on Russia's current conditions. Sergei Karaganov, founder of Russia's Council on Foreign and Defense Policy, attacked the Yeltsin administration in 1992 for continuing the idealistic policy of Soviet New Thinking while Russia faced "entirely new conditions." He stressed that "my criticism of our current foreign policy also applies to the whole policy of our state." Karaganov continued, "The result is that Moscow, which commands vast intellectual and diplomatic potential, has relinquished all initiative to the outside world. Luckily the outside world is careful not to press us too hard. . . . This is certain to result sooner or later in our being disregarded and imposed on."[70]

Centrist and conservative politicians also criticized Kozyrev's foreign policy as idealism. Ruslan Khasbulatov, chairman of the Supreme Soviet, agreed that Russia, in rejecting the communist foreign policy doctrine of the past, "should not give in to any wide-ranging, high-sounding ideas that generally fail to serve our socio-economic and inner political interests."[71] For Khasbulatov and other statists, Russia's primary ingroup was not the West but the CIS and those countries bordering on it, the "countries offering us optimum chances of building up real economic power in accordance with our long-term interests as a nation-state."[72] The liberal economic and foreign policy positions of the Yeltsin administration were attacked for opening up the country to Western exploitation and for not protecting the industrial base that formed Russia's might.[73] In 1993, VTsIOM found that 60 percent of Russian political elites had a negative view of Russia's policies regarding relations with the former Soviet republics and only 20 percent viewed them positively. A plurality thought that liberal foreign economic policy reforms were destabilizing Russia.[74]

In the 1995 parliamentary election campaign, all parties criticized the liberal internationalist course and took harder lines on relations with the former Soviet republics and the West than those advocated by Kozyrev.[75] The moderate democratic parties stressed CIS integration and aid to the Russian-speaking diaspora as their primary national interests.[76] The nationalist and communist parties were joined by the democratic developmentalist Yabloko, the statist Congress of Russian Communities (KRO), and even the pro-government (and statist developmentalist) Our Home is Russia (NDR) parties in advocating great power patriotism, with either an imperialist or Eurasian flavor.[77] The election returns strengthened national restorationists and weakened Westernizers in the new parliament. Statists again served as the main counterweight to the national restorationist parties. In 1996, Kozyrev was replaced by Eurasian statist Evgenii Primakov. Under Primakov, Russian foreign policy became more assertive regionally and globally, and Russian rhetoric became more anti-American.

Liberal Internationalist Domestic Policy In economic policy, political elites found liberal internationalist efforts to adopt Western models and advice in their entirety to be ineffective in that they were harmful and difficult to carry out under Russian conditions. While almost three-quarters of Russian political elites supported Western-style market reforms in principle, they were highly critical of the policies that were carried out.[78] The liberal internationalist reformers were self-conscious promoters of the wholesale adoption of Western political-economic templates and in particular advocated a controversial "shock therapy" premised on the notion that radical and rapid price liberalization and the opening of Russian markets to foreign competition followed by quick voucher privatization would effectively create a tabula rasa on which liberal market institutions could be inscribed. For many Russians, the reforms and their results were directly associated with liberal internationalist reformers and the United States, the IMF, and the capitalist West more generally, as many of the Russian administration's advisors, such as Harvard's Jeffrey Sachs, were American. Yeltsin's team did secure Russia's membership in the World Bank and IMF. These organizations promptly assisted Russia in stabilizing prices and finances on condition of continued radical reform, but Russia's international debt ballooned.

In the crucial early years of the new Russia, these radical Westernizers were accused of excessive idealism in economic policy from across the political spectrum. Russian political elites challenged the "universal" applicability of radically liberalizing "shock therapy" and the orientation toward American-style liberal capitalism.[79] As one moderate democrat said, "Our young economists, who had been studying Karl Marx only, could not suggest anything different to the nation, even if they wanted to. They read works by Milton Friedman and Friedrich von Hayek, who had become fashionable after the pendulum had swung to the Right [in the West], adopted their views not as the latest in economic fashion, but rather as the latest achievement of economic science and trusted in them without reservation."[80] Another democrat was less polite, condemning the liberal Westernizers' adoption of American economic advice as "romantic" and "infantile."[81] Extremists on the right blamed them for believing that Russia's "complete salvation lies in complete reconstruction according to the models that exist in the lands of plenty."[82]

The outcome of liberal internationalist reforms seemed to confirm that their ideas did not suit Russian conditions. Liberal economic reforms, particularly the price liberalization of the ruble in late 1991, led to hyperinflation in 1992 and 1993 and impoverished millions of Russians. The Russian economy from 1991 to 1995 suffered a decline worse than the American Great Depression. Real wages fell by 50 percent, adjusting for inflation.[83] Millions of state employees were not paid; factories could not sell their goods. VTsIOM found in 1993 that Russian political elites generally thought their country to be in crisis; over 85 percent believed that price liberalization had been the most destabilizing reform introduced by the government.[84]

Western advisors to the Russian government argued with some justification that the hyperinflation resulted not from the "shock" of price liberalization and tight monetary policy but from the modifications to the reforms undertaken in May and June 1992 as a result of parliamentary opposition.[85] Inflation, they pointed out, had already reached 160 percent in 1991 as a result of Gorbachev's reforms and could not be solely attributed to liberal internationalist policies.[86]

Russian political elites, however, linked the reforms to the overtly pro-Western policy of the reformers and the reliance on Western advice and funds. The centrist-conservative political party Civic Union argued that the liberal Westernizer reform program depended on unrealistic amounts of Western aid for its success. This, in turn, risked impoverishing Russia by increasing its debt burden, which would destroy its scientific-technological infrastructure, subsequently undermining the sources of its national strength and international status.[87] Such loans were characterized by national restorationists as Western efforts to undermine Russia. Ziuganov attacked Yeltsin's submission to the "Gauleiters from the IMF," equating the Western institution with Nazi paramilitary leaders.[88]

Even democratic developmentalist Grigorii Yavlinskii, the leader of the pro-reform Yabloko, argued that radical liberalization had no place in the Soviet economy, because unlike those in Central Eastern Europe, the Soviet system had been created *de novo* in the 1920s and 1930s. It was unprecedented in its degree of centralized integration and monopolization and therefore could not be reformed without comprehensive state involvement. The liberal economic model simply did not apply in these conditions.[89] Most political elites favored continuing the reforms, but in a more gradual manner.[90]

Throughout the 1990s, continuing disagreement over the nature and pace of reform prevented any coherent implementation of economic strategy or agreement on what strategy was both suitable for Russia and sustainable. Liberal internationalists insisted that Russia's economy was to be governed by the building of stable institutions according to a Western liberal blueprint rather than by the balancing of political forces and adaptation to Russian conditions.[91] After the 1993 elections, their reforms proceeded in fits and starts, impeding the success of liberal internationalist policies and further contributing to doubts about the capacity of Western national self-images to be effectively enacted in accordance with their own principles.

Another major policy contributing significantly to negative perceptions of the liberal internationalist self-image was the aforementioned loans-for-shares privatization of 1995 and 1996, the brainchild of liberal internationalist Anatolii Chubais. The plan in effect sold shares in major government enterprises, most importantly in the lucrative energy and minerals sectors, to a small group of bankers (the "oligarchs"), who loaned the government money to finance its government bonds and the 1996 presidential campaign. The oligarchs then sold the shares to themselves at cut-rate prices. The plan had the effect of rapidly privatizing much of the state-controlled energy and minerals industries, a feat that made Chubais a hero in the Western press and financial circles.

In Russia, however, the loans-for-shares policy was viewed as a huge sell-off of key state sectors to favored businessmen for a song. This, like previous rounds of privatization, did little to create competitive markets or reduce state subsidies.[92] The insider nature of the deal made Russia's Westernizing reformers, particularly Chubais, morally suspect and further discredited the legitimacy of a putatively liberal market model.[93] Subsequent state auctions continued to raise questions about insider deals and the lack of market transparency. From then on, Yeltsin's regime was associated with oligarchic capitalism and massive corruption. This perception was so pervasive that in 1997 Yeltsin brought into his government Boris Nemtsov, a young reformer famous for fighting corruption. Nemtsov promptly declared that the administration would fight the "oligarchic capitalism," authored by Chubais, with "people's capitalism."[94] Yet Chubais and Nemtsov served side by side as deputy prime ministers. The effect was to create widespread agreement that liberalization—as it occurred in Russia—was, in practice if not in principle, illegitimate.

Continuing economic and diplomatic failures consolidated agreement on Russia's national interest in great power status maintenance. Just as the Russian economy was beginning to gain ground in 1997, an international currency crisis halted the positive growth, and in August 1998, Russia devalued its currency and defaulted on its loans after the IMF refused to extend emergency financing. This crisis highlighted the government's unseemly dependence on the West for its solvency, for which the Yeltsin administration had already been harshly criticized. Disappointment over Russian Westernizers' inability to deliver Western assistance was deepened by outrage over Western actions, including NATO's role in the Yu-

ing brought about Kozyrev's downfall.[109] While Yeltsin and his economic advisors continued to stress cooperation with the West, Russian diplomacy stiffened on the Russian diaspora, Bosnia, NATO enlargement, and—especially after Primakov's appointment—international sanctions against Iraq, Cuba, Serbia, and Libya.

Foreign and then Prime Minister Evgenii Primakov epitomized the great power aspiration, with his Eurasian statist definition of Russia as global great power in a multipolar world.[110] Primakov's stature across party and ideological lines as well as his political survival and promotion after the fall of the Chernomyrdin government in March 1998 was both an indicator of elite aspirations regarding international status as well as the "lowest common denominator" aspect of his Eurasian statism.[111] Primakov based his foreign policy on the premise that "Russia, despite present-day difficulties, was and remains a great power. Her policy in the outside world must correspond to this status."[112] Russia's foreign policy orientation toward the West was to be based on "equality," not on "a partnership where one leads and another is led," as Primakov declared in his first appearance before the State Duma's International Affairs Committee.[113]

The Historical Legitimacy of Statist National Self-Images in Post-Soviet Russia

As noted in chapter 4, Primakov adopted a strategy of social creativity relative to the United States in order to gain domestic and international recognition of Russia's status. The national interest was defined as maintaining Russia's global status by repeatedly pointing out Russia's Eurasian geography and historical role in both Europe and Asia as a great power. Primakov sought to gain recognition mainly through symbolic assertions of Russia's status. He signed declarations with China about their joint commitment to a multipolar world and condemned U.S. unilateralism while doggedly pursuing Russia's "special relationship" with NATO and equal status in other Western institutions. The government repeatedly stressed its inclusion in the Western economic clubs (the London and Paris Clubs, in addition to the G-8) in an effort to prove to domestic critics that the other powers recognized Russia's great power status. Primakov and his successors continuously used the UN Security Council to remind the world of Russia's status as one of the five global powers with a veto. Primakov's stance epitomized the political elite aspiration regarding great power status.[114]

Primakov made his social creativity strategy of a "multipolar world"—in which Russia played the starring role as system stabilizer and upholder of international law—the calling card of Russian foreign policy.[115] He depicted the United States, with its emphasis on humanitarian intervention, democracy promotion, and use of force without United Nations authorization, as acting in a manner unbefitting a great power, as it was not fulfilling its duty to stabilize world politics. Russia, in contrast, was acting as a status quo great power should, upholding international order and the established rules of a great power concert system.[116] To that end, Primakov declared a strategic partnership with China and generally pursued efforts to counteract perceived U.S. efforts to erode Russia's status. Primakov also made Russia's dominance in the former Soviet republics a key priority of foreign policy. Russia stepped up its opposition to NATO expansion and continued to pursue efforts to establish a privileged relationship with NATO.

During his tenure as foreign minister (1996–1998) and then as prime minister (1998–1999), Primakov reoriented official foreign policy away from the liberal internationalists' conciliation with the West—away from the United States in particular—and toward competition bounded by cooperation with the West. Primakov stressed the need to consolidate Russia's position in the CIS and diversify Russia's foreign policy so as to assure recognition of Russia's great power status.

Primakov's social creativity strategy in the waning years of the twentieth century entailed an image of world politics taken from nineteenth-century European politics, in which great powers had special duties to act in concert to preserve the balance of power while maintaining special rights to interfere in their own spheres of influence. His actions received broad support across party and ideological lines, thanks to both elite aspirations regarding international status and the "lowest common denominator" aspect of his status-driven national self-image.[117] He was known to be more conservative than the "young reformers" but had supported Gorbachev's New Thinking. He was essentially a man for all seasons, respected for his professionalism. For the conservatives, he represented the face of past Soviet power and prestige. For liberals and moderates, he offered the pragmatism and nonpartisan comportment that Kozyrev had lacked. Primakov was viewed as keeping foreign policy separate from domestic political battles. Above all, he was perceived as restoring Russia's dignity on the international stage, and his social creativity strategy therefore passed the test of historical legitimacy. He was widely seen as more professional than his predecessor, a key factor in assessments of his ability to successfully enact the identity he supported.[118] As Aleksei Arbatov phrased it, Primakov's cross-partisan appeal "testifies to the new minister's own professional prestige rather than to any emerging consensus on Russia's external relations."[119] Russian elites were content to separate their criticisms of domestic policies from foreign policy so long as the latter was focused on the limited interest of great power status maintenance. Primakov did not specify concrete national interests other than this.

In practice, Primakov's policy meant a rejection of the overtly hostile ideological and material conflict of the Cold War in favor of competition to gain recognition of Russia's role as a global great power. As such, the main foreign policy disposition toward the West was a reflexive one of status competition, but within a framework of cooperation with the West. Russia was to attend to "all azimuths" of the world more on principle than for objective interests.[120] In many areas, this strategy impeded productive Russian cooperation with the West, as Russian officials reacted to perceived slights to Russia's prestige rather than acting on more realistic assessments of Russian capabilities and needs. Instead, as chapters 6 and 7 cover in detail, Russian elites often pursued recognition of status at the expense of more concrete goals.

Despite the lack of consensus on political purpose, the historical legitimacy of the social creativity strategy put forward by Evgenii Primakov gave respite to a beleaguered Yeltsin administration, satisfying most mainstream critics. But it did little to make Russia's foreign policy proactive, as there remained no agreement on what Russia's fundamental interests beyond global great power status and territorial integrity were.[121]

Pursuit of status as a great power required competition with the United States, while recognition of Russian limitations mandated that such competition be bounded. This definition of the national interest—and Primakov's social creativity strategy—continued into the Putin administration. The primary difference between the Primakov and Putin years lay in the nature of competition, which shifted from symbolic to internal development, and in the level of official rhetoric, where the constant assertions of Russia's great power status and rights were reduced. In addition to Primakov's social creativity strategy, Putin sought to adopt a social competition strategy, one focused on Russia's internal development as the key to its global recognition.

For much of the 1990s, a handful of political elites challenged the cross-partisan aspiration regarding Russia's global great power status. Moderate members of the political elite consistently applied an efficacy test of Russia's objective weakness in combination with a history test of the illegitimacy of the past Soviet purpose of East-West confrontation to moderate the competitive orientation produced by common great power aspirations.[122] "We stubbornly repeat that our country is a great power," Duma deputy Evgenii Kozhokin noted in 1992. "And the more stubbornly we repeat this, the stronger the feeling that we aim to banish to the subconscious the realization of what has suddenly come out: our inferiority and weakness in the face of the United States, the only superpower today."[123] Others argued that Russia had no real basis for claiming global great power status other than a rusting nuclear arsenal.[124] Viacheslav Nikonov, a prominent policy expert, posited that "owing to economic and military weakness, Russia cannot aspire to the role of even a regional superpower."[125] Efficacy testers pointed to NATO's expansion and its intervention in Yugoslavia as events that Russia was powerless to prevent.[126] Instead, they argued, Russia should take the path of cooperation with the world's most powerful military and political alliance as the way to the economic recovery necessary for Russia to return to global great power status.[127]

Moderate voices, predominantly those of democratic and statist developmentalists, such as Vladimir Lukin and Sergei Karaganov, criticized Primakov's and later Putin's social creativity strategy and assertion of a multipolar world as an ineffective model of world politics that would be damaging to Russia. They argued that the preservation of Russia's great power and anti-American posture interfered with Russia's national interest in integration into the Western political and economic order.[128] In a turnaround from their criticism of Kozyrev's focus on the West, they accused Primakov and even Putin of overemphasizing relations with the East and the former Soviet allies. As Aleksei Arbatov complained, "What's Vietnam to us?"[129] They sought to focus on the ineffective nature of the statist social creativity strategy, as it did not conform to Russia's present capacities or the nature of the international system. As another Russian analyst put it in 1999, "The great-power model of development is no longer working. . . . Russia will be forced to recognize that it is not a global power center. It will be necessary to evaluate its real capabilities and prospects more precisely and compare its new 'international weight' to the weight not only of the United States but also of many other countries."[130]

Such efficacy-testing succeeded in moderating the reactive strategy of social creativity, which hindered Russia's integration into the West.[131] Sergei Karaganov argued in 2001 that Russia's choice lay between being one of the last fiddles in the first world of the global economy or forging a political alliance led by China. The first option would be politically possible but "morally" difficult, he said, while the second would be dangerous, as it would encourage authoritarianism domestically. He therefore criticized statists for pursuing a status-driven policy of courting former Soviet allies that would lead to friction with the United States, which was the only desirable ally for Russia.[132]

However, such voices were not able to remove the weight of historical aspirations from consideration of Russia's identity and interests in the twenty-first century. A speech Primakov gave in 2001 indicates how many political elites remained focused on Russia's historical status rather than on the current conditions shaping its effective capabilities, such as Russia's external debt. His focus on geopolitics rather than Russia's economy led prominent liberal democrat Irina Khakamada to retort to the same gathering that political elites' inability to focus on Russia's economic situation demonstrated their inability to understand the modern international reality of economic globalization.[133] The appeal of Primakov's strategy becomes clearer in light of the finding that 46 percent of Russian political elites believed in 2001 that "there is no direct connection between the economic potential of a country and its international position." Not surprisingly, of the group that saw the source of Russia's international position as residing in military might, culture, and educational levels, 58 percent also felt that Russia should follow its own path of development.[134] Such views sharply contrast with Western views about the centrality of economic development to international political influence.

Vladimir Putin, on becoming prime minister in 1999 and then president in 2000, followed Primakov's lead in offering something for everyone, neither rejecting the West entirely nor denying the importance of Russia's past greatness. While the 2000 Foreign Policy Concept stressed pragmatism and an international role commensurate to Russia's diminished means, the broad outlines of Primakov's social creativity strategy continued under the new president.[135] Despite the widely touted "pragmatism" of Putin's foreign policy, it remained largely a reactive one, premised on recognition of Russia's proper place in the international system and also laced with latent resentment of the United States for not sufficiently recognizing that status. As one Russian analyst noted, Russia under Putin still "covet[ed] respect."[136]

The main difference between Primakov's and Putin's identity management strategies was that Putin more often argued that the basis for such respect could only come through modernizing the Russian economy and strengthening the Russian state. As explained in chapter 4, Putin advocated an identity management strategy similar to Primakov's, but one focused on the criteria for inclusion not only in the great power club (Primakov's focus) but also in the Western global economy. His strategy incorporated Primakov's social creativity but grounded Russian identity in social competition in order to be recognized as both modern *and* great.

Yet, to a greater degree than at any time previously, this policy was based on recognition of Russia's diminished capacities. Putin closed bases in Vietnam and Cuba and emphasized the vital importance of economic growth in consolidating and strengthening the Russian state as a great power. Official foreign policy discourse shifted away from hostile rhetoric about countering U.S. power to strategic cooperation and efforts to facilitate Russia's economic development.[137] He mollified domestic critics with his strong statist position on restoring Russia's might, his skillful manipulation of national symbols, and, most fundamentally, his unequivocal stand on squelching the insurgency in Chechnya. While not all political elites fully supported this change in foreign policy orientation, Andrei Tsygankov argues persuasively that Putin moved away from merely asserting Russia's primacy—as Primakov had done—to actively building the basis for its international status.[138] Putin insisted at the turn of the century that Russia's role in the world had to be based on its economic capabilities, not merely its military might and territorial expanse, a message that appealed to Westernizers and Western-oriented statists.

With regard to Russia's domestic development, the Putin era was marked by an effort to turn away from the revolutionary destruction of Soviet institutions to stabilization. In contrast to Yeltsin, Putin viewed liberalization not as an end in itself but as a crucial means of strengthening the Russian state and ensuring its global might and authority. He took office with an agenda of consolidating and expanding the economic reforms of the 1990s. He oversaw passage of a package of liberal economic laws, including stabilization of property rights, reduction of welfare benefits and subsidies, and enforcement of a reformed tax code that introduced a flat tax. In an important shift from the Yeltsin years, these reforms were made law rather than being implemented by administrative fiat.[139]

Putin became extremely popular, aided in large measure by the upturn in the economy after 1999, as the currency devaluation discouraged the consumption of expensive imports and helped domestic industries. The government improved tax collection and adopted more effective budgets. However, the main cause of Russia's post-1998 growth was sustained high oil prices. Oil and gas exports accounted for over half of Russia's total exports.[140] The government was finally able to pay state employees the salaries that had gone unpaid during the 1990s.

Putin appealed to both liberal and moderate Westernizers by declaring he would strengthen the state by encouraging state-led economic development conducted in cooperation with business and by liberalizing government regulation and reforming the judicial system.[141] At the same time, Putin argued that the purpose of modernization was to maintain Russia as a great power, which earned him the backing of statists and national restorationists alike.[142]

In foreign policy matters, Putin distanced himself somewhat from the multipolar rhetoric of Primakov but sought to use Russia's energy and diplomatic resources to diversify and strengthen Russia's economy and international political influence. He cultivated friendly relations with the leaders of Germany, China, and the United States. Even before the attacks on the United States of September 11, 2001, Putin adopted a more conciliatory posture toward the United States. In contrast to previous Russian leaders, he reacted mildly to the 1999 and 2004 rounds of NATO expansion and U.S. determination to withdraw from the Anti-Ballistic Missile (ABM) treaty.

Immediately after the September 11 terrorist attacks, Russian-U.S. relations improved. Putin supported the U.S. war against the Taliban and

Al Qaeda in Afghanistan and did not object to the establishment of U.S. bases in the former Soviet Central Asian republics. In response to the U.S. withdrawal from the ABM treaty in 2002, Putin withdrew Russia from the START II treaty but signed the Russo-U.S. Strategic Offensive Reduction Treaty. He did not support, however, the U.S. war against Iraq in 2003 and threatened to veto any UN security resolution authorizing the use of force. Western realists saw this as evidence of Russian efforts to divide the NATO allies and create a Moscow-Berlin-Paris counterbalance to U.S. power or as an effort to preserve Russian economic interests in Iraq. They depicted the Iraq War as the greatest crisis in Russian-U.S. in the post–Cold War era.[143] However, Russian-U.S. relations recovered much more quickly after the Iraq crisis than U.S. relations with its NATO allies, Germany and France. After the war, political elites praised Putin for carefully "stage-managing" the war with the United States and for raising Russia's status to that of "a privileged security partner of the mightiest state in the contemporary world."[144]

Russian-Western relations were not severely damaged until 2004, a consequence of affairs in the former Soviet republics and in Russia itself. Given the psychological importance of hegemony in the FSU for Russian elite aspirations, President Putin's willingness to allow U.S. military bases in Central Asia after the 9/11 attacks was seen domestically as a fundamental shift toward the United States and was roundly criticized by many elites. Initially, the administration and its allies in the Duma argued that this was merely getting the United States to deal with the problem of international terrorism in Afghanistan in a way that Russia was unable to do.[145] Prior to Putin's speech on September 24, 2001, only advocates of Western national self-images had called for support of the United States. The rest of political elites called for neutrality and rejected any U.S. presence in Central Asia.[146] At the end of 2004, talk of a new Cold War had begun, relations between the U.S. and Russia were "at their worst since 1991," and Russian elites were decrying the fact that the West still judged Russia according to values rather than interests.[147] Putin and Russian elites returned to a familiar complaint that the West was seeking to impose domestic reforms within Russia and simultaneously trying to reduce Russia's status in the FSU.

What produced the 2004 crisis in Russian-Western relations was not the Iraq War, as some Western realists claimed, but fraudulent presidential elections that led to Ukraine's Orange Revolution and the West's attitude toward the breakaway province of Chechnya.[148] The "color revolutions" in Georgia, Ukraine, and Kyrgyzstan in 2003 and 2004 were perceived in Moscow as U.S. efforts to install anti-Russian forces and to isolate Russia from its own backyard.[149] All three countries had seen street demonstrations install pro-Western governments. The Kremlin branded the revolution in Ukraine as "a Western ploy to install pro-American regimes on Russia's periphery and then to engineer a regime change in Russia itself." Russia rejected the West's support for pro-Western Ukrainian politicians, while the West objected to Putin's heavy-handed support for the pro-Russian candidate. Russian attempts to use economic blackmail against Ukraine in the form of natural gas price hikes in December 2005 worsened relations further and raised questions about Russia's self-proclaimed role as a reliable alternative to Middle East suppliers of energy. Mutual recriminations over efforts to democratize the former Soviet republics mounted, and Russia was again criticized for its actions in Chechnya and its move toward authoritarianism.[150]

Also far more important than Iraq for Russian political elites was the West's attitude toward Chechnya. In 1999, the Second Chechen War began when Chechen rebels extended their operations into neighboring Dagestan. Prime minister at the time, Putin sent close to a hundred thousand troops to Chechnya to conduct what he called "antiterrorist operations." Counterterrorism became a leitmotif of Putin's policy after he was elected president in 2000. Putin declared major combat operations to be over in 2003, but popular support for his antiterrorism efforts remained high until 2004. From September 11, 2001, to 2003, the West muted its criticism of Russian actions in Chechnya, and U.S. President George W. Bush accepted Putin's definition of the long-running separatist war there as a counterterrorist operation. In 2003, however, the West increasingly criticized the human rights violations that were being committed by Russian forces there, while Britain harbored a former Chechen leader wanted by Russian authorities.

From 1999 to 2004, a series of terrorist attacks in Russia perpetuated public support for Putin's policies in Chechnya. In September 2004, on the first day of school, Chechen rebels seized a school in the North Caucasian town of Beslan, and 331 hostages—half of them children—were killed in a shootout between the rebels and Russian security forces.[151]

After Beslan, elite and public support for the government's position in Chechnya began to wane.[152] Putin also succumbed to the power of historical memory, as suggested by his remarks about the West's designs on Russia after Beslan. After lukewarm expressions of outrage in the West over Beslan and statements to the effect that political means should be used to bring an end to the Chechen war, Putin personally blamed the West for deliberately channeling Muslim terrorists toward Russia.[153] A presidential advisor stated that any efforts to "roll back" Russia in the former Soviet republics would be met with force.[154] The public announcement of cooperation with the United States after 9/11 was replaced by public rebukes of Western interference in the FSU. Russia moved to reduce U.S. influence in the FSU, working to establish multilateral regional organizations that included the Central Asian republics and China and to remove U.S. bases from Central Asia.

Despite the efforts of Westernizers and democratically oriented statists, and contrary to arguments that Putin made a dramatic choice in favor of the West after the September 11 terrorist attacks on the United States, there was little real shift in the Russian political discourse or in the status-driven definition of the national interest after Putin took office.[155] Russian political elites continued to reject policies that suggested Russia was "junior partner" to the West, while the Putin administration continued to insist that its support of the Bush administration after the 9/11 attacks was not as a second-rate partner. Given this consensus, in his annual address to the Federal Assembly in April 2005, President Putin felt compelled to state that "it goes without saying that the civilizing mission of the Russian nation in the Eurasian continent should be continued."[156] Foreign Minister Igor Ivanov stated, "Russia will seek to form a multipolar system of international relations that truly reflects the diversity of the modern world with its diverse interests."[157] Putin himself became Russia's most active diplomat and followed through on diversifying Russian foreign policy, visiting or hosting leaders from China, India, Iran, North Korea, Iraq, Cuba, and Vietnam in his first year and a half in office.[158] The government also continued to declare Russia's great power status and the need to prevent the United States from establishing a unipolar world.[159]

Putin's strategy of social creativity and social competition, following on that of Primakov, was well received by political elites. In 2001, 77 percent of Russian political elites believed that there had been positive changes in Russian foreign policy in the preceding decade. These changes were attributed to the periods when statists asserted Russia's great power status. Thirty-five percent of political elites associated positive changes in Russian foreign policy with Putin's tenure as president, while only 16 percent associated them with the early Yeltsin years. Twenty-five percent attributed the change to Foreign Minister Evgenii Primakov's tenure.[160] A majority of political elites agreed that Russian foreign policy corresponded more to its national interests and was more balanced with regard to East and West. This agreement bridged the traditionalist-Westernizer divide, with more than half of political elites accepting these propositions—although the portion of traditionalists adopting this view exceeded the share of Westernizers by 10 points. Sixty-six percent rejected the premise that Russian foreign policy had become more confrontational with regard to the West.[161]

This positive assessment appeared to stem more from an application of a test of effective legitimacy to Putin's and Primakov's conduct of diplomacy and use of available resources than a material change in Russia's international position. When asked what resources were available for strengthening Russia's international position, political elites most often chose the "new, more flexible and pragmatic style of Russian foreign policy," which narrowly edged out "more meaningful use of the natural resource potential of the country."[162] However, this positive assessment of the more assertive Russian foreign policy and effective use of existing Russian material resources did not translate into a rational assessment of Russia's material position globally. As noted below, 46 percent of Russian political elites believed that "there is not direct connection between a country's economic potential and its international position"; when broken down according to whether Russia should remain distinctive and follow a "Russian path" or follow the West, 58 percent of those favoring a distinctive Russian path believed that there was no link between economic potential and international status.[163]

Efficacy-Testing and the Limitation of Confrontation with the West

Political elite application of efficacy tests in Russia's foreign policy discourse also played a role in shaping Russian identity and national interests. Efficacy tests applied by moderate Westernizers and statists served to check extremist views on both ends of the political spectrum and to ameliorate confrontational behavior stemming from the aspiration for great power status. At the turn of the century, democratic and statist developmentalists sought, with some success, to revise the status-driven interest in great power social competition in light of the newly perceived "reality" of globalization.[164] Table 5.1 suggests that after the shocks of the late 1990s, the shift begun under Primakov to uphold Russia's status aspirations, together with efficacy-testing, somewhat reduced the weight of historical aspirations in shaping Russia's national interests. The proportion of elites supporting Russia's status as one of the five leading powers fell by half between 1993 and 2001. In part this may stem from a change in the wording of the options available to respondents in the 2001 survey. What is notable about the change in the last option is what the change in phrasing represented. In 1993 and 1996 Russian elites rejected a status of being merely a sovereign nation, preferring a much higher status. When the choice was rephrased in such a way as to make the option more positive ("renouncing global ambitions," which cues historical memories of Soviet ideological messianism) in order to focus on internal problems, the numbers favoring the higher-status categories dropped and those favoring internal development jumped. While a small number of elites remained committed in 2001 to restoring Russia's superpower status, far more favored a more modest status.[165]

Yet the aspirations derived from Russia's past international status and elite division over other sources of Russia's national distinctiveness continued to limit the weight of the "self-in-context" and prevent what rationalists would call cost-benefit analysis from serving as the main basis Russia's identity and interests. Great power status remained the primary basis for Russian national identity into the new millennium, as elites could not agree on other bases for positive distinctiveness. Statist and democratic developmentalists, including most prominently Vladimir Putin, sought with some success to put forward economic criteria as the basis for Russia's comparison with the West. In his first address to the Russian nation, he did what no other Russia or Soviet leader had done: he bluntly pointed to Russia's current standing: "It will take us approximately fifteen years and an annual growth of our Gross Domestic Product by 8 percent a year to reach the per capita GDP level of present-day Portu-

TABLE 5.1. *Elite Views on Russia's International Status over Time*

	1993	1996	2001
Goals in the national interest that Russia should strive for in the next 10–15 years (%)			
Restore USSR-like superpower status	4	7	13
Belong to one of the five great powers	55	57	21
Belong to the 10 to 15 most developed countries in the world	30	24	28
Be the leader within the borders of the CIS	6	6	5
Be one of the many sovereign [*ravnopravnie*] countries of the world / Renounce global ambitions and concentrate on solving domestic problems*	4	2	24
No answer	1	3	9

Source: Mikhail K. Gorshkov, *Vneshniaia Politika Rossii: Mneniia Ekspertov* (Moscow: RNICINP po zakazu moskovskovo predstavitel'stva Fonda im. F. Eberta, 2001).

Note: Due to rounding, some percentage totals may not equal 100.

*In 2001, this choice was changed to "Renounce global ambitions and concentrate on solving domestic problems."

gal or Spain, which are not among the world's industrialized leaders. If during the same fifteen years we manage to ensure the annual growth of our GDP by 10 percent, we will then catch up with Britain or France."[166]

This efficacy-testing was not, however, broadly accepted among Russian political elites. Many of them preferred Primakov's more creative criteria for the definition of Russia's great power status, which offered more rationales for a positive evaluation of Russia. As already noted, in 2001 Russian elites divided evenly over whether economics was at all related to its international rank.[167] Forty-six percent believed that it was *not,* that the sources of Russia's great power status were its military capabilities, culture, and educational system.[168] From a social psychology perspective, this result conforms to the expectation that people will seek other, positive dimensions on which to compare themselves with others through the deployment of social creativity strategies.[169] On economics, Russia was clearly outpaced by Western countries, even ones as small as Portugal, as their president reminded them. To relate Russia's international weight to its military capabilities, culture, and advanced educational system and high literacy rate is therefore not surprising. What is more hopeful is that 44 percent disagreed, saying that Russia's current international influence was a function of its global economic position. Such figures suggest that efficacy-testing had had an impact, albeit a limited one, on elite perceptions of Russia's international status and the definition of its national identity. However, such "realism" was still very much subject to historical aspirations to Russia's great power status, particularly when current events raised the question of that status among the former Soviet republics.

Westernizers and Western-oriented statists conducted efficacy tests, suggesting that Putin and most Russian political elites viewed Chechnya and the former Soviet republics in nineteenth-century sphere-of-influence terms rather than through the Western perspective of self-determination. Russian political elites viewed world politics as a nineteenth-century world in which sovereign states could take whatever steps necessary to maintain control within their own territory, one in which great powers had spheres of influence. In that sense, most Russian political elites were living in a different historical epoch than the West, and Westernizers and moderate statist developmentalists challenged the accuracy and practicality of their worldview.[170]

As the Putin era progressed, Westernizers and moderate statist developmentalists argued that Putin was becoming too much like Primakov and focusing less on reality than on wounded pride.[171] In 2005, moderate statists and Westernizers felt compelled to remind their fellow elites that Russia's position was that of a middle-income country like Brazil, Indonesia, and South Africa and that Western-style economic development would allow Russia to improve its international position and become a pole of attraction more than emphasis on Russia's status relative to the United States.[172] Their efforts, however, only served to bound competitive orientations toward the United States and the West rather than displace the aspiration to retain Russia's historical distinctiveness as a global great power.

National Self-Esteem and Russia's Lack of Political Purpose

In the 1990s, Russian political elites expended endless effort on the subject of national identity, or Russia's "national idea." According to Aleksei Arbatov, "Reflections on this subject by political scientists, state figures, philosophers, and historians of the past and present can be cited ad infinitum."[173] President Yeltsin even established a "Presidential Commission on the National Idea" in 1996, and after a survey of just the pro-government press, it found that there was no consensus on a national idea—or whether one should even exist.[174]

At the root of much of Russia's political instability and inconsistency in foreign policy throughout Russia's "revolutionary decade" was the inability of its elites to agree on whether Russia could accept a form of economic and political development—a political purpose—that is not *unique to Russia* but adopted from the West. Russian political elites are attracted to the Western form of economic and political development and the advancement and international status it has produced. But they remain divided over whether pursuing a Western-style political purpose befits Russia's historical status as a distinctive great power, one carved out of the Eurasian heartland through often brutal state repression and control in the periods of Peter the Great, Catherine the Great, and the Soviet Union.

This past self produced historical aspirations to a status commensurate with those high points in Russia's past, while managing to avoid the ideological confrontation of the Cold War period, widely seen as ruinous for Russian development. Such aspirations left plenty of ambiguity as to how Russians should attain them. What these aspirations did do, however, was rule out national self-images that downplayed pursuit of great power status and identity management strategies that negated the positive achievements of Russian history, including its international role. Russia's past self also left marked ambivalence about whether "following" the West, rather than creating and leading others along an alternate path of development, best suited Russia's status aspirations.

Liberal internationalism was the early casualty of the need for national self-esteem and the maintenance of the positive distinctiveness of Russia's historical status as a great power; as a result, the legitimacy of Westernization more generally was always in question throughout this period. Liberal internationalists failed to persuade political elites that their national self-image offered Russia a historically appropriate international status and viable political purpose. They failed to respond adequately to charges that their program undermined Russia's legitimate status as a great power. Their economic policies exacerbated an already bad situation and seemed ineffective and damaging in post-Soviet conditions. Their political prescriptions for openness and democracy were undermined by the administration's unwillingness, most vividly expressed in the violent October 1993 standoff, to share power with more moderate and conservative elements in the parliament.

The decline of liberal internationalism did not represent Russian political elite agreement on Russia's national identity. Instead, it produced a consensus on a partial identity, Russia as a modern and distinctive great power. This consensus strengthened the persuasiveness of statist self-images that asserted that status. The consensus on status, however, did not correspond with elite agreement on what Russia's political purpose should be. Political elites had agreed on a national interest of status maintenance early in the decade, and by the end of the 1990s, they had achieved a very general consensus on strengthening Russia's weak central government and modernizing the economy.

However, there was no consensus on the appropriate means or end result of doing so. While the West was generally accepted as the standard by which Russia's status was judged and as the benchmark for political and economic development more generally, elite desire for positive distinctiveness—manifested as support for recovering a special Russian path—prevented durable agreement on any one national self-image's depiction of Russia's proper political purpose. Much of the elite debate about Russia's national identity revolved around this question of whether Russia should follow the West or take an independent path, or somehow combine the two, as table 5.2 and other survey research suggests.[175] This produced the long and unresolved debate about what Russia's "national idea" really was, a debate that was ultimately stifled after Putin centralized power and marginalized opposition beginning in 2004.

In their search for national self-esteem, Russian political elites judged Western national self-images to be insufficiently distinctive or respectful of Russian traditions. National restorationist, neocommunist, and Slavophile national self-images, on the other hand, were too distinctive. As noted in chapter 3, many Russian political elites negatively identified with Soviet ideological confrontation with the West. These national self-images offered paths of development that were viewed as impractical and harmful in being too ideological and too different from the West's. Like Goldilocks and the three bears, Russian political elites rejected these alternatives as too hot and too cold, leaving the nebulous statist advocacy of "a strong state" as the political purpose that was closest to "just right." In the absence of consensus on political purpose, aspirations about regaining Russia's historical status as a great power, about which Russian political elites did agree, filled in for a political purpose. It is in this context that the popularity of Evgenii Primakov's "lowest-common-denominator" statism

TABLE 5.2. *Dynamics of Elite Attitudes regarding Russia's Proper Political Purpose (%)*

	1993	1996	2001
Russia must search for its own path, for an alternative to a Western model of development (traditionalists)	44	52	46
Russia must strive to integrate with the leading Western countries and get rid of the "Russian uniqueness syndrome" (Westernizers)	51	41	40
Hard to say / Other opinion	5	6	14

Source: Mikhail K. Gorshkov, *Vneshniaia Politika Rossii: Mneniia Ekspertov* (Moscow: RNICiNP po zakazu moskovskovo predstavitel'stva Fonda im. F. Eberta, 2001).

Note: Due to rounding, some percentage totals may not equal 100.

and the subsequent dominance of Putin's liberal statist developmentalism should be understood.

Conclusion

The aims of this chapter have been threefold. First and most generally, the chapter sought to illustrate the empirical plausibility of an aspirational constructivist account of Russian national identity interests during the period from 1991 to 2004. Second, the chapter demonstrated how aspirations and history and efficacy tests, which together make up the correspondence process of legitimacy-testing, affected the persuasiveness of the primary contenders for Russian national identity: Western and statist national self-images and their associated identity management strategies. Third, the chapter explained in aspirational constructivist terms why one set of these national self-images, statism, and its identity management strategies of social competition and social creativity were viewed as more legitimate than its primary competitor, liberal internationalism, and came to act as Russia's national identity and shape its national self-interest from 1999 onward.

The debate about national identity in Russia produced a confusing and contradictory national interest toward the West, one that was both socially competitive and cooperative, what here has been termed a national interest of "competitive engagement" or "competition within a framework of cooperation." Their aspirations for Russia to regain its historical status as a peer of the United States led Russian political elites to compete with the United States for social recognition. Two countervailing tendencies, the identification of the West as at least a partial ingroup in many Russian national self-images and the efficacy tests conducted by Westernizers and moderate statists regarding Russia's need for inclusion into the West, limited this competitive orientation and kept it bounded within an overarching desire to engage with the West and integrate into its political and economic clubs.

The impact of these struggles over Russia's national distinctiveness and its aspirations set the stage for the conduct of security policies that were not driven by effective assessments of Russia's material and political capabilities. Instead, as the next two chapters highlight, historical aspirations to a significant extent determined the definition of Russian security interests in two critical issue areas, European security and strategic nuclear arms control. The next two chapters explore the effects of Russian political elite settlement on a status-driven national identity on Russian policy in these areas.

SIX

The Post-Soviet Creation of Russia's Security Interests in Europe

Europe after the end of the Cold War saw major transformations in the definitions of security interests. Ethnic conflict, humanitarian crises, extension of the liberal zone of peace, and transnational terrorism replaced territorial defense and power balancing as the primary security concerns for European security officials over the 1991–2004 period. Despite the changed security environment in Europe and internal agreement that Europe posed no threat to Russia, Russian political elites throughout the post–Cold War era did not share Europeans' new definitions of security interests. Their predominant frame of European security in Russia invoked the nineteenth—rather than the twenty-first—century by reducing Europe to the key area in which the global hierarchy of international status was to be determined. The perception grew over the 1990s that, when it came to security concerns, Europeans and Russians were living in different historical epochs.[1]

During this period, Europeans and Americans were focused on post–Cold War security tasks, in the form of civil wars and ethnic cleansing in the former Yugoslavia, transforming NATO from an anti-Soviet alliance to take on humanitarian and counterterrorism roles, facilitating democratization of the postcommunist countries through enlargement of European security institutions, figuring out a common European foreign and defense policy, strengthening Russia's democratic transformation, and preventing proliferation of nuclear materials.

Russian political elites, in contrast, were seeking to restore a positive image of themselves as a vital European and therefore global world power, as Russia had been since Peter the Great. European security issues were not considered in their own right but rather in terms of their contribution to Russia's ranking relative to the United States in a global status hierarchy. Instead of adapting to the new environment in Europe and new definitions of security and calculating their interests on the basis of material threats and capabilities, Russian political elites defined Russia's European security interests in terms of their historical aspirations to reclaim Russia's global status as a great power. As a result, European security, for Russian political elites, was reduced to the effect NATO had on Russia's standing as a great power. Russian security policy toward Europe (and globally) throughout the post-Soviet period was driven by this status competition. This competitive orientation was bounded within an overarching commitment to cooperation with the West, however, and Russian foreign policy regarding European security alternated between moves for closer and deeper cooperation and hostile rhetoric and demands for recognition of Russia's equal right to shape Europe's future.

This chapter seeks to explain why Russian political elites defined Russia's national interests regarding European security issues as part of a competition for social status with the United States and why Russian policy remained oriented toward "competition within cooperation" or "competitive engagement" throughout the post-Soviet period. It argues that historical aspirations drove Russian political elites to view European security in largely nineteenth-century terms as reflecting Russia's standing in a global power concert and oriented them toward status competition with the United States. That this competition remained bounded by an overarching interest in cooperation was the result of two factors: the designation of the West, particularly Europe, as one of Russia's ingroups in Western and statist national self-images; and the efficacy tests applied by Westernizers and statist developmentalists to calls for confrontation with the West.

Alternative Explanations of Russian Interests in European Security

A structural constructivist explanation of identity and interests assumes that identity develops through the process of "mirror-imaging." In this view, Russia develops its sense of who it is and how it should behave based on how others behave toward it. The behavior of NATO members should generate Russia's identity and interests regarding European security.[2] This explanation would expect successive rounds of NATO expansion, NATO's war against Serbia, and its operations in the former Soviet republics and Afghanistan to produce a Russian security identity as the foe of "U.S.-led NATO" and to produce interests in confronting NATO. While NATO's behavior did produce hostility among Russian officials and political elites, such hostility largely remained rhetorical and never turned into confrontation. Moreover, Russians developed a quite different identity than that of the enemy of NATO or the United States, and this identity—of Russia as a great power—was not inherently hostile toward the West. Indeed, Russia's status-driven national identity created an interest in partnership with the United States and NATO as a necessary component of great power status. As a result, Russian foreign policy regarding European security zigged and zagged between competition and cooperation.

Realist explanations based on structural conditions and threat perceptions as the source of Russia's European security interests also cannot account for the behaviors and orientations that Russia exhibited. For realists, dramatic shifts in international power are tightly correlated with wars among rising and declining powers. Realists expect that "when the political status quo in a key region is ambiguous or fluid, great powers can easily conclude that their only viable strategic options are either expanding or accepting geopolitical losses. . . . Thus, when the status quo is unstable, the security dilemma is tight: policies that enhance one's own position necessarily jeopardize that of one's opponent. Under such conditions, aggressiveness is at a premium, and errors of overextension should be common."[3] Based on this logic, in the early 1990s, offensive realists expected that the collapse of the Soviet Union would lead Russia to engage in risky actions to hold on to its international positions in Europe and the former Soviet republics, despite its declining power, which would significantly increase the likelihood of war with the West.[4] Clearly, such an outcome did not occur.

Realists of a more defensive orientation argued that such structural factors did not explain cooperation and conflict. They instead focused on the role of material capabilities and perceptions of hostile intentions as a critical factor in determining states' interests in cooperation or competition. In a similar vein to structural constructivism, according to defensive realism, when a state perceives hostile intentions in the behavior of nearby militarily powerful countries, this generates perceptions of threat. These perceptions in turn produce national interests in competing militarily through internal defense buildups or the creation of external military alliances against the threatening state or states.[5]

For both sets of reasons, realists argued against NATO expansion, as they feared it would prompt serious conflict with Russia.[6] Given the East-West nature of the Cold War rivalry, Russia's loss of military power and strategic depth after 1989, and NATO's expansion, realists expected Russians in the post–Cold War period to perceive the West and the Western alliance as a genuine security threat and to respond accordingly.

During the post–Cold War period, these realist expectations regarding the changing distribution of power and threat were not met. As noted in chapter 4, perceptions of external threat were at an all-time low in 1991.[7] In 1993, the overwhelming majority of political elites believed that the likelihood of foreign aggression was low and that most of the security threats were internal. Almost one-third believed that there were no security threats to Russia (see table 6.1). Exactly one-half believed that the likelihood of foreign aggression was "rather low," and another 36 percent believed it was "generally absent" (*vovse nikakaia*).[8] Internal issues persistently ranked first as the main threat to Russia's security throughout the post-Soviet period.[9] This was reflected in official national security and military doctrines. In 1993 and 1997, these doctrines stated that Russia faced no enemies or threat of attack from the West. In 1993, the mil-

TABLE 6.1. *Perceived Sources of Russian Security Threats in 1993 (%)*

	Domestic	Foreign	Both	None
Total	*39*	*12*	*19*	*29*
Executive branch	30	12	22	34
Communist-oriented party leaders	20	20	48	12
Noncommunist party leaders	64	12	12	12
State enterprise directors	46	2	12	40
Private entrepreneurs	48	0	20	28
Military commanders	40	36	22	2
Press	26	14	14	42
Scholars and cultural figures	40	4	14	42

Source: Adapted from Vox Populi, "USIA Survey no. I93060: NATO" (Moscow: United States Information Agency, 1993), question 9.

Note: Due to rounding, some percentage totals may not equal 100.

itary doctrine stated that "the main current source of danger is local wars and regional conflict. This danger is constantly growing." In the 1997 National Security Concept, these remained the main source of external danger, but the emphasis was on Russia's internal difficulties. The April 2000 Military Doctrine stated that "in modern conditions, the threat of a direct military aggression, in its traditional forms, against the Russian Federation and its allies has ebbed."[10]

Moreover, contrary to early fears of a revanchist Russia, in 1993 Russian political elites preferred cooperation with the West, rather than counterbalancing it, as the best means of guaranteeing Russian security (see table 6.2). Half of political elites believed that NATO was still necessary after the Cold War, as it was the primary guarantor of peace in Europe (see table 6.3). Despite qualms about a reunified Germany, 80 percent of political elites approved of German reunification, according to a 1993 survey.[11] The same year VTsIOM found that Germany was most often identified as "friend number 1" by political elites.[12] Throughout the post-Soviet period, the majority of political elites believed that a return to Cold War confrontation was unlikely.[13] In April 2001, when asked about threats to Russia, political elites ranked the growth of international terrorism, the spread of Islamic fundamentalism within Russia, economic noncompetitiveness, and Russia's growing scientific and technological backwardness ahead of the accession of former Soviet republics into NATO.[14]

Only after announcements of plans for its enlargement were made did NATO register in Russian threat perceptions. Yet these perceptions of NATO enlargement, while negative, were inconstant and were likely perceived as threats to Russia's rightful place in European and global politics rather than as genuine security threats. William Zimmerman found in 2004 surveys of foreign policy elites that the proportion of the respondents viewing NATO expansion as a threat had declined five years after NATO's air war against Serbia, though between 35 and 45 percent of respondents still believed that NATO expansion and NATO intervention in ethnic conflicts in Europe was a great threat to Russia. Zimmerman noted, however, that "across the board, the intensity of concern about NATO has diminished."[15]

More tellingly, Russian elites favored continued cooperation with the Western alliance despite wavering perceptions of NATO as a threat. In

TABLE 6.2. *Elite Perceptions of Guarantors of Russia's External Security in 1993 (%)*

		Cooperate with West				
	CIS military alliance	Military alliance with Europe	Partnership with U.S.	Membership in NATO	Subtotal	Other
Total	*29*	*18*	*21*	*15*	*54*	*13*
Executive branch	50	28	12	8	48	0
Communist-oriented party leaders	40	4	12	4	20	36
Noncommunist party leaders	16	32	8	12	52	32
State enterprise directors	36	16	18	8	42	18
Private entrepreneurs	18	12	16	32	60	8
Military commanders	46	14	18	10	42	12
Press	18	20	26	16	66	14
Scholars and cultural figures	10	16	46	20	82	4

Source: Adapted from Vox Populi, "USIA Survey no. I93060: NATO" (Moscow: United States Information Agency, 1993), question 8.

Note: Due to rounding, some percentage totals may not equal 100.

TABLE 6.3. *Elite Attitudes toward the Need for NATO in 1993*

Is NATO still necessary?				
NATO is still necessary for guaranteeing European security			NATO no longer plays a critical role and is no longer necessary	
50%			36%	
Why is it necessary to preserve NATO?				
It preserves peace in Europe	It guarantees cooperation between Europe and America	Other	It defends Western Europe	It guarantees the U.S.'s participation in Europe's defense
47%	16%	16%	12%	5%
Why is it not necessary to preserve NATO?				
Other	It allows the U.S. to play a bigger role	Its members may become involved in conflicts	It is a waste of money	It represents a threat to peace
30%	26%	18%	12%	6%

Source: Vox Populi, "USIA Survey no. I93060: NATO" (Moscow: United States Information Agency, 1993), questions 13 to 15. Only those who thought NATO was still necessary were asked to list the "best reason" for its continued existence, while only those who thought NATO was not necessary were asked to list the "best reason for ending NATO."

1996, after NATO announced that it would proceed to admit new members, 92 percent of political elites believed that "cooperating with the US and West European countries" was important (of that number, 40 percent thought this was "very important").[16] Three times as many respondents believed that cooperation with NATO strengthened Russia's security than the 12 percent who thought it weakened it.[17] The same year, only 1 percent of political elites viewed the Commonwealth of Independent States (CIS) as a defensive alliance.[18] Even in September 1999, at the peak of Russian anti-American and anti-NATO sentiment over the intervention in Kosovo, respondents in a survey of Russian regional elites overwhelmingly opted for cooperating with NATO. Seventy-eight percent thought Russia should cooperate with but not join NATO, and 9 percent thought Russia should join NATO; only 11 percent opposed all cooperation with the Western alliance.[19]

Other evidence also suggests that Russia did not fulfill realist expectations after the Cold War. Despite negative perceptions of NATO throughout the 1990s, increasing asymmetry in the distribution of power between Russia and the West, and Western efforts to bring a Cold War alliance closer to Russia's borders, Russia did nothing to counteract the West. It did not pursue internal and external balancing throughout the 1990s. Russian military spending was radically reduced from $171 billion in 1990 to $26.1 billion in 2004—even as U.S. military expenditures remained relatively constant, dipping from $457.7 billion in 1990 to $328.6 billion in 1998 and rising to $480.5 billion in 2004 (in constant 2005 prices and exchange rates). William Zimmerman found that "there was no statistical relationship between assessments by elites of the distribution of power between the United States and Russia and their assessment of NATO expansion into Eastern Europe as a threat."[20] Russian policy reflected this absence of a perception of genuine military threat. Russian armed forces personnel were reduced from 2.6 million in 1992 to less than nine hundred thousand in 2003, and those on the Western flank from 1,383,283 to 579,852. Tanks, aircraft, and helicopters on Russia's Western border were reduced from Soviet levels by as much as 48 to 63 percent from 1990 to 2004, and all conventional military hardware there fell below the ceilings allowed by the Conventional Forces in Europe Treaty during the same period.[21] No serious attention was devoted to turning the CIS into a military or political counterweight to NATO, and efforts to build alliances with China against the United States and NATO remained rhetorical.[22] The balance of military threat played little role in the Russian political elite's definition of its interests in European security or its views of NATO.

Despite the loss of a considerable portion of territory, population, and military infrastructure in 1991, Russian political elites felt threatened by NATO and the United States not primarily in *military* terms but in *status* terms.[23] Political elites were generally less concerned about traditional forms of Western aggression against Russia than the possibility of isolation from the West and the consequences this would entail for Russian internal modernization and its global status. It is in this light that NATO expansion was perceived as a threat, as it entailed both Russia's increased isolation from Europe and the legitimation of neo-imperialist and anti-Western views at home. The genuine absence of a *military* threat from the West was widely agreed upon by political elites, including military and government officials. In general (and with the exception of international terrorism after 2001), Russian policy analyst Mikhail Karpov's 1995 observation remained true throughout the post-Soviet period: "The legitimacy of the proposition that all the main threats to Russia's security continue to emanate from within [goes] virtually unchallenged."[24] Zimmerman noted a sharp drop from 1999 levels in elite perceptions of a threat from NATO in 2004. Particularly remarkable was the drop by 49 percent of the military elite respondents who said the United States was a threat to Russia and that Russia should balance the United States.[25]

Despite its waning power in Europe, Russia did not undertake risky revanchist adventures after the Cold War, as offensive realists feared. As Sergei Medvedev noted, from a "metahistorical perspective, change in Russian foreign policy amounts to no less than a revolution, which occurred without war, occupation, or incorporation into a dominant regime. . . . Painful as it was, Russia's post-imperial transformation was surprisingly stable. A surprise night move of 200 Russian paratroopers from . . . Bosnia to the Pristina airport in Kosovo ahead of NATO forces in June 1999 was probably the high point of Russia's defiance of the West."[26] Instead of revanchism, Russia expended considerable diplomatic effort to develop a partnership with NATO and the United States in managing security affairs.

Aspirational Constructivism and Russian Interests in European Security

The definition of Russia's national interest regarding Europe was not driven by fears of a unified Germany, threatening behavior on the part of the United States, or even real fears of an anti-Russian NATO expanding throughout Russia's former sphere of influence. Russians, despite their twentieth-century history, did not perceive material threats to their national security emanating from the West. In contrast to the expectations of structural constructivism and realism, Russia's identity and interests were not formed in response to the West's behavior or its power.

Instead, Russian identity and interests regarding Europe were formed in response to Russia's own history. As with the general debate over Russia's post-Soviet identity, two questions animated the political elite debate over Russia's interests in European security: Was Russia Western? What was Russia's international role? Russia's identity and interests regarding Europe were based on historical aspirations to maintain Russia's past international status as a global great power and acceptance, albeit sometimes reluctant, that this status could only be achieved through inclusion in the West. Russian aspirations produced a desire to compete for social recognition in the West of Russia's great power status; they also produced among many Russian political elites a nineteenth-century view of global great power status turning on Russia's position in Europe. After Primakov became foreign minister in January 1996, political elites, including many high officials, began deliberately citing the example of Prince Gorchakov, who as foreign minister in the 1850s and 1860s was credited with preserving tsarist Russia's great power status after its crushing defeat in the Crimean War.[27] Elites often quoted Gorchakov's famous words, "*La Russie ne boude pas, mais se recueille*" ("Russia is not sulking, she is collecting herself") when discussing Russia's present-day efforts to maintain its international status.[28] Russian elites interpreted Western behavior through this nineteenth century-lens, in which world politics was based on a great power concert.

Russian policy on European security became reactive to perceived Western efforts to undermine Russia's aspirations regarding its global status. Western behavior reinforced this view but did not create it. The reactive and competitive nature of Russian national interests remained limited. The West as a desired ingroup and efficacy tests applied to policies associated with anti-Western national self-images produced interests in cooperation with Europe and the United States, which served to prevent the status aspirations from producing national interests in confrontation. Throughout the post-Soviet period, these counteracting factors produced a definition of Russia's national interests as cooperation with the West while competing for status with the United States.

Historical Aspirations and the Creation of Russia's European Security Interests

From the very start, Russia's interests in European security were turned into a question of Russia's aspirations to be an independent global power whose interests were taken into account by the transatlantic great powers. Russian political elites still viewed Russia's traditional status as a European and global great power as highly legitimate. As Aleksei Arbatov predicted, "Russian participation in world affairs is crucial to its prestige and status as something more than just a regional power, and will greatly affect its relations with the United States and other Western states."[29] Most political elites assumed that Russia, together with the United States, would continue to regulate European, if not global, security.[30]

Historical aspirations disposed Russian political elites to favor competition with the United States and NATO for recognition of Russia's proper status. As one Foreign Ministry official put it, "Moscow's view is that the entry of Russia into Western institutions should not be made at the expense of losing its major power status." NATO should not therefore "attempt to put Russia (with its potential for considerable influence on world events) in the position of 'equal among equals.'"[31] Those espousing national self-images that painted the West as an outgroup sought to fan this competition into hostile confrontation. Such an outcome did not occur, though Russian policy regarding NATO at times took on hostile and even belligerent tones, and Russian positions hardened on NATO for most of the post-Soviet period.

However, another counterbalancing aspiration shaped most elites' views of the extent of Russia's status competition. Chapter 3 noted a broad, though not universal, Russian political elite consensus on the illegitimacy of the Soviet ideologically driven purpose of confronting the West. This produced a widespread aspiration to avoid confrontation with the West. For most political elites, a national interest defined in terms of the Soviet-era purpose of open confrontation with the West was completely ruled out.[32] This aspiration, reinforced by the belief of half of Russian political elites that Russia should join the West—their designation of the West as an ingroup—produced a broadly cooperative orientation toward the West.[33] Mainstream critiques of Russia's relations with the West were over how, not whether, to cooperate.[34]

Elite aspirations regarding Russia's historical status resulted in the political discourse about Russia's interests in European security being marked, as all foreign policy debates were, by the deep ambivalence among Russian political elites about the historical appropriateness of "following" the West versus pursuing an independent and unique "Russian path."[35] As noted in the previous chapter, Russian political elites sought to overcome negative national self-esteem by rejecting a secondary status to the United States. Rejecting this secondary status was particularly important in Europe, as it was in this region historically that Russia and then the Soviet Union became a peer, at least in the eyes of Russians, to the leading great powers of the day.[36]

For most political elites, the aspiration to maintain Russia's historical status required some degree of Westernization.[37] This made "preventing Russia's disengagement from the rest of Europe . . . undoubtedly the country's major objective interest. . . . Consequently, ensuring cooperative engagement and compatibility with the West should be considered Russia's main goal in the region." However, given the rejection of a status secondary to the United States, "this basic proposition is the most controversial thesis in Russia's debates on its foreign and security policy priorities."[38] This was not the case in the initial years of the post-Soviet period.

At the outset of the post-Soviet period, Russian political elites assumed that Russia's interests lay in cooperating with the West on European security. In 1992, as a foreign policy interest among political elites, cooperation with NATO was largely taken for granted, based on an assumption of Russia's continued status as a global and European great power.[39] There was widespread agreement, except among radical national restorationists, that Russia should not return to Cold War confrontation with the West, which meant maintaining cooperation with the United States, NATO, and Western Europe.

This assumption began to be questioned with the consolidation of the Eurasian statist critique of the Yeltsin administration's liberal internationalist foreign policy in 1992 and 1993, discussed in chapter 5. The issue of European security first became prominent in the political discourse in 1992 when the Yeltsin government voted for economic sanctions against Yugoslavia for its role in the Bosnian war. The essence of this critique was that the Yeltsin administration was not behaving in accordance with Russia's historical role as a great power—not that the United States or the West had threatened Russia. Statists and national restorationists condemned Foreign Minister Andrei Kozyrev's unthinking "orientation towards close cooperation and alliance with NATO countries, above all the United States and Germany" as a general part of their domestic critique of the "Westernizing democrats."[40] Moderate liberals and centrists argued that the Yeltsin administration's passive policy of being Washington's "junior partner" with regard to Bosnia not only strengthened national restorationists and conservative statists in Russia, it also weakened Russia's "standing in international relations and in its relations with the West."[41] They criticized the administration for passively following the United States and thereby undermining Russia's capacity for future influence and status as a great power, a critique based on the legitimacy of Russia's past status. Parliamentarian Evgenii Kozhokin argued that Kozyrev's foreign policy was far too "pragmatic" in its acceptance of Russia's weakness and had therefore mistakenly abandoned "traditional interests" in Europe.[42] This critique extended across the political spectrum, incorporating democratic developmentalists, statists, and national restorationists.[43]

In response to this criticism, the Yeltsin administration began to pursue a more independent line on Bosnia, but one that still conformed to the Western consensus. The main change in official policy on Bosnia was Russia's demand for (and receipt of) recognition of its equal status in diplomatic negotiations. In 1994, Russian special envoy Vitalii Churkin persuaded the Bosnian Serbs to comply with UN demands to withdraw heavy artillery from the hills around Sarajevo. His action averted threatened NATO air strikes, and Russian political elites jubilantly declared that Russia's great power status had been restored.[44] This elite perception of Russia's first diplomatic success indicates the significance of equal participation in European security for Russia's international status and its national identity.[45]

Preoccupation with NATO

European security as an issue became a dominant fixture of the debate over Russia's national identity and interests only when Boris Yeltsin declared during a trip to Poland in 1993 that the Poles were free to join NATO if they wished.[46] NATO promptly announced plans for the "Partnership for Peace"—a program for cooperation with postcommunist countries and potential new members of the alliance—that fall. NATO thereafter was coterminous with European security for Russian political elites. As one analyst noted, Russian political elites united in opposition to NATO expansion: "Russia saw the emergence of its first foreign policy consensus bringing together representatives of all major political forces—from communists to democrats, and from liberally oriented enthusiasts of market reform to proponents of 'Russia's specific (i.e., "not-like-the-others") identity.' In terms of Russia's fragmented political life, this phenomenon is rare indeed."[47] The majority of political elites remained opposed to NATO expansion in 2005.[48] NATO's war against Serbia consolidated this opposition.[49] As Vladimir Baranovskii wrote in 2001, "This opposition has endured throughout almost the entire decade of the 1990s and has combined the logic of rational arguments with an acute emotional reaction."[50]

Social psychology suggests that such an "acute emotional reaction" would occur in response to a threat to one's identity.[51] For Russians, NATO came to symbolize a threat to Russia's identity as a global great power rather than as a genuine military threat, as it represented a challenge to Russian elites' perception of their special role in stabilizing European, and thereby global, security. This in turn implied that Russia no longer had the positive distinctiveness it had previously possessed—a huge blow to national self-esteem, as this was the single shared positive distinction Russian elites took from their past.

By increasing the role of the United States and reducing Russia's role, the expansion of NATO's membership and missions challenged elite historical aspirations to great power status on a par with the United States.

This aspiration was made explicit in 1996 by Sergei Kortunov, at the time advisor to the Russian Security Council. He said, in reference to "the two traditionally principal players of world politics," that "the Russo-American ligament could be the backbone of a security community encompassing all the northern hemisphere, and in the future, of global security also."[52] When Evgenii Primakov took office in January 12, 1996, he emphasized this aspiration in his first news conference. Stating that "Russia is a great power and that its policy should accord with that status," he also revealed the substance of his first telephone conversation as foreign minister with U.S. Secretary of State Warren Christopher. Primakov recounted that "the Secretary of State emphasized that our two great powers, and, I quote him, 'carry special responsibility for stabilizing the situation in the world.' We absolutely support this formulation of the question."[53] As a result, Russia's *equal* participation in European security was seen as a vital component in maintaining Russia's global status as a peer to the United States and its national self-esteem.

In order to elevate Russia above other countries and highlight its unique great power status, Russian national self-esteem required a distinctive relationship with NATO "that would be deeper and more substantive than the Alliance's relations with any of its other partners."[54] Russia expended considerable diplomatic effort in pursuit of this aim. It insisted on a special agreement symbolizing its difference from the former Soviet satellites that had joined NATO's Partnership for Peace (PFP) program so that Russia would not be "in the position of 'equal among equals'" with the countries of Central East Europe.[55] When PFP was formally launched in January 1994, the Central Eastern European countries immediately joined, while Russia held out until June for recognition of its "special status."[56] In 1997, Primakov sought this distinction with the enactment of the NATO-Russia Founding Act, which created the NATO-Russia Permanent Joint Council. Putin followed suit in 2002 with the establishment of the NATO-Russia Council, an advisory group designed, according to Defense Minister Sergei Ivanov, to give Russia a voice equal to that of member states, which its predecessor had not.[57]

As noted earlier, Russian political elites framed European security almost entirely in terms of Russia's global status, which in turn was seen as dependent on its status as an equal partner to the United States in NATO. This framing explains the political elite's difficulty in securing a stable, cooperative orientation toward European security. Its conception of European security was inseparable from its social status relative to the United States and therefore NATO and the West more generally.[58]

Constraints on Historical Aspirations

Despite their aspirations to a status equal to the United States, Russian elites found that their interest in status competition with the United States was constrained by acceptance that Russia's global status depended in large part on Russia's incorporation into Western international society. Two factors contributed to the bounding of competition within a larger framework of cooperation. The construction of Europe—and the West more generally—as an ingroup in Western and statist national self-images moderated competitive inclinations among Russian political elites who favored those self-images. A second factor limiting confrontational and competitive orientations was the sustained efficacy-testing they conducted regarding Russia's inability to balance U.S. influence in Europe. Both helped limit hostile and confrontational attitudes toward the United States and Europe throughout the 1990s. As a result, competition for status within a broader strategic framework of cooperation remained the general orientation. One leg of this foreign policy orientation was opposition to NATO expansion; the second leg, as we have seen, was an effort at a special Russian relationship with NATO and continued engagement with the West.

Efficacy-Testing and the Avoidance of Confrontation over European Security

As in the general debate over Russia's identity and national interests, Russian political elites relied on practical assessments in addition to historical legitimacy to vet national self-images regarding their prescriptions for European security.[59] Efficacy tests confirming the limited benefit to Russia of opposing NATO helped form the dominant foreign policy orientation of competition-within-cooperation or "competitive engagement" on European security.[60]

Moderates and centrists kept attempting to shift the political elite discourse from the post-1992 consensus on a national interest devoted to preserving Russia's great power status to one focused on Western-style economic development.[61] As one democratically oriented statist put it, "Russia will be an equal partner in any negotiations only when we have stopped being an economic 'poor cousin.'"[62] Throughout the Primakov and Putin eras, these political elites argued that defining Russia's interests at the European level was more effective and more appropriate than continuing to define the national interest as globally restraining U.S. unipolarity.[63]

As noted in previous chapters, Evgenii Primakov made pursuit of Russia's global status the centerpiece of his foreign policy from 1996 to 1999. Under Primakov, Russian emphasis on its interest in global status maintenance was largely manifested in incessant assertions that "Russia is a great power" on the part of the government and elites.[64] NATO and European security remain intimately connected with the conception on the part of Primakov and other Russian political elites of Russia as a *global* great power.[65] Russia's interests regarding NATO and European security continued to be defined in terms of competition for recognition of Russia's global status. Primakov's rhetoric had the effect of tipping Russian elite discourse on European security toward conservative statist and national restorationist positions, even though he never advocated confrontation with the West.

Primakov's strategy of social creativity sought to reimagine the basis for Russia's status as one based on its role as a friendly stabilizer of the international system bent on restraining its fellow great power, the United States, from overreaching in the interests of international order.[66] His assertion of Russia's great power status served as the lowest common denominator uniting Russian political elites and made him popular among them. Russia's official opposition to NATO enlargement and its war against Serbia were central elements of this strategy.

Critics recognized that this status-driven definition of Russia's interests could lead to a purely reactive foreign policy, one that lacked a concrete proactive agenda.[67] Two moderates warned, in reference to European security, that "as long as status considerations are the most important criteria for Russia's international behavior, it might easily misjudge its real security challenges and options."[68] These democratic and statist developmentalists argued that defining Russia's interests at the European level was more effective and more appropriate than a competition for status on par with the United States. They criticized the reactive, anti-American character of Primakov's efforts at great power maintenance.[69] In 2001, however, only a quarter of political elites saw these claims as the primary cause of Russia's poor relations with Europe, and this portion consisted mainly of Westernizers and Western-oriented statists.[70]

In contrast, conservative statists, neocommunists, and national restorationists rationalized cooperation with NATO and Western Europe as a divide-and-conquer tactic to separate Western Europe from the United States. Their calls for Russia to pursue such a policy began with NATO expansion and increased with the Kosovo conflict. Neocommunist Gennadii Seleznev suggested that Russia could foot the bill for a European security system and even offer its nuclear shield to Europe. "Greater links between Russia and Europe," he claimed, "would strengthen the military-political potential of Europe, its position vis-à-vis the United States, and geostrategic opportunities in the 21st century."[71] These Russian political elites reluctantly accepted "compulsory cooperation" with NATO in order to pursue its aspiration to regain its great power status and then confront the West.[72]

National Self-Images and the West as an Ingroup

The national self-images of many Russian elites depict the West as an ingroup or partial ingroup. This predisposed their adherents to favor engagement and oppose confrontation with the West. As shown in table 4.1, only national restorationist and neocommunist national self-images construct the West as an outgroup; all others view Russia as at least partly Western. Social identity theory expects such identification to produce cooperative orientations toward the ingroup; indeed, ingroup identification is a key motivation for collective action.[73]

As explained in chapter 4, for Westernizers, cooperation with the West is a given, as their desire is to assimilate into the West by adopting its values and principles for social order. For statists, Russia is to greater or lesser extent a Western country—more so for statist developmentalists than Eurasianists—but in both statist self-images, Russia belongs in the West as a modern, rational country. For statist developmentalists, the West represents the apex of modern development, and they desire to rank Russia as an advanced Western country on the grounds of its economic and technological capacity.[74] For Eurasian statists, Western rationalism provides the counterbalance to Eastern emotionalism in Russia's identity, and exclusion from the West would therefore relegate Russia to being purely Eastern.[75] The West also represents for statists Russia's natural great power peer group, as this is the region in which Russia first became a great power historically. For Eurasian statists such as Primakov, and those referencing Gorchakov, engagement with the West remained essential for Russia's great power status. Gorchakov's modus operandi was that Russia's foreign policy should create optimal conditions for domestic reform, for "the first duty of Russia is to accomplish the work of internal reorganization, which contains the germ of her destiny in the future."[76] Russia therefore should pursue, in the words of Prince Gorchakov, "careful and nonprovocative policies" to prevent its exclusion from coalitions of wealthy industrialized nations.[77] Even Slavophiles, while decrying the corrupting decadence of the West, view Russia as closer to the Christian West than the non-Christian world. Given these designations of the West as an ingroup in these national self-images, aspirational constructivism would expect significant numbers of Russian political elites to be disposed toward engagement and cooperation with the West and to view exclusion from their ingroup negatively.

Not surprisingly, given the depiction of the West as an ingroup in these national self-images, significant numbers of Russian political elites maintained that it was in Russia's interests to cooperate with NATO regardless of their negative views of the alliance's expansion. Russian political elites division over this question of cooperation with NATO stemmed largely from the form such cooperation should take—whether it would be undertaken in a manner befitting Russia's special status or represent an unseemly "bowing" to the West's leadership. This question of Russia's distinctiveness tracked elite divisions over relations with NATO, first over the PFP in 1994, then again and again over successive rounds of NATO expansion in 1995, 1999, and 2004; the NATO-Russia Founding Act in 1997; NATO's campaign in Kosovo in 1999; and the NATO-Russia Council in 2002.[78]

Throughout the post-Soviet period, between 40 and 51 percent of Russian political elites agreed that "Russia must strive to integrate with the leading Western countries and get rid of the 'Russian uniqueness syndrome,'" while 44 to 52 percent favored the statement that "Russia must search for its own path, for an alternative to a Western model of development."[79] William Zimmerman found that this divide, more than preferences regarding Russia's form of political economic development, was the most significant predictor of elite foreign policy orientations throughout the post-Soviet period, including those toward NATO.[80] Such a correspondence between attitudes toward cooperation with NATO and Russia's Westernness or "uniqueness" fit with an aspirational constructivist expectation that cooperative orientations should go along with the West's designation as an ingroup in Russian national self-images. In line with these expectations, moderate and centrist statists and Westernizers argued for continued cooperation with NATO, while conservative statists and national restorationists argued that Russia should compete with or confront NATO, respectively.[81]

Russian political elites broadly agreed that Russia had to maintain a role in Europe to secure the domestic reforms necessary to secure Russia's reemergence as a great power. These reforms and Russia's great power role could only be accomplished in conjunction with an improving external security environment and integration into the West.[82] Russian political elites therefore generally rejected national restorationist prescriptions for confrontation with the West. Responding to national restorationist calls to side with the Bosnian Serbs against the West, special envoy Vitalii Churkin said that Russia "will never get into a confrontation with the world community over the map of Bosnia."[83] The influential centrist-statist Council on Foreign and Defense Policy argued that Russia was endangered by such "Soviet-type rhetoric of confrontation that will infringe Russia's national interests in all senses."[84] Presidential spokesman Sergei Yastrzhembskii said upon the signing of the NATO-Russia Founding Act that in the negotiations, the "supreme aim, the aim of preserving trust between Russia and the West, between Russia and the NATO states, was like a lode star" guiding the negotiators. Prominent Eurasian statists, such as Andranik Migranian, and even some neocommunists, such as Duma Speaker Gennadii Seleznev, also rejected confronting the West.[85]

Instead of fearing Western military power, Russian political elites feared political and economic *exclusion* from the West and from Europe. Reasons for this fear of exclusion varied. Westernizers believed it would prevent Russia's internal democratization and economic liberalization. Statist developmentalists believed it would impede Russia's economic modernization and integration into the Western global economy and subsequent reclamation of great power status. As then Prime Minister Putin said in 1999, "Despite problems and mistakes, [Russia] has entered the highway by which the whole of humanity is travelling. Only this way offers the possibility of dynamic economic growth and higher living standards, as the world experience convincingly shows. . . . In the present world the might of a country as a great power is manifested more in its ability to be the leader in creating and using advanced technologies, ensuring a high level of people's well-being, reliably protecting its security and upholding its national interests in the international arena, than in its military strength."[86]

These reasons, most Westernizers and statists reasoned, required close cooperation with NATO, if not membership in it and other multilateral European organizations.[87] They viewed exclusion from the West as signifying an end to Russia's desired global position and worsening the internal conditions for Russia's development. As Evgenii Primakov said upon becoming foreign minister in 1996, the issue of Russia's great power status "is also a question of the need to create an external environment which to the highest degree would favor the development of the economic and democratic processes in Russian society." Such development requires "partnerly relations with former opponents" in the West.[88]

In 2001, when NATO's intervention in Kosovo was still fresh in their collective memory, the proportion of elite respondents who felt that Russia should seek to regain the USSR's status—a proxy for confrontation with the United States—doubled. Yet this doubling only yielded a post-Soviet record of 13 percent who favored such a policy.[89] In contrast, 65 percent favored a strategic partnership with Europe, 49 percent wanted a strategic partnership with the United States, and 43 percent favored partnership with NATO.[90] Only national restorationists premised the definition of Russia's interests in Europe on confrontation between the West and the East—that is, between the United States and Russia.[91]

The dire predictions of realists about a revanchist Russia at the end of the Cold War period were not borne out. As one Russian observer noted, post-Soviet Russian foreign policy "never steered off the course chosen in the late Gorbachev and early Yeltsin periods and stayed within the broad framework of cooperation with the West."[92] These orientations toward cooperating with a desired ingroup were bolstered by the efficacy tests liberals and moderates applied to those advocating an ideology- or status-driven confrontation with the West.

Despite the arguments of efficacy testers, NATO and European security remained intimately connected with the Russian political elite's aspirations for Russia's role as a global great power.[93] The behavior of the United States and NATO strengthened—but did not create—the status-driven definition of Russia's national interests and the competitive orientation of the elites.

Impact of the West on Russian Security Interests in Europe

Russian political elites' almost singleminded focus on NATO, and by extension the United States, meant that the latter's behavior in European and international security consolidated the predominance of a nineteenth-century style framing of world politics among post-Soviet Russian political elites.[94] Assen Ignatow captured how the behavior of Western great powers (the other) was seen as directed at Russia (the self). He writes, "Russia is still in the habit of thinking of itself as a superpower and therefore continues to orient itself to the 'other' superpower, the USA, or toward the NATO as the 'Atlantic' community encompassing more than only Europe. Russia is no longer a superpower but it goes on behaving as if it were. Like a person with an amputated limb, it continues to feel the pain of loss—in this case the loss of political power."[95] Given these self-centered standards, NATO's behavior was perceived as evidence that statists and national-socialists were right, respectively, in their identification of the West as a competitor or enemy.

NATO's behavior since 1994 served not only to reinforce the Russian consensus on great power status but added some effective legitimacy to the basis for Russia's oppositionist foreign policy orientation on European security. According to centrist Sergei Rogov, an advisor to influential statists such as Arkadii Volskii, "The decision on the enlargement of NATO is seen by Russia as . . . an aspiration to consolidate the fruits of victory over the Soviet Union in the cold war and to isolate Moscow."[96] NATO expansion served to make national restorationist claims of Western geopolitical designs on Russia appear more credible, at least temporarily. The Council on Foreign and Defense Policy, normally oriented toward engagement with the West, reflected this growing legitimacy in 1995 when one of its reports stated that "there is an intention, particularly noticeable in the United States, to capitalize on the geopolitical acquisitions achieved through the 'victory' in the Cold War, so that Russia, even after sorting out the current crisis, would not be able to proportionately increase her political influence in Europe."[97] NATO's behavior in Kosovo provided the more conservative and national restorationist members of the Russian political elite with a "realistic" claim for the need to maintain and increase Russia's global status, where previously their claims to global status had been justified only in terms of Russia's "historical rights."[98]

It seemed to Russian political elites immediately after NATO's air war against Serbia that Primakov's image of a rogue United States was being confirmed by real-world events. A plurality of them (42 percent) saw Kosovo as creating a "new international balance of power under U.S. dominance." This was both a sign that asymmetries in the distribution of material power had begun to sink in but also reflected the nineteenth-century view of European security issues as the epicenter of global politics. Not surprisingly, this view was more prevalent among traditionalists—those favoring a "Russian path" of development—than among Westernizers.[99] "As seen from Moscow," wrote Dmitrii Trenin in 1998, "the Kosovo conflict is not primarily about the Serbs and Albanians, . . . but about the U.S. role in the world."[100]

This nineteenth-century interpretation of Kosovo reinforced the view that Russians and Europeans perceived European security crises, such as Kosovo, in radically different terms. As Max Jakobson, former Finnish ambassador to the United Nations, wrote in 1999, "The Kosovo conflict revealed a fundamental gap between Western and Russian perceptions of the evolution of international relations. The concept of humanitarian intervention was alien to Russian thinking. It was dismissed by Russian politicians and generals as a disguise for America's geopolitical ambitions. . . . The primacy of human rights in Western policies is a function of the profound integration that has taken place between open societies. Russia has not yet been transformed by that process."[101] Sergei Karaganov agreed, stating in 2005 that "the political classes in Russia and the EU have a noticeable difference in basic values."[102]

Post-Kosovo, Russian officials began more frequently to speak of the United States as a force destabilizing the international system, and NATO as "a group of states [that] will use force at their own will and without limitations to destroy the economic potentials and cultural values of any country."[103] Official denunciations of Western efforts to impose "Western ideas of democracy and unified political and social systems" on "all states irrespective of their historical, cultural, and social features" arose with Kosovo, subsided, then returned in 2003 and 2004 after the U.S. invasion of Iraq, the admission of the Baltic states to NATO, and the revolutions in Georgia and Ukraine produced pro-Western governments.[104]

Russian political elites accepted Primakov's social creativity strategy, which Putin more pragmatically implemented. This strategy added to the status-driven definition of Russia's interests the role of upholding the international system of sovereign states against a revisionist United States and its proxy, NATO. However, as we have seen, Russian elites still favored cooperation and engagement with the West and NATO rather than confrontation. Efficacy-testing, but especially Russian elites' perceptions of the legitimacy of Vladimir Putin's statist developmentalism, helped restrain confrontational orientations toward NATO and the United States.

As noted in previous chapters, Putin continued Primakov's social creativity strategy and emphasized Russia's equal status with the United States. But he also emphasized Russia's need for economic modernization, which required engagement with the West. Putin viewed Russia's interest in European security and NATO as part of his effort to restore its global position. This long-term interest necessitated cooperation with European security institutions.[105]

Putin wanted to base Russia's greatness on economic rather than military criteria, as, in his words, "in the present world the might of a country as a great power is manifested more in its ability to be the leader in creating and using advanced technologies, ensuring a high level of people's wellbeing, reliably protecting its security and upholding its national interests in the international arena, than in its military strength."[106] In emphasizing Russia's greatness and right to special treatment on that basis, Putin was fulfilling the psychological need to assert Russia's distinctiveness from the smaller countries of Europe. He continued Primakov's policy of demanding special status with European institutions and, in the form of the 2002 NATO-Russia Council, sought to establish Russia's "equality" in European security deliberations. Putin raised expectations (as had Yeltsin with the 1997 NATO-Russian Founding Act and Joint Permanent Council) that the NATO-Russia Council would provide participation for Russia on key security issues on an equal basis with the members of NATO.

Through such efficacy-testing and the pursuit of a special relationship with the United States in fighting global terror, Putin managed to cushion the impact of Kosovo and the 2004 round of NATO expansion, though NATO was still negatively perceived by the overwhelming majority of Russian political elites.[107] As such, the Putin administration could claim to be upholding Russia's great power status and defending Russia's interests rather than merely "following" the West or becoming a "junior partner" to the United States.[108] After 2003, elite concern over NATO began to wane. In part this reduced concern regarding NATO reflected the political elite's conviction that Putin had significantly improved Russia's international standing; his statist developmentalist national self-image had passed a history and an efficacy test (see chapter 5).[109]

While Putin was able to satisfy the political elite's demand for a diplomacy befitting its historical status and one that seemed capable of enactment under present conditions, he also strengthened the arguments of Westernizers. He continually discussed Russia's economic weakness and liberal economic modernization as the foundation on which its international position depended. Such liberal modernization required good relations with the West, including NATO, as Westernizers had long argued.[110] The majority of the political elites reacted positively to Putin's foreign policy, especially his insistence on Russia's equal status within the European security community and claim to an equal partnership with the United States.[111]

Putin emphasized Russia's broader interests in rapprochement with the West and Russia's comparative economic and military weakness.[112] In addition, he consistently argued that European security, and NATO in particular, must be transformed from a system of mutual deterrence into a more cooperative arrangement while still characterizing NATO expansion as a negative development.[113] He also sought to manage "the reality of NATO," hoping to convince Russian political elites that they had spent too much time on NATO rather than on more important issues. Karaganov captured Putin's view: "All Russia's European policies and foreign policy [were] focused on this issue alone, so Russian government resources were diverted from many other issues, some of which were much more relevant."[114]

Putin also sought to create a new, positive global identity for Russia as a co-guarantor of global security and the system of sovereign states. While cooperation with NATO remained official policy, under Putin Russia attempted to refocus European security away from NATO toward the

European Union. Little real progress was made in defining Russia's concrete security interests in Europe, however, as Putin quickly gave priority to a relationship with the United States on global security issues.[115]

The 9/11 attacks on the United States put Putin in a more legitimate position to frame U.S., European, and Russian security interests genuinely as a single common interest: combating the real threat of international terrorism. As Dov Lynch put it in 2003, the idea of "this common cause has inspired Russian and NATO officials to rhetorical heights," likening antiterrorism to the Allied war against fascism in the 1940s.[116] Putin was one of the most prominent efficacy testers in Russia, but his aim was the preservation of Russia's great power status through economic modernization, rather than Westernization, for the sake of Russian citizens and society.[117] His emphasis on Russia's status, and his pragmatic efforts to reach it, generated broad support among Russian political elites.[118]

Despite the greater realism in Putin's vision for Russia, historical aspirations still dominated the definition of national interests in the greater European region. They were largely premised on Russia's history as a huge continental empire that controlled the destinies of the peoples on and within its periphery.[119] Putin himself premised Russian identity on Russia's global great power status and its rights in the former Soviet Union and responsibilities in Europe. As noted in chapter 3, the former Soviet republics were a primary ingroup in all Russian national self-images except the liberal internationalist one, and within that ingroup, Russia was the unquestioned hegemon. As social identity theory would expect, perceived threats to that ingroup status prompted hostility. Moreover, Putin, like Primakov, portrayed Russia as standing for the world order of the nineteenth century, when state sovereignty putatively meant non-interference in another state's political-economic system and great powers respected one another's sphere of influence while jointly managing global security.

Both factors set the stage for the only genuine source of confrontation between the West and Russia: NATO and Western involvement in the former Soviet republics. As noted in the previous chapter, the most serious crisis in Russian relations with the West therefore arose over Western assistance to democratic forces in the former Soviet republics in 2003 and 2004 during the "colored revolutions." In Moscow, this assistance was viewed not as assistance to democratization but as an effort to undercut Russia's position as the leading power in its own backyard and reduce Russia's global status still further. In a major break with the neoliberal and pro-Western views that had emanated from Putin's Kremlin before this time, the powerful deputy head of the presidential administration, Vladimir Surkov, who had orchestrated the utter defeat of the left- and right-wing parties opposed to Putin in the 2003 parliamentary elections, said in September 2004 that U.S. and European "decision makers . . . take credit for the nearly bloodless collapse of the Soviet Union and want to further that achievement. Their goal is the destruction of our country." Surkov went on to accuse the West of deliberately intervening in the affairs of the former Soviet republics to bring about Russia's collapse, by a means that "has been used repeatedly in the 19th and 20th centuries." Surkov claimed that all opponents of Putin's regime on both the left and the right were acting as a "fifth column" for the West. "They have a common hatred for 'Putin's Russia,' as they call it, and common foreign backers."[120] Language that used to be the preserve of national restorationist discourse became part of official and mainstream discourse.

The Kremlin's unofficial spokesman, Gleb Pavlovsky, announced in 2005 a new Russian doctrine for the former Soviet Union in the wake of Ukraine's Orange Revolution; he stated that any country that would "promote the doctrine of Russia's rollback will certainly create a conflict in relations with this country. This must be clearly understood." He proceeded to say that this sphere of influence included former Soviet republics—the Baltic states—that were already members of NATO and the European Union.[121]

The reactive nature of Russia's status-driven foreign policy prompted Westernizers and moderate statists to denounce the appearance of such anti-Western rhetoric under both Primakov and Putin. Westernizers sharply criticized the Putin administration as well as conservatives and hardliners in 2003 and 2004 for risking Russia's relations with the United States and the West over the "Orange Revolution" in Ukraine.[122] Vladimir Ryzhkov, then first deputy speaker of the Duma and senior member of the centrist Our Home is Russia party, said in June 1999, "We should renounce the loudmouth quality of our foreign policy. . . . We should renounce the impulse to pose as a superpower when we cannot put our own house in order."[123] Moderate democrats, such as Dmitrii Trenin, argued that the elite consensus on great power status and its obsession with NATO expansion revived "geopolitical fundamentalism" and produced a reactive, irrational foreign policy. This critique helped to limit status competition with the United States and helped moderate hostility toward the West.

These Westernizers and moderates were strengthened in their efforts to reduce the competitive nature of Russia's historical aspirations, both by current events and by Putin's own policies. Current events, particularly the August 1998 financial crisis that saw Western capital flee Russia overnight and Russia default on its debt, and Russia's failure to prevent NATO's war against Serbia and enlargement, underscored their claims regarding Russia's weakness and internal decline. Russian political elites became more aware of Russia's weakness.[124] Westernizers and moderates, as we have seen, had recognized this weakness much earlier in the post-Soviet period. In 2001, political elites identified Kosovo and NATO expansion as the two greatest defeats for Russian foreign policy in the 1990s.[125] Such policy outcomes affected the effective legitimacy of social creativity strategies premised either on confrontation with the West or on Russia's special role as international stabilizer.

The challenge to the effectiveness of statism's status-driven foreign policy became somewhat more widespread in the late 1990s, as some political elites who were former supporters of the reactive great power consensus took to criticizing the "obsession with NATO" as well as the policy of balancing the United States.[126] Vladimir Lukin blamed "Eastern emotionalism" for the Russian elite's response to NATO expansion and called on elites to adopt "Western rationalism" when defining its interests regarding the West.[127] Lukin lamented that because of elite focus on the USSR's past status, Russia was unable to define its post-Soviet global role.[128] Sergei Karaganov reminded Russians that the "USA is the world's most powerful country, and hence it would be a senseless expenditure of strength to try to fight it. And bad relations with the USA would only slow down rapprochement with many countries, including in Europe."[129] Despite the small numbers of their moderate advocates and aided in no small measure by the designation of the West as a partial ingroup in the dominant national self-image of statism, these appeals to reason deflected conservative and extremist calls for pure competition or open confrontation with the West and helped to sustain the cooperative framework within which competition would take place.[130] They failed, however, to undo the perceived legitimacy of Russia's role as a nineteenth-century-style stabilizer of global order and to dislodge the aspiration to great power status on which this creative strategy was premised.

Conclusion

Despite sustained efficacy-testing and the designation of the West as an ingroup throughout the post-Soviet period, the historical legitimacy of Russia's past global power status drove the definition of Russia's security interests regarding Europe and its continued competition with the United States to recognize Russia's status.[131] Since 1993, Russian views of European security were reduced to the question of the role of the United States in the post–Cold War world. NATO was increasingly identified among Russian political elites as a proxy for the United States. As Anatolii Chekhoev, the deputy chairman of the Parliamentary Committee for CIS Affairs stated in 2003, "NATO is the USA. . . . They interfered in Afghanistan, then they arrived in Central Asia, they went ahead with the war in Iraq, and their troops are in Georgia today. . . . [T]he USA is NATO."[132] As such, "U.S.-led NATO" played a key role in sustaining early historically derived aspirations regarding Russia's status as a global rather than regional power and the orientation toward global status competition with the United States. Most Russian political elites continued to believe that Russia remained the significant other for both Europe and the United States, even as the United States had shifted its focus to Russia's eastern neighbor, China. As well, "U.S.-led NATO" played a key role in sustaining the consensus on Russia's status as a *global* rather than regional power and the orientation toward status competition. Foreign and then Prime Minister Primakov's insistence on countering "unipolarity" and opposition to a "NATO-centric" world amply demonstrated this.[133]

Westernizers and moderate statist developmentalists lamented the political elite's Russia-centric view of U.S. behavior. Unlike political elites, they argued, the public realized that it was not living "in the 19th century."[134] They were largely unsuccessful in dislodging the definition of national interests in European security as a status competition with the United States. Russia's historical status as a global great power remained legitimate among Russian political elites, even though many recognized that it was impractical.[135] Efficacy testers did succeed in limiting this competition to one still couched in terms of engagement with the West.

Once the consensus on Russia's interests in maintaining its historical global great power status was achieved in late 1992 to early 1993, it set the stage for a self-fulfilling prophecy generated from its views of the West's behavior. Russian political elite aspirations regarding great power maintenance defaulted to a set of nineteenth-century, status-driven criteria for judging the West's behavior. These criteria were applied whether the West's actions were directed at Russia or not, as the political elite's reactions to Kosovo and the U.S. wars in Afghanistan and Iraq all suggest. These nineteenth-century criteria were premised on the assumptions that the West's behavior was directly or indirectly aimed at Russia, and was driven by a zero-sum logic of global status rankings in which the West could only gain influence at Russia's expense.[136] NATO's 1999 armed intervention in Kosovo followed by the West's political interventions in the former Soviet republics in 2003 and 2004 sustained the interest in status competition with the United States and tested the orientation toward engagement with NATO and the West.

This status-driven nineteenth-century perception of the West's behavior solidified the political elite's historical aspirations and definition of a national interest in reasserting Russia's status as a global power. As Trenin put it, "The discussion 'on NATO' really aids in consolidating in domestic political thinking, military-strategic, geopolitical and ideological approaches, more suitable to the situation at the end of the 19th, and not the 21st century."[137]

Aside from consolidating the national interest in maintaining a global great power status, the increasing effective legitimacy of statist identity management strategies depicting Russia as a status quo power and therefore noble upholder of the international order was the main change wrought by Western behavior. It was an important change, as it offered Russian political elites the language and positive basis with which to construct a new anti-American mission fulfilling the need for status maintenance while claiming a greater, more altruistic end.

As we saw above, most political elites in 2001, particularly traditionalists, saw Kosovo as marking a dramatic shift in the global balance of power, now dominated by the United States and its instrument, NATO. This produced greater realism among political elites regarding Russia's capacity to play a major role in world politics but also continued resentment of the United States and NATO as detriments to Russia's international status.[138]

At the same time, throughout the post-Soviet period, political elites grudgingly accepted as legitimate the "efficacy tests" applied by moderates that, given its inherent weakness and need to integrate into the West, Russia had to cooperate with NATO in order to have influence on European and global security.[139] Moreover, roughly half of elites saw the West as an ingroup and favored cooperation with NATO despite its behavior (in contrast to what structural constructivists would expect). But this cooperative orientation was neither taken for granted nor deeply institutionalized. It required continuous re-legitimation or re-rationalization in domestic discourse through the "efficacy tests" of Westernizers and moderates that offered "proof" of the benefits of engagement. Russian officials and sympathetic members of the political elite expended considerable effort in painting the NATO-Russia Founding Act and then the NATO-Russia Council as a major diplomatic success, in light of what officials claimed was a de facto veto over NATO actions, or as a considerable victory, given the weakness of Russia's bargaining position.[140]

Despite the considerable number of elites who identify Russia as belonging in the Western ingroup and their constant process of efficacy-based legitimation of a national interest in cooperation, historical aspirations for global great power status and consequent interest in status competition remained the default frame for Russia's interests in European security. This historical frame was reinforced by U.S. and NATO behavior. Moderates' efficacy-testing did not succeed in altering the historical aspirations at the root of Russia's national interests or in shifting its focus from the global to the regional. However, this testing, together with the designation of the West as Russia's desired ingroup in a number of national self-images, limited Russia's status competition with the United States and confined it within an overarching framework of cooperation with the West.[141] As noted in the next chapter, the same basic pattern played out in Russian politics regarding the subject of nuclear arms control.

SEVEN

The Post-Soviet Creation of Russia's Interests in Nuclear Arms Control

Nuclear weapons were the epicenter of the relationship between the two Cold War superpowers, the United States and the Soviet Union. Efforts to control them, particularly the category of strategic arms that were capable of reaching each other's homelands, were taken as key indicators of the state of the superpower relationship and of international stability more broadly. As such, aspirational constructivism would expect, in contrast to rationalist accounts, that aspirations to retain Russia's global great power status would have a significant impact on post-Soviet Russian attitudes toward nuclear weapons.[1] From an aspirational constructivist perspective, nuclear weapons, more than any other issue, symbolized for Russians their country's historical attainment of their desired status as a peer of the United States.

U.S.-Soviet arms control measures similarly symbolized for Russians the joint responsibility the two superpowers shared in ensuring not only strategic stability but also prevention of global nuclear war.[2] Rationally, one would expect Russian political elites to opt to constrain the growing asymmetry between Russia and the United States through prompt ratification and negotiation of strategic arms reduction treaties that would bind the relatively greater power of the United States within a controlled process of mutual reductions. Nuclear policy, more than any other issue, would be expected to be kept within the bounds of rational calculations of the costs and benefits to national security. Instead, preoccupation with Russia's historical status led Russian political elites to use arms control as a means of expressing its pique in its status competition with the United States.

Soviet-American negotiations on limiting strategic nuclear weapons began in the late 1960s with the Strategic Arms Limitation Talks (SALT) and culminated with the Strategic Offensive Reduction Treaty (SORT) in 2002. The SALT process produced the SALT I and II and the Anti-Ballistic Missile (ABM) treaties in the 1970s. During the 1980s, the United States and the Soviet Union negotiated the July 1991 Strategic Arms Reductions Treaty (START I), which was signed only five months before the collapse of the Soviet Union. The START II treaty quickly followed; it was signed by the United States and Russia in January 1993 but never entered into force. In May 2002, both countries signed the SORT treaty, which marked a reversal in the trend underway in previous treaties to more intrusive verification and inspection of nuclear arms reduction; in the view of many arms control experts, it signified "the death of arms control."[3]

This chapter argues that historical aspirations to retain Russia's status as a great power were a key variable determining Russia's national security interests in strategic arms control and attitudes toward nuclear weapons more generally. Russia's security discourse was largely focused on Russia's historically given place in the world rather than on a rational appraisal of conditions in Russia and abroad after the collapse of the Soviet Union. Elite consensual aspirations to global great power status led members of the Russian Duma to use their ratification power regarding START II to respond to U.S. actions on issues as diverse as the Bosnian conflict, NATO expansion, Iraq, and the ABM Treaty. In so doing, Russian political elites failed to act according to realist expectations and missed important opportunities to conclude an arms reduction agreement with the Clinton administration that would have preserved the strategic framework of the Cold War era and, implicitly, Russia's Cold War status as co-guarantor of international strategic stability.

The post-Soviet debate on strategic nuclear weapons was largely one about Russia's international status. Structural constructivists often expect definitions of interests to be determined by the behavior of a state's primary other—the most significant state in the international system for that state on a given issue. In strategic nuclear arms control, according to this logic, the behavior of the United States toward Russia should have largely determined how post-Soviet Russian political elites defined their interests in strategic arms control.

However, post-Soviet Russia's identity and interests in strategic arms control were defined by political elite aspirations regarding Russia's international status, which were formed mainly through an appraisal of its own past rather through U.S. behavior toward Russia. Among others, political analyst Lilia Shevtsova noted that Russia's past served as the main cognitive reference point for Russian political elites when considering Russia's future.[4] Russia's past status as a global great power was tightly bound up with its immense nuclear arsenal. As moderate democrat Dmitrii Trenin wrote in 2005, "For the post-Soviet Russian elite, nuclear weapons play a major politico-psychological role as one of only two remaining attributes of their country's great power and global status (the other being a permanent seat on the UN Security Council)."[5] This was true of the mass public as well, who were united in their views of nuclear weapons. As a recent report noted, "Russia's possession of a WMD arsenal is viewed by Russian citizens as evidence of its retention of great power status. . . . This is the source of the predominant view in favor of retaining Russia's nuclear arsenal, at least at current levels."[6]

As previous chapters have explained, this historical appraisal took place in the process of domestic competition among political entrepreneurs vying to have their particular image of Russia's past and future shape the national interest. The other, the United States, was a significant variable in sustaining and reinforcing Russia elites' historically legitimated sense of self as a global great power. The behavior of the other did not, however, initiate this consensus on self-image. The other's behavior was important only insofar as elites used it to help validate or invalidate the various candidate national self-images competing for dominance. In the case of strategic arms control, the behavior of the United States was a key factor delaying a rational reassessment of Russia's post-Soviet status. Once Russian political elites' aspirations that Russia should maintain its status as a global great power came to the fore in 1993, strategic nuclear interests were largely framed in terms of status maintenance rather than in terms of a rational calculation of costs and benefits to Russian national security.

This chapter explains this outcome in aspirational constructivist terms. The first part of the chapter covers the agreements between the Soviet Union / Russia and the United States and the post-Soviet Russian political elites' definition of their national interests in strategic nuclear arms reduction. The remainder of the chapter addresses the role historical aspirations and efficacy tests played in the development of these interests. It focuses in particular on the symbolic importance of parity in Russian elite debates about strategic arms control.

From 1991 to 2002, progress in Russia on strategic arms control, in the form of the 1993 START II treaty, was held hostage to the dominance of historical aspirations regarding Russia's international status in the Russian domestic political discourse. Despite repeated arguments from moderate Westernizers and statists regarding the cost savings, enhanced security, and status benefits of START II, the Russian parliament did not ratify the treaty until April 14, 2000. In its ratification, the Duma made Russia's adherence to START II conditional on the United States not withdrawing from or violating the 1972 ABM Treaty (already almost a certainty in 1999) and on the conclusion of START III negotiations by 2003. In essence, the parliament ratified START II "on terms which make its prompt entry into force practically impossible."[7] Strategic arms control went from being the key means of stabilizing Soviet-U.S. relations to becoming the primary means of asserting Russian equal status and demonstrating its pique with the United States.

The 1993 and 1997 Strategic Arms Reduction Treaties (START I and II)

On January 3, 1993, U.S. President George H. W. Bush and Russian President Boris Yeltsin signed the Treaty on Further Strategic Nuclear Arms Limitations and Reductions (START II). START II followed the START I agreement concluded in July 1991. The START process, unlike all proceeding arms control agreements, committed both sides to reduce, rather than just limit, their deployed strategic arsenals and to establish an intrusive verification and monitoring regime. It covered the entire triad of strategic weapons systems: air, ground, and sea launched strategic nuclear weapons. Under START I, both sides were to reduce their warheads from over 10,000 to 6,000, and under START II, to between 3,000 and3,500.[8] Initially, the 3,000–3,500 level was to be reached by January 1, 2003. START II, if it had entered into force, would have entirely eliminated what were considered the most destabilizing strategic nuclear weapons (for their preemptive strike ability): intercontinental ballistic missiles (ICBMs) outfitted with multiple independently targetable reentry vehicles (MIRVs). MIRVs are collections of several nuclear warheads meant for different targets that can be carried on a single ICBM.

Under START II, the United States was required to eliminate all 500 of its MX missiles and Russia all 1,800 of its SS-18 missiles. START II also would have limited the number of warheads deployed on submarine-launched ballistic missiles (SLBMs) to the 1,700–1,750 range (from a START I level of 3,600 for the United States and 2,700 for Russia). Unlike START I, which substantially undercounted bomber weapons to U.S. advantage, START II required an accurate accounting of warheads on heavy bombers.[9] Russia also announced its intention to give up its insistence on exact strategic nuclear parity with the United States, thereby taking the position that Russian security could be guaranteed through minimal deterrence alone.[10] (The importance of parity in the Russian nuclear debate is discussed below.) "As a result, START II would require both countries, but Russia especially, to reconfigure their strategic triads into a more stable composition of mobile and silo-based ICBMs, as well as submarine-launched ballistic missiles."[11] For Russia, the treaty would have fundamentally altered its nuclear force posture from one anchored on ground-based ICBMs to one relying on sea-based SLBMs, a posture that mimicked that of the United States—and divided the Russian military.[12]

The U.S. Senate ratified the original START II agreement on January 26, 1996, by an 87–4 vote. At a March 1997 Helsinki summit, Presidents Bill Clinton and Boris Yeltsin agreed that the next round of START negotiations would reduce deployed strategic nuclear warheads to the 2,000–2,500 level. The Clinton administration made the launch of negotiations on START III contingent upon Russian ratification of START II. The two presidents also agreed to continue negotiations on clarifying the ABM Treaty through official demarcation of "strategic" or "national" (ABM-violating) missile defenses (NMDs) from "nonstrategic" or "theater" missiles systems (TMDs). These negotiations were finalized in a September 26, 1997, meeting between U.S. Secretary of State Madeleine Albright and Russian Foreign Minister Evgenii Primakov in New York.

Under the New York protocols, the United States agreed to accept "lower-velocity" TMDs (those with interceptor speeds of 3 km per second or less as opposed to the 5 km-per-second high-velocity system that the United States had wanted) as the benchmark for judging strategic versus nonstrategic missile defense systems. Russia agreed to allow deployment of lower-velocity TMDs as long as they were not tested against high-velocity target missiles or missiles with a range of 3,500 km. Essentially, the agreement retroactively approved defense systems that the United States had unilaterally declared to be ABM-compliant.[13] Under these protocols, the two sides were also prohibited from testing high-velocity TMDs against high-velocity targets or long-range missiles and space-based TMD interceptors. The New York protocols made official the Helsinki Accords' deadline extension for completion of START II reductions from January 1, 2003, to December 31, 2007. Finally, the two sides, plus Ukraine, Belarus, and Kazakhstan, signed a Memorandum of Understanding (MOU) on Succession to the ABM Treaty. The United States agreed to submit the package of agreements to the U.S. Senate for approval after the Russian Duma ratified START II. The U.S. Senate later failed to approve the Helsinki and New York amendments and indicated that it would not ratify the amended treaty.[14]

In 2000, the Russian Duma finally ratified the amended START II treaty, conditioned on the implementation and adherence to several stipulations. Article 9 of the Duma's resolution of ratification stated that the treaty would only enter into force after the U.S. Senate ratified the New York protocols and the Helsinki Accords. In the United States, the MOU and the demarcation agreements on TMDs were particularly controversial and made ratification unlikely. Conservative Republicans in the U.S. Congress opposed any limitations on missile defense systems, a condition of which the Russian parliament was fully aware.[15] Article 2 of the Russian Duma's resolution on ratification contained a provision specifically stating that U.S. withdrawal from or violation of the ABM Treaty would constitute grounds for Russia to withdraw from START II, which Russia could technically claim had already occurred as recognized in the New York protocols. The resolution also required negotiations on START III to be completed by 2003, the original implementation deadline of START II and an unrealistic deadline for negotiations. It also called for these negotiations not just to cover lower weapons ceilings but also to incorporate tactical nuclear weapons and transparency issues.[16] Given the terms of ratification, START II was effectively dead.

The 2001 Strategic Offensive Reduction Treaty (SORT)

At a November 2001 summit in Crawford, Texas, Presidents George W. Bush and Vladimir Putin agreed to reduce deployed strategic nuclear warheads to between 1,700 and 2,200 over the following ten years and launched a series of talks on these reductions. In these negotiations, the Russian side sought a legally binding document that would make reductions irreversible and transparent and prohibit uploading of stockpiled warheads, following the START I and II models. The Bush administration, in contrast to the Clinton administration, preferred a less formal process and maximum flexibility to manage the size and structure of its nuclear forces and to retain stockpiles. The United States moved somewhat toward the Russian position in early February 2002, despite opposition from the U.S. Defense Department.[17] On May 24, 2002, Presidents Bush and Putin signed the Strategic Offensive Reductions Treaty (SORT, also known as the Moscow Treaty), in which the two parties agreed to reduce their deployed nuclear warheads independently to the 1,700–2,200 range. In a 95–0 vote, the U.S. Senate ratified the Moscow Treaty on March 6, 2003, with a number of binding conditions.[18] On May 14, the Russian Duma ratified the Treaty by a vote of 294–134, with 22 abstentions.[19] The treaty was widely seen as merely window-dressing, as the two-page document contained no requirements for destruction of warheads, verification, or schedules for completion, and tacitly allowed stockpiling of nondeployed warheads. As Trenin wrote in 2005, "SORT, with the minimum restrictions and maximum margin of maneuver it provides, has become the epitaph to the classical nuclear arms control."[20] The treaty essentially freed each side to pursue its strategic nuclear weapons policy as it unilaterally saw fit within the agreed numerical limits. Russia had lost its opportunity to keep the United States within an arms control framework that allowed mutual verification and jointly scheduled reductions in nuclear arsenals.

The 2002 U.S. Withdrawal from the Anti-Ballistic Missile Treaty (ABM)

On June 13, 2002, the United States formally withdrew from the ABM Treaty. The treaty had long been viewed as the cornerstone of strategic stability and one of the most significant achievements in strategic arms control. It was unique in prohibiting the Soviet Union and the United States from building defensive missiles systems designed to defend against nuclear attack. Not only did the treaty ban a weapon system, it also rested entirely on the logic of mutually assured destruction (MAD). According to this logic, mutual vulnerability to each other's nuclear strikes and their horrific destructive capacity was the key to successful and effective nuclear deterrence and avoidance of nuclear war. The United States sought to reverse this logic in the 1980s during the Reagan administration with the Strategic Defense Initiative (the "Star Wars" program) and a doctrine of fighting and winning limited nuclear war. Consequently, the Soviet/Russian linkage of START and the ABM Treaty dated from 1986. The Soviet Union dropped the linkage between the START I negotiations and a narrow interpretation of the ABM Treaty in 1987 but issued a unilateral statement on the occasion of the signing of START I in 1991 to the effect that compliance with the ABM Treaty was necessary for compliance with START I.[21] The day after the United States withdrew from the ABM Treaty, Russia declared START II to be null and void.

The remainder of this chapter explores the importance of Russia's historical status (which in this issue area, equates with nuclear parity) and efficacy tests, in the form of economic and strategic costs, in the domestic political debate surrounding Russia's definition of its interests in nuclear arms control.

Correspondence Tests of Legitimacy and Russia's Interest in Strategic Nuclear Arms Control

As many observers and participants have noted, the Russian debate on strategic arms control in the post-Soviet period was highly politicized. The center of expert debate on Russia's interests was dominated by competing definitions—based on different national self-images—of the costs and benefits of strategic arms control. Two different benchmarks underlay this debate. The first was the Soviet principle of parity with the West, which continued to be widely viewed as critical for the maintenance of great power status.[22] Both the United States and the Soviet Union considered nuclear parity an indicator of great power status and an important objective during the Cold War. In the post-Soviet period, much of the political center and right continued to hold on to parity as an important principle. Only Westernizers rejected it. The second benchmark of the debate was the economic cost of arms reductions. This part of the debate was carried on in much more rational terms than the debate on European security discussed in the previous chapter. The defense and arms control communities argued in terms of both the actual capabilities of the new Russian state either to maintain or to destroy its nuclear arsenal and the actual opportunity costs to the Russian economy.

Ultimately, however, this relatively rational discourse was held hostage to Russian political elites' aspiration to maintain Russia's historical great power status with regard to the United States. This historical aspiration created the context in which domestic opposition to Westernizers in the government combined with the general behavior of the United States produced glacial movement on strategic arms control in Russia. As a result, Russian interests in strategic arms control were defined in terms of Russia's historical aspirations to equal status—less as a means of maintaining security and reducing the threat of nuclear war than as an instrument for countering perceived efforts of the United States to reduce Russia's great power status.[23] As one authoritative observer commented in 1999, "A growing perception that the mighty West was seeking to capitalize on Russia's weaknesses deeply affected Moscow's decision making. In that environment START II became a symbol of the increased inequality in the U.S.-Russian relationship."[24]

The political elite's consensus on Russia's status as an independent great power and guarantor of global security meant strategic nuclear arms control was defined as part of the political elite's broader interest in maintaining and demonstrating Russia's international status rather than achieving concrete arms control objectives. The Russian parliament used its power over ratification to retaliate against the United States when it was perceived to treat Russia as less than an equal partner on issues often far from the realm of nuclear security—the Bosnian conflict, NATO expansion, the U.S. 2003 invasion of Iraq—as well as its withdrawal from the ABM Treaty. In the process, Russian political elites prevented the Russian government from concluding an arms reduction agreement with the Clinton administration that would have preserved Russia's status as co-guarantor of international stability and the bilateral strategic framework of the Cold War era in which the United States and Russia were equally bound to concrete bilateral arms reduction and limitation measures.

There were two phases in the domestic debate on Russia's interests in strategic arms control. The first, in 1992 and 1993, was dominated, along with every other issue on Russia's agenda, by the ideological struggle between conservative statists and national restorationists in the parliament and liberal internationalists in the Yeltsin administration. In this period, the statists and national restorationists who opposed the Westernizing policies of key members of the Yeltsin administration prevented movement on arms control to retaliate for liberal domestic reforms.[25] From 1993 on, Russia's interests in strategic arms control were defined in large measure by the general aspiration to maintain Russia's great power status, making interests in arms control subject to a status-driven reaction to the behavior of the United States on other issues. Rear Admiral Alexei Ovcharenko noted that START II had become "a convenient vehicle for expressing general displeasure with U.S.-Russian relations."[26] While the earlier dynamic of political contestation over Westernizing reforms continued to play a significant role in this phase, the key factor preventing and then conditioning ratification of START II was the political elite's perception that U.S. actions were always aimed against Russia, a perception derived from aspirations to historical great power status.[27] After START II ratification, Russia continued to link the issue of future arms control agreements to U.S. adherence to the ABM Treaty and NATO expansion.[28] In a replay of the battles over START II, the Duma postponed ratification of SORT to protest the U.S. war in Iraq, a position lauded at the time by Russian Foreign Minister Igor Ivanov but opposed by President Putin.[29] The Ministry of Foreign Affairs attempted to use its harsh opposition to the U.S. withdrawal from the ABM Treaty to increase its political influence among Russian political elites, reflecting the continuing salience of Russia's status vis-à-vis the United States to Russian national identity.[30] Putin, in contrast, reacted mildly, hoping to limit hostility and remain engaged with the United States and the West, in line with his identity management strategy of social competition.

There was no consensus on nuclear arms control under Soviet President Mikhail Gorbachev and after 1991, with hardliners charging that the USSR/Russia had conceded too much to the United States and radical liberals arguing that it had not conceded enough.[31] In 1993, an elite survey by VTsIOM found that about one-third of elites supported unconditional ratification of START II, exactly one-half favored conditional ratification, and about one-fifth opposed any ratification.[32] For Westernizers and moderate statists, arms control was seen as a crucial weapon to break the control of the Soviet military-industrial complex, which they believed was responsible for a mindless arms race with the United States and destroying the Soviet economy. As security analyst Genrikh Trofimenko put it in 1991, "Our conception of security as something merely providing military safeguards and hence concentrating on military buildup resulted in undermining and distorting our economy, the rock bed of the country's security and independence."[33] They also viewed strategic arms control as a key to good bilateral relations with the United States and consequently to Russia's global political and economic integration.[34]

Westernizers initially loathed the "primitive" notion of "parity" in relations with the United States, which in practice meant matching the United States missile for missile. As Russian analyst Sergei Kortunov wrote in 1991, "It is time that the country's legislative and executive authorities fully realized that strategic parity with the United States was won under a command system allowing military programmes to be funded without control and to the detriment of the civilian sector of the economy." He continued, "The democratic reforms in the Soviet Union leading to a law-governed state . . . will distribute funds and resources in strict accordance with national security priorities approved by the Supreme Soviet, not in the interest of the military industrial complex."[35] In the post-Soviet period, while Westernizers and moderate statists were very critical of START II, they generally favored ratification. In 1993 and 1994, they called for rapid ratification and immediate initiation of negotiations on START III to rectify the problems with START II.[36] Later, Westernizers and moderate statists generally shifted toward conditional ratification, linking START II compliance with ABM compliance and an extension of the completion of weapons reductions, for reasons that will be explained.[37]

From the outset, conservative statists and national restorationists who opposed the liberal internationalist Yeltsin administration rejected START II on ideological grounds. In the VTsIOM survey, none of those completely opposed to ratifying START II approved of Yeltsin as president, while over half of those favoring unconditional ratification did approve of his governance.[38] Strategic arms control became a stick with which the conservative statist and national restorationist opposition could beat the Westernizers among political elites and in the executive branch. The administration was blamed for concluding an unequal treaty that signed away Russia's nuclear superpower status. National restorationist

Iurii Glukhov viewed START II as an act of "unilateral disarmament . . . made without any reciprocal steps or commitments by the United States and NATO. It is being made at a time when Washington has begun to acquire a taste [for] a policy based on strength."[39] In 1993, Supreme Soviet Speaker Ruslan Khasbulatov explicitly conditioned the parliament's ratification of START II on the removal of liberal internationalist Foreign Minister Andrei Kozyrev.[40]

Radical national restorationists, motivated by extreme anti-Westernism, persistently viewed START II as outright capitulation to the United States, through which Yeltsin's "occupation regime has once again openly and brazenly shown its traitorous essence."[41] Arms control in general was repudiated as an American plot to destroy Russia's military might. Some, such as national restorationist General Albert Makashov, rejected START II's ban on ICBMs with MIRVs and reductions beyond the START II level of 3,000 to 3,500 warheads.[42] From 1995 to 1999, when national restorationists controlled the Duma, they played a significant role in preventing ratification of START II. Most national restorationists, led by Community Party of the Russian Federation (KPRF) leader Gennadii Ziuganov, voted against the treaty's ratification in 2000.[43] Ziuganov called the ratification "Russia's next defeat."[44]

National restorationists and conservative statists were particularly upset by START II's rejection of the principle of parity, seen in the ban on MIRVs and the complete elimination of SS-18s, which had traditionally formed the core of the Soviet strategic triad and in which Russia had numerical superiority.[45] These "great power patriots" generally believed that these concessions "no doubt . . . will be used at every opportunity to exert political pressure" on Russia by the United States.[46] As defense analyst Pavel Felgengauer noted in 1995, the "START II Treaty has yet to be ratified and may not ever be, since in its current form it clearly undermines the principle of Russian-American parity, which any patriot of our country holds so dear."[47] In this view, parity was equated with nuclear great power status.[48] In 2001 and 2002, according to Trenin, "part of the military establishment was considering dropping the parity requirement in favor of drastic cuts in the Russian nuclear arsenal."[49] However, by late 2003, it was clear that these voices had been silenced and the size of the Russian nuclear arsenal would not be decoupled from that of the United States.[50]

Within the strategic arms control community, security experts criticized START II even before its signing in January 1993. Conservative experts argued that the treaty required the Soviet force posture to be radically altered by eliminating the core of those forces, the SS-18 with MIRVs, and shifting to greater reliance on the naval portion of the strategic triad. Initially, these critics argued that maintaining the START I level of warheads at 6,000 would cost three times less than reducing warheads and delivery systems to the START II level.[51]

Moderates and liberals from the outset criticized the cost of implementing START II but urged early ratification on the grounds that Russia's MIRVed SS-18s would have to be decommissioned by 2007 and SS-24s by 2003 in any event. They also argued that the treaty would both ensure bilateral as opposed to unilateral reductions and pave the way for early negotiations on deeper reductions under more favorable terms. They countered the conservative cost argument by claiming that the costs of maintaining counterstrike forces and "the possibility of a disarming first strike (either American or Russian)" was significantly reduced under START II.[52] Experts argued over whether a sea-based triad would be more vulnerable than a land-based one.[53]

The turning point in the expert debate came in 1994, as strategic arms control was increasingly tied to issues outside of the strategic nuclear relationship and to the broader political elite interest in maintaining Russia's great power status. After the announcement of NATO's Partnership for Peace, the U.S. threat of NATO air strikes against the Bosnian Serbs, and the U.S. congressional Republicans' 1994 Contract with America (which promised Americans a national missile defense system), moderates and liberals who had supported early ratification switched to advocating conditional ratification. They and moderates in the military continued to rely on "efficacy tests" of Russia's economic weakness to argue that conditional ratification was the best means to preserve Russia's national security and nuclear great power status.

These arguments largely persuaded most politicians subscribing to various national self-images, and in 1995, 1997, and 1998, the press and government officials predicted easy ratification of START II.[54] In 1995, the Duma appeared ready to ratify the treaty with a condition regarding ABM Treaty compliance and a denunciation of NATO's expansion plans. "However, NATO air strikes against the Bosnian Serbs in August 1995 . . .

significantly changed attitudes in Moscow towards START II. . . . [B]oth the Duma and the administration decided to postpone the ratification process to protest the U.S. and NATO policy in Bosnia."[55] The Duma elections in December 1995 meant that "the new legislature no longer contained a strong minority of unconditional treaty supporters."[56] Chances for unconditional ratification had disappeared.[57]

After the 1995 parliamentary elections, "Duma debates were . . . increasingly affected by disagreements between the United States and Russia over NATO expansion" and the deadlock in negotiations on ABM demarcation.[58] Communist Party leader Ziuganov linked START II to NATO expansion, while national restorationist Sergei Baburin called for renegotiating the treaty to take into account the changed situation.[59] Statist administration officials, including Defense Ministers Pavel Grachev and Igor Rodionov, linked NATO expansion to Russian refusal to ratify START II.[60] Whereas in 1993, 79 percent of political elites favored ratifying START II (with almost 29 percent favoring unconditional ratification), in 1996, the share of political elites supporting ratification had fallen to 63 percent.[61]

By 1996, two stances on ratification had formed: complete opposition and conditional ratification. Opponents pointed to U.S. moves in Bosnia and NATO expansion to argue that the European security environment called for rethinking strategic arms control.[62] As Ziuganov put it, the "main thing of concern to the Russian statist opposition is . . . the West's long-standing, traditional desire to take advantage of the unsettled situation in Russia to destroy the last remnants of our state's nuclear might."[63] Others, including members of the military High Command, disagreed. In 1996, General Igor Sergeev, commander of the Strategic Rocket Forces, "explicitly warned against linking START and NATO enlargement, arguing that the START agreement was in Russia's interest and assured a balance of forces."[64]

Nuclear Parity and National Interests

The question of the numerical balance of nuclear forces was a central issue in Russia's perception of itself as a great power on a par with the United States. As a result, nuclear parity played an enormous symbolic role in the Russian political discourse. Nuclear parity for many elites symbolized their historical status as a great power on a par with the leading powers in the international system, which, since World War II, meant the United States. Throughout the Soviet and post-Soviet period, the question of nuclear parity revolved around the issue of whether the Soviet Union must match the United States missile for missile and warhead for warhead, or whether it could rely on a force structure that provided a minimum level of mutually assured destruction, a position known as "minimal deterrence."

The Soviet and then Russian debate over nuclear parity versus minimal deterrence was never resolved. The Soviet leadership intermittently adopted a minimal deterrence position: deterrence could be achieved by maintaining the ability to inflict requisite damage on the opponent rather than establishing equality in nuclear numbers. This stance was in place from 1953 to 1954 (under Malenkov), from 1959 to 1964 (under Khrushchev), and finally from 1987 to 1991 (under Gorbachev). The Yeltsin administration adopted the minimal deterrence position as well in 1993 and explicitly reiterated it in the National Security Concept of 1997. In signing the 2000 Military Doctrine, Putin approved a more qualified phrasing that called for minimal ceilings to be met in conjunction with the United States and other nuclear powers, rather than unilaterally.[65]

Russian political elites remained divided on the issue, and the nuclear doctrines since 1993 increasingly emphasized the role of nuclear weapons in the defense of Russia's security and national interests. Pavel Podvig, an arms control expert, reported that there was no consensus in 2005 on whether Russia could afford to rid itself of the ICBMs that made up the backbone of Russia's nuclear parity.[66] This lack of consensus largely correlates with the deep division over Russia's political purpose noted in previous chapters; on the issue of nuclear parity, the division was largely between Westernizers and liberal statists, who favored following the West and abandoning parity, and statists and national restorationists who emphasized Russia's national mission to create its own path and its need to preserve parity with the United States.

Parity and Great Power Status

The question of nuclear parity was fundamental to both the expert and more general political discourse on strategic arms control. In 2005, Trenin noted the place nuclear weapons played in Russian identity politics throughout the post-Soviet period. "Over the past 15 years, Russian leaders have been repeatedly 'reminding' others, in particular the United States, that Russia is still a nuclear power on par with the U.S. . . . Nuclear weapons," he wrote, "are a symbol of Russia's strategic independence from the United States and NATO, and their still-formidable capabilities alone assure for Russia a special relationship with America."[67] Russia's large nuclear arsenal meant that it was not just a great power but a global great power—even, in the eyes of national restorationists and some statists, a superpower.[68]

Despite early resistance to it on the part of Westernizers, the principle of numerical parity remained a cross-partisan baseline assumption in the political elite debate over the costs and benefits of START II. In 1993, the majority of Russian foreign policy elites favored maintaining a strategic weapons balance with the West.[69] The nature of that balance was more controversial; Russian political elites were divided over the issue of minimum deterrence, with 47 percent favoring parity and 42 percent favoring minimal deterrence. As on other issues, the division among political elites largely fell along the lines set by another debate: whether the respondent believed Russia should follow its own path (traditionalists) or a Western path of modernization (Westernizers). Twice as many traditionalists as Westernizers chose parity (60 percent) to minimal deterrence (34 percent).[70] Sixty-seven percent of foreign policy institute directors (who tended to be a more liberal group) favored minimal deterrence, while 60 percent of political party members favored parity. In 1996, 85 percent of political elites thought that maintaining parity with the United States was important; 47 percent said that it was "very important."[71] By September 2000, support for parity had declined somewhat, while still remaining quite high. That month, 68 percent of political elites believed that achieving military parity with the West was one of Russia's most important foreign policy goals.[72]

An indicator of the parity baseline was that, almost unanimously, political elite cost estimates of implementing START II assumed that Russia would build new weapons in order to maintain treaty levels of warheads rather than allow Russian forces to drop below U.S. levels. Both advocates and critics of START II criticized the treaty's requirement that Russia eliminate all of its MIRVed ICBMs by 2003, as they assumed that this would necessitate the extremely costly production and deployment of 500 single-warhead ICBMs in order for Russia to maintain the 3,000-warhead START II ceiling.[73] For this reason, moderate Westernizer and arms control expert Aleksandr Pikayev said of START II that "for Russia, it was not a disarmament but a rearmament agreement."[74]

Aleksei Arbatov, at the time a democratic member of the Duma and an arms control expert, made explicit the link between nuclear parity and Russia's continued great power status in 1996. In response to U.S. critics who challenged the need for Russia to build up the START II ceilings, he wrote, "What these American critics fail to understand is that Russian nuclear equality with the United States is the only remaining legacy of Russia's great power status." Furthermore, "this equality . . . requires that the United States continue to treat Russia with respect."[75] As Pikayev noted, "Weaknesses in Russia's economy and conventional military forces are leading Moscow to rely more on its nuclear capabilities in an attempt to maintain its international role and to gain a stronger positions vis-à-vis perceived Western pressure."[76] As Westernizer Dmitrii Trenin put it, "If you look at the state of the nation which is ranked sixteenth in terms of GDP, which has male life expectancy just under sixty years, there's not much left besides nuclear weapons to substantiate the claims to a status of great power."[77]

Strategic Stability

In addition to great power prestige, rough nuclear parity was long perceived in Russia as the essence of strategic and hence global stability. Since the advent of the doctrine of mutual assured destruction, strategic stability between the United States and the Soviet Union was premised on maintaining enough nuclear forces to guarantee unacceptable retaliatory damage to the other side after a first strike. For much of the Soviet period, strategic stability required matching unit for unit the nuclear forces of the United States, France, and Great Britain.[78] This demand for exact numerical parity of Russian nuclear forces began to disappear from the mainstream political elite debate in the late 1990s as economic issues dominated Russian politics, but it persisted among hardline national restorationists such as General Makashov.[79]

Most political elites, however, continued to accept that rough, rather than exact, parity was sufficient for strategic stability. According to Arbatov, it was the parity argument that finally won parliamentarians over to ratification of START II. As he said shortly after the Duma ratified the treaty, "The principal argument in favor of START II, which proved so instrumental, was that without START II, Russian forces, with a shortage of funding, would go down in ten years to 1,000 warheads on their own. . . . At the same time, the United States can easily afford to maintain the present level of its strategic forces. In this way, if there is no further arms control agreement, in ten years the United States may, inadvertently, acquire nuclear forces that are five or six times over that of Russia—basically free, without spending additional money."[80]

Putin used this parity argument when he appealed to the Duma to ratify the treaty in 2000. He argued that the United States would have a retaliatory second-strike capacity fifteen times greater than Russia's under START I—but only three times greater under START II. The negotiation of START III, which the United States tied to START II ratification, would allow Russia to regain approximate parity at a lower cost and in a more flexible way than under START II. As Duma member Arbatov noted, Putin's argument "was very persuasive for members of Parliament, making a big impression on them." He added that "fear of American nuclear superiority . . . was the principal motive for many members of Parliament to vote for START II."[81]

Parity and the Anti-Ballistic Missile Treaty

The ABM Treaty of 1972 was based on the MAD logic of guaranteeing national security through mutual vulnerability. According to this logic, both sides became more secure with increased vulnerability to each other's nuclear weapons. Building anti-ballistic missile systems capable of destroying incoming nuclear warheads would reduce the other side's ability to retaliate after a first strike by the side shielded by missile defenses, thereby upsetting strategic stability. The ABM Treaty was also credited with having prevented a defensive arms race and an exacerbation of the offensive arms race by preventing the development of both ABM and anti-ABM systems and the greater numbers of offensive weapons necessary to overcome anti-missile defenses.

As the Soviet Union was unraveling, Gorbachev indicated for the first time that the Soviets were willing to discuss U.S. President George H. W.

Bush's plan for a Global Protection against Limited Strikes system (GPALS), a global anti-missile system. The Soviets until then had steadfastly opposed any weakening of the ABM Treaty.[82] Initially, the new post-Soviet Russian administration had also signaled its interest in a global ABM system. In his address to the UN Security Council in January 1992, President Yeltsin stated that Russia is "ready to develop, then create and jointly operate a global defense system, instead of the SDI system."[83] In June 1992, Bush and Yeltsin signed a memorandum suggesting joint efforts by the United States, Russia, and other countries to develop such a system, which would include space-based components. This agreement was incorporated into the preamble of the START II treaty.

Liberal internationalists in the Ministry of Foreign Affairs (MFA) supported such cooperation. One MFA official went so far as to advocate playing a "second or even third role" to the United States in such a joint project.[84] Many others rejected such a secondary status, and supported such cooperation only if it were based on the assumption of a superpower condominium, in which Russia's status as a nuclear superpower equal with the United States was unquestioned and even reinforced.[85]

In this desire for cooperation with the United States, the historical aspirations of Russian political elites are evident. Aspirational constructivism highlights the psychological need for positive distinctiveness, here expressed in terms of Russia's equal status to its historical peer, the United States, and their *joint* responsibility for global strategic stability. Such aspirations create motivations to enact an identity that embodies such positive distinctiveness. Russian actions on strategic nuclear arms control and ABM reflect these aspirations more than they do rational calculations of Russia's security needs and bargaining power.

In 1992, Russia officially supported cooperation on missile defenses while at the same time stressing the importance of the ABM Treaty.[86] That year the Bush administration indicated its desire to eliminate ABM restraints and allow deployment of space-based defenses within ten years. According to one Russian expert, this did not meet with great Russian enthusiasm at the initial high-level meeting on GPALS cooperation in September 1992.[87] A group of experts tasked by the Russian government with evaluating the GPALS idea advocated only bilateral Russian-U.S. development of ground-based missile defenses and opposed both the militarization of space implicit in GPALS and the costs associated with global missile defenses. They also threw cold water on the expectations of liberal Westernizers and some in the military industrial complex that the United States would support Russian research and development of such programs, citing the experience of NATO allies who never received such U.S. technological support.[88]

The new Clinton administration immediately backed off from the idea of global missile defenses and instead advocated theater missile defenses, which would require demarcation talks on delimiting strategic from theater missile defenses.[89] By the fall of 1994, it was clear that these talks would not be quickly concluded. The Russian Duma was linking START II to the ABM Treaty, and the Contract with America, issued by the Republicans, who now controlled Congress, raised Russian concerns that the United States was using the demarcation issue to circumvent the ABM Treaty. By 1995, both the Russian Duma and Yeltsin tightly linked ABM compliance to ratification of START II. In 1995, the United States unilaterally declared two TMDs—THAAD (Theater High Altitude Area Defense) and the Navy's Upper Tier system—to be ABM-compliant and conducted the first test of THAAD. At the Helsinki summit in 1997, the United States traded extension of the START II deadline for Russian acceptance of a demarcation agreement that did not specifically rule out high-speed systems or space-based sensors.[90]

As noted above, the Duma made continued U.S. ABM compliance a condition for START II's entry into force. After the Duma ratified START II, the Putin administration began to waver in its opposition to modifying the ABM Treaty. Despite repeated official statements that the ABM Treaty was the "cornerstone of strategic stability," Putin indicated his willingness to alter it in his proposal that Russia and the United States work together to create a European theater defense system and even suggested joint U.S.-Russian cooperation on a system that would intercept missiles during the initial, or boost, phase of flight.[91] As Podvig noted, Russia's official position on the ABM Treaty was inconsistent. Russia rejected the U.S. assessment of a serious intercontinental missile threat from "rogue nations," while it accepted the threat of short- and intermediate-range missiles. It therefore rejected national but not theater missile defenses. "Apparently," Podvig concluded, "Russia believed (though it is hard to tell why) that this emphasis on the differences between theater and strategic defenses would help support the ABM Treaty."[92]

A few Russian political elites argued that the fuss over ABMs was a result of status deprivation and the military's desire to divert resources to the military industrial complex.[93] According to policy experts Andrei Piontkovskii and Vitalii Tsygichko, "Practically all major analysts think that the creation of a national missile defense by the U.S. will not damage global strategic stability because Russia is capable of overcoming any form of prospective missile defense. . . . That is why confrontation with the U.S. on amendments to the ABM Treaty is not productive, and does not suit Russia's national interests."[94] Moderate statists and Westernizers argued that Russia should not allow national missile defenses to interfere with deeper arms reductions or cooperation against nuclear proliferation.[95] Defense analyst Aleksandr Golts emphasized the relationship between nuclear parity and the Russian establishment's assumption of its right to great power privileges on other issues:

> Of all the Russian politicians, military officials and experts who say the American plan represents a military threat to Russia, it's unlikely any of them seriously believe this. . . . The real issue lies elsewhere. Over the past decade, the nuclear arms balance has taken on a very specific role. Moscow has come to believe that because it has the capability to destroy the United States, it should have special privileges in its relations with Washington. Over recent years, this approach has become formulated as the concept of "enlarged deterrent," based on the idea that the nuclear factor is a part of any military and political negotiations, and that parity with the United States automatically gives Russia some advantages.[96]

According to a 2001 survey of foreign policy elites, only 28 percent of respondents saw U.S. plans to withdraw from the ABM Treaty as a real danger.[97] Liberal and moderate Westernizers argued that the anti-American and Cold War focus on nuclear parity and adherence to the ABM Treaty undercut Russia's true national interests. As one commentator succinctly put it, the "U.S. missile defense plans are unrealistic and will be a huge waste of money. The real danger to Russia is that Russia's political leaders will face great pressure from the military-industrial complex, for missile defense funding. Russia should keep calm and concentrate on improving its economy."[98]

Sergei Rogov, a prominent defense expert and moderate statist, urged

Russians not to overreact to U.S. national missile defense plans, as this would lead to needless confrontation and harm Russia's economic interests. "The aim," according to Rogov, "is to force the U.S. to consider the opinion and interests of Russia on major issues. In order to do this, it is necessary to definitely determine Russia's own priorities, as well as the real abilities of Russia and the U.S. . . . Unfortunately, there is an impression that in a number of cases the position of Russia has not been well thought out."[99] Defense analyst Pavel Felgengauer, while condemning the Bush administration for its unilateralism, argued that Russia, in turn, was acting no less irresponsibly by providing pretexts for U.S. hawks to ruin international security.[100]

Conservative statists and national restorationists viewed U.S. abrogation of or withdrawal from the ABM Treaty as an attempt to destroy the bipolar balance of power and establish global hegemony. As one commentator put it, the U.S. national missile defense plan "makes Russia's sole remaining superpower attributes all but worthless."[101] Ziuganov called George W. Bush's announcement of U.S. plans to develop a national missile defense "an extremely dangerous move leading to . . . the final destruction of the effective international security system that developed after World War II."[102] In 2001, unnamed "military political sources" were more forthright: "The ABM treaty is truly a hurdle to a U.S. monopoly in global politics."[103] They argued that "today it is clear that the new U.S. administration has set itself on the course of destroying the whole system of strategic stability [and] is betting on the factor of military strength in attaining global leadership."[104] Some conservative proponents of nuclear parity, such as retired Strategic Rocket Forces General Vladimir Dvorkin, a longtime opponent of START II, welcomed the demise of the ABM Treaty. Russian withdrawal from START II would allow Russia to retain its MIRVed ICBMs, the cheapest means of maintaining rough parity with the United States.[105] These critics advocated abandoning the ABM Treaty, once again equipping ICBMs with MIRVs, and directing state funds back to the military industrial complex.[106]

Conservative statists and national restorationists also called on Russia to withdraw not only from START I and II but perhaps from the CFE, INF, and SALT treaties as well, in retaliation for U.S. withdrawal from the ABM Treaty.[107] Many Russian officials and analysts thought that after the attacks of September 11, 2001, and Putin's aid to the United States in its war against the Taliban, the United States would strike a deal with Russia to keep the ABM Treaty alive. When the United States withdrew from the treaty so soon after its major operations in Afghanistan were over, it "made the Russians feel used. Coming so quickly on the heels of the dramatic post–September 11 U.S.-Russian rapprochement, it was an embarrassing slap in the face and a disappointment for Putin." While Russia withdrew from START II, this was hardly retaliation, as the U.S. Senate was not likely to ratify the treaty in any event. In contrast to the expectations of the structural constructivist or realist explanations, "the reaction from Russians has been much more positive than expected."[108]

Strategic Nuclear Weapons Policy and Russian Identity Politics

Domestic identity politics surrounding nuclear weapons affected Russian policy both before and after the U.S. withdrawal from the ABM Treaty. For most of the 1990s, the issue of strategic nuclear weapons remained the preserve of technical and military experts and was somewhat insulated from broader elite debates about the symbolic importance of nuclear parity to Russian historical aspirations. Until 1998, Russian nuclear policy focused on a minimal defense policy under the guidance of the commander of the Strategic Rocket Forces, General Igor Sergeev.[109] However, NATO's intervention in Kosovo produced in Russia a "Kosovo syndrome," which led to a dramatic debate within the senior military leadership and among broader political elites about the role of Russian nuclear forces and a marked increase in the prominence of nuclear weapons in its defense policy.[110] As noted earlier, Russia's nuclear weapons were clearly perceived by political elites and much of the military as the factor ensuring Russia's status as a global great power.[111] Beginning with its 1993 Military Doctrine, Russia increasingly relied on its nuclear deterrent, particularly the posture of launching a first strategic nuclear strike on the basis of a warning of a potential attack.[112] The 1993 Military Doctrine removed the Soviet no-first-use pledge and clearly moved Russia to reliance on nuclear weapons to deter a large-scale nuclear or conventional attack (which was still assumed to emanate from the West). In the 2000 Military Doctrine, reliance on nuclear deterrence was even more pronounced and was to be used to deter attacks at all levels.[113] The primacy of nuclear weapons in Russian security doctrine reflected the central role nuclear weapons played in domestic struggles not only over Russia's identity and foreign policy but also over reforming the foundations of Russia's great power status.

In 1998, as NATO's conflict with Serbia intensified, proponents of maintaining the preeminence of nuclear forces became ascendant, reversing official policy of gradually deemphasizing nuclear weapons as symbols of Russia's status and retiring weapons as their lifetimes expired.[114] In 2000, the "great nuclear debate" between Minister of Defense Igor Sergeev and Chief of the General Staff Anatolii Kvashnin broke out into the open. Kvashnin, a veteran of the war in Chechnya, favored transforming the Russian military into a modern conventional force capable of fighting wars—Chechnya being the prominent example—that Russia was more likely to encounter in the twenty-first century. He suggested folding the Strategic Rocket Forces into the Air Force—a double insult, as the Strategic Air Forces were already the least respected unit of Russia's strategic triad.[115] In 2001, it appeared as if Kvashnin had won the debate. Sergeev was replaced by Sergei Ivanov, the first civilian minister of defense in post-Soviet Russia.

By October 2003, however, it was clear that Putin wanted a compromise that respected Russia's historical status as a nuclear and military great power. He rejected Kvashnin's "de-nuclearization" plan and favored actively maintaining a reduced strategic nuclear force while modernizing conventional forces.[116] Putin dismissed Kvashnin in 2004, signaling the end of the "great nuclear debate." He reversed the policy of the Yeltsin administration, which had slashed military spending throughout the 1990s. The 2005 defense budget called for increased spending on new SLBMs and ICBMs as well as on modernizing conventional forces. Putin increased spending on the military by 400 percent after taking office in 1999. Such spending was necessary, in the words of Defense Minister Ivanov, "to maintain genuine nuclear parity, not parity as we had in the Cold War but taking into account the security interests of the state."[117] Putin had decided to preserve the symbolism of nuclear parity.[118] Podvig noted in 2005 that the strategic nuclear forces "have managed to avoid radical transformation."[119]

Russian nuclear policy, despite being more rational than its strategic arms control policy, still reflected the historical aspirations to retain a status equal to that of the United States. While official rhetoric and the 2003 security doctrine highlighted nontraditional threats such as international terrorism and the proliferation of weapons of mass destruction, Trenin suggested that this focus was superficial; after all, a core defense mission remained "the Cold War agenda of managing American power." He argued that the "central mission of Russian nuclear forces remains essentially unchanged from the days of the Cold War. Deterrence, albeit at a numerically reduced level, is key to this mission." A key reason, he explained, was Russia's "inconsistent and often ambiguous" attitude toward the United States—wanting on the one hand to compete for recognition of its equal status and on the other seeking cooperation to continue Russia's political and economic inclusion into the Western international order.[120]

These "inconsistent and ambiguous" views echoed the social creativity strategies that Primakov and then Putin pursued after the Kosovo crisis and that were consolidated with the U.S. war against Iraq and the West's political interventions in the former Soviet republics: not only was Russia a great power, it was also a status-quo power facing a revisionist United States. Partnership with the United States was "part of the solution" of providing global stability. In this light, Russian nuclear and military forces now took on a new role. Instead of ensuring security against all manner of physical threats great and small, nuclear weapons were, according to the 2003 Defense White Paper, the sole means of preventing the destruction of the contemporary "system of international relations based on international law."[121] The deeply ambivalent policy of competition with the United States for status while maintaining a framework of cooperation in order to join the West—the orientation toward "competitive engagement"—was again apparent.

After the United States withdrew from the ABM Treaty in 2002, Russian interest in cooperation with the United States on a missile defense system was driven by great power status considerations, rather than any belief that missile defenses were necessary.[122] Statists, including most prominently Vladimir Putin, sought to restore Russia's former position as the co-guarantor of global stability and to fulfill their social creativity strategies.[123] However, instead of global stability being defined as joint strategic arms *reduction,* statists clamored for cooperation with the United States on joint *missile defenses*—a complete reversal from Russian opposition to U.S. withdrawal from the ABM Treaty.

The quest for parity and status continued, albeit in a different form.

Retired Strategic Rocket Forces general Vladimir Dvorkin had long opposed START II and cooperation on missile defenses as well as Kvashnin's plans for strategic modernization because such actions undermined nuclear parity. In 2005, he changed his position and advocated for Russian cooperation with the United States to create a global missile defense system. In contrast to realist arguments that Russia sought to balance the United States and divide NATO through its offer of cooperation on theater missile defenses, Dvorkin argued that the only arena for genuinely equal—and therefore worthy—cooperation was with the United States on missile defense. He rejected all other areas of cooperation. Only in missile defense could Russia avoid playing a secondary role; as Dvorkin stated, "This is, in fact, an area of cooperation where Russia could play a leading role, principally because the Russian MAWS [missile attack warning system] radars deployed in the south of the country possess a unique capability to monitor the southeastern, southern, and southwestern regions where the danger of a missile launch exists. These capabilities substantially exceed those of the United States or other Western partners. This technology could be made more effective with the joint operation of Russian and U.S. early warning systems."[124] Podvig suggested that interest in cooperation on missile defenses was motivated more by concerns for status than on practicality. "As far as Russia is concerned," he wrote with regard to missile defense in 2003, "a joint project of almost any kind had to demonstrate that Russia and the United States are equal partners."[125] As these statements indicate, strategic arms control and missile defense were not interests to be pursued in their own right. Rather, Russian political elites clearly saw them as two of the primary means of achieving their aspiration to maintain Russia's global status relative to the United States.[126]

Conclusion

Strategic arms control remained tightly linked to political elite debates about Russia's national identity as a great power. With the decline of liberal internationalism beginning in 1993 and the increasing policy impact of historical aspirations regarding Russia's historical great power status, such security issues ceased to be issues in their own right. With regard to strategic arms control, Russian political elites had not defined the national interest primarily in terms of increasing Russia's security. From a realist perspective, Russian opposition to START II was a serious miscalculation, given Russia's weak bargaining position; Russian political elites erred in not making a deal with the Clinton administration that would have preserved the ABM Treaty and more verifiable, mutually binding, and far-reaching arms reductions. Moreover, Putin and many Russian political elites miscalculated in believing that the United States would reward Russia for its cooperation after September 11 and agree to modify the ABM Treaty rather than withdraw from it outright.[127]

Instead, Russian interests in strategic arms control were largely subsumed under the broader interest in maintaining Russia's status relative to its own past. Strategic arms control was defined less as an interest in its own right than a means to retaliate or to demonstrate Russia's equality with its prior peer, the United States. Lack of a domestic consensus on Russia's political purpose prevented the development of a more rational Russian political discourse based on efficacy-testing. This absence and Russian elite aspirations prevented rational definition of Russia's national interests, even on military issues and nuclear doctrine, where rationalists most expect rationality to prevail. The elite division on Russia's political purpose meant that any advocates of compromise on the START or ABM treaties were likely to be disparaged as undermining Russia's international position and caving to the United States. The great power definition of the national interest and the nineteenth-century worldview underpinning it prolonged Russian political elites' preoccupation with asserting international prestige rather than focusing on more pressing and more likely threats. In other words, national interests, even in the most critical areas of national security, were not defined primarily through a cost-benefit analysis of Russia's realistic capabilities and threats (a calculus put forward mainly by moderate Westernizers and moderate statists and expected by rationalists). Rather, historical aspirations and the dominance of a cost-benefit calculus framed by Russia's own past shaped national interests in strategic nuclear weapons.

EIGHT

Conclusion

Aspirational Constructivism and International Institutional Change

This study began by asking how national interests are formed. The answer proposed here—in the form of aspirational constructivism—is that to understand what states want, scholars must start by investigating what the sources of a country's national identity are and how they influence its national interests. In trying to explain how national interests are created, aspirational constructivism has looked to research in social psychology—research new to the field of international relations—to answer three fundamental questions: What are the sources of national identity? Why do multiple identities come into contention? How does one of these candidate national identities come to dominate the others and become "social fact," acting as "the" national identity that defines a country's core national interests?[1] The proposed answers to these questions constitute the aspirational constructivist theory of identity and interest formation.

Aspirational constructivism begins with the premise that political elites are motivated by both value rationality and the psychological need for collective self-esteem to create collective identities, which in turn shape their interests and behavior.[2] A central source of collective self-esteem, according to aspirational constructivism, are the intersubjective memories of the past national self and the aspirations they generate for the future. These motivations drive political elites to create or alter national identities and national interests in order to promote national self-esteem and further their preferred form of social order, particularly in times of change.

As a result of these motivations, political elites attempt to craft and recraft national identities through the introduction of national self-images, sets of ideas about the correct international status and political purpose of their country. They promote their preferred national self-image in the public discourse through the deployment of identity management strategies, which are the means to persuade other political elites that their national self-image enhances collective self-esteem and can provide the basis for a valid social order. The many national self-images and identity management strategies that elites introduce into the political discourse depict other countries as similar or dissimilar to the national self, and this depiction creates orientations to behave in a generally cooperative fashion toward ingroup members and a generally competitive manner toward outgroup members.

It is not enough to propose what the sources of national identity and interests are and why multiple competing identities come into existence to build an aspirational constructivist theory of identity and interest formation. A complete theory must address the third question of why a particular candidate national identity becomes epistemically dominant and serves as "the" national identity that defines core national interests. This requires the theoretical elaboration of a "selection mechanism" that can explain why one particular social institution—in this case, a candidate national identity—comes to "stick" while others do not.[3] According to aspirational constructivism, whether these national self-images and their behavioral orientations toward the outside world come to be epistemically dominant rests on their perceived legitimacy among the majority of political elites. This legitimacy is established in public through the political discourse, as political elites seek to establish whether a national self-image is both historically appropriate—in that it satisfies historical aspirations shared among elites—and capable of being realistically carried out under the conditions their country currently faces.

According to aspirational constructivism, this process, or mechanism of institutional selection, is one of correspondence tests of historical and effective legitimacy (or history- and efficacy-testing) that political elites apply to the national self-images in contention in the political discourse. The most consensual, stable, and durable national self-image (and the interests following from it) is one that rests on both historical and effective legitimacy, a self-image that passes both history and efficacy tests in the eyes of political elites.

This aspirational constructivist theory of identity and interest formation generated three theoretical expectations (explored in chapters 3 through 7): (1) political elites, motivated by the need for self-esteem and value rationality, should seek to create new bases of national self-esteem and valid social orders through the introduction of national self-images and their promotion via identity management strategies; (2) those efforts (the advocacy of national self-images and identity management strategies) should generate national interests and behavioral orientations toward the ingroups and outgroups constructed in the self-images; and (3) a national self-image is most likely to become epistemically dominant and become institutionalized when most political elites perceive it as both consonant with historical aspirations and practicable given the current conditions their country faces. With regard to the third expectation, aspirational constructivism suggests that if historical aspirations clash with the practical enactment of a national self-image, the degree of institutional flux is likely to determine whether history or efficacy matters more in the political elite definition of the nation's identity and interests. Historical aspirations should matter more than efficacy tests in more fluid periods, while in more stable periods, both should matter equally.

Plausibility Probe of Aspirational Constructivism

As the primary purpose of this book is to build a new theory, it has not attempted to test aspirational constructivism in any rigorous fashion against situational theories, be they structural constructivist or rationalist. Instead, the book empirically represents a plausibility probe of aspirational constructivism. The empirical findings suggest that aspirational constructivism can bear fruit.

Russian political elites did introduce new national self-images in the post-Soviet period, images that sought to create post-Soviet bases for national self-esteem and a new social order. Russian political elites offered several national self-images: Western (with liberal internationalist and democratic developmentalist variants), statist (with Eurasian statist and statist developmentalist variants), Slavophile, neocommunist, and national restorationist. The Western national self-images suggested that Russia's national self-esteem and the foundation for its post-Soviet social order should be the emulation of Western political, economic, and social values and institutions. Statist national self-images found the basis for

Russia's national self-esteem in the maintenance of its historical status as a great power and proposed that a post-Soviet social order be premised on internal strengthening of the state. The Slavophile, neocommunist, and national restorationist self-images all relied on portions of Russia's tsarist or Soviet past as the basis for Russia's positive distinctiveness and sought to create a post-Soviet social order that would restore particular features of the past. Russian political elites used a variety of identity management strategies to promote their preferred national self-images. Liberal internationalists favored complete assimilation strategies, while statists adopted social creativity and social competition strategies.

All the post-Soviet Russian national self-images constructed Russia in relation to three groups: the great powers, the West, and the former Soviet republics. For all but the neocommunist and national restorationist self-images, the West was an ingroup or a partial ingroup for Russia. These depictions created orientations toward cooperation toward the West. Neocommunist and national restorationist self-images constructed the West as an outgroup and disposed their adherents toward competition if not outright confrontation with the West. The liberal internationalist national self-image was the only one not to construct the group of great powers and the former Soviet republics as Russia's ingroups, in which Russia would play a leading role. As social identity theory would suggest, perceived challenges to Russia's position in its ingroups generated competitive orientations toward countries, particularly the United States, that were seen as threatening Russia's status among the great powers, in the West, and especially in the former Soviet Union.

With respect to aspirational constructivism's third expectation, that a correspondence process of legitimacy-testing acts to "select" a particular national self-image from among its competitors, this too was borne out in the empirical analysis. Of particular importance to the process of correspondence-testing are historical aspirations of Russian political elites. Historical memories of Russia's prior self, rather than the behavior of others or material threats, served as the primary source of post-Soviet national identity and national interest formation. With the exception of radical liberal internationalists, Russian political elites viewed Russia's historical status as a great power responsible for European and global order as a positive feature of its past and as Russia's most distinguishing feature. This intersubjective memory regarding Russia's past created historical aspirations to retain that positive and distinctive status.

This aspiration regarding Russia's international status served as the key benchmark that political elites used in assessing the legitimacy of competing national self-images. No such common aspiration existed with regard to Russia's political purpose, the other element of national identity. Russian political elites subjected the liberal internationalist national self-image, dominant in the new Russian government at the outset of the post-Soviet period, to history tests. As early as 1992, they quickly found liberal internationalism wanting in historical legitimacy, as it portrayed Russia's historical quest for great power status as a key source of its authoritarian misfortunes. Russian political elites believed that the status of the tsarist empire and the former Soviet Union as a global great power and independent pole in the international system still were sources of Russian positive distinctiveness—of national self-esteem—after the Soviet collapse.

Liberal internationalist foreign policy, as enacted by Foreign Minister Andrei Kozyrev, was judged to be historically inappropriate, not because Russian political elites perceived the West to be hostile or materially threatening but because it cast Russia as an unquestioning follower of the United States. The historical aspiration to great power status also served to bolster national self-images, particularly statist ones, that proclaimed Russia's great power status a central feature of Russian identity and sought to assert that status. Another shared historical memory—regarding the harmful effects of ideologically driven foreign policy—was not quite as widely held among Russian political elites, but it also played a role in shaping the legitimacy of contending national self-images. It helped cast doubt on national self-images premised on an ideological confrontation with the West.

Liberal internationalism's illegitimacy in the eyes of Russian political elites was not solely a function of its rejection of Russia's historical search for great power status. A key factor in the delegitimation of liberal internationalism was the inability of its advocates to demonstrate its effectiveness under current conditions. The ability to verify the proposed self in its present context is an important source of self-esteem (what social identity theory calls self-efficacy, or efficacy-based self-esteem), and as a result aspirational constructivism expects that national self-images must be seen as capable of enactment under current conditions if they are to muster effective legitimacy. Russian political elites assessed the behavior of liberal internationalists against their professed principles and found that they did not practice what they preached. Practitioners of liberal internationalist foreign policy were seen as lacking in professionalism and driven by idealism rather than pragmatism. In addition, the domestic policy outcomes associated with liberal internationalism, particularly "shock therapy" and privatization, were seen as harmful and destabilizing. As a result, liberal internationalists were removed from office, statists were elevated to official positions, and the center of the Russian political discourse in 1993 began shifting away from the reformist end of the spectrum.

Statists were the primary beneficiaries of the demise of liberal internationalism. Their prominent advocates, first Evgenii Primakov, and then later Vladimir Putin, adopted identity management strategies that highlighted Russia's positive distinctiveness as a great power, one that was a status quo and therefore "better" great power than Russia's status rival, the United States. However, their national self-images also cast Russia as at least partly Western, and they therefore rejected confrontation with the United States and favored status competition with it while remaining cooperatively disposed toward the West as an ingroup. Their national self-images were widely seen as historically legitimate by Russian political elites.

Russian foreign policy as a result became much more assertive after 1994, as statists gained ascendancy, even though Russia's economic and military position was weakening. Russian foreign policy zigged and zagged between cooperation and competition with the West, as Russian political elites reacted to perceived slights to Russia's international status. The impact on Russian foreign behavior, most clearly shown in post-Soviet Russia's handling of strategic arms control, was that historical aspirations often trumped realism in determining foreign policy. Russian interests in strategic arms control were defined less as a means of maintaining security and reducing the threat of nuclear war and more as an instrument to prevent the United States from undermining Russia's historical status in other areas. As a result, Russian political elites sacrificed the opportunity to seal an arms control agreement that would have preserved the bipolar Cold War strategic framework and Russia's Cold War status as a co-guarantor of global stability. They did so just to express their displeasure over events—often well beyond the area of arms control—that they could not control. Similarly, on the issue of European security, Russian political elites perceived little real danger to Russia from an expanding NATO. Rather, half of them perceived it as an effort to undermine Russia's global great power status as co-manager of global security, of which Europe, in their eyes, remained a critical part. For the other, Western-oriented half, NATO expansion was opposed because it hampered Russia's integration into the West and its pursuit of a liberal democratic path of modernization.

However, efficacy tests of the contending self-images (what social identity theory would term verification of the self-in-context) applied by Westernizers and moderate statists served to check the effective legitimacy of statists' interest in status competition and of national restorationists' interest in confrontation with the West. Westernizers and moderate statists used efficacy tests to move Russian elites away from focusing only on an antagonistic and reactive quest for a status on a par with the United States. These political elites continuously reminded their more conservative elites that Russia was effectively incapable of achieving its desired status as an equal to the United States without lengthy internal modernization and transformation. They emphasized Russian weakness and interdependence in a world of globalization to generate support for a more proactive agenda of rebuilding the state as a means of achieving global great power status.[4] They pointed to the harmful consequences a reactive, status-driven foreign policy was having on Russia's "true" national interests—its integration into the West and development as a modern, economically advanced country—as well as on more concrete issues such as reconceptualizing Russia's interests in European security and maintaining strategic arms control with the United States.

Such efficacy-testing helped keep most Russian political elites oriented toward "competitive engagement" or "competition within a framework of cooperation" with the West and NATO. Yet Westernizers' and moderates' application of such efficacy tests did not generate any consensus on Russia's political purpose; along with the illegitimacy of ideological and military confrontation with the West, it served to deflate the most hostile orientations implicit in a status-driven identity and to maintain the national interest as one of competitive engagement.[5]

In sum, the empirical chapters highlight that post-Soviet Russia's identity and interests through 2004 were largely based on Russia's appropriate international status as defined by elite historical aspirations. Russian political elites never settled on the second element of national identity, Russia's political purpose. They were profoundly split, as they had been throughout the nineteenth century, over whether Russia had a unique political purpose to carve an independent path of development or whether it could adopt the values, practices, and institutions of the West and still retain its sense of self-worth.

Even after the revolutionary post-Soviet decade ended and Vladimir Putin focused on stabilization, Russian political elites remained deeply divided over Russia's political purpose, in particular whether its historical mission was to emulate the West or to develop according to its own traditions. This continued division left pursuit of great power status as the common denominator in political elite definitions of Russia's national identity. The deep division over political purpose contributed to the elites' failure to replace a national identity of global great power status and a reactive definition of national interests with a more measured one based on the actual condition of the nation and its most appropriate form of political and economic modernization. Andrei Mel'vil's 1997 complaint remained viable in the early twentieth century: "If there is not any definite notion of *Russia's new identity,* around which there could exist even relative agreement among elites and society, then from whence can foreign policy strategy and recognition of national interests and aims be taken? As of yet, Russia has neither one nor the other, and as a result, she has either unfounded nostalgic ambitions or an almost reflexive reaction to foreign irritants."[6] Efficacy-testing by Westernizers and moderates succeeded only in altering but not in replacing historical aspirations to retain Russia's great power status as the key source of Russia's national identity and national interests.

As a result, Russian political elites settled on a *partial* Russian national identity, with the national interest defined as maintaining international status. Halfway through the first decade of the twenty-first century, post-Soviet Russia had still not formed a national identity grounded on a firm agreement of where Russia stood and what its purpose was. Rather, its political elites arrived at a point where Russia's historical status largely substituted for political purpose in the definition of national interests regarding domestic politics and relations with the outside world.

The empirical application of aspirational constructivism to post-Soviet Russia highlights the central roles that historical aspirations, international status, and efficacy tests of the self-in-context have had in shaping Russian national identity and national interests. Whether these findings hold elsewhere and at other times, and whether aspirational constructivist theory is more generally applicable—these are subjects for further research.

Areas for Further Research

This work has introduced aspirational constructivism to a larger audience. In doing so, it has highlighted new areas of research for constructivists and rationalists. Further research, however, is also required to assess whether aspirational constructivism's emphases on history, agency, and identity are useful in understanding other countries' identities and interests (India, the United Kingdom, France, Germany, China, Japan, and the United States all come to mind as potential cases).

In the case of Russia, aspirations derived from its past have been the sources of its national identity and have outweighed the role of its present situation in shaping its national identity and interests. This produces two questions for future research: Are historical aspirations always more important that practical enactment of a candidate identity under current conditions in defining the legitimacy of competing national self-images? And what conditions would make practical enactment under current conditions as opposed to historical aspirations more important? The assumption here is that the experience of change makes the historical self more important than practical enactment in the present in shaping identity.[7] Whether this is always the case in times of institutional change or even during more stable times requires further investigation. Such research would produce a more precise understanding of the time frame in which identity is created, institutionalized, destabilized, and dethroned and whether identity formation—and the establishment of other social institutions—is a rapid and sudden or a slow and almost imperceptible process. In addition further research could investigate to what extent the process is syncretic.[8]

The Russian case also highlights that international status has been the core source of its national self-esteem. Further research is also necessary to assess whether international status is usually or always more important than political purpose in shaping a country's national identity and interests, as well as what conditions make status more important than purpose and vice versa. Another area for further research is the possibility of bridging structural and aspirational constructivist accounts of identity formation. Such an effort could flow from similar efforts currently under way in social psychology: social psychologists are investigating whether the literatures that underpin aspirational constructivism (the Tajfel and Turner school of social identity theory, which focuses on group identities) and structural constructivism (Stryker's structural symbolic interactionism, which focuses on role identities) are commensurable and capable of fruitful combination.[9]

Aspirational Constructivism's Contribution to Understanding National Interests

Aspirational constructivism moves scholarship concerning national interests forward in ways that contribute both to constructivist and rationalist approaches. Much constructivist and rationalist research, as noted in the introduction, is situational and structural in nature—focusing on the effects of particular situations and normative or material structures on actors' identities and interests. From the perspective of aspirational constructivism, world politics is a complex web of social relationships crossing the boundaries between domestic and international politics, and its trends and outcomes are better captured by analyzing processes than material or social structures. We see in the comments of Ernst Haas an understanding of international relations that is a precursor of aspirational constructivism: "What matters is process. The actors' perceptions of reality result in policies that shape events; these effects create a new reality whose impact will then be perceived all over again, ad infinitum. . . ."[10] This notion of interactive process is central to social identity theory as well, where strong identities that persist over time "are expressions of the identity *process* rather than fixed aspects of cognitive structure or personality."[11]

This attention to the spread of collective knowledge through process and interaction, interest definition and redefinition, highlight essential elements of an aspirational constructivist research program. Scholars such as Haas recognized that the process of social interaction is the essence of international politics and that human agents can alter the quality of international life, even if they are unable to eradicate the power of the social structures they build.

Contributions to Constructivist Scholarship

If constructivism is to impart important sociological and social psychological insights into international relations theory, then situational versions of structural constructivism are a thin and ahistorical view of social structure.[12] If scholars really want to take social norms, culture, and history seriously in international relations theory, they must pay more attention to the weight of the past, to historical aspiration and its effect on what actors want. Scholars in comparative politics have undertaken a research agenda to demonstrate how the past affects current politics.[13] Constructivists need to follow suit and move beyond the implicit assumption of the importance of history and make it a part of their theoretical framework of how social structures and socially constituted interests evolve.[14]

The Logic of Aspirations and Institutional Change

Aspirational constructivism takes a first step in this direction by offering a new logic of aspirations with which to understand what actors want and how they behave. This logic of aspirations—in focusing on historically derived aspirations and human reflection—helps explain when and why people come to accept a social identity as *self*-defining, ensuring that constructivists add agency into their accounts of institutional formation and change.[15] In contrast to structural constructivist theories that explain the self's adoption of identities and interests as a result of how other countries behave toward the self or the international normative structure that the self encounters, aspirational constructivism highlights how a preexisting self-concept can create aspirations that are independent of the international social structure and that can hamper the self's willingness to conform to it or accept the identities others would give it.

In Russia, post-Soviet political elites struggled to shift away from identifying Russia's national self-esteem with an idea of Russia drawn from its past, one in which it was positive and distinct owing to great power and its unique amalgamated civilization. This need for positive distinctiveness that matched historical aspirations and post-Soviet conditions made the search for a "national idea" in Russia particularly tortured. Martha Finnemore argues that the international social structure in place today is grounded in a meta-structure of Western rationality. Entrants into international society are socialized according to this global structure and become "civilized."[16] Yet in Russia, the international structure of Western rationality competed with the weight of Russia's past—its internal sense of being a distinct civilization, unique and alternative to the West, that had achieved its greatness in a manner at least partly distinct from Western rationalism. One contribution of aspirational constructivism to constructivism is to highlight that the weight of the past and the self's agency in accepting a new identity as self-defining may slow or alter the nature of socialization into existing social structures and may alter those structures themselves. This in turn can affect the nature and pace of international transformation.

The past self, if viewed today as legitimate, frames the self's interactions with others and with international institutional structures in ways that may or may not be conducive to international transformation, a central area of research for constructivists.[17] In the post-Soviet Russian context, the failure of radical Westernizers to legitimate the ideas of Gorbachev's New Thinking on international affairs and the success of the historically legitimate statist national self-image of Russia as a global great power suggest the obstacles that history can throw in the path of cognitive evolution and, subsequently, international systemic transformation.[18] These intrinsic features of a state's identity, particularly its history, matter quite a bit if we are interested in the possibility of change in the nature of identification of others, and, consequently, in the likelihood of transforming the Westphalian state system. In this sense, structural constructivists err in suggesting that the "intrinsic" identities of states and their histories do not matter to a theory of how the system of states can be transformed.[19]

Microfoundations for Structure and Agency

Aspirational constructivism also contributes to broader constructivist (and international relations) scholarship by introducing a body of social psychological theory and research that is new to the international relations discipline. Aspirational constructivism, in drawing on social psychology, particularly social identity theory, provides microfoundations for a constructivist theory of identity and interest formation that incorporate both structure and agency. As noted above, aspirational constructivism is premised on the insight from social identity theory that collective identities must be accepted by individuals as self-defining in order for them to have psychological or behavioral consequences.[20] In contrast, structural constructivist work that draws on symbolic interactionism (such as Alexander Wendt's) or cognitive psychology (such as Ted Hopf's) argue, respectively, that the self automatically takes on the role identity given it by others and that identities are cognitive structures that are automatically adopted.

Aspirational constructivism draws on a body of recent psychological research that accepts a role for genuine human agency in the construction of identities and interests. Aspirational constructivism combines this agency with the impact of preexisting structures (preexisting social identities) to create a genuinely constructivist account of how agency and structure together create new social identities and interests. Aspirational constructivism does so through its emphasis on the historical aspirations created by intersubjectively held memories of the past self and the importance of verifying the sense of the self in light of its current conditions.

Mechanism of Institutional Selection

In addition, aspirational constructivism proposes an institutional selection mechanism—the correspondence process of historical and effective legitimacy-testing—through which one of many competing national identities comes to be epistemically dominant and define national interests. In doing so, it responds to calls to specify the mechanisms through which social institutions change.[21] Constructivists tend to focus on the importance of the spread of collective ideas—in the form of international norms, scientific knowledge, identity, and culture—for the possibility of transforming the nature of international relations and the institutions that structure them.[22] Emanuel Adler quite rightly argues that constructivists require a theory of institutional selection that accounts for why some social identities and other forms of collective ideas "stick," while others do not or, as he terms it, why we see "the political selection of similar epistemic and normative premises."[23] Aspirational constructivism proposes that political elites' legitimacy tests of the historical appropriateness and practicality of competing national self-images serve to "select" which self-image becomes dominant.

Identity Alteration, Reproduction, and Change

Aspirational constructivism also emphasizes that national identities can be altered, reproduced, or changed as identity is an interactive product of the self and its context.[24] This has important implications for constructivist efforts to understand the circumstances under which international social structures change. John Gerard Ruggie has focused on psychological change as means of what he calls "transforming" the social structure of international relations. Such transformative change requires what he calls "change in social epistemology" or "the mental equipment that people drew on in imagining and symbolizing forms of political community" and in conceiving forms of "social time," different time frames over which appropriateness and policy responses are considered.[25]

This aspirational constructivist study of post-Soviet Russia indicates that most Russian elites had not changed their perception of political space *or* social time. Many in the West have come to see the post–Cold War world as a postmodern future of softened sovereignty, with globalized processes and problems creating widened interests. In Russia, most political elites viewed international relations through a nineteenth-century lens of modern sovereign states. Russian Westernizers and Western-oriented statists pointed out the dangers of relying on a modern, as opposed to postmodern, view of Russia's purpose and place in the system and emphasized the imperatives of globalization and interdependence.[26] Yet Russian elites, by and large, looked to their past for their vision of the Russian self and had not institutionalized the new social epistemology that Gorbachev and liberal internationalists introduced in the late 1980s and early 1990s, changes that might have produced international institutional transformation. In focusing on aspirations drawn from their past, Russian political elites altered, but did not fundamentally transform, their sense of self. This in turns affected the possibility of broader international systemic transformation.

Identity and the Moderation of Behavior

However, and in contrast to other constructivist work focusing on the social construction of "realist" identities, aspirational constructivism highlights that identities, even “realist” ones, do not necessarily produce interests in competition and conflict and that behavioral orientations can be moderated through the application of legitimacy tests.[27] Efficacy-testing played an important role throughout the post-Soviet period in shaping the behavioral orientations arising out of the definition of national interest as great power status maintenance. Westernizers and moderate statists were successful in applying “efficacy tests” concerning Russia’s weakness and in sustaining consensus on the need for engagement with the West.[28] They moderated the competitive and confrontational foreign policy orientations entailed in the status-driven aspirations to regain Russia’s historical status as equal to the United States. Their testing was responsible for status competition being maintained as a “competitive engagement” orientation toward the West and for tamping down antagonistic and reactive orientations to the West as self-defeating.[29]

Contributions to Rationalist Scholarship

Aspirational constructivism also offers new areas of engagement with non-constructivist scholars. Aspirational constructivism provides significant potential for building bridges between rationalism and constructivism through its focus on historical aspirations and historical memory as well as elite perceptions of the suitability of identities in light of current conditions, the focus of “situational” and rationalist approaches.

The Logic of Consequences and Assessments of the Self-in-Context

Rationalism emphasizes that actors forecast the consequences that logically flow from a given situation and choose strategies that best meet their interests, given these situational constraints. These interests are generally assumed to be material welfare, power, and security. Changes in the material situations actors face should produce changes in their definitions of their interests. With respect to Russia, rationalists would expect Russia to adapt to its changed position in the international distribution of material power, “learning through weakness” to reduce its national interests to those commensurate with its new capabilities. A rationalist would assume that attachment to the past will continue until the costs associated with that historical stance, be they political or economic, become too great. As the costs associated with historical aspirations or the insistence on status maintenance rise, elite definition of identity and interests should begin to shift to one based more on reality than history. In other words, Russia should learn through rational assessment of present-day material conditions what its current national interests are.

The empirical findings here suggest that the picture is more complicated than rationalists expect. It appeared that Russian political elites favored aspiration-driven interests on security issues more than situation-based ones, despite Russia's growing weakness in the security realm. At root, the rationalist explanation is unsatisfying, as the definition of costs, and the level at which they are too high to bear, is never objectively given. Nor is it intersubjectively fixed among Russian political elites for all time. Rather, the definition of costs and benefits and the country's "threshold of pain" are subject to the ongoing political debate over whether a national self-image is both historically appropriate and effective. For most of the post-Soviet period, Russia's weakness did not cause Russian political elites to redefine core aspirations or core interests. Indeed, the elites remained in agreement that pursuit of Russia's status was an overarching national interest regardless of the situation they faced, though they disagreed on how to pursue it.[30]

Aspirational constructivism agrees with rationalism that people act strategically and rationally to pursue their interests given current conditions. Aspirational constructivism incorporates from social psychology the importance of "verification of the self-in-context," of the self's ability to enact its identity under current conditions, in its emphasis on efficacy tests as shaping the legitimacy of a national self-image and its attendant behavioral orientations. This offers the potential for dialogue with rationalists on the nature in which costs and benefits are calculated.

However, in contrast to rationalism, aspirational constructivism suggests that instead of merely responding to situations, actors attempt to change them so as to achieve their aspirations. Social psychology emphasizes that when people have difficulty verifying their identities under current conditions, they will take steps to change their environment in order to bring the self-in-context back in line with their identity prototype.[31] Aspirational constructivism draws from social identity theory the insight that people's interests, and their strategic calculations, stem from their sense of self—their social identities—and that these social identities "influence the way they perceive their social environment." As a result, "people not only passively observe social situations, but are also active participants in these situations."[32] Instead of reacting to the situations they encounter, as in rationalism, people will attempt to change the situation and their position in it to bring it into conformity with their sense of self.[33] Rationalists need to consider how aspirations and the need for self-esteem may shape the calculus that actors use when considering the strategies to adopt in the situations they face. Aspirational constructivism suggests that historical aspirations are a significant factor shaping that calculus.

International Status and International Prestige

Aspirational constructivism also offers the potential for a constructive dialogue with realists and others concerned with the roles and behavioral consequences of status and prestige on international cooperation and conflict. In contrast to realist arguments regarding the structural sources of national prestige or status, aspirational constructivism suggests that the concern for international status and prestige is based on a desire for national self-esteem.[34] The issue of international prestige is understudied in international relations theory, even though Max Weber, in an oft-forgotten passage, long ago noted that "a nation will forgive damage to its interest, but not injury to its honour."[35]

Aspirational constructivism suggests that, based on recent work in social psychology, the need to establish national self-esteem may indeed be the everyday stuff of world politics, as Robert Gilpin suggests.[36] However, social identity theory suggests that the audience for national self-esteem is primarily domestic, rather than international, as Gilpin and other realists propose, and that its consequences may not be as pernicious as realists (and Weber) expect.[37] This is particularly the case if a country's national identity constructs its rivals for prestige as ingroup members, since such construction generally has moderating effects on status competition.[38] Aspirational constructivism suggests that international prestige is not determined by the international distribution of material power or victory in the last war, as realism suggests. Instead, scholars must examine the national self-images and identity management strategies that dominate in a given country to know what that country's sources of prestige are and what behavior may result. It is likely that the legitimacy of the country's identity and the prominence of international status within that identity shape the importance of prestige in foreign policy. This offers a new area for further research and productive exchange between constructivists and realists. It also suggests important policy implications for practitioners and scholars alike.

Policy Implications

The question of whether states are driven to compete for international status or prestige has important real-world implications. The empirical application of aspirational constructivism has highlighted the crucial importance of elite aspirations to restore Russia's historical great power status to the definition of its post-Soviet identity and national interests. Such aspirations stoked fears that Russia would take a revanchist tack in its relations with the outside world. Russian policymakers' constant proclamations of its great power status and its efforts to keep its status on a par with the United States suggested Russia was embarked on a confrontational course with the United States. This prompted repeated talk about "a return to the Cold War." Drawing on recent research in social psychology, aspirational constructivism suggests, however, that such declarations may well be directed primarily to a domestic audience, as they are efforts to enhance Russians' own sense of their country's self-worth.[39] Policymakers need to look beyond the surface of such proclamations and behavior if they are to avoid misperceiving the sources and reasons for a country's pursuit of international status—in this case, Russia's.

Aspirational constructivism offers some moderately good news in this respect. Contrary to more pessimistic assessments of Russian foreign policy, aspirational constructivism highlights that Russia is not a revisionist power seeking to challenge the United States and the West and create a non-Western international order. Instead, Russia seeks to join the West, but in a manner that allows its leaders to maintain national self-esteem in the eyes of Russian political elites, primarily through Russia's involvement in the management of global affairs and its partial Westernization. This suggests that strategies of face-saving or "respect-enhancing" engagement (such as Russia's addition to the G-7, or the Russia-NATO Founding Act) can allay tension. The development of a Russian national identity as a partly Western great power does not rule out competition with the United States and the West, but it does suggest that such competition will take place on the terms of existing Western-dominated international society and will be bounded in an overarching desire to remain engaged with the West.

The bad news is that promoting Russia's resurgence as a great power within the existing international order has been the domestically legitimate identity management strategy when Russia was weak, as it was throughout the 1990s, and as it grew stronger thereafter. Russian political elites reject rapid and total Westernization and following a pro-Western line in foreign policy as unbefitting Russia's greatness, even though most are positively inclined toward the West. For Western decisionmakers, the primary problem is that Russian political elites want to participate in the contemporary, Western-dominated international society, but they view this society through a nineteenth-century lens rather than one that takes into account the impact that democratization, economic liberalization, increasing interdependence, globalization, and softened sovereignty are having on that society.[40] Russian political elites view the countries of the former Soviet Union through this nineteenth-century lens, as part of the historical basis of Russia's great power status and unique Eurasian form of development. Western encroachments in this region are equated with loss of Russia's historical status and therefore threaten national self-esteem. It is not surprising, from this perspective, that Russian policymakers would risk its relations with the West over countries that are considered core to its identity as a great power, as it did in its war with Georgia in 2008. It is in the former Soviet Union, therefore, that Russia is most likely to compete with the West, and it is the only region where genuine confrontation is likely. Such competition is unlikely to reach levels approaching that of the Cold War, as the Russian political elites seek entry into the Western political order rather than replacing it with one of their own. However, Western policymakers should expect Russian leaders to continue to make pronouncements about Russia's historical right to be treated as a great power, in the former Soviet Union and globally.

Policymakers trying to understand the behavior of Russia (or Iran or any country) need to consider the social psychological reasons why Russian decisionmakers engage in such esteem-enhancing actions. Practitioners need to consider the following: Is such behavior part of an identity-management strategy intended primarily to boost the legitimacy of its advocates' preferred national self-image back home? Are such efforts viewed by domestic political elites as either historically or practically appropriate, or as harmful and dangerous? Answers to both sets of questions yield a more accurate understanding of the likely real-world importance of esteem-enhancing behavior and rhetoric. Genuine fear and hostility are most likely to occur toward countries viewed as an outgroup when they are perceived, rightly or wrongly, as threatening a country's sense of self.[41] In this regard, it is important for policymakers to know whether their country is perceived to be an outgroup by another country's elites, or whether it is seen as belonging to an ingroup or possibly a partial ingroup.

In post-Soviet Russia, for the majority of political elites, the depiction of the West as an ingroup or partial ingroup and the illegitimacy of national self-images premised on ideological confrontation with the West produced more moderate foreign policy orientations toward the West than many pundits expected, given the often belligerent great power rhetoric of its policymakers.[42] However, a key source of Russian political elites' sense of positive distinctiveness and national self-esteem is Russia's leading role in the former Soviet republic ingroup. As such, perceived threats to Russia's identity as playing the leading role in the former Soviet republics are the most likely sources for genuine conflict between Russia and the West.

Taking these insights together, policymakers and analysts need to uncover widely held historical aspirations among a foreign country's political elites if they wish to understand its national interests. However, they also need to consider the domestic legitimacy of the national self-image and identity management strategy a decisionmaker promotes, as well as whether dominant self-images cast a foreign country as an ingroup member or not. These factors can significantly shape whether a country, be it Russia, China, the United States, or India, seeks to attain its historical aspirations in a manner that is cooperative, competitive, or confrontational and, at a more fundamental level, whether it has a revisionist or status quo national identity and national interest. A country's external behavior is shaped by the interaction between its identity and its social context, including its *domestic* not just international context; for policymakers, this means that, in contrast to essentialist studies of strategic or political culture, a national identity does not yield an unchanging, "primordial," or cognitively determined interest in conflict or cooperation with particular countries or the outside world.[43] As a result, policymakers' efforts to understand historical aspirations and the legitimacy of national self-images can produce better understanding of other countries' foreign policy and aid in the design of policies that allay perceptions of threat to a country's identity and the fear and hostility that such perceptions can produce.

Appendix: Methodology

This book is an attempt to build a new aspirational constructivist theory of national identity and interest formation. In theory-building exercises, the emphasis is less on definitive tests of the theory-in-progress than on establishing its logical and empirical plausibility. The empirical study of post-Soviet Russia in this volume represents a "plausibility probe" of aspirational constructivism. Plausibility probes are especially appropriate when building theories as opposed to evaluating established ones. Eckstein defined plausibility probes as "attempts to determine whether potential validity may reasonably be considered great enough to warrant the pains and costs of testing."[1]

Studying the process of identity and interest formation requires the expenditure of considerable time and resources. Analysts cannot simply take a snapshot of national identity at a particular point in time and generalize from the point to other periods, as Ted Hopf rightly notes.[2] Nor can the content of national identities be deductively arrived at and modeled and then generalized to a number of countries. Detailed analysis of a broad swath of elite discourse over a considerable stretch of time is necessary to uncover what the content of national self-images are and how they actually take shape and come to dominate the definition of national interests. Analysts must conduct in-depth analysis of the country or countries in question, which requires extended field research and the acquisition of language skills. Therefore, aspirational constructivism is first evaluated in a plausibility probe of a single country study, that of Russia, from 1991 to 2004.

Methodology

In order to explain why and how post-Soviet Russian identity and interests have been created, this study employed qualitative content analysis in combination with Weberian ideal types.

In order to code the ideas that make up national identities and inform national interests and to code changes in the political discourse over time, following Max Weber, I first constructed ideal-type indicators of the two key elements of national identity: international status and political purpose. The remainder of this appendix develops these indicators in detail. Data was collected, sorted, and coded according to these ideal-type indicators. These ideal types were used as indicators throughout to measure the elements of actual Russian national self-images across time and place. The ideal-type indicators, combined in different ways, describe a wide array of possible national self-images. The content of national self-images is contingent on the historical period and country studied, but the abstract elements that constitute them may be applied to other cases across time and space; they therefore provide a useful heuristic for categorizing any state's political discourse, not just Russia's. The ideal-type indicators were used in chapter 3 to create a typology of Russian national self-images. In the remainder of the empirical chapters, these indicators, and the national self-images constructed out of them, were used to code the diverse views in Russian elite discourse.

The second methodological step was inductive: determining what national self-images existed in the post-Soviet Russian political discourse from 1991 to 2004 and what identity management strategies they entail. As will become apparent, none of the Russian national self-images neatly map onto the pure abstract ideal types. Qualitative content analysis was the primary method used throughout.[3] The elements of the elite political discourse included: discussions of Russian national identity, citizenship, borders, international rank, international role, and economic, political, and social system. In addition, I evaluated elite statements for declarations of what Russia and its others are and ought to be, how the various players do and should act, the modes of reasoning elites were employing in their analysis or advocacy (including the use of realist, Marxist, liberal, Kantian, historical, and utilitarian logic or analogies) and the basis they used to justify or legitimate their views (the use of material, ideal, historical, racist, cultural, or other rationales).

The results of this analysis led to the identification of five national self-images (Westernizer, statist, national restorationist, neocommunist, and Slavophile) discussed in chapter 3. Chapter 3 also investigates what commonalities exist among the national self-images to determine what, if any, aspirations are common to them. To determine what the content of historical aspirations are, I considered elite statements and elite survey research regarding the constituent elements of the Soviet Union's political purpose and international status and Russia's present situation and coded them as negative or positive in order to assess whether members of the elite viewed the current situation as reflecting a position of loss or gain.

Knowing which national self-images are in circulation does not in and of itself tell us which are most likely to dominate elite discourse—still less why. To determine whether in fact one particular national self-image came to dominate the political discourse, I used the ideal-type indicators to qualitatively analyze the political discourse from 1991 to 2004 for evidence of fluctuations. I followed and coded elite views over time according to ideal-type indicators in order to determine whether and when an elite consensus on Russia's national identity developed and whether this consensus endured both over time and in the face of external shocks.[4]

Chapter 4 considers the identity management strategies employed by advocates of Russian national self-images. In order to assess whether elites were using an identity management strategy of assimilation, I analyzed their discourse for indicators of what they desired Russia should be considered like or beliefs that Russia was like other countries or categories (for example, statements that Russia was a Western country or that it rightfully belonged in the West). Indicators of social competition strategies included statements that Russia would show that it was equal to or better than some category and that it would demonstrate this to others (for example, statements that Russia was a great power in a multipolar world). Indicators of social creativity strategies included statements recategorizing Russia on a higher level (for example, statements that suggest that Russia is superior to the West culturally or morally) while ignoring dimensions on which Russia is inferior or that create a new dimension for comparing Russia with its desired peer, (for example, statements suggesting that Russia is performing a new, better role in the international social hierarchy than others).[5]

Using the ideal-type national self-images constructed in chapter 3, I analyzed the elite political discourse to establish whether the range of national self-images in play remained constant or some dropped out, and whether the language and reasoning underpinning one self-image diffused across party lines. I assessed the prevalence of national self-images in the political discourse by analyzing elite statements published in a variety of scholarly and journalistic media of differing ideological persuasions in six-month segments to establish which national self-images persisted in discourse, which were less prevalent, and which dominated others. In assessing how widely accepted a particular national self-image was, I compared discourses among elites who differed in party affiliation and ideology. If a cross-party convergence on national self-images exists at a given point in time, then this is considered an indicator that it dominates the discourse. I also examined elite discourse and used elite survey research, where available, for evidence of elite notions of the historical appropriateness of competing national self-images over time (to see if history-testing was occurring) and of the policy outcomes and personages associated with them in order to determine whether elites believed they were practicable under current conditions (to see if efficacy tests were being applied). The results of this analysis provide the empirical findings reported in chapters 3 through 7.

Since the development of national identities is a public act, public statements and news accounts are the primary sources used throughout the analysis.[6] Data was drawn from over a thousand elite statements made from 1991 to 2004 in news media of varying ideological affiliation, scholarly and policy journals, books, and party platforms from 1993, 1995, 1996, 1999, 2000, 2003, and 2004, collected in part during a year of field research in Moscow in 1997 and 1998. Further evidence was obtained from personal interviews conducted with Russian political elites in 1997, 1998, 2004, and 2005, and survey research on elite attitudes, where these were available and reliable (the surveys used were conducted by the most credible Russian survey research organizations, including VTsIOM, before it was effectively nationalized during the Putin years, and ROMIR, which has conducted surveys for Gallup International and scholar William Zimmerman, Vox Populi, and Fond "Obshchestvennoe Mnenie").

The views of prominent proponents of different political ideologies were followed over time to see if their national self-image changed. The sample included prominent members of ideologically different political parties (such as Aleksei Arbatov, Vladimir Lukin, Gennadii Ziuganov, Aleksandr Lebed', Gennadii Seleznev, Vladimir Zhirinovskii, Aleksei Mitrofanov, Sergei Baburin, and Vladimir Ryzhkov), policy analysts and media pundits (Andranik Migranian, Konstantin Zatulin, Sergei and Andrei Kortunov, Andrei Kokoshin, Vladimir Baranovskii, Sergei Karaganov, Aleksei Pushkov, Dmitrii Trenin, Sergei Rogov, and Lilia Shevtsova), public intellectuals (such as Natalia Narochnitskaia, Emil Pain, Elgiz Pozdniakov, Valerii Tishkov, Aleksandr Solzhenitsyn, and Andrei Zagorskii), and office holders, including presidents Yeltsin and Putin, their senior leadership, members of their governments, national security and defense councils and high-ranking officials in the armed forces and ministries. (A number of these persons moved across these categories.)

Measuring the Content of National Identity

The national self-images focused on in this work are those of political elites, who are the primary creators and reproducers of a national collective identity. The important role of political elites has been recognized in a number of studies of social identity.[7] Political elites consist of politically active and influential individuals in government, the media, and the intelligentsia.

In order to ascertain what different national self-images are in contention, this study codes elite discourse and attitudes according to several ideal-type categories. Following Max Weber, ideal types of national self-images that consist of purely abstract elements were constructed according to the constituent elements of national identities: political purpose and international status. These ideal types offer benchmarks against which we can measure actual elements of national self-images and are a useful heuristic for categorizing the political discourse. The ideal-type elements can be combined to form a wide array of possible national self-images. Using these ideal types, chapter 3 develops a typology of Russian national self-images. The content of those Russian images is historically contingent, but the abstract elements that constitute them are generalizable across time and space. The same indicators were the basis for the coding of elite views in chapters 4 through 7. The ideal-type indicators of political purpose are dealt with first, followed by those for international status.

Ideal-Type Indicators of Political Purpose

The indicators used to construct images of political purpose are ideas about the country's appropriate political-economic system, its national mission (if any), proper territorial boundaries, and criteria for membership in the body politic.

Political-Economic System

This indicator is constructed on the opposition of public versus private control of the country's political and socioeconomic spheres. Russian elite discourse and opinions were coded as to whether they favor one of the ideal types of political-economic systems. The ideal categories range from low to high on the dimensions of state versus private control of the economy, provision of social welfare, and extent of democracy. The ideal types are liberal democracy, social democracy, statist democracy, liberal statism, social statism, and total statism. For example, the ideal type of liberal democracy rests on a country with a market economy dominated by private actors, low public involvement in the provision of social services and welfare, and a robust democracy. The countries most closely approximating this ideal type are the United States and the United Kingdom from the 1980s onward. The ideal types and the countries most representative of them are listed below.

- Liberal democracy: high private-led market, low welfare, high democracy (post-1980 United States and United Kingdom)
- Social democracy: medium private-led market, medium welfare, high democracy (Germany)
- Statist democracy: low private-led market, medium welfare, high democracy (France)

- Liberal statism: low state-led market, low welfare, low democracy (South Korea and Taiwan, 1950–1970)
- Social statism: medium-high state-led market, high welfare, low democracy (USSR, 1990–91)
- Total statism: high state-led economy, high welfare, no democracy (USSR before 1985; PRC before 1982)

National Mission

Mission derives from a combination of founding myths and historical interactions. It is not usually based in "objective" reality but is rather the realm of "inventing tradition."[8] It pertains to claims of predestination, messianism, and core tasks of the state as well as the historical relations with other states that make these tasks necessary or manifest them. Elite statements and attitudes regarding such claims are used to identify what national mission, if any, is subscribed to. I coded national mission on a scale using the missions of autonomy, inclusion into some larger grouping, and expansion. The endpoints are along territorial, cultural, economic, and political-ideological lines. Candidate missions for Russia might include: international socialism, Eurasian bridge, Great Russian gatherer of the lands, pan-Slav protector, nativist cultural autarchy, imperialism, restoration, Westernization, European savior, economic development, and great power status. Different missions, or a combination thereof, indicate which foreign models are usable and which roles the state should play at home and abroad.

Territorial Boundaries

The claims of the state's rightful boundaries can be status quo or revisionist. Revisionist claims can be to shrink or enlarge the present borders. I used elite statements and elite survey data concerning lands and territory that properly or historically "belong" or "do not belong," the right of secession, and the relation between sovereignty and territorial integrity to position members of the elite and their ideas on this dimension.

Membership in the Body Politic

Membership is coded on a civic-statist-ethnic scale. Civic definitions include all citizens as defined by law without regard to ethnicity or bloodlines. Statist definitions include all those loyal to the state *qua* state. In Russia, this generally means all Russian-speaking residents of the Russian state in its various historical forms, including the Soviet Union and the Russian empire.[9] Here it is the affiliation with the state, in all its incarnations, that matters. Ethnic definitions include members of one or more ethnic groups and exclude others or give them secondary status.

Claims for assimilation into the dominant culture or for multicultural tolerance, as well as prescriptive definitions of who comprises the "core" or primary group, are used to judge a person's position on this scale.

Ideal-Type Elements of International Status

The indicators of ideal-type international status are ideas about what roles are appropriate for the country to occupy in world affairs, what rank the country should hold in international society, and what is the characteristic nature or "logic" of international affairs.

Proper Roles in International Affairs

Roles are a function of which ingroups a state believes it should be a member of, a state's mission, and its relationship with other states in these groupings. They entail implicit and explicit privileges and obligations, rights, and duties. These groupings may be based on geography, economics, politics, culture, ideology, or material power. Elite views of their country's proper mission, roles, rights, and obligations are used to place them on this dimension.

Rank

Rank is the position a state occupies or should occupy in an imagined hierarchy within the international system as well as within regional and global groupings. Rank typically is coded as super, great, medium, or small power along global or regional lines, but within an ingroup it is coded as positive or negative. Statements by elites about international hierarchies and their country's place in them are used to establish their views on their country's proper rank.

The Nature of International Relations

The nature of international relations refers to elite ideas and folk theorems about the fundamental principles governing interstate relations. Is the state of nature (human nature, the international environment) hostile or benign or a mix? Different conceptions of international relations are coded as to the weight they give to ideas, interaction, and materialism as causes of international cooperation and conflict.[10] Materialist views include racist, realist, dependency theory, and geocultural explanations of conflict. Idealist folk theories are premised on "birds of a feather flocking together," suggesting that ideological affinity creates peace and dissimilarity creates conflict. Interactionist theories focus on increased interaction as creating more beneficial relations, which can take cosmopolitan form (interaction creates understanding, which creates peace, especially if institutionalized) and utilitarian liberal form (pursuit of individual gain through exchange produces social gain, which can create peace, if institutionalized). Interactionists and idealists are more likely to emphasize the common fate produced by interdependence; utilitarian liberals stress that interdependence creates opportunity as well as insecurity and the possibility of exploiting others. Materialists tend to view interdependence as a source of conflict. I used elite views on the "logic of international relations" (whether it is inherently conflictual or not, zero- or positive-sum in nature) and their characterization and ranking of threats (whether they are seen as common to all humanity, national, individual, military, economic, social, ideological, cultural, racial) as indicators of this category.

Notes

Chapter 1: Introduction

1. Gilpin, *War and Change in World Politics,* 34, and Paul, "Soft Balancing in the Age of U.S. Primacy."

2. Trenin and Lo, *The Landscape of Russian Foreign Policy Decision-Making,* 5.

3. Parrish, "Chaos in Foreign Policy Decision-Making," 30, and Larrabee and Karasik, *Foreign and Security Policy Decisionmaking under Yeltsin.*

4. For international relations approaches that draw on cognitive psychology, see George, *Presidential Decisionmaking in Foreign Policy,* Jervis, *Perception and Misperception in International Politics,* Jervis, Lebow, and Stein, eds., *Psychology and Deterrence,* Larson, *Anatomy of Mistrust,* McDermott, "Prospect Theory in Political Science," and Stein, "Political Learning by Doing." On the differences between aspirational constructivism's and Jonathan Mercer's uses of social identity theory, see chapter 2 as well as Oakes, "Psychological Groups and Political Psychology," 810–12, and Brewer, "Importance of Being 'We.'"

5. The differences between the rationalist logic of consequences and the sociological logic of appropriateness are laid out in March and Olsen, "The Institutional Dynamics of International Political Orders."

6. Larson and Shevchenko, "Shortcut to Greatness," 80.

7. Wohlforth, "Realism and the End of the Cold War," Copeland, "Trade Expectations and the Outbreak of Peace," and Brooks and Wohlforth, "Power, Globalization, and the End of the Cold War."

8. Larson and Shevchenko, "Shortcut to Greatness."

9. Levy, "Declining Power and the Preventive Motive for War," Jervis, "The Implications of Prospect Theory for Human Nature and Values," and Parrish, "The USSR and the Security Dilemma," 161–68, 209–47.

10. Jervis and Bialer, *Soviet-American Relations after the Cold War.*

11. Wendt, *Social Theory of International Politics*.

12. Finnemore, *National Interests in International Society*, and Finnemore, "Norms, Culture, and World Politics."

13. Risse, "Let's Argue!" Kratochwil, *Rules, Norms, and Decisions*, Reus-Smit, "The Constitutional Structure of International Society and the Nature of Fundamental Institutions," and Checkel, "Why Comply?"

14. Important constructivist contributions that do focus on the internal development of national identities and strategic cultures include Kier, *Imagining War*, Johnston, *Cultural Realism*, and Hopf, *Social Construction of International Politics*.

15. Jepperson, Wendt, and Katzenstein, "Norms, Identity, and Culture in National Security," and Wendt, *Social Theory*.

16. Wendt, *Social Theory*. See also Stryker, "Identity Salience and Role Performance," and Stryker, *Symbolic Interactionism*.

17. Finnemore, "Norms."

18. Ellemers and van Knippenberg, "Stereotyping in Social Context," 209. See also Huddy, "From Social to Political Identity."

19. For Hopf's discussion of historical others, see his *Social Construction*, ch. 4.

20. Ibid., 5–6.

21. Ibid., 11.

22. Gray, "National Style in Strategy," Gray, *Nuclear Strategy and National Style*, Huntington, *The Clash of Civilizations and the Remaking of World Order*, and Pipes, *Russia under the Old Regime*.

23. For a discussion of the differences among primordial, instrumentalist, and constructivist theories of nationalism, see Smith, *Nationalism and Modernism*.

24. Checkel, "The Constructivist Turn in International Relations Theory."

25. Katzenstein, ed., *Cultural Norms and National Security*, Berger, *Cultures of Antimilitarism*, Abdelal, *National Purpose in the World Economy*, Tsygankov, *Pathways after Empire*, and Hopf, *Social Construction*.

26. Wendt, *Social Theory*.

27. For reviews of this literature, see Brewer, "The Many Faces of Social Identity," Hogg, Terry, and White, "A Tale of Two Theories," Stryker and Burke, "The Past, Present, and Future of an Identity Theory," Huddy, "From Social to Political Identity," and Stets and Burke, "Identity Theory and Social Identity Theory."

28. I owe Jeffrey Knopf a great debt for suggesting that I was using a "logic of aspiration" in developing this theory.

29. The need for collective self-esteem is a core tenet of social psychology. See Baumeister, "Preface," Cast and Burke, "A Theory of Self-Esteem," Elliott,

"Self-Esteem and Self-Consistency," Gecas and Schwalbe, "Beyond the Looking-Glass Self," Rosenberg et al., "Global Self-Esteem and Specific Self-Esteem," and Smelser, "Self-Esteem and Social Problems."

30. Tajfel, *Differentiation between Social Groups,* and van Knippenberg, "Strategies of Identity Management."

31. Stets and Burke, "Identity Theory," 233–34, and Oakes, "Psychological Groups."

32. Larson and Shevchenko, "Shortcut to Greatness."

33. Tajfel, *Differentiation between Social Groups,* Tajfel and Turner, "The Social Identity Theory of Intergroup Behavior," and Huddy, "Context and Meaning in Social Identity Theory."

34. Aspiration is a core feature of prospect theory, which emphasizes the importance of aspiration levels in decisionmaking. See Tversky and Kahneman, "Judgment under Uncertainty," Tversky and Kahneman, "The Framing of Decisions and the Psychology of Choice," Tversky and Kahneman, "Loss Aversion in Riskless Choice," McDermott, "Editor's Introduction," and Levy, "Loss Aversion, Framing Effects, and International Conflict."

35. Wendt, *Social Theory.*

36. Berger, *Cultures of Antimilitarism,* Katzenstein, *Cultural Norms,* Hopf, *Social Construction,* Abdelal, *National Purpose,* Tsygankov, *Russia's Foreign Policy,* and Tsygankov, *Pathways after Empire.*

37. Oakes, "Psychological Groups," 817.

38. May, *"Lessons" of the Past,* Jervis, *Perception and Misperception,* and Khong, *Analogies at War.*

39. Bandura, "Social Cognitive Theory," and Bandura, "Towards a Psychology of Human Agency."

40. Ruggie, "What Makes the World Hang Together?" 856.

41. On valid social orders and value rationality, see Zelditch, "Theories of Legitimacy," 43–44, and Weber, *Economy and Society.*

42. Bandura, "Towards a Psychology," 165.

43. In particular, see Wendt, *Social Theory,* and Hopf, *Social Construction.*

44. Legitimacy is a key determinant of social identities in social identity theory, as it is the criterion for establishing appropriate social status. See Zelditch, "Theories of Legitimacy," and Tyler and Blader, "Autonomous vs. Comparative Status."

45. Bandura, "Social Cognitive Theory," Bandura, "Towards a Psychology," and Levy, "Learning and Foreign Policy," 283–85.

46. On humans as rational creatures inhabiting a socially constructed world, see Onuf, *World of Our Making.* On human desires to change identities, see Kiecolt, "Stress and the Decision to Change Oneself."

47. Bandura, "Towards a Psychology."

48. Oakes, "Psychological Groups," 813–17, Ellemers and van Knippenberg, "Stereotyping," 209, and Stets and Burke, "Identity Theory," 229–32. See more generally Tajfel and Turner, "Social Identity Theory," and Cast, Stets, and Burke, "Does the Self Conform to the Views of Others?"

49. For an earlier statement of the ontological position on human capacity for reality testing, see Boulding, "The Learning and Reality-Testing Process in the International System."

50. Levy, "Learning."

51. Kratochwil, *Rules, Norms, and Decisions,* Risse, "Let's Argue!" Finnemore, "Norms," and March and Olsen, "Institutional Dynamics."

52. Bandura, "Towards a Psychology," 165.

53. For more on plausibility probes, see Eckstein, "Case Study," and George, "Case Studies and Theory Development."

54. Eckstein, "Case Study and Theory in Political Science," 108.

55. On critical junctures, see Collier and Collier, *Shaping the Political Arena,* ch. 2.

56. Swidler, "Culture in Action," 278.

57. Collier and Collier, *Shaping the Political Arena,* ch. 2.

58. The author worked in 1989 and 1990 at the Office of Soviet Union Affairs, U.S. Department of State, and then from June 1990 to January 1993 for nongovernmental organizations setting up civil society programs throughout the former communist bloc, where she personally observed the widespread nature of these views.

59. Marcussen et al., "Constructing Europe?"

60. Wendt, "Anarchy Is What States Make of It," 404.

61. Collier and Collier, *Shaping the Political Arena,* ch. 2. See also Sewell, "Historical Events as Transformations of Structures," 843, and Searle, *The Construction of Social Reality,* 92.

62. Thelen, *How Institutions Evolve,* 35–37, Pierson, *Politics in Time,* 137–38, and Berke and Galvin, "A Field Guide to Creative Syncretism."

63. Haas, "Words Can Hurt You," 241.

64. Tversky and Kahneman, "Framing of Decisions," McDermott, "Editor's Introduction," and Levy, "Loss Aversion."

Chapter 2: Aspirational Constructivism

1. For discussion of these weaknesses, see Huddy, "From Social to Political Identity," 137–38, and Huddy, "Context and Meaning in Social Identity Theory."

2. For primordialist accounts of national identity, see Calhoun, "National-

ism and Ethnicity," Smith, *The Ethnic Origins of Nations,* and Smith, *National Identity.*

3. Baumeister, "Preface," Cast and Burke, "Theory of Self-Esteem," Elliott, "Self-Esteem and Self-Consistency," Gecas and Schwalbe, "Beyond the Looking-Glass Self," Rosenberg et al., "Global Self-Esteem and Specific Self-Esteem," and Smelser, "Self-Esteem and Social Problems."

4. This literature includes structural symbolic interactionism, social identity theory, and identity theory. For discussions of the similar insights of these theories, particularly regarding self-esteem, the self-concept, the reflexitivity of human agents, and the social construction of social roles and categories, see Stets and Burke, "Identity Theory," Stryker and Burke, "Past, Present, and Future," and Hogg, Terry, and White, "Tale of Two Theories."

5. Gecas, "The Self-Concept," and Rosenberg et al., "Global Self-Esteem."

6. Cast and Burke, "Theory of Self-Esteem," 1047, and Stets and Burke, "Identity Theory," 234.

7. Personal self-esteem is the primary focus of identity theory, while social identity theorists study both personal and collective self-esteem. Here I focus exclusively on collective self-esteem.

8. Turner, "Henri Tajfel."

9. Hogg, Terry, and White, "Tale of Two Theories," 259–60.

10. Tajfel, *Differentiation,* and van Knippenberg, "Strategies of Identity Management."

11. Tajfel, *Differentiation,* Tajfel, ed., *Social Identity and Intergroup Relations,* Oakes, "Psychological Groups," Burke and Stets, "Trust and Commitment through Self-Verification," Cast and Burke, "A Theory of Self-Esteem," Bandura, "Self-Efficacy," and Bandura, "Self-Efficacy Mechanism in Human Agency."

12. Marilynn B. Brewer, " Many Faces of Social Identity," cited in Spinner-Halev and Theiss-Morse, "National Identity," 519.

13. Tyler and Blader, "Autonomous vs. Comparative Status," Ellemers, "The Influence of Socio-Structural Variables on Identity Management Strategies," and Stets and Harrod, "Verification."

14. Mead, *Mind, Self, and Society.*

15. Wendt, *Social Theory,* Stryker, *Symbolic Interactionism,* Wendt, "Anarchy Is What States Make of It," and Wendt, "Collective Identity Formation and the International State." For a critique based on social identity theory, see Mercer, "Anarchy and Identity."

16. Hopf, *Social Construction,* 11.

17. Ellemers and van Knippenberg, "Stereotyping in Social Context," 209.

18. Spinner-Halev and Theiss-Morse, "National Identity," 530, Tyler and

Blader, "Autonomous vs. Comparative Status," and Cast and Burke, "A Theory of Self-Esteem."

19. Tversky, "Features of Similarity." See also Beike and Neidenthal, "The Process of Temporal Self-Comparison in Self-Evaluation and Life Satisfaction."

20. Oakes, "Psychological Groups," 812.

21. Ibid., 813.

22. Tajfel, *Differentiation,* 61, cited in Oakes, "Psychological Groups," 813.

23. Oakes, "Psychological Groups," 813.

24. Ibid., 816.

25. Ibid., 814–20, emphasis in original.

26. See Bandura, "Social Cognitive Theory," Bandura, "Towards a Psychology of Human Agency," and Searle, *Construction of Social Reality.* Bandura directly identifies himself with Searle's work.

27. Social identity theory holds that legitimacy is a key factor affecting acceptance of a social identity. Ellemers, "Individual Upward Mobility and the Perceived Legitimacy of Intergroup Relations," and Mummendey and Otten, "Aversive Discrimination."

28. Locke, *Essay concerning Human Understanding,* cited in Kihlstrom, Beer, and Klein, "Self and Identity as Memory," 71.

29. James, *The Principles of Psychology,* ch. 9, Albert, "Temporal Comparison Theory," Beike and Neidenthal, "Process of Temporal Self-Comparison," and Kahneman and Tversky, "Prospect Theory."

30. Albert, "Temporal Comparison," Howard and Hollander, "Marking Time," and Karniol and Ross, "The Motivational Impact of Temporal Focus."

31. Cited in Spinner-Halev and Theiss-Morse, "National Identity," 521.

32. Albert, "Temporal Comparison," 502, and Huddy, "From Social to Political Identity," 130–32.

33. Albert, "Temporal Comparison," 502, Howard and Hollander, "Marking Time," Beike and Neidenthal, "Process of Temporal Self-Comparison," Brown and Haeger, "Compared to What?" and Klauer, Ferring, and Filipp, "Still Stable."

34. Stets and Burke, "Identity Theory," 225, Huddy, "From Social to Political Identity," 142–43, and Huddy, "Context and Meaning," 829. For a constructivist equivalent of this argument, but with reference to collective ideas rather than identities, see Jeffrey W. Legro, "The Transformation of Policy Ideas," 425.

35. Klauer, Ferring, and Filipp, "Still Stable," 341–43, and Dube, Jodoin, and Kairouz, "On the Cognitive Basis of Subjective Well-Being Analysis."

36. For classic statements of prospect theory, see Kahneman and Tversky, "Prospect Theory," Kahneman and Tversky, "Framing of Decisions."

37. Kahneman and Tversky, "Prospect Theory," Kahneman, Slovic, and Tversky, *Judgment under Uncertainty,* Kahneman and Tversky, *Choices,* Tversky

and Kahneman, "Judgment," and Tversky and Kahneman, "Framing of Decisions."

38. For an argument that comparison to the Self is more significant in shaping self-esteem than comparison to others, see Tyler and Blader, "Autonomous vs. Comparative Status," Beike and Neidenthal, "Process of Temporal Self-Comparison," and Tversky, "Features of Similarity."

39. Spinner-Halev and Theiss-Morse, "National Identity," 519.

40. Emerson, *From Empire to Nation,* and Tajfel, *Differentiation,* both cited in Spinner-Halev and Theiss-Morse, "National Identity," 519.

41. I recognize that the use of the term "national" identity and interests may be contested by scholars who dismiss intrinsic (including "national") features of a state's identity as having any bearing on state interests. Personal communication with Alexander Wendt, November 22, 1997, and Wendt, *Social Theory.* Whether in fact that a state or a nation-state exists is less important than the fact that the existence of a national identity creates interests in creating and maintaining a state.

42. Lustick, "Hegemony and the Riddle of Nationalism," 7.

43. Demo, "The Self-Concept over Time," 305–6.

44. Marx, "The Eighteenth Brumaire of Louis Bonaparte."

45. Burke, "The Self," 20. See also Demo, "Self-Concept," 305.

46. Bandura, "Social Cognitive Theory."

47. Wendt, *Social Theory.*

48. Hopf, *Social Construction.*

49. Oakes, "Psychological Groups," and Huddy, "Context and Meaning."

50. Legro, "Transformation."

51. The adjective *national* here indicates that the self-images that concern us refer to a collectivity, not to an individual. I follow Ralph Turner in using the concept of self-image as distinct from more stable identity. Turner refers to a "self-image" as an individual's picture of herself at any particular moment and to a "self-conception" as a person's relatively stable "sense of the real me." See Turner, "The Self in Social Interaction," cited in Demo, "Self-Concept," 305.

52. Citrin, Wong, and Duff, "The Meaning of American National Identity," Citrin et al., "Multiculturalism in American Public Opinion," Citrin et al., "Is American Nationalism Changing?" and Huddy, "From Social to Political Identity."

53. Hopf, *Social Construction.*

54. For a discussion of this debate regarding identity, see Demo, "Self-Concept," Huddy, "From Social to Political Identity," and Oakes, "Psychological Groups." For the broader question of change in institutions, see Pierson, *Politics in Time,* chs. 4–5, as well as the discussion in Sewell, "Historical Events," 843.

55. Swidler, "Culture in Action."

56. Pierson, *Politics in Time.*

57. "One of the most important messages of the social identity approach is that identities are emergent, context specific outcomes of the interaction between the perceiver and social reality." Oakes, "Psychological Groups," 815.

58. This parallels the processual model in social psychology, which argues that self-concepts are always undergoing change. Demo, "Self-Concept," 305.

59. Burke, "The Self," cited in Demo, "Self-Concept," 305.

60. Sewell, "Historical Events," 843, cited in Mahoney, "Uses of Path Dependency in Historical Sociology," 18.

61. Searle, *Construction of Social Reality,* 92.

62. On this point with regard to identities, see Huddy, "From Social to Political Identity," and Huddy, "Context and Meaning." With regard to institutions more generally, see Thelen, *How Institutions Evolve,* 35–37, and Pierson, *Politics in Time,* 137–38.

63. Demo, "Self-Concept," 305.

64. Ibid., 306.

65. Jervis, "Implications of Prospect Theory," and Mercer, "Prospect Theory and Political Science."

66. This definition draws on John Gerard Ruggie's concept of social purpose and Ernst Haas's concept of national myth. See Ruggie, "International Regimes, Transactions, and Change," and Haas, *Nationalism, Liberalism, and Progress.*

67. Weber, *Economy and Society.*

68. Ibid.

69. Zelditch, "Theories of Legitimacy," 44.

70. On the notion of valid social orders, see Weber, *Theory,* and Zelditch, "Theories of Legitimacy."

71. Lustick, "Hegemony," 9.

72. Oakes, "Psychological Groups," 812, and Brewer, "Many Faces of Social Identity," 119.

73. Weber, "The Social Psychology of the World's Religions," cited in Goldstein and Keohane, eds., *Ideas and Foreign Policy,* 12.

74. Huddy, "From Social to Political Identity." Psychologists have long recognized that people can adopt or discard identities and that identities are not cognitive structures that are permanent and unchanging. See Kiecolt, "Stress," 50, Turner, "Role Change," and Bandura, "Social Cognitive Theory."

75. Tajfel and Turner, "Social Identity Theory of Intergroup Behavior," and Mummendey et al., "Strategies to Cope with Negative Social Identity."

76. That these social groups and their statuses are socially constructed is amply demonstrated by the favored measurement strategy of social identity theorists, the minimal group paradigm. In experiments based on this paradigm, researchers found that strangers were willing to use any measure, from a preference

for Kandinsky over Monet or eye color, to construct social groups and thereby provide meaning in their environment. Tajfel, *Differentiation,* Huddy, "From Social to Political Identity," and Oakes, "Psychological Groups," 812.

77. Mummendey et al., "Strategies," 229.

78. Tajfel and Turner, "Social Identity Theory," and van Knippenberg, "Strategies of Identity Management." Identity theorists have put forward similar strategies to maintain self-esteem. See Cast and Burke, "Theory of Self-Esteem," 1050.

79. Ellemers, "Individual Upward Mobility," 207.

80. Ibid.

81. Ibid. See also Blanz et al., " Responding to Negative Social Identity," 701.

82. Ellemers, "Individual Upward Mobility," 207. See also van Knippenberg, "Strategies of Identity Management."

83. Blanz et al., "Responding to Negative Social Identity," 702, and van Knippenberg, "Strategies of Identity Management."

84. Larson and Shevchenko, "Shortcut to Greatness." Larson and Shevchenko suggest that development of military capabilities reflects a strategy of social competition (they conflate social and realistic competition). However, in line with social identity theory, the development of military capabilities can reflect the effort to rise to the ranks of great powers, not just social or realistic competition. This is particularly true of nuclear weapons capabilities (see pp. 91–95). They also err in suggesting that there is a requisite linear progression from one (failed) strategy to the next.

85. Ellemers, "Individual Upward Mobility."

86. Oakes, "Psychological Groups," 814–17.

87. Ibid., 816–17.

88. Salience is "simply a convenient way of talking about the dominant self-categorization when self-perception reflects the conflicts and compromises among several competing, alternative ways of categorizing self in a situation." Turner et al., "Self and Collective," cited in Oakes, "Psychological Groups," 819.

89. Huddy, "Context and Meaning," 829.

90. On the logic of consequences and appropriateness, see March and Olsen, "The Institutional Dynamics of International Political Orders," *International Organization* 52, no. 4 (1998).

91. Huddy, "From Social to Political Identity," 141–43, and Mummendey and Otten, "Aversive Discrimination," 126.

92. Huddy, "From Social to Political Identity," 142.

93. Huddy, "From Social to Political Identity," 141–45, Huddy, "Context and Meaning," 828–31.

94. Douglas, *How Institutions Think.*

95. Klauer, Ferring, and Filipp, "Still Stable."

96. Kahneman and Tversky, "Prospect Theory," Kahneman and Tversky, "Framing," and Kahneman and Tversky, *Choices.*

97. Karniol and Ross, "Motivational Impact," Albert, "Temporal Comparison," Beike and Neidenthal, "Process of Temporal Self-Comparison," and Klauer, Ferring, and Filipp, "Still Stable."

98. Tajfel and Turner, "Social Identity Theory," and Mummendey et al., "Strategies."

99. Haas, "Words Can Hurt You," 25–26.

100. Cast and Burke, "A Theory of Self-Esteem," Burke and Stets, "Trust," Stets and Burke, "Identity Theory," Bandura, "Self-Efficacy," Bandura, "Social Cognitive Theory," and Bandura, "Self-Efficacy Mechanism."

101. Stets and Burke, "Identity Theory," 231.

102. Stryker and Burke, "Past, Present, and Future," 292.

103. Cast and Burke, "Theory of Self-Esteem," 1046–47.

104. Kratochwil, *Rules, Norms, and Decisions,* Risse, "Let's Argue!" and Reus-Smit, "Constitutional Structure."

105. Legro, "Transformation," 424.

106. Haas, *When Knowledge Is Power,* 1–23.

107. Legro, "Transformation," 425.

108. Stryker and Burke, "Past, Present, and Future," 293.

109. If people lack information about skills and performance levels available for enacting the identity, then individuals will draw on collective memory of past status and self-esteem to judge the potential for effective enactment of an identity. See Ibid.

110. John J. Mearsheimer, "Back to the Future," and Walt, "Alliance Formation and the Balance of World Power."

111. For a discussion of this research, see Spinner-Halev and Theiss-Morse, "National Identity," 520.

112. Albert, "Temporal Comparison," and Stets and Burke, "Identity Theory."

113. For this view of Gorbachev's New Thinking, see Larson and Shevchenko, "Shortcut to Greatness."

114. Tajfel and Turner, "Social Identity Theory."

115. Mercer, "Anarchy and Identity," 237, Sherif, *Group Conflict and Cooperation,* and Sherif and Sherif, *Groups in Harmony and Tension.*

116. Oakes, "Psychological Groups," 810–12, and Spinner-Halev and Theiss-Morse, "National Identity," 520–21.

117. Brewer, "Importance of Being 'We.'" See also Brewer, "Many Faces of

Social Identity," 122–23, Huddy, "From Social to Political Identity," 145, and Oakes, "Psychological Groups," 812–13, 818.

118. Oakes, "Psychological Groups," 818, and Spinner-Halev and Theiss-Morse, "National Identity," 520.

119. Veenstra and Haslam, "Willingness to Participate in Industrial Protest," cited in Oakes, "Psychological Groups," 818.

120. Brewer, "The Social Self," and Brewer, "Social Identity, Distinctiveness, and In-Group Homogeneity."

121. Spinner-Halev and Theiss-Morse, "National Identity," 520.

122. Ibid., 523–24.

123. Brewer, "Many Faces of Social Identity," 122–23.

124. Spinner-Halev and Theiss-Morse, "National Identity," 423.

125. Ibid., 424.

Chapter 3: Russian National Self-Images in the 1990s

1. Vserossiiskii tsentr izucheniia obshchestvennogo mneniia (hereafter VTsIOM), "Vneshnopoliticheskaia Elita i Vneshniaia Politika," 33–34. This report analyzes the results of a June 1993 survey of policy elites first presented in VTsIOM, *Vneshniaia Politika Rossii—1993: Analiz Politikov i Ekspertov,* 35.

2. Fond "Obshchestvennoe Mnenie" (hereafter FOM), "The Treaty of Belovezhsk."

3. The possible responses were that the Soviet Union collapsed because of "irresponsible actions by politicians who did not understand that our strength is only in unity" (50%), "criminal actions, which ought to have been stopped by any means, including armed force" (6%), and "the empire was doomed, the majority of the peoples aspired to sovereignty" (39%). VTsIOM, *Vneshniaia Politika Rossii,* 35. The third response does not necessarily convey the negative value judgment of the others, but those choosing this response may still have regretted the USSR's collapse.

4. FOM, "Referendum on the Fate of the USSR," and FOM, "Treaty of Belovezhsk." The reports of the elite surveys only give graphical presentations rather than precise percentages of responses, hence the approximation. FOM, "Dynamics of Russian Attitudes on the USSR's Collapse."

5. VTsIOM, "Vneshnopoliticheskaia Elita," 33–34.

6. For a discussion of the longstanding nature of this aspiration, see Larson and Shevchenko, "Shortcut to Greatness," 91–95. For the importance of modernity to Russian identity, see Hopf, *Social Construction,* 45–47.

7. Kullberg, *The End of New Thinking,* 5, 21. Kullberg conducted a survey of Soviet elites in June 1991, six months before the breakup of the Soviet Union.

8. VTsIOM, *Vneshniaia Politika Rossii,* 22. This sentiment was also widespread among the general public. In an August 1992 poll, 69 percent of respondents agreed that "Russia should ensure that she remains a great power, even if this leads to a worsening of her relations with the surrounding world," 20 percent disagreed, and 11 percent were undecided. *Moskovsie Novosti* 30 (1992): 2, cited in Ryan, *Social Trends in Contemporary Russia.*

9. VTsIOM, *Vneshniaia Politika Rossii,* 22.

10. Kullberg, *End of New Thinking,* 5, 21.

11. VTsIOM, *Vneshniaia Politika Rossii,* 22.

12. Ibid., 22–23, 26–27.

13. Kullberg, *End of New Thinking,* 18, and Brudny, *Reinventing Russia,* 20, 245.

14. VTsIOM, "Analiz Rezultatov Oprosov. Eksperty o Kharaktere Peremen v Rossii," 13.

15. VTsIOM, "Vneshnopoliticheskaia Elita," 34.

16. Kullberg, *End of New Thinking,* 17–18. See also the comments of Igor Malashenko on the counterproductiveness of Soviet ideology in "Perestroika, Sixth Winter," 100, 104–5.

17. Perhaps this is one of the reasons that Russians react so bitterly to the statements that the United States remains the sole superpower. For many Russian elites, Russia/USSR was not "beaten" in the Cold War, did not "lose," but was rather the key force ending the Cold War and transforming the international system. In this view, Russia should not be seen as having its great power status diminished; rather, the country should be lauded.

18. VTsIOM, "Analiz Rezultatov Oprosov."

19. VTsIOM, *Vneshniaia Politika Rossii,* 34.

20. Levy, "Declining Power," and Scott D. Parrish, "The USSR and the Security Dilemma," 161–68, 209–47.

21. See, for example, Piadyshev, "We Need a National Security Concept," and Kortunov and Iziumov, "What Is Meant."

22. Malashenko, "Soviet-American Relations after Totalitarianism and the Cold War," 14.

23. Kortunov and Iziumov, "What Is Meant."

24. VTsIOM, "Vneshnopoliticheskaia Elita," 32.

25. VTsIOM, *Vneshniaia Politika Rossii,* 21–22.

26. Razuvaev notes that the term *Russian* incorporates the tsarist and Soviet past: "Here the definition of 'Russian' implies the entire 'cross-section' of the historic past connected with Rus and Russia and a multiethnic, multilinguistic and polyconfessional community which is mostly situated on the territory of the RSFSR." Razuvaev, "Russia and Europe," 41.

27. Ibid., 43.

28. Malashenko, "Soviet-American Relations," 14.

29. VTsIOM, *Vneshniaia Politika Rossii,* 21.

30. See for example the views of Prokhanov, "Tragediia Tsentralizma." Prokhanov was known as the "the nightingale of the General Staff" for his defense of the military and his glorification of the Soviet war in Afghanistan as befitting the USSR's civilizing mission. He became one of the most prominent proponents of national restorationism in post-Soviet Russia.

31. VTsIOM, *Vneshniaia Politika Rossii,* 21.

32. Viktor Alksnis, quoted in Emelin, "Moscow Also Betrays Them."

33. Kortunov and Iziumov, "What Is Meant."

34. "Perestroika, Sixth Winter," 101.

35. Kovalev and Sebentsov, "The Shadows of the Past on the Road into the Future," and Lavrov, " 'Seven-Plus-One' Plus UN," 17.

36. VTsIOM, "Vneshnopoliticheskaia Elita," 21–22.

37. Kullberg, *End of New Thinking,* 17.

38. VTsIOM, "Vneshnopoliticheskaia Elita," 32.

39. The typology presented here is based on an inductive analysis of Russian elite discourse based on the ideal-type indicators and data sources discussed in the appendix. These indicators were developed in an effort to make them applicable to other countries. A plethora of typologies have been developed by foreign scholars and participants in Russia's national identity debate. Among others, see Arbatov, "Russia's Foreign Policy Alternatives," Buszynski, *Russian Foreign Policy after the Cold War,* Kortunov, "Budet' Li Smena Kursa?" Prizel, *National Identity and Foreign Policy,* Sergounin, "Post-Communist Security Thinking in Russia," Shlapentokh, " 'Old', 'New' and 'Post' Liberal Attitudes toward the West," Torbakov, "The 'Statists' and the Ideology of Russian Imperial Nationalism," Tsygankov, *Pathways after Empire,* Tsygankov, *Whose World Order,* Wallander, ed., *The Sources of Russian Foreign Policy after the Cold War,* Vujacic, "Serving Mother Russia," and Zevelev, "The Redefinition of the Russian Nation, International Security, and Stability."

40. Some of these commonalities and distinctions are covered in Tsygankov, "Finding a Civilizational Idea."

41. Sergei Karaganov was a presidential advisor to Yeltsin who founded and currently chairs the Council on Foreign and Defense Policy. Arkadii Volskii is the leader of the influential Union of Labor-Trade Unions and Industrialists.

42. The markers of ethnicity range from language and culture in the moderate versions to race and genetics in the extremist forms.

43. Nationalist publicists have taken Lev Gumilev's popular theory of ethnicity to promote anti-Semitism. In this formulation, unlike the other Soviet na-

tionalities, Jews are a "chimera," inassimilable into the Russian "superethnos." Jews, therefore, are parasitic and pose a vital danger to the Russian nation. For this view, see Igor Shishkin, "Simbiosis, Xenia, i Khimera: Lev Gumilev ob etnosakh Rossii," *Zavtra,* no. 4 (60), 1995, 4.

44. Ziuganov, *Derzhava,* cited in Vujacic, "Serving Mother Russia," 290.

45. Author interview with Vladimir Zhirinovskii, June 19, 1997. See also Zhirinovskii, *Vladimir Zhirinovsky Speaks with Russia.*

46. Ziuganov, Podberezkin, Tuleev, Govorukhin, Rutskoi, and Lapshin formed the People's Patriotic Union of Russia in August 1996. Rutskoi is not included in the advocates of a national restorationist image, as he and his party advocated a combination of Slavophile and statist national self-images.

47. For an overview of Russian national restorationists, see Vujacic, "Serving Mother Russia." For a proto-fascist geopolitical rationale for Russia's "special path," see Baburin, *Territoriia Gosudarstva,* 404–75.

48. The Russian language is "a window to the world, a means of advancement into world culture." Author interview with Egor Ligachev, June 24, 1997.

49. Tuleev was a member of the oppositionist KPRF, but he has worked in government. He was Minister for CIS Affairs from 1996 to 1997, and has been governor of Kemerovo oblast. Rybkin was speaker of the Duma in 1994, was appointed secretary of the Security Council (1996–98), and later chaired the Duma Committee on CIS Affairs. On instructions from Yeltsin, he tried and failed to set up a center-left party as an alternative to the KPRF.

50. Author interview with Egor Ligachev, June 24, 1997. Note that according to the 1977 Constitution, the Soviet Union was a "voluntary" union that also enshrined the right of secession.

51. Interfax, reported by BBC Summary of World Broadcasts, no. SU/D4044/B, January 15, 2001.

52. Viktor V. Aksiuchits, *Ideokratiia v Rossii,* 15–16, emphasis in original. The Bolshevik doctrine is seen as an alien, materialist, and atheist ideology imported from the West via "denationalized" intellectuals. Aksiuchits, *Ideokratiia v Rossii,* 18, 138–39. Aksiuchits was formerly leader of the Christian Democratic Movement and later an advisor to Deputy Prime Minister Boris Nemtsov during the late Yeltsin years. Author interview with Viktor Aksiuchits, June 26, 1997.

53. Aksiuchits, *Ideokratiia v Rossii,* 16.

54. Ibid., 128–31.

55. Aksiuchits speaks of "hostile forces" including "the international financial oligarchy"—that is, the Jews—who are seeking to "finally exterminate the Russian national spirit." Ibid., 138–39.

56. "Defend the New Yugoslavia—Appeal to the Seventh Congress of Russian Federation People's Deputies," *Pravda,* December 2, 1992.

57. Aksiuchits, *Ideokratiia v Rossii,* 130. "Moscow is the Third Rome" is a Russian slogan dating back more than four hundred years attesting Russia's world-historical role as the leader of true Christianity.

58. "Russia's National Interests," 142.

59. Aksiuchits, *Ideokratiia v Rossii,* 16.

60. Author interview with Viktor Aksiuchits, June 26, 1997.

61. As with any ideal type, considerable variations on this national self-image exist in reality. While Aksiuchits is overtly protectionist and opposed to admitting international finance but unclear as to his preferred economic model, Moscow mayor Iurii Luzhkov is a consummate capitalist and welcomes foreign investment and favors a market economy. Aksiuchits advocates monarchy, while Luzhkov is a centrist who favors democracy.

62. Luzhkov is the influential mayor of Moscow and leader of the Fatherland Party. Vladimir Volkov is director of the Institute of Slavic and Balkan Studies.

63. It is confusing to refer to Russian politics using the Western concepts of "left" and "right," since a more or less permanent feature of 1990s Russian politics was a "left-right" or "red-brown" alliance between Vladimir Zhirinovskii's Liberal Democratic Party of Russia (LDPR) and the Communist Party of the Russian Federation (KPRF), led by Gennadii Ziuganov. Figure 3.1 presents an alternative mapping of Russian politics, using a spectrum bracketed by preferences for reform and restoration. Ziuganov is ideologically a national-socialist, as are his followers in the KPRF, further confusing the political picture, as the "Communist" Party reflects predominantly national-socialist ideology. For confirmation of Ziuganov's national-socialist ideology, see Vujacic, "Serving Mother Russia."

64. Slavophiles are a particularly difficult group to represent spatially, as there are liberal, moderate, and conservative Slavophiles. However, they are between the national restorationist and Westernizing extremes and orient themselves more toward Europe and Christianity than toward the East.

Chapter 4: Russia's Foreign Policy Orientations

1. As in chapter 3, the empirical conclusions drawn in this chapter are based on the qualitative content analysis outlined in the appendix.

2. Brewer, "Many Faces of Social Identity," 119.

3. Spinner-Halev and Theiss-Morse, "National Identity," 520.

4. Brewer, "Psychology of Prejudice," cited in Spinner-Halev and Theiss-Morse, "National Identity," 520.

5. Brewer, "Many Faces of Social Identity," 122–23, Brewer, "Psychology of Prejudice," Brewer, "Importance of Being 'We,'" and Spinner-Halev and Theiss-Morse, "National Identity," 523–24.

6. Spinner-Halev and Theiss-Morse, "National Identity," 423–24.

7. This point has been extensively documented and discussed in Western scholarship. For just one example, see Neumann, *Russia and the Idea of Europe.*

8. VTsIOM, "Analiz Rezultatov Oprosov."

9. Even liberal internationalism accepts that Russia, once it has transformed itself into a civilized market democracy, belongs among the great powers.

10. Lukin and Utkin, *Rossiia i Zapad.*

11. Tajfel, *Differentiation,* and Tajfel and Turner, "Integrative Theory of Intergroup Conflict."

12. Tajfel, *Differentiation,* 93–94. Note that social identity theorists characterize the other mobility strategy ("mobility," or leaving one group and joining another) as a purely individual-level strategy that cannot be employed by groups. Blanz et al., "Responding to Negative Social Identity," 700. According to Tajfel, however, the strategy of assimilation can be pursued by groups.

13. Larson and Shevchenko, "Shortcut to Greatness," 91–95. In line with social identity theory, the development of military capabilities can reflect a social mobility rather than a social or realistic competition strategy. In this sense, the pursuit of military capabilities is driven by desire for social status and recognition rather than threat perceptions or insecurity. This is likely to be particularly true of high-status weapons systems, such as nuclear weapons. This strategy conforms to structural constructivist explanations that states will seek to conform to normative standards of what it means to be a great power in order to gain social recognition through isomorphism. See Finnemore, "Norms."

14. On different identity management strategies, see Tajfel and Turner, "Integrative Theory of Intergroup Conflict."

15. Hatch and Schultz, "Introduction," 13.

16. Blanz et al., "Responding to Negative Social Identity," 701.

17. Hogg and Abrams, *Social Identifications,* 55.

18. Ibid., 50.

19. For a nice comparison of the importance of territorial expanse in Russian and American national myths, see Bassin, "Turner, Solov'ev, and the 'Frontier Hypothesis.'"

20. Stankevich, "Derzhava v Poiskakh Sebia."

21. All quotations in this paragraph and the next come from statements made by Kozyrev in "A Transformed Russia in a New World," 85–89, and Kozyrev, "Russia Looks West."

22. Arbatov, "Russia's Foreign Policy Alternatives," 11.

23. Kortunov and Volodin, *Contemporary Russia,* 13.

24. Larson and Shevchenko somewhat mischaracterize social competition

and social mobility identity management strategies in their recent work. They conflate social (or evaluative) competition with realistic (or instrumental) competition, an important flaw, as the latter is more likely to produce conflict. They also use social mobility in a manner inconsistent with social identity theory, as simply leaving one (backward) group and joining another, and suggest that this is achieved through "hard work." Social identity theorists argue that groups cannot simply leave one group and join another (only individuals can do this). The only available social mobility strategy for a group is assimilation, which implies identity transformation, rather than simply hard work to acquire the material resources necessary for being a group member. Their portrayal of much of Russian history falls more accurately under social and realistic competition than mobility. See Larson and Shevchenko, "Shortcut to Greatness." For a clarification of the distinctions among identity management strategies, see Blanz et al., "Responding to Negative Social Identity," 700.

25. Stankevich, "Derzhava v Poiskakh Sebia."

26. Blanz et al., "Responding to Negative Social Identity," 726–27.

27. Primakov, "Mnogopoliarnii Mir i OON."

28. Putin, "Annual Address to the Federal Assembly," 2002, and Primakov, "Rossiia Byla i Ostaetsia Velikoi Derzhavoi."

29. Putin, "Annual Address to the Federal Assembly," 2002.

30. On U.S.-Soviet cooperation to avoid nuclear danger, see Nye, "Nuclear Learning and U.S.-Soviet Security Regimes."

31. Putin, "Russia at the Turn of the Millennium."

32. Spinner-Halev and Theiss-Morse, "National Identity."

33. The quotations in this paragraph are from "A Transformed Russia in a New World," 85–89, and Kozyrev, "Russia Looks West."

34. "A Transformed Russia in a New World," 88, 100. See also Kozyrev, "Russia Looks West," and Zagorskii, "Rossiia i Evropa."

35. Arbatov, "Russia's Foreign Policy Alternatives," 11.

36. "A Transformed Russia in a New World," 93.

37. Ibid., 92.

38. For reviews of their attitudes toward the West, see Urban, "Remythologising the Russian State," Arbatov, "Parliament and Politics in Russia," and Tolz, "Forging the Nation."

39. Stankevich, "Derzhava v Poiskakh Sebia," 1.

40. Primakov consistently developed this theme. See for example Primakov, "Mnogopoliarnii Mir."

41. Trenin, "Russia's French Accent."

42. For one of many pronouncements to this effect, see Primakov, "Rossiia."

On Putin, see Interfax, July 10, 2000, Official Kremlin International News Broadcast, "Press Conference with Foreign Minister Igor Ivanov," Treisman, "What Is Different About Putin's Russia?" and Lapidus, "Putin's War on Terrorism."

43. Stankevich, "Derzhava v Poiskakh Sebia."

44. Putin, "Annual Address to the Federal Assembly," 2002.

Chapter 5: Post-Soviet Russia's "Revolutionary Decade" and the Creation of National Identity

1. Larrabee highlights that instability in Russian foreign policy was widespread and not merely a function of bureaucratic infighting. Larrabee and Karasik, *Foreign and Security Policy,* 1.

2. Parrish, "Chaos in Foreign Policy Decision-Making," 30.

3. Council on Foreign and Defense Policy, "Russia and NATO," 4.

4. Stets and Burke, "Identity Theory and Social Identity Theory," 232, Abrams and Hogg, *Social Identity Theory,* Abrams and Brown, "Social Self-Regulation," and Abrams, "Processes of Social Identification."

5. For a particularly clear recognition of this and the incoherent effect the absence of a "consensual 'national/civilizational identity'" was having on Russian foreign policy, see Kortunov and Volodin, *Contemporary Russia,* 7–9.

6. This lack of consensus was widely recognized and led to efforts in the mid- to late 1990s to find both a "national idea" for Russia and to foster national reconciliation. Arbatov, "The National Idea and National Security." See also Trenin, "Rossiia i Amerika," and Putin, "Russia at the Turn of the Millennium."

7. This characterization of the post-Soviet period as a revolutionary one can be found in Igrunov, "Russia after the 2000 Presidential Elections—The Yeltsin Succession and What Comes Next."

8. As chapters 1 and 2 highlight, the need for positive distinctiveness, or self-esteem, is a core psychological need motivating the search for identity and behaviors to achieve it.

9. VTsIOM, *Vneshniaia Politika Rossii,* and VTsIOM, "Analiz Rezultatov Oprosov."

10. Author interview with Leonid Smirniagin, member of the Presidential Commission on the National Idea, June 4, 1998.

11. "Five Questions Put to Well-Known Persons," *Moskovskii Komsomolets,* August 8, 2000.

12. On historical ruptures, see Sewell, "Historical Events." On the possibility of past institutions being reused and renegotiated, see Thelen, *How Institutions Evolve,* 31–37.

13. Other prominent official advocates of a liberal internationalist self-

image included Mikhail Poltoranin, Vitalii Churkin, Georgii Kunadze, Fedor Shelov-Kovalev, Galina Starovoitova, and St. Petersburg mayor Anatolii Sobchak. In the Supreme Soviet, liberal internationalists made up a small faction, including Viktor Sheinis, Sergei Yushenkov, Vladimir Kuztnetsov, and Gleb Yakunin. In academia Andrei Zagorskii, Andrei Kortunov, Nikolai Kosolapov, Konstantin Sarkisov, Evgenii Velikhov, Nikita Moiseev, Sergei Blagovolin, and Aleksandr Saveliev took liberal internationalist positions. Representatives of this national self-image in the media included Andrei Nuikin, Otto Latsis, Iurii Kariakin, Vitalii Korotich and Evgenii Kiselev. See Arbatov, "Russia's Foreign Policy Alternatives," Checkel, "Russian Foreign Policy," Rahr, "'Atlanticists' Versus 'Eurasians' in Russian Foreign Policy," Lukin, "Forcing the Pace of Democratization," 36, and Shlapentokh, "'Old', 'New' and 'Post.'"

14. A study of elite attitudes in 1991 that notes these divisions is Kullberg, *The End of New Thinking*.

15. Arbatov, "Russia's Foreign Policy Alternatives," 24.

16. Lukin, "Forcing," 36–37.

17. VTsIOM, *Vneshniaia Politika Rossii,* and VTsIOM, "Vneshnopoliticheskaia Elita."

18. Kullberg, *End of New Thinking,* 21.

19. VTsIOM, "Vneshnopoliticheskaia Elita." In the VTsIOM poll, 5 to 6 percent pointed to the three Baltic states and Ukraine as their primary enemy. One person out of the 113 sampled identified the United States as Russia's primary enemy. The only other country identified as an enemy was Turkey (5%). VTsIOM, *Vneshniaia Politika Rossii,* 29–30, N=113. The survey participants were broken down as follows: 16 percent were from the Ministries of Foreign Affairs and Foreign Economic Relations and the Security Council; 12 percent came from the presidential administration, the Council of Ministers, the Ministry of Defense, the Foreign Intelligence Service, and unspecified others; 13 percent were Supreme Soviet deputies associated with foreign policy and the leadership of the Supreme Soviet; 13 percent were members of political factions within the Supreme Soviet; 13 percent were leaders of political parties; 18 percent were leaders of research institutes and foreign policy think tanks; and 14 percent were members of the press. For an abbreviated version of the VTsIOM report, see Popov, "Vneshniaia Politika Rossii (Analiz Politikov i Ekspertov)," pts. 1 and 2. These articles unfortunately lack the data tables in the appendix of the original survey and the particulars on specific issues such as the Persian Gulf War, the Yugoslav crisis and START II. The overall conclusions of the 1993 survey were published separately in VTsIOM, "Vneshnopoliticheskaia Elita."

20. Vox Populi, "USIA Survey no. I93060: NATO," table 10, N=350. Survey participants were drawn equally from officials of the executive branch (min-

istries, state committees, federal agencies and commissions), members of twenty-six political parties (eight of which had a communist orientation), directors of state-owned enterprises (the majority from industrial enterprises), private entrepreneurs and bankers, high military commanders (including the general staff of the CIS military forces and the Russian Federation, the Ministries of Defense and Interior, and directors of eight military academies), media directors, and scientific and cultural figures. The survey found a greater portion of the political elite viewed the Middle Eastern countries of Afghanistan, Iran, and Turkey (40% chose this group), the former Soviet republics (24%), and the Far East (22%) as the biggest threat to Russia than the United States (19%). Directors of state enterprises were most likely to view the United States as the biggest threat (presumably out of a fear of market competition). Over half of them identified the United States as the greatest threat, compared with only 17 percent of military officers and 18 percent of those in communist parties. The military and the communists all viewed the Middle Eastern countries (35% and 38%, respectively) and the former Soviet republics (35% and 36%) as the greatest threat. The executive agencies overwhelmingly (71%) viewed the Middle Eastern group as the primary threat.

21. Ibid.

22. Ibid., table 11.

23. Kozhokin, "The Russian Parliament and Foreign Policy," Karaganov, "Russia Needs a Foreign Policy Consensus," and Reddaway and Glinski, *The Tragedy of Russia's Reforms.*

24. VTsIOM, "Vneshnopoliticheskaia Elita," 33.

25. Malcolm, "New Thinking and After: Debate in Moscow about Europe."

26. For Grachev's comments, see ITAR-TASS, June 29, 1992. For Lebed's comments, see *RFE/RL Daily Report,* June 29, 1992.

27. Stankevich was a very prominent democrat; he had been a leader of the Interregional Deputies' Group (IRDG) in the Soviet Supreme Soviet who had criticized Yeltsin for relying on Communist Party apparatchiks in his administration. *RFE/RL Newsline,* September 26, 1991.

28. Eurasianism had previously been the purview of national restorationist journalists (and their political followers) and academics in research institutes dealing with Asia or the Islamic world. See Rahr, "'Atlanticists' Versus 'Eurasians' in Russian Foreign Policy," and Tolz and Teague, "Russian Intellectuals Adjust to the Loss of Empire."

29. "A Transformed Russia in a New World," 100.

30. Ibid., 99.

31. Holden, *Russia after the Cold War.*

32. Stankevich, "Derzhava v Poiskakh Sebia."

33. As noted in chapters 1 and 2, such a desire to distinguish oneself posi-

tively is a core expectation of social identity theory. See Tajfel, *Differentiation,* and Tajfel and Turner, "Social Identity Theory."

34. Malcolm, "New Thinking."

35. This criticism was evident in "A Transformed Russia in a New World," 93, 100.

36. Among those arguing for greater attention to Asia and the South were Supreme Soviet Chairman Ruslan Khasbulatov, a Chechen; deputy director of the Africa Institute Aleksandr Vasiliev; sinologist Sergei Goncharov of the Far Eastern Institute; and Ambassador to the United States Vladimir Lukin, who had earned his doctorate on the political economy of Southeast Asia. They began outlining the Eurasian statist national self-image shortly after the collapse of the Soviet Union. For representative examples, see Bogaturov and Kozhokin, "Vostochnyi Vopros dlia Rossii," Goncharov, "Osobye Interesy Rossii—v Chem Oni Zakluchaiutsia?" Malashenko, "Rossiia i Islam," Simoniia, "Sever-Iug: Konflikt Neizbezhen?" and Vasil'ev, "Rossiia i Musul'mansky Mir—Partnery ili Protivniki?"

37. VTsIOM, *Vneshniaia Politika Rossii,* and VTsIOM, "Vneshnopoliticheskaia Elita."

38. "A Strategy for Russia," authored under Sergei Karaganov's direction by the Council on Foreign and Defense Policy in 1992, served as the first articulation of this consensus. Council on Foreign and Defense Policy, "Strategiia dlia Rossii." For a convenient roundup of views in English representing this consensus, see the articles by Stankevich, Rogov, Travkin, and Shokhin in Sestanovich, ed., *Rethinking Russia's National Interests.*

39. Malcolm, "New Thinking," 169–70.

40. Karaganov, "Russia Needs."

41. Kozhokin, "The Russian Parliament and Foreign Policy," 41–42.

42. Good examples of both views were voiced at a conference on Russian national identity I attended in 1997 at the Carnegie Center in Moscow. A member of the audience took the opportunity to vent his ire at Russia's "humiliation" at the hands of the West and the Russian liberals. A moment later, Fedor Shelov-Kovediaev, a prominent member of Kozyrev's team, leaned over to me (a presumably sympathetic Westerner) and asked, "What humiliation? I don't think we have been humiliated, do you?"

43. Kozyrev argued that "the experience of many countries, such as Germany or Japan, shows that only by taking the road to civilized, democratic development can a country fully bring its distinctive character as a nation state to bear." "A Transformed Russia in a New World," 85–89. For a similar argument, see Zagorskii, "Rossiia i Evropa," and Zagorskii et al., *After the Disintegration of the Soviet Union.*

44. Stankevich, "Derzhava v Poiskakh Sebia." See also Holden, *Russia.*

45. Kozhokin, "The Russian Parliament and Foreign Policy," 39.

46. Arbatov, "Russia's Foreign Policy Alternatives," 11. See also Lukin's comments in "A Transformed Russia in a New World," 91.

47. Responses were open-ended. VTsIOM, *Vneshniaia Politika Rossii*, 38–41.

48. VTsIOM, "Vneshnopoliticheskaia Elita," 33, emphasis added.

49. Ibid., and VTsIOM, *Vneshniaia Politika Rossii*, 38–41.

50. Trenin, "Rossiia i Amerika," and Karaganov, "Russia Needs."

51. Rasputin, "After Events, on the Eve of Events." Rasputin blames the West for imposing this inferiority complex; therefore, restoration of honor and glory entails confronting the West.

52. Trenin, "Rossiia i Amerika."

53. Reddaway and Glinski, *Tragedy*.

54. VTsIOM, "Analiz Rezultatov Oprosov," 18.

55. Breslauer, "Personalism Versus Proceduralism."

56. Hesli, *Governments and Politics in Russian and the Post-Soviet Region*, 69.

57. Arbatov, "The Vicissitudes of Russian Politics," 78–80.

58. Shevtsova, "Vybornoe Samoderzhavie pri Putine." See also Reddaway and Glinski, *Tragedy*.

59. For evidence of such thinking, see Official Kremlin International News Broadcast, "On the Alignment of Forces in Parliament and Possible Scenarios of Developments at the 6th Congress of People's Deputies of the Russian Federation." For the continuation of this polarization, see the discussion of the battle between the ideologies of "people's capitalism" and "oligarchic capitalism" in Ostapchuk and Krasnikov, "Kremlin Tries to Promote People's Capitalism," and Urban, "Remythologising the Russian State."

60. Lipman and McFaul, "Putin and the Media."

61. Treisman, "Blaming Russia First."

62. While Treisman correctly points out that the alternative to this corrupt scheme would have been worse (Yeltsin reportedly was urged to cancel elections entirely), this does not alter elite perceptions that liberal international principles were not applied by those advocating them. See ibid.

63. VTsIOM, "Analiz Rezultatov Oprosov," and Schulze, ed., *Die Außen- und Sicherheitspolitik im Neuen Russland*.

64. The quotation is from Andranik Migranian in "We and the World: Russia's Foreign Policy: Three Views."

65. The view that the FSU should be Russia's top priority is amply represented in "Russia's National Interests."

66. Furman, "'Dinner Jacket' and 'Camouflage Suit,'" and Karaganov, "Russia Needs."

67. Zagorskii, "Rossiia i Evropa."

68. VTsIOM, *Vneshniaia Politika Rossii,* 27–29.

69. For a review of this debate, see Crow, "Competing Blueprints for Russian Foreign Policy," and Crow, "Russia Debates Its National Interests."

70. Karaganov made this critique at a roundtable of "*institutchiki*" on Russian foreign policy. See "Russia's National Interests."

71. "A Transformed Russia in a New World," 82. Khasbulatov later led the parliament in its struggle for supremacy over the executive branch under Yeltsin. He became associated with the red nationalism of Vice President Rutskoi during the armed confrontation between parliament and the president on October 3 and 4, 1993. But here he rejected Russian military intervention or even arbitration in the post-Soviet republics, favoring a small army under civilian control, laws protecting individuals from arbitrary state power, and democratic institutions.

72. Ibid., 82–83.

73. Cf. Malcolm, "New Thinking," Prizel, *National Identity,* and Zevelev, "The Redefinition of the Russian Nation."

74. VTsIOM, "Analiz Rezultatov Oprosov," 15–18. On the question of liberalization of foreign economic affairs, 41 percent believed these were destabilizing, 31 percent said they were stabilizing, 14 percent thought they had no effect, 9 percent believed liberalization was not taking place, and 6 percent didn't know.

75. Borisov, "Vneshniaia Politika i Predvybornaia Bor'ba."

76. Ibid., 29–30.

77. Kortunov, "Budet' Li Smena Kursa?" For a full explication of a democratic Eurasian statism, see Lukin and Utkin, *Rossiia i Zapad.*

78. VTsIOM, "Analiz Rezultatov Oprosov," 15.

79. The April 1992 Congress of People's Deputies provides a vivid example of these attacks on the liberal internationalists; they led to the dismissal or demotion of Gaidar, Burbulis, and Shakrai. Telen, "Controversy at Congress."

80. Arbatov, "Cold War May Become a Reality Yet Again."

81. Vladimir Lukin cited in Steele, "The Bear's Necessities."

82. Rasputin, "After Events, on the Eve of Events."

83. Gerber and Hout, "More Shock Than Therapy."

84. VTsIOM, "Analiz Rezultatov Oprosov," 18.

85. Åslund, *How Russia Became a Market Economy,* and Treisman, "Blaming Russia First."

86. See Kullberg, *End of New Thinking,* 28, and Treisman, "Blaming Russia First."

87. Grazhdanskii Soiuz, *Programma Deistvii po Vyvody Ekonomiki Rossii iz Krizisa.*

88. Cited in Berger, "Candidates for the Russian Presidency Hold a Debate in the Davos, Switzerland 'Polling Place.'"

89. Yavlinskii, *Uroki Ekonomicheskoi Reformy,* 51–56, 64–69.

90. VTsIOM, *Vneshniaia Politika Rossii,* 50.

91. Shmelev, "Russia: The Emerging Consensus on National Reconstruction."

92. Boone and Rodionov, "Rent Seeking Russia and the CIS."

93. Freeland, *Sale of the Century,* and Treisman, "Blaming Russia First."

94. Ostapchuk and Krasnikov, "Kremlin Tries to Promote People's Capitalism."

95. Arbatov, "Russian Foreign Policy Thinking in Transition," 143–44.

96. According to Arbatov, conservatives forced Yeltsin's last-minute cancellation of a trip to Japan, where he was reportedly willing to resolve the longstanding dispute over the Kurile Islands on terms favorable to the Japanese. Most analysts concur that the decline of the liberal nationalist self-image in foreign policy discourse occurred in 1992. Some pinpoint Yeltsin's aborted trip to Japan as the turning point, while others point to the Foreign Policy Concept issued in December 1993. See Arbatov, "Russia's Foreign Policy Alternatives."

97. Russian politics was widely reported as a Manichean struggle between the democrats and patriots, both in Western accounts and in the Russian press. See, for example, Arbatov, "Russia's Foreign Policy Alternatives," Kozhokin, "The Russian Parliament and Foreign Policy," Stankevich, "Derzhava v Poiskakh Sebia," Tolz, "Russia," and Vyzhutovich, "Liberal Jitters."

98. Holden, *Russia,* 173.

99. This statement was reprinted on the inside cover of *International Affairs* (Moscow), no. 11 (1992).

100. For Kozyrev's statement regarding the draft Foreign Policy Concept, see *Rossiiskie vesti,* December 3, 1992, and Holden, *Russia,* 167–68.

101. Arbatov, "Russia's Foreign Policy Alternatives," 24, and more generally his article in Baranovsky, ed., *Russia and Europe.*

102. They included Evgenii Ambartsumov, Sergei Karaganov, and Andranik Migranian. Migranian's rise was a notable symbol of the shift away from liberal internationalism, as he had penned an imperialist, anti-American polemic in September 1992. In it he called for Russia to declare a Monroe Doctrine of its own regarding the CIS and to oppose any military alliances on the territory of the FSU that excluded Russia, either among the CIS states themselves or with external powers. He challenged the legitimacy of the post-Soviet borders and suggested annexing those territories where ethnic Russians or the local population had declared independence (Crimea in Ukraine, Karabakh in Azerbaijan, Transdniestria in Moldova, South Ossetia in Georgia) and said that "under no circumstances

should Russia leave Crimea." See Migranian, "Real and Illusory Guidelines in Foreign Policy." Ambartsumov was another "defector" from the democratic camp. His rhetoric reflects a moderate statist self-image. Unlike Migranian, he called for cooperation with the United States in order for Russia to act as the Eurasian stabilizer on the territory of the USSR. See Eggert, "Rossiia v Roli 'Evraziiskogo Zhandarma'?" Sergei Karaganov came from the generally pro-West Institute of Europe, but his post-Soviet writing suggests a reluctant acceptance of democratically oriented statist developmentalism. He criticized the liberal internationalists on realist grounds, and while he called for greater attention to the CIS, he did not want this focus to exclude relations with the West. See his comments in "Russia's National Interests," 134–36. He is the main link between democratic developmentalists, such as Arbatov and Khakamada, and statist developmentalists like Arkadii Volskii, Viktor Chernomyrdin, and Vladimir Putin. He argued for an "enlightened post-imperial" role in the post-Soviet space and attention to the South and the East in light of the instability there. See Holden, *Russia,* 176. Karaganov has continued to play a prominent role in Russian foreign policy. He founded the Council on Foreign and Defense Policy, a nonpartisan think tank incorporating political and business figures from across the political spectrum, and has managed to carve out a space for moderate discussion of foreign policy. The CDFP's report "A Strategy for Russia" was partially incorporated into the 1993 Foreign Policy Concept. See Crow, "Competing Blueprints."

103. The process of drafting the Foreign Policy Concept also suggests the administration's shifting views. Drafts were privately circulated and critics given the opportunity to provide input. On the politics behind the drafting of the Foreign Policy Concept, see Checkel, "Russian Foreign Policy," Crow, "Competing Blueprints," and Crow, "Russia Debates."

104. Skokov was dismissed in July 1993 after criticizing Yeltsin in a speech to the Supreme Soviet. Oleg Lobov took over the position in September 1993 and continued to represent conservative and great power views. Both Skokov and Lobov were associated with Civic Union, a coalition of centrists representing the industrial lobby, the federal military, and civilian bureaucracies as well as some moderate democrats. Karaganov is credited with laying the intellectual foundation for Civic Union's foreign policy positions. Sergounin, "Post-Communist Security Thinking in Russia," 18.

105. See Arbatov, "Vicissitudes," 80, and Arbatov, "Russian Foreign Policy," 143–44.

106. Holden, *Russia,* Malcolm and Pravda, "Democratization and Russian Foreign Policy," and Prizel, *National Identity.*

107. As one headline put it after the newly appointed foreign minister's first appearance before the State Duma International Affairs Committee: "Deputies

Are Promised a Great Power. Evgenii Primakov Finds Common Diplomatic Language with Duma's International Committee," *Izvestiia,* February 10, 1996, 3.

108. Arbatov, "Russia's Foreign Policy Alternatives," 23, and Pushkov, "Tame Foreign Minister Seeks New Image."

109. Karaganov, "The Problems Facing Primakov."

110. For one of many pronouncements to this effect, see Primakov, "Rossiia Byla i Ostaetsia Velikoi Derzhavoi," 1–2.

111. This observation is based on my discussions with Lilia Shevtsova and Dmitrii Trenin during my work at the Moscow Carnegie Center in the spring of 1998. The dismissal of Chernomyrdin came as a huge surprise to political analysts, but the retention of Primakov did not; indeed, it was welcomed across the board.

112. Primakov, "Rossiia."

113. Official Kremlin International News Broadcast, "Remarks by Foreign Minister Evgenii Primakov at the Duma Committee for International Affairs."

114. For one of many pronouncements to this effect, see Primakov, "Rossiia."

115. As a former Finnish Ambassador to the United Nations noted, "Ironically, Chinese and Russian leaders now present themselves as faithful champions of the UN Charter." See Jakobson, "Is Kosovo a Turning Point for International Relations?"

116. Primakov consistently developed this theme. For an example, see Evgenii Primakov, "Mnogopoliarnii Mir i OON."

117. This observation is based on my discussions with Lilia Shevtsova and Dmitrii Trenin.

118. Cast and Burke, "Theory of Self-Esteem," and Oakes, "Psychological Groups."

119. Arbatov, "Russian Foreign Policy," 144.

120. Primakov, "Mnogopoliarnii Mir."

121. As Igor Chubais, an ardent fan of a "national idea," said at a conference I attended in 1998, "Because we don't have an identity we can't solve any problems properly. We have a multisystemic crisis because we don't know what country we are in." Chubais, "New Russian Identity and the Geopolitics of the Post-Soviet Space."

122. Baranovskii, "Kosovo," 8–9, and Baranovsky and Arbatov, "The Changing Security Perspective in Europe," 47.

123. Kozhokin, "The Russian Parliament and Foreign Policy," 41.

124. See Andrei Mel'vil's contribution to Shevtsova, *Rossiia: Desat' Voprosov o Samom Vazhnom,* 72.

125. Ibid., 74.

126. See the comments of Georgii Arbatov in "Russian Reaction to NATO's Summit in Prague."

127. Danilov, "Russia and European Security," 82, and Karaganov, "Russia and the International Order," 41–43.

128. Kortunov, "Rossiia: Ne Serdit'sia, a Sosredotochit'sia."

129. Federal News Service, "Press Conference with State Duma Vice Chairman Aleksei Arbatov on Vladimir Putin's Foreign Policy." See Lukin's criticism of Putin's foreign policy as too focused on Asia in "Putin Pays Yeltsin's Debts," *Segodnia,* December 28, 2000. See also Sergei Karaganov's interview in Tarasov, "Lovushki Globalizatsii."

130. Trenin, "Rossiia i Amerika."

131. Ibid.

132. "Sergei Karaganov Divides the World into Three Parts," strana.ru, February 6, 2001.

133. "Russian Political Elite Analysing Russia's Place in Today's World," *Izvestiia,* February 6, 2001.

134. Forty-four percent disagreed, viewing economic potential and international influence as related. Not surprisingly, 61 percent of those who observed a link between economic potential and international influence believed that Russia should follow the path of the West. Schulze, ed., *Außen- und Sicherheitspolitik,* 25–26.

135. Some recognized these contradictions in the new foreign policy concept. See Stepanov and Iusin, "Pragmatizm v Monopolarnom Mire."

136. Trenin, "Reading Russia Right."

137. Trenin, "What You See Is What You Get," and Trenin and Lo, *Landscape,* 18.

138. Tsygankov, "Vladimir Putin's Vision of Russia as a Normal Great Power," 134.

139. Woodruff, "Pension Reform in Russia," Woodruff, "The End of 'Primitive Capitalist Accumulation'?" and Tompson, "The Russian Economy under Vladimir Putin."

140. Hesli, *Governments and Politics in Russia,* 239.

141. Balzer, "The Putin Thesis and Russian Energy Policy."

142. Tsygankov, "Vladimir Putin's Vision," 140–41, and Trenin, "Traditionalism Makes a Comeback."

143. Ambrosio, "The Russo-American Dispute over the Invasion of Iraq," and Katz, "Playing the Angles."

144. Karaganov, "Russia," 30.

145. Channel One, "Russian Foreign Minister Participates in TV Review of Foreign Relations in 2002."

146. O'Loughlin, Ó Tuathail, and Kolossov, "A 'Risky Westward Turn'?"

147. Trenin, "Reading Russia."

148. Trenin, "Traditionalism," and Ryzhkov, "More of the Andropov Approach, Less Security." For the realist analysis that the 2003 U.S. war against Iraq was the most serious crisis in U.S.-Russian relations, see Ambrosio, "Russo-American Dispute."

149. Trenin, "Reading Russia," 5.

150. Yasmann, "Analysis: The Kremlin after Beslan," Coalson, "Analysis: Running against Washington," and Yasmann, "Moscow Looks at the World."

151. BBC News, "State Forces Blamed over Beslan," available at http://news.bbc.co.uk/go/pr/fr/-/1/hi/world/europe/4481800.stm, accessed August 27, 2008, and "Putin Meets Angry Beslan Mothers," available at http://news.bbc.co.uk/go/pr/fr/-/1/hi/world/europe/4207112.stm, accessed August 27, 2008.

152. Ryzhkov, "More of the Andropov Approach."

153. Trenin, "Reading Russia," 1.

154. Yasmann, "Analysis," and Socor, "Kremlin Redefining Policy in 'Post-Soviet Space.'"

155. McFaul, "Putin's Risky Westward Turn," and Trenin, "'Novyi Kurs' Putina." See also Anatolii Chubais, quoted in Treisman, "What Is Different About Putin's Russia?" 67, and Lapidus, "Putin's War."

156. Putin, "Annual Address to the Federal Assembly," 2005.

157. Official Kremlin International News Broadcast, "Press Conference with Foreign Minister Igor Ivanov."

158. "Novaia vneshniaia politika Moskva," strana.ru, November 14, 2000, as well as the press conference with State Duma Committee for Defense Vice Chairman Aleksei Arbatov on Vladimir Putin's Foreign Policy, Press Development Institute, March 5, 2001, available at www.fednews.ru.

159. In introducing the new foreign policy doctrine in July 2000, Foreign Minister Igor Ivanov made a point of stating that even though the term *great power* had not been mentioned in his introductory remarks, "it does not mean that we have given up this concept." Official Kremlin International News Broadcast, "Press Conference with Foreign Minister Igor Ivanov," and Interfax, July 10, 2000.

160. Gorshkov, *Vneshniaia Politika Rossii: Mneniia Ekspertov,* tables 4 and 5.

161. Ibid.

162. Respondents were allowed to choose multiple responses. Fifty percent chose the new style of Russian diplomacy (the answer most often chosen), and 48 percent chose better use of Russian oil and gas resources. Schulze, ed., *Außen- und Sicherheitspolitik*, 27.

163. Ibid., 26.

164. The early signs of this shift were visible in the reasoning of foreign policy experts such as Vladimir Lukin, Sergei Karaganov, Aleksei Arbatov, and Dmitrii Trenin, all of whom are moderate or centrist democrats.

165. Gorshkov, *Vneshniaia Politika Rossii,* table 6. The data presented in tables 5.1 and 5.2 of this book are all commensurable, as Gorshkov's report relied on data commissioned from VTsIOM; Gorshkov's full report was not published in Russian but was translated and published in German by Peter Schulze of the Friedrich Ebert Stiftung. Both these works incorporate surveys done in 1993 and 1996 by VTsIOM; the 1993 surveys were published separately as VTsIOM, *Vneshniaia Politika Rossii,* and VTsIOM, "Vneshnopoliticheskaia Elita."

166. Putin, "Russia at the Turn of the Millennium."

167. Figures are from Schulze, ed., *Außen- und Sicherheitspolitik,* 26–27.

168. For an example of such thinking, see Leontyev, "Restoring Russia's Future."

169. Tajfel, *Differentiation,* Tajfel and Turner, "Social Identity Theory," Turner, "Social Comparison and Social Identity," Blanz et al., "Responding to Negative Social Identity," and Amelie Mummendey et al., "Strategies to Cope with Negative Social Identity."

170. Karaganov, "Russia," 33, and Trenin, "Russia and Anti-Terrorism."

171. Trenin, "Traditionalism," Mikhailenko, "Russia in the New World Order," Ryzhkov, "More of the Andropov Approach," and Karaganov, "New Contours of the World Order."

172. Ivanenko, "The Importance of Being Normal."

173. Arbatov, "National Idea." He attempts to debunk the mysticism surrounding much of the discourse on the "Russian idea" and Russia's historical mission. The debate on the national idea was quite prominent and demonstrated no consensus. In 1996 Andrei Kortunov and Andrei Volodin argued that this lack of consensus on a "national idea" interfered with "the country's ability to influence the course of international events." Kortunov and Volodin, *Contemporary Russia.* Examples of the lack of consensus on Russia's national idea abound, including Sergei Kortunov's outline of the global spiritual-cultural mission of the Russian people, Roy Medvedev's call for democratic socialism, Igor Chubais's appeal for anti-Soviet liberal state-building, Aleksei Podberezkin's advocacy of an pan-Slavic and autarkic "state-patriotism," Aleksei Mitrofanov's demand for anti-American and Eurasian "national egoism," and Natalia Narochnitskaia's design for a national mission of pan-Orthodox leadership. Georgii Mirskii rejected the entire notion of a "national idea" as a cover for imperialist great power chauvinism and called for Western democratic state. Sergei Kortunov, *Russia's National*

Identity in a New Era, 5, and Kortunov, "Russia's Way"; Roy Medvedev, "Russia Again at the Crossroads"; Igor Chubais, *Ot Russkoi Idei—K Idee Novoi Rossii*; Georgii I. Mirskii, " 'Obshchnost' Sud'by' i Natsional'noe Samosoznanie"; Aleksei Podberezkin, *Russia's New Path*; Aleksei Mitrofanov, *Russia's New Geopolitics*; and Natalia Narochnitskaia, "Russia and the Worldwide Eastern Question." For other discussions on the "national idea" see, among others, "Russkaia Ideia: Mify i Real'nost'," and Solov'ev, "Integrativnaia Ideologiia."

174. Author interview with Leonid Smirniagin, June 4, 1998. For the findings of the Presidential Commission, see Satarov, ed., *Rossiia v Poiskakh Idei.*

175. Gorshkov, *Vneshniaia Politika Rossii,* Schulze, ed., *Außen- und Sicherheitspolitik,* VTsIOM, *Vneshniaia Politika Rossii,* VTsIOM, "Analiz Rezultatov Oprosov," VTsIOM, "Vneshnopoliticheskaia Elita," Zimmerman, "Survey Research and Russian Perspectives on NATO Expansion," Zimmerman, "Slavophiles and Westernizers Redux," Zimmerman, *The Russian People and Foreign Policy,* and Lukin, "Russia between East and West."

Chapter 6: The Post-Soviet Creation of Russia's Security Interests in Europe

1. Medvedev, "Rossiia v Kontse Epokhi Moderna."

2. Wendt, "Collective Identity Formation."

3. Snyder, *Myths of Empire,* 219.

4. Jervis and Bialer, *Soviet-American Relations,* Jervis and Snyder, *Dominoes and Bandwagons,* Mearsheimer, "Back to the Future," and Mearsheimer, "The Case for a Ukrainian Nuclear Deterrent."

5. Walt, "Alliance Formation."

6. Mandelbaum, "Preserving the New Peace."

7. Kullberg, *End of New Thinking,* 21.

8. Vox Populi, "USIA Survey no. I93060: NATO."

9. ROMIR, *Chto Ugrozhaet Bezopastnosti Rossii?* and Zimmerman, "Survey Research," table 1.

10. Citations of the various doctrines and concepts are taken from Bakshi, "Russia's National Security Concepts and Military Doctrines." For the full text of the 1993 doctrine, see "Osnovnye Polozheniia Voennoi Doktriny Rossiiskoi Federatsii." See also "National Security Concept of the Russian Federation."

11. VTsIOM, *Vneshniaia Politika Rossii,* 43.

12. VTsIOM, "Vneshnopoliticheskaia Elita," 33.

13. The portion believing that a return to the Cold War to be unlikely or completely impossible was 68 percent in 1993 and 54 percent in 2001. Schulze, ed., *Außen- und Sicherheitspolitik,* table 9.

14. Ibid., 13–14.

15. Zimmerman, "Slavophiles and Westernizers Redux," 198–202, 207. The portion advocating a "special Russian path" who saw NATO as a threat dropped by almost half to 47 percent in 2004.

16. Dobson, "Is Russia Turning the Corner?" 70, table 41.

17. Ibid., 23.

18. Schulze, ed., *Außen- und Sicherheitspolitik,* 30.

19. Results of a ROMIR survey of regional elites in September 1999. Cited in Zimmerman, *Russian People,* 207–8.

20. Ibid., 219.

21. All data from SIPRI, *Military Expenditure Database;* the Bonn International Center for Conversion (BICC) provides the data on total armed forces personnel numbers; SIPRI provides the data on CFE ceilings and holdings and military expenditures.

22. Such behavior prompted realists to invent a new category of behavior, "soft balancing," to account for the failure of states to fulfill expectations regarding internal and external "hard" balancing. See Paul, "Soft Balancing."

23. See Sergei Rogov's and Dmitri Riurikov's comments in RIA Novosti, "NATO Enlargement and Russia's National Security." See also Legvold, Kaiser, and Arbatov, "Introduction."

24. Karpov, "Smolensk-Sennaia Square Catches Hell Again." For a representative statement about the lack of a threat from the West, see Lukin and Utkin, *Rossiia i Zapad,* 47.

25. Zimmerman, "Slavophiles and Westernizers," 207–8.

26. Medvedev, "Rossiia."

27. Statists such as Sergei Karaganov have argued that Russia must follow Gorchakov's example and compensate for its internal weakness through an active foreign policy in order to preserve her international status. Karaganov, "The Problems Facing Primakov."

28. See for example *Mezhdunarodnaia Zhizn',* no. 5 (1998), devoted to Gorchakov, and articles by Minister of Foreign Affairs Igor Ivanov, St. Petersburg mayor Yakovlev, and diplomat Petr Stegnii in *Mezhdunarodnaia Zhizn',* nos. 11–12 (1998), honoring Gorchakov's 200th jubilee. For discussion of Gorchakov, see Fuller, *Strategy and Power in Russia, 1600–1914,* 267–70.

29. Arbatov, "Russian Foreign Policy Priorities," 13.

30. Arbatov, "Russian Foreign Policy Priorities for the 1990s," 24, Davydov, "Russian Security and East-Central Europe," 279, Zagorskii, "Russia and Europe," 43, and Ignatow, Das Russische Europa-Bild Heute, 30. For a Westernizer critique of this view, see Yazkova, "Where Will the New 'Security Line' in Europe Run?"

31. Chasnikov, "Sifting through the Relics of Confrontation."

32. Shevtsova, *Rossiia,* 71.

33. Medvedev, "Rossiia."

34. Kozhokin, " Russian Parliament and Foreign Policy." For more on this, see chapter 5.

35. Zimmerman, "Survey Research," and Zimmerman, "Slavophiles and Westernizers."

36. Larson and Shevchenko, "Shortcut to Greatness."

37. VTsIOM, "Analiz Rezultatov Oprosov," 14.

38. Baranovsky and Arbatov, "The Changing Security Perspective in Europe," 52.

39. The only exceptions were national restorationists, who argued against any cooperation with the United States. However, in 1992, their influence was still marginal.

40. Kozhokin, "The Russian Parliament and Foreign Policy." For more on this, see "A Transformed Russia in a New World," and chapter 5.

41. Arbatov, "Russia's Foreign Policy Alternatives," 32.

42. Kozhokin, "The Russian Parliament and Foreign Policy."

43. Arbatov, "Russia's Foreign Policy Alternatives," 32.

44. Pushkov, "Russia Confirms Great Power Status."

45. Baranovskii, "Kosovo: Russia's Interests," 9.

46. Yazkova, "Where Will the New 'Security Line' in Europe Run?" and Kobrinskaia, "Rossiia—Tsentral'naia Evropa—NATO," 9–10.

47. Baranovsky, "Russia's View," 10.

48. Danilov, "Russia and European Security," 82.

49. Baranovsky, "Russia's View," 10.

50. Ibid.

51. Spinner-Halev and Theiss-Morse, "National Identity."

52. Kortunov, "Russia–United States."

53. Primakov, "Rossiia."

54. Baranovsky, "Russia's View," 11.

55. Chasnikov, "Sifting through the Relics of Confrontation."

56. Zagorski, "Russia and European Institutions."

57. Ivanov, "As NATO Grows, So Do Russia's Worries."

58. Danilov, "Russia and European Security," 79.

59. Gorshkov, *Vneshniaia Politika Rossii,* pt. 3.

60. Baranovskii, "Kosovo: Russia's Interests," 9, and Baranovsky and Arbatov, "Changing Security," 60.

61. Baranovsky and Arbatov, "Changing Security," 54–55. Viktor Kuvaldin of the Gorbachev Foundation (one of Russia's few social democrats) and Iurii Fedorov of MGIMO both argue this line in Shevtsova, *Rossiia,* 71, 75.

62. Rogov, "Soglasovannyi Primakovym i Solanoi Dokument Po-Raznomu Traktuiut v Moskve i Vashingtone."

63. Baranovsky and Arbatov, "Changing Security," 55. See also Arbatov, "The National Idea," Trenin, "Rossiia i Novaia Evropeiskaia Sistema," and Trenin, "Rossiia i Amerika."

64. This slogan even made it onto the cover of the MFA's journal, *International Affairs,* in January 1993: "Russia has entered the Year 1993 to be a Renewed Great Power." For more such claims, see Dmitri Riurikov's comments in "NATO Enlargement and Russia's National Security," Russian Executive and Legislative Newsletter, February 24, 1997, RIA Novosti. accessible at www.ria.ru. See also Kozhokin, "The Russian Parliament and Foreign Policy," Primakov, "Rossiia," and Official Kremlin International News Broadcast, "Remarks by Foreign Minister Evgenii Primakov at the Duma Committee for International Affairs."

65. See for example, Kuzar, "NATO an Instrument of Global U.S. Strategy," Pushkov, "Novyi Evropeiskii Poriadok," and Rogov, "Soglasovannyi Primakovym i Solanoi."

66. Primakov, "Rossiia," and Primakov, "Mnogopoliarnii Mir."

67. Arbatov, "S Tochki Zreniia Parlamentariia."

68. Baranovsky and Arbatov, "Changing Security," 55.

69. Yabloko in 1995 called for basing relations with the West and Asia on Russia's real interests, rather than in reaction to NATO. Solodovnik, "Yabloko Favors Pragmatism in Foreign Policy." See also Zagorskii, "Rossiia i Evropa," and Zagorskii, "Rossiia i Rasshirenie NATO—Endshpil'."

70. Schulze, ed., *Außen- und Sicherheitspolitik,* 31.

71. Gennadii Seleznev's comments in Official Kremlin International News Broadcast, "Main Speeches at the International Conference 'New Security.'" For another example, see Pankov, "Europe Is Closer to Russia."

72. Pushkov, "Novyi Evropeiskii Poriadok."

73. Brewer, "Psychology of Prejudice," and Spinner-Halev and Theiss-Morse, "National Identity."

74. For a classic statement of Russia being both Western and different, see Putin, "Russia at the Turn."

75. Lukin and Utkin, *Rossiia i Zapad,* 25, 123.

76. Fuller, *Strategy and Power in Russia, 1600–1914,* 267–70.

77. Ibid.

78. Zimmerman, "Slavophiles and Westernizers," 198, and Schulze, ed., *Außen- und Sicherheitspolitik,* 26.

79. Gorshkov, *Vneshniaia politika Rossii,* table 2.

80. Zimmerman, *Russian People,* 149–86, and Zimmerman, "Slavophiles and Westernizers."

81. National restorationists rely on theoretical arguments such as Elgiz Pozdniakov's and Natalia Narochnitskaia's arch-geopolitical Eurasianism as the basis for a national interest driven by anti-Americanism. For their theoretical explications of structurally determined conflict between the "Atlantic" rimland and the "Eurasian" heartland, see Narochnitskaia's comments in "Rossiia Predopredeleno Igrat' v Mire Vazhnuiu i Samostoiatel'nuiu Rol'," and Narochnitskaia, "Russia's National Interests." Pozniakov's views can be found in his articles "We Must Rebuild What We Have Destroyed with Our Own Hands," "The Geopolitical Collapse and Russia," "Russia Is a Great Power," and "Russia Today and Tomorrow."

82. See "What Foreign Policy Should Russia Pursue," 9.

83. *Izvestiia,* April 21, 1993.

84. Council on Foreign and Defense Policy, "Russia and NATO," 1.

85. For both Yastrzhembskii's and Migranian's comments, see Official Kremlin International News Broadcast, "Round-Table Regarding Russia/NATO Founding Act." For Seleznev's comments, see Official Kremlin International News Broadcast, "Main Speeches."

86. Putin, "Russia at the Turn."

87. Alekseev, "The North Atlantic Cooperation Council and the Future of Europe," Alekseev, "The New Dimension of NATO," Kozin, "New Dimensions of NATO," and Putin, "Annual Address to the Federal Assembly," 2002.

88. Primakov, "Rossiia." See also Andranik Migranian's comments in Official Kremlin International News Broadcast, "Round-Table," and Gennadii Seleznev's comments in Official Kremlin International News Broadcast, "Main Speeches."

89. Gorshkov, *Vneshniaia Politika Rossii,* table 6.

90. Schulze, ed., *Außen- und Sicherheitspolitik,* 16–19.

91. See, among others, Narochnitskaia, "Russia and the Worldwide Eastern Question," and Pozdniakov, "Russia Is a Great Power."

92. Medvedev, "Rossiia," 46.

93. Examples include Kuzar, "NATO an Instrument of Global U.S. Strategy," Pushkov, "Novyi Evropeiskii Poriadok," and Rogov, "Soglasovannyi Primakovym i Solanoi."

94. Rogov, "Rossiia i NATO."

95. Ignatow, *Das Russische Europa-Bild,* 29.

96. Rogov, "Rossiia i NATO."

97. Council on Foreign and Defense Policy, "Russia and NATO," 2.

98. Baranovsky and Arbatov, "Changing Security," and Baranovskii, "Kosovo. Rossiiskie Interesy Slishkom Znachitel'ny."

99. Forty-nine percent of traditionalists vs. 35 percent of Westernizers ac-

cepted this interpretation of Kosovo. Schulze, ed., *Außen- und Sicherheitspolitik,* 24.

100. Trenin, "Russia's French Accent."

101. Jakobson, "Russia Heads Off toward a Solution of Its Own."

102. Karaganov, "Russia and the International Order," 33.

103. Kazantsev, "Obvious Bias to the Use of Force," 1–2. Kazantsev at the time of writing was Deputy Director of the Foreign Ministry's Department of European Cooperation.

104. Ibid., 4.

105. Lynch, ed., *Russia Faces Europe.*

106. Putin, "Russia at the Turn."

107. Danilov, "Russia and European Security," 82–83.

108. "Russian Foreign Minister Participates in TV Review of Foreign Relations in 2002," *BBC Monitoring,* December 22, 2002, and Danilov, "Russia and European Security," 79–86.

109. Gorshkov, *Vneshniaia politika Rossii,* tables 4 and 5.

110. Trenin and Lo, *Landscape,* 18. For Putin's views, see Putin, "Russia at the Turn," and Putin, "Annual Address," 2002.

111. Gorshkov, "What Russians Say About the Results of 2000 and Their Hopes for 2001."

112. Putin, "Russia at the Turn," and Putin, "Annual Address," 2002 and 2004.

113. Danilov, "Russia and European Security," 80–86.

114. Cited in Lynch, ed., *Russia Faces Europe,* 34.

115. Danilov, "Russia and European Security," 79–80.

116. Lynch, ed., *Russia Faces Europe,* 35.

117. Putin, "Annual Address," 2002 and 2005, and Tsygankov, "Vladimir Putin's Vision."

118. Rose, Munro, and Mishle, "Resigned Acceptance of an Incomplete Democracy."

119. Bassin, "Turner, Solov'ev, and the 'Frontier Hypothesis.'"

120. Cited in Yasmann, "Kremlin Articulates Its Ideological Platform."

121. Cited in Socor, "Kremlin Redefining Policy."

122. Golan, "Russia and the Iraq War," 438–50, and Kortunov, "Rossiia: Ne Serdit'sia."

123. Ryzhkov, "Real'nosti Chetvertoi Rossiikoi Respubliki," 12.

124. Schulze, ed., *Außen- und Sicherheitspolitik,* 17.

125. Ibid., 5, 26.

126. Trenin, "Rossiia," 119, and Arbatov, "Tochki Zreniia."

127. Lukin and Utkin, *Rossiia i Zapad,* 25, 123.

128. See Lukin's comments in "Five Questions Put to Well-Known Persons."

129. See Karaganov's interview in *Segodnia,* April 6, 2001.

130. Ryzhkov, "Real'nosti," 12, and Baranovskii, "Kosovo: Russia's Interests," 9.

131. Arbatov, "Tochki Zreniia."

132. "Russian TV Studio Discussion Divided on NATO," *Foreign Broadcast Information Service,* April 3, 2003.

133. Gornostaev, "Russian Foreign Minister Formulates Russia's New Strategic Objectives in International Arena."

134. Bovt, "Naked Politics."

135. Tsygankov, "Vladimir Putin's Vision."

136. Trenin, "Rossiia," 109.

137. Ibid.

138. Schulze, ed., *Außen- und Sicherheitspolitik,* 24, and Zimmerman, "Slavophiles and Westernizers," 198.

139. Sergei Rogov makes this point very clearly in his defense of Russia's concluding the NATO-Russia Founding Act in 1997. Rogov, "Soglasovannyi Primakovym i Solanoi."

140. For an example of the latter, see ibid. For official views, see Primakov's account given to the Duma, reported by Interfax, May 23, 1997, and to the public on Russian Television May, 24, 1997, BBC World Monitoring; Official Kremlin International News Broadcast, "Interview Granted by Sergei Prikhodko, Assistant to the RF President for International Affairs," Official Kremlin International News Broadcast, "Round-Table," and Afanasievskii, "Osnovopolagaiushchii Akt Rossiia-NATO."

141. Zagorski, "Russia and the Shared Neighbourhood," 68–69.

Chapter 7: The Post-Soviet Creation of Russia's Interests in Nuclear Arms Control

1. Relatively little attention has been devoted to the symbolic importance of nuclear weapons to national identity. For early accounts that begin to grapple with this question, see Jervis, *The Meaning of the Nuclear Revolution,* ch. 6, and Sagan, "Why Do States Build Nuclear Weapons?" 64–67.

2. Bunce, "Domestic Reform and International Change," and Larson and Shevchenko, "Shortcut to Greatness," 94–95.

3. Dhanapala, *Prospects for Arms Control and Disarmament.*

4. Shevtsova, *Rossiia,* 77.

5. Trenin, "Russia's Nuclear Policy in the 21st Century Environment," 5.

6. See Akhtamzyan, *Opinion Poll: "Attitudes in the Russian Federation To-*

wards WMD Proliferation and Terrorism," 12–16. In 2006, 76 percent of Russians believed that Russia needs nuclear weapons, primarily because they provide Russia with more "clout" and deterrence (37–40%), as opposed to concrete military advantages (19%). The report covers the results of two surveys of the mass public conducted in 2000 and 2006 by VTsIOM for the PIR Center. The report found that those inclined to see nuclear weapons as important for Russian security and to favor increasing its arsenal as a rule were more educated and prosperous and more likely to live in Moscow or St. Petersburg. This group was also the least inclined to view the United States as a threat.

7. Maslin and Safranchuk, "Nuclear Deadlock."

8. See the Arms Control Association's Fact Sheets on Strategic Arms Control, available at www.armscontrol.org/factsheets, accessed September 18, 2008.

9. The texts of the START treaties and related documents are available at the U.S. Department of State's website, www.state.gov/www/global/arms/bureau_ac/treaties_ac.html, accessed August 27, 2008.

10. Pikayev, "The Rise and Fall of START II." Aleksandr Pikayev was formerly Yabloko's chief counselor to the Duma's Defense Committee and its Subcommittee on Arms Control and International Security. He provides an authoritative insider's description of the internal debate on START II from 1993 to 1999.

11. Ibid.

12. See Ovcharenko, "A Russian Naval Perspective." Ovrachenko acknowledges that while the Navy approves of the new force posture, the other military branches do not. This was confirmed by Col. Petr Romashkin, an advisor to Aleksei Arbatov, then deputy chairman of the Duma Defense Committee. He argued against mimicking the U.S. sea-based force posture, arguing instead that the most stable force posture would be 1,000 silo-based single-warhead ICBMs on both sides—indicating both the desire for precise parity and land-based systems, the area of Russia's traditional strength. Romashkin, "Objectives of Future Reductions."

13. See section on First Agreed Statement of Demarcation, The Arms Control Association, "The START/ABM Package at a Glance," available at www.armscontrol.org/factsheets/pack, accessed September 18, 2008.

14. "Russian START II Vote Nears."

15. See Pikayev, "Rise and Fall," 27. U.S. opponents objected to the Memorandum of Understanding on Succession to the ABM because, as one argument went, the ABM Treaty ceased to be in force as soon as the Soviet Union ceased to exist. See Senator Trent Lott et al., letter to the President, September 25, 1998, cited in Rivkin and Casey, "Six Reasons Why Arms Control Advocates Are Wrong."

16. See "START II Resolution on Ratification."

17. Woolf, "Nuclear Arms Control," 4.

18. For the U.S. Senate's conditions, see Nuclear Threat Initiative, "5/14/2003: Duma Ratifies Moscow Treaty after Delays." The text of the Moscow Treaty is available at www.armscontrol.org/documents/sort.asp, accessed August 27, 2008.

19. Sokov, "The Duma Ratifies the Moscow Treaty."

20. Trenin, "Russia's Nuclear Policy," 19.

21. See Podvig, "A History of the ABM Treaty in Russia."

22. Trenin, "Russia's Nuclear Policy," 19.

23. Trenin, *Russia's Security Relations with the West after Kosovo and Chechnya,* 26–28. This is true of those in the parliament as well as those in the administration. Pikayev says Yeltsin did not submit START II to the new Duma in 1993 because Yeltsin was piqued about NATO enlargement. Pikayev, "Rise and Fall."

24. Pikayev, "Rise and Fall," 35.

25. Ibid., 7, 15.

26. Ovcharenko, "A Russian Naval Perspective."

27. See Pikayev, "Rise and Fall."

28. See Woolf, "Nuclear Arms Control."

29. Petrovskaia, "Ivanov Perestal Byt Pokladistym," and "Vladimir Putin: RF Zainteresovana v Ratifikatsii Dogovora o Sokrashchenii SNP."

30. Podvig, "Who Is In Charge?"

31. For Soviet acknowledgment of these divisions, see Nazarkin, "A Treaty the World Needs." Nazarkin headed the Soviet delegation on nuclear and space-based armaments from 1989 to 1991. For the Russian Foreign Ministry's early response on START II to critics, see Sokolov and Kliukin, "Starting Off for a Secure Future."

32. VTsIOM, *Vneshniaia Politika Rossii,* 25–26.

33. Trofimenko, "What Military Doctrine Do We Need?" 77. Trofimenko argued that the Soviet Union had built its navy purely for prestige reasons. See also Kozyrev, "Washington Summit," 4.

34. Pikayev, "Rise and Fall," 7. Kozyrev especially saw U.S.-Russian relations in this light. See Kozyrev, "Washington Summit," 1, 7–8.

35. Sergei Kortunov, "Toward a New Pattern of Strategic Relationship," 4, 22. Kortunov later was an advisor to the Russian Federation Security Council.

36. A report was prepared by Aleksei Arbatov and other arms control experts for the Foreign Policy Association (headed by former Soviet Foreign Minister Aleksandr Bessmertnykh). See Arbatov et al., "Expert Appraisal."

37. See for example, Pavel Felgengauer, *Segodnia,* November 18, 1995, 2, and Arbatov, "Eurasia Letter."

38. VTsIOM, *Vneshniaia Politika Rossii,* 25–26.

39. *Pravda,* May 26, 1993, 3.

40. Nadein, "Our Speaker Finally Puts American Congress in Its Place."

41. *Den,* January 1–9, 1993, 1.

42. For a characteristic expression of this view, see member of the Duma General Albert Makashov's comments in " 'Za' i 'Protiv' Razoruzheniia. Kto Seichas Ugrozhaet Rossii." His views are contrasted with those of Duma member General Eduard Borob"ev, who favored leapfrogging START II to negotiate START III rather than ratifying with conditions.

43. Arbatov, "Parliament and Politics in Russia."

44. Two prominent and moderate members of the KPRF, Iurii Masliukov and Gennadii Seleznev, did not take part in the vote. Masliukov had earlier come out in favor of ratification. See ibid., 24. For a discussion of who voted for and against ratification, see Reuters, "Breakdown of Voting in Russia Duma on START-2."

45. See for example, Belous, "Price of Security."

46. Grigoriev, "START II Has No Analogues."

47. *Segodnia,* November 18, 1995, 2.

48. Kondrashov, "Tough Choice of the Times."

49. Trenin, "Russia's Nuclear Policy."

50. Goettemoeller, "Nuclear Necessity in Putin's Russia."

51. Pikayev, "Rise and Fall," 9. For examples of such arguments, see Belous, "Price of Security," and Grigoriev, "START II."

52. See the views of START I negotiator Aleksandr Savelev in Guk, "It Wouldn't Be Out of Place to Estimate the Expense," and Arbatov, "Expert Appraisal."

53. Pikayev, "Rise and Fall," 10.

54. Koretskii, "START II Hearings." Koretskii reported that "it can be already be said with confidence that the treaty, despite the pessimistic predictions of its opponents, will be ratified by the current State Duma without any particular problems." See also Pikayev, "Rise and Fall," and Gornostaev, "Security."

55. Pikayev, "Rise and Fall," 16.

56. Ibid., 17.

57. Ibid.

58. Ibid., 18.

59. See Abaftnov, "Russian Ratification of START II Is Problematic."

60. Velekhov, "Russian Defense Minister Promises 'Appropriate Measures' in Response to NATO Expansion," and Clayton, "Rodionov."

61. For the 1993 data, see VTsIOM, *Vneshniaia Politika Rossii,* 25–26. For the 1996 data, see Dobson, "Is Russia Turning," 19.

62. Pikayev, "Rise and Fall," 17. See also "'Za' i 'Protiv' Razoruzheniia. Kto Seichas Ugrozhaet Rossii," and Ziuganov, "What to Expect from the Moscow Meeting of the Group of Seven Countries."

63. Ziuganov, "What to Expect," 3.

64. Larrabee and Karasik, *Foreign and Security Policy*, 25.

65. George Breslauer, personal communication, July 21, 2001. On the 2000 Doctrine, see Sokov, "An Assessment of the Draft Russian Military Doctrine," and Sokov, "Russia's New National Security Concept."

66. Author interview with Pavel Podvig, March 9, 2005. For examples of this lack of elite consensus, see Iurii Nazarkin (who helped negotiate START II) and Vitalii Tsygichko (who helped model strategic policy for the Soviet government and served as an advisor to the Federation Council International Affairs Committee), "ABM Treaty Isn't Holy Writ—Russia Cannot Afford Confrontation With the West," *Segodnia*, November 18, 1999 versus the views of Krylov in "Dead-End Branch." For a helpful overview of Russia's post-Soviet national security and military doctrines, see Bakshi, "Russia's National Security Concepts."

67. Trenin, "Russia's Nuclear Policy."

68. Kokoshin, "What Is Russia."

69. VTsIOM, "Vneshnopoliticheskaia Elita," 33.

70. VTsIOM, *Vneshniaia Politika Rossii*, 25.

71. Dobson, "Is Russia Turning," 19.

72. ROMIR, "Tseli Vneshnei Politiki Rossii."

73. Arbatov, "Eurasia Letter," 109.

74. Pikayev, "Rise and Fall," 9.

75. Arbatov, "Eurasia Letter," 110.

76. Pikayev, "Rise and Fall," 35, as well as author interview with Pavel Podvig. See also Arbatov, "Russian Military Doctrine and Strategic Nuclear Forces to the Year 2000 and Beyond," and Goettemoeller, "Nuclear Weapons in Current Russian Policy."

77. Comments at Carnegie Endowment for International Peace Roundtable on START II and Russian National Security, May 19 1998, attended by the author.

78. As noted earlier, parity has been championed by more conservative Soviet leaders. National restorationists and military hardliners harshly criticized Gorbachev for his promotion of minimal deterrence.

79. "'Za' I 'Protiv' Razoruzheniia. Kto Seichas Ugrozhaet Rossii." See also Krylov, "Dead-End Branch."

80. Arbatov, "The Next Steps in Arms Control."

81. Ibid. For the public portion of Putin's speech to the Duma, see the transcript printed in *Kommersant-Daily*, April 15, 2000, 2.

82. Nazarkin, "A Treaty the World Needs," 26. For an in-depth study of mis-

sile defenses in Russian-U.S. relations, see Podvig, "Protivoraketnaia Oborona kak Faktor Strategicheskikh Vsaimootnoshenii SSSR/Rossii i SShA v 1945–2003 gg."

83. Podvig, "History of ABM."

84. Federiakov, "Strategic Defence and Political Realities," 31.

85. Gaidukov, "The Concepts of Strategy and Military Doctrine in a Changing World," 67–68.

86. Podvig, "History of ABM."

87. Ibid.

88. Prikhodko, "Global Protection System," 85–87.

89. Podvig, "History of ABM."

90. Ibid.

91. Podvig, "Putin's Boost Phase Defense."

92. Ibid.

93. Pavel Felgengauer, "Kremlin Delivers Another Rebuff to Imperialists."

94. Piontkovskii and Tsygichko, "Tango c Rossiei." Piontkovskii was the director to the Center for Strategic Research in the post-Soviet period.

95. See the comments of General Piskunov, a member of the Duma, in Odnokolenko, "To Forget and Give In." See also the interview with Sergei Karaganov in Tarasov, "Lovushki Globalizatsii."

96. Golts, "Let U.S. Have Its NMD."

97. Schulze, ed., *Außen- und Sicherheitspolitik*, 21.

98. Felgengauer, "Kremlin."

99. Rogov, "Ne Stoit Vpadat' v Isteriku."

100. Felgengauer, "Kremlin."

101. Urusov, "How Does the American Missile Shield Threaten Russia?"

102. "Russian Communists Urge Government to Adopt National Security Program," ITAR-TASS, May 3, 2001.

103. Litovkin, "Playing the 'Security Door.'"

104. Patrick Lannin, "Russian Reaction Mixed after Bush's Missile Speech," *Reuters*, May 2, 2001. Lannin notes that other "military-diplomatic sources" were much more cautious and optimistic in their interpretation of Bush's national missile defense speech.

105. Podvig, "Russian Strategic Forces in the Next Decade," and Goettemoeller, "Nuclear Weapons," 189.

106. See the views of Vladimir Belous, director of the Center for Strategic Studies, in Odnokolenko, "Star Wars."

107. Shaburkin, "Russian Generals Testing Europeans' Nerves."

108. Kuchins, "Explaining Mr. Putin."

109. Sokov, "The Fate of Russian Nuclear Weapons."

110. Ibid.

111. Trenin, "Russia's Nuclear Policy," 9–10.

112. Arbatov and Dvorkin, *Iadernoe Sderzhivanie i Nerasprostranenie,* 24–32, 56–62, and Trenin, "Russia's Nuclear Policy."

113. Main, "Russia's Military Doctrine." English text of the 2000 Military Doctrine available at armscontrol.org/act/2000_05/dc3ma00, accessed September 19, 2008.

114. Goettemoeller, "Nuclear Weapons," 187, and Sokov, " 'Kosovo Syndrome' and the Great Nuclear Debate of 2000."

115. Goettemoeller, "Nuclear Weapons," 187–89, and author interview with Pavel Podvig.

116. Goettemoeller, "Nuclear Weapons," 190, Sokov, "Fate," and Sokov, " 'Denuclearization' of Russia's Defense Policy?"

117. Galeotti, "Russia's Emerging Security Doctrine."

118. Goettemoeller, "Nuclear Weapons," 189.

119. Podvig, "Russian Strategic Forces."

120. Trenin, "Russia's Nuclear Policy," and Kokoshin, "What Is Russia."

121. Trenin, "Russia's Nuclear Policy," 9–10.

122. Podvig, "U.S.-Russian Cooperation in Missile Defense," and Podvig, "Protivoraketnaia Oborona," 156–200.

123. Trenin, "Russia's Nuclear Policy," 9.

124. Vladimir Dvorkin, "An Outlook for Joint Countering of Security Threats," 50.

125. Podvig, "U.S.-Russian Cooperation."

126. Podvig, "Russian Strategic Forces."

127. Author Interview with Pavel Podvig, and Kuchins, "Explaining Mr. Putin."

Chapter 8: Conclusion

1. On social facts, see Searle, *Construction of Social Reality*. Social facts, including national identities, are social institutions that are created out of intersubjectively held beliefs that have become sufficiently institutionalized so that they are taken for granted.

2. Aspirational constructivism seeks to combine the microfoundations of social psychology with a Weberian and constructivist emphasis on the importance of values and ideas in shaping social structures and interests. As elaborated in chapter 2, the psychological need for collective self-esteem involves both the need to feel valuable and worthy and the need to feel competent and effective. This need is fulfilled, according to social psychology, when one feels part of a group that one values positively and sees as distinctive from other groups. On Weber's

value rationality, and the desire to create valid social orders, see the discussion in chapter 2 and, more generally, Weber, *Economy and Society,* and Zelditch, "Theories of Legitimacy."

3. Adler, "Cognitive Evolution," 27.

4. Karaganov, "New Contours of the World Order."

5. Trenin, "Russian Foreign Policy after Ukraine."

6. See his contribution to Shevtsova, ed., *Rossiia,* 72–73. Emphasis in original.

7. Albert, "Temporal Comparison Theory," Beike and Neidenthal, "Process of Temporal Self-Comparison," Klauer, Ferring, and Filipp, "Still Stable," and Howard and Hollander, "Marking Time."

8. Pierson, *Politics in Time,* and Berke and Galvin, "Field Guide."

9. Stets and Burke, "Identity Theory and Social Identity Theory," Stryker, "Developments in 'Two Social Psychologies,'" Stryker and Burke, "Past, Present, and Future," Brewer, "Many Faces of Social Identity," and Hogg, Terry, and White, "Tale of Two Theories."

10. Haas, "Words Can Hurt You," 241.

11. Oakes, "Psychological Groups," 817. Emphasis in original.

12. Checkel, "Why Comply?"

13. Pierson, *Politics in Time,* Thelen, *How Institutions Evolve,* and Mahoney, "Uses of Path Dependency in Historical Sociology."

14. John Ruggie's work on social time represents an innovative theoretical approach. See Ruggie, "International Structure and International Transformation," and Ruggie, "Territoriality and Beyond."

15. Oakes, "Psychological Groups," 813–17.

16. Finnemore, *National Interests,* 28. See also Meyer et al., "World Society and the Nation-State."

17. Ruggie, "Continuity and Transformation in the World Polity," Ruggie, "International Structure," Ruggie, "Territoriality and Beyond," and Wendt, "Anarchy."

18. Ruggie, "Territoriality and Beyond," 157, Adler, "Cognitive Evolution," and Haas, "Reason and Change in International Life."

19. Wendt, "Collective Identity," 385.

20. Oakes, "Psychological Groups," 812–17, and Bandura, "Towards a Psychology of Human Agency."

21. Adler, "Seizing the Middle Ground," 27.

22. On the spread of norms, see Finnemore and Sikkink, "International Norm Dynamics and Political Change." On scientific knowledge, see Adler and Haas, "Conclusion." On identity, see Wendt, *Social Theory,* and Haas, *Nationalism.* On culture of various kinds, see, among others, Katzenstein, *Cultural Norms,* Katzenstein, ed., *Culture of National Security,* and Kier, *Imagining War.*

For a discussion of how knowledge does and does not spread in organizations, see Haas, *When Knowledge Is Power*.

23. Adler, "Seizing the Middle Ground," 27.

24. On identity as changing and an interactive product, see Oakes, "Psychological Groups," 814–20.

25. Ruggie, "Territoriality and Beyond," 157. For constructivist work that has revealed the social construction of "realist" identities in China, see Johnston, *Cultural Realism*.

26. Medvedev, "Rossiia v Kontse Epokhi Moderna," 41–67, and Tsygankov, "Vladimir Putin's Vision," 132–58.

27. For constructivist work that has revealed the social construction of "realist" identities in China, see Johnston, *Cultural Realism*.

28. Medvedev, "Rossiia," 57–65.

29. Trenin, "Russian Foreign Policy."

30. Tsygankov, "Vladimir Putin's Vision," 139.

31. Stets and Burke, "Identity Theory," 232.

32. Ellemers and van Knippenberg, "Stereotyping in Social Context," 209.

33. Stets and Burke, "Identity Theory," 232.

34. Robert Gilpin is the main theorist suggesting prestige as a key driver of world politics. See Gilpin, *War and Change in World Politics*, 3–33.

35. Weber, "The Profession and Vocation of Politics," 351.

36. Gilpin, *War and Change*, 3–33.

37. Marilynn B. Brewer, "Importance of Being 'We.'"

38. Spinner-Halev and Theiss-Morse, "National Identity," 523–24.

39. Brewer, " Psychology of Prejudice," and Brewer, "Importance of Being 'We.'"

40. Medvedev, "Rossiia," and Trenin, "Rossiia i Novaia Evropeiskaia Sistema."

41. Brewer, "Psychology of Prejudice," 435–36, and Spinner-Halev and Theiss-Morse, "National Identity," 520.

42. For an example of how a focus on rhetoric and realist assumptions about international prestige can produce misreadings of sources of genuine conflict in Russian-American relations, see Ambrosio, "Russo-American Dispute."

43. Veenstra and Haslam, "Willingness to Participate," cited in Oakes, "Psychological Groups," 818.

Appendix

1. Eckstein, "Case Study and Theory in Political Science," 108.

2. Hopf, *Social Construction*, ch. 1.

3. See in particular the discussions of grounded theory, qualitative content analysis and critical discourse analysis in Titscher et al., *Methods of Text and Discourse Analysis*.

4. Chapter 4 of my dissertation, which discusses shifts in political discourse, was organized according to the list of ideal-type indicators. It therefore presents a more detailed account of the divergence in elite views regarding Russia's political purpose than the present volume. See Clunan, "Identity and the Emergence of National Interests in Post-Soviet Russia."

5. I relied on the work Amelie Mummendey in constructing these indicators of identity management strategies. See Mummendey et al., "Strategies to Cope," 244.

6. This attention to the news media and elite views as sources of data on social identity is supported by Huddy, "From Social to Political Identity," 143–44.

7. Spinner-Halev and Theiss-Morse, "National Identity," 519, Billig, *Banal Nationalism,* and Haslam and Platow, "Link between Leadership and Followership."

8. Hobsbawm, "Introduction."

9. The comments of Viacheslav Igrunov, then deputy chairman of the Duma Committee for CIS Affairs and Relations with Compatriots (member of Yabloko) represent an example of an elite statement indicating a civic definition in the first sentence and a statist definition in the second: "Citizenship should be granted without checks. There should be only one basis: affiliation to the former Soviet Union, Russia, the RSFSR, the Russian Empire, and so forth." Cited in Nekrasova, "Together and Apart." Taken together, they are coded as statist. A purely civic definition does not claim citizens outside of the former Russian Soviet Federative Socialist Republic.

10. Note that I am not describing social scientific theories here so much as "folk theories" about how the world works. These folk theories entail policy prescriptions, which not all social science theories make claims to do.

Bibliography

Abaftnov, Vladimir. "Russian Ratification of START II is Problematic." *Segodnia,* January 31, 1996, 2.

Abdelal, Rawi. *National Purpose in the World Economy: Post-Soviet States in Comparative Perspective, Cornell Studies in Political Economy.* Ithaca, NY: Cornell University Press, 2001.

Abrams, Dominic. "Processes of Social Identification." In *Social Psychology and the Self-Concept,* edited by Glynis M. Breakwell, 55–99. London: Surrey University Press, 1992.

Abrams, Dominic, and Rupert Brown. "Social Self-Regulation." *Personality and Social Psychology Bulletin* 20 (1994): 473–83.

Abrams, Dominic, and Michael A. Hogg. *Social Identity Theory: Constructive and Critical Advances.* London: Harverster-Wheatsheaf, 1990.

Adler, Emanuel. "Cognitive Evolution." In *Progress in Postwar International Relations,* edited by Emanuel Adler and Beverly Crawford, 43–88. New York: Columbia University Press, 1991.

———. "Seizing the Middle Ground: Constructivism in World Politics." *European Journal of International Relations,* no. 3 (1997): 319–63.

Adler, Emanuel, and Peter M. Haas. "Conclusion: Epistemic Communities, World Order, and the Creation of a Reflective Research Program." *International Organization* 46, no. 1 (1992): 367–90.

Afanasievskii, N. "Osnovopolagaiushchii Akt Rossiia-NATO—Polozhitel'nyi Itog Trudnykh Peregovorov." *Mezhdunarodnaia Zhizn',* no. 6 (1997): 8–12.

Akhtamzyan, Idlar. *Opinion Poll: "Attitudes in the Russian Federation Towards WMD Proliferation and Terrorism."* Translated by Cristina Chuen and Laura Binnington. Moscow: PIR Center Report / Human Rights Publishers, 2006.

Aksiuchits, Viktor V. *Ideokratiia v Rossii.* Moscow: Izdatel'stvo "Vybor," 1995.

———. Interview by Anne Clunan. June 26, 1997.

Albert, Stuart. "Temporal Comparison Theory." *Psychological Review* 84, no. 6 (1977): 485–503.

Alekseev, Aleksandr. "The New Dimension of NATO." *International Affairs* (Moscow), no. 2 (1992): 45–52.

———. "The North Atlantic Cooperation Council and the Future of Europe." *International Affairs* (Moscow), nos. 4–5 (1992): 121–28.

Ambrosio, Thomas. "The Russo-American Dispute over the Invasion of Iraq: International Status and the Role of Positional Goods." *Europe-Asia Studies* 57, no. 8 (2005): 1189–1210.

Arbatov, Aleksei. "Eurasia Letter: A Russian-U.S. Security Agenda." *Foreign Policy,* no. 104 (Fall 1996): 102–17.

———. "The National Idea and National Security." *Mirovaia Ekonomika i Mezhdunarodnaia Otnosheniia,* no. 5 (1998): 5–21.

———. "The Next Steps in Arms Control: A Russian Perspective." Paper presented at the Carnegie Endowment for International Peace Non-Proliferation Program, Washington, D.C., May 9, 2000.

———. "Parliament and Politics in Russia." Paper presented at the conference on "Strategic Arms Control—Moment of Decision?" Carnegie Endowment for International Peace Nuclear seminar, Washington, D.C., June 11, 1997.

———. "Russian Foreign Policy Priorities for the 1990s." In *Russian Security after the Cold War: Seven Views from Moscow,* edited by Teresa Pelton Johnson and Steven E. Miller, 1–41. Washington and London: Brassey's and the Center for Science and International Affairs, Harvard University, John F. Kennedy School of Government, 1994.

———. "Russian Foreign Policy Thinking in Transition." In *Russia and Europe: The Emerging Security Agenda,* edited by Vladimir Baranovsky, 135–61. London and New York: Oxford University Press for SIPRI, 1997.

———. "Russian Military Doctrine and Strategic Nuclear Forces to the Year 2000 and Beyond." Paper presented at the conference on "The Russian Defense Policy Towards the Year 2000." Naval Postgraduate School, Monterey, California, March 26–27, 1997.

———. "Russia's Foreign Policy Alternatives." *International Security* 18, no. 2 (Fall 1993): 5–43.

———. "S Tochki Zreniia Parlamentariia." *Mezhdunarodnaia Zhizn',* no. 3 (1999): 89–93.

———. "The Vicissitudes of Russian Politics." In *Russia and Europe: The Emerging Security Agenda,* edited by Vladimir Baranovsky, 77–89. London and New York: Oxford University Press for SIPRI, 1997.

Arbatov, Aleksei, and Vladimir Dvorkin. *Iadernoe Sderzhivanie i Nerasprostrane-*

nie. Moscow: Carnegie Endowment for International Peace Moscow Center, 2005.

Arbatov, Aleksei, et al. "Expert Appraisal: START II and Russia's National Interests." *Nezavisimaia Gazeta,* March 23, 1993, 5.

Arbatov, Georgii. "Cold War May Become a Reality yet Again." *Nezavisimaia Gazeta,* June 17, 1998.

The Arms Control Association, "The START/ABM Package at a Glance." Available at www.armscontrol.org/factsheets/pack.

Åslund, Anders. *How Russia Became a Market Economy*. Washington, D.C.: Brookings Institution, 1995.

Baburin, Sergei N. *Territoriia Gosudarstva: Pravovye i Geopoliticheskie Problemy*. Moscow: Izdatel'stvo Moskovskogo Universiteta, 1997.

Bakshi, Jyotna. "Russia's National Security Concepts and Military Doctrines: Continuity and Change." *Strategic Analysis* 24, no. 7 (October 2000).

Balzer, Harley. "The Putin Thesis and Russian Energy Policy." *Post-Soviet Affairs* 21, no. 3 (2005): 210–25.

Bandura, Albert. "Self-Efficacy: Toward a Unifying Theory of Behavioral Change." *Psychological Review* 84 (1977): 191–215.

———. "Self-Efficacy Mechanism in Human Agency." *American Psychologist* 37, no. 2 (1982): 122–47.

———. "Social Cognitive Theory: An Agentic Perspective." *Annual Review of Psychology* 52, no. 1 (2001): 1–26.

———. "Towards a Psychology of Human Agency." *Perspectives on Psychological Science* 1 (2006): 164–80.

Baranovskii, Vladimir. "Kosovo. Rossiiskie Interesy Slishkom Znachitel'ny." *Mezhdunarodnaia Zhizn'*, no. 6 (1999): 34–46.

———. "Kosovo: Russia's Interests Are Very Important." *International Affairs* (Moscow), no. 3 (1999): 1–10.

Baranovsky, Vladimir. "Russia's View." *ESF Working Paper NATO Enlargement Series,* 2001, 9–15.

Baranovsky, Vladimir, ed. *Russia and Europe: The Emerging Security Agenda.* New York: Oxford University Press, 1997.

Baranovsky, Vladimir G., and Alexei G. Arbatov. "The Changing Security Perspective in Europe." In *Russia and the West: The 21st Century Security Environment,* edited by Alexei G. Arbatov, Karl Kaiser, and Robert Legvold, 44–73. Armonk, NY, and London: M.E. Sharpe, 1999.

Bassin, Mark. "Turner, Solov'ev, and the 'Frontier Hypothesis': The Nationalist Significance of Open Spaces." *Journal of Modern History* 65, no. 3 (1993): 473–511.

Baumeister, Roy F. "Preface." In *Self-Esteem: The Puzzle of Low Self-Regard,* edited by Roy F. Baumeister. New York: Plenum, 1993.

Beike, Denise R., and Paul M. Neidenthal. "The Process of Temporal Self-Comparison in Self-Evaluation and Life Satisfaction." In *The Human Quest for Meaning: A Handbook of Psychological Research and Clinical Applications,* edited by Paul T. P. Wong and Prem S. Fry, 71–90. Mahwah, NJ: Lawrence Erlbaum Associates, 1998.

Belous, Vladimir. "Price of Security." *Nezavisimaia Gazeta,* December 30, 1992, 4.

Berger, Mikhail. "Candidates for the Russian Presidency Hold a Debate in the Davos, Switzerland 'Polling Place.'" *Izvestiia,* February 6, 1996, 1–2.

Berger, Thomas U. *Cultures of Antimilitarism: National Security in Germany and Japan.* Baltimore: Johns Hopkins University Press, 1998.

Berke, Gerald, and Dennis Galvin. "A Field Guide to Creative Syncretism or How and When People Remake Institutions." Paper presented at the 100th Annual Meeting of the American Political Science Association, Chicago, Illinois, September 2–5, 2004.

Billig, Michael. *Banal Nationalism.* London: SAGE Publications, 1995.

Blanz, Mathias, Amelie Mummendey, Rosemarie Mielke, and Andreas Klink. "Responding to Negative Social Identity: A Taxonomy of Identity Management Strategies." *European Journal of Social Psychology* 28 (1998): 697–729.

Bogaturov, Aleksei, and Mikhail Kozhokin. "Vostochnyi Vopros dlia Rossii." *Nezavisimaia Gazeta,* March 26, 1992.

Boone, Peter, and Denis Rodionov. "Rent Seeking Russia and the CIS." Paper presented at the Tenth Anniversary Meeting of the EBRD, London, December 2001.

Borisov, Vadim. "Vneshniaia Politika i Predvybornaia Bor'ba." *Mezhdunarodnaia Zhizn',* nos. 11–12 (1995): 27–32.

Boulding, Kenneth E. "The Learning and Reality-Testing Process in the International System." In *Image and Reality in World Politics,* edited by John C. Farrell and Asa P. Smith, 1–15. New York: Columbia University Press, 1968.

Bovt, Georgii. "Naked Politics." *Segodnia,* June 16, 1998.

Breslauer, George W. "Personalism versus Proceduralism: Boris Yeltsin and the Institutional Fragility of the Russian System." In *Russia in the New Century, Stability of Disorder?* edited by Victoria E. Bonnell and George W. Breslauer, 35–58. Boulder, CO: Westview Press, 2000.

Brewer, Marilynn B. "Importance of Being 'We': Social Identity and Intergroup Relations." Paper presented at the American Psychological Association Convention, San Francisco, California, August 17–20, 2007.

———. "The Many Faces of Social Identity: Implications for Political Psychology." *Political Psychology* 22, no. 1 (2001): 115–25.

———. "The Psychology of Prejudice: Ingroup Love or Outgroup Hate?" *Journal of Social Issues* 55, no. 3 (1999): 429–44.

———. "Social Identity, Distinctiveness, and In-Group Homogeneity." *Social Cognition* 11, no. 11 (1993): 150–64.

———. "The Social Self: On Being the Same and Different at the Same Time." *Personality and Social Psychology Bulletin* 17, no. 5 (1991): 475–82.

Brooks, Stephen G., and William C. Wohlforth. "Power, Globalization, and the End of the Cold War: Reevaluating a Landmark Case for Ideas." *International Security* 25, no. 3 (2000/01): 5–53.

Brown, Rupert, and Gabi Haeger. " 'Compared to What?': Comparison Choice in an Internation Context." *European Journal of Social Psychology* 29, no. 1 (1999): 31–42.

Brudny, Yitzhak M. *Reinventing Russia: Russian Nationalism and the Soviet State, 1953–1991*. Cambridge, MA: Harvard University Press, 1998.

Bunce, Valerie. "Domestic Reform and International Change: The Gorbachev Reforms in Historical Perspective." *International Organization* 47, no. 1 (1993): 107–38.

Burke, Peter J. "The Self: Measurement Requirements from an Interactionist Perspective." *Social Psychology Quarterly* 43, no. 1 (1980): 18–29.

Burke, Peter J., and Jan E. Stets. "Trust and Commitment through Self-Verification." *Social Psychology Quarterly* 62 (1999): 347–60.

Buszynski, Leszek. *Russian Foreign Policy after the Cold War*. Westport, CT: Praeger, 1996.

Calhoun, Craig. "Nationalism and Ethnicity." *Annual Review of Sociology* 19 (1993): 211–39.

Cast, Alicia D., and Peter J. Burke. "A Theory of Self-Esteem." *Social Forces* 80, no. 3 (2002): 1041–68.

Cast, Alicia D., Jan E. Stets, and Peter J. Burke. "Does the Self Conform to the Views of Others?" *Social Psychology Quarterly* 62, no. 1 (1999): 68–82.

Channel One [television station]. "Russian Foreign Minister Participates in TV Review of Foreign Relations in 2002." *Foreign Broadcast Information Service*, December 22, 2002, CEP20021222000072.

Chasnikov, Sergey V. "Sifting through the Relics of Confrontation." *Comparative Strategy* 14 (1995): 91–93.

Checkel, Jeff. "Russian Foreign Policy: Back to the Future?" *RFE/RL Research Report,* October 16 1992, 15–29.

Checkel, Jeffrey T. "The Constructivist Turn in International Relations Theory." *World Politics* 50, no. 2 (1998): 324–48.

———. "Why Comply? Social Learning and European Identity Change." *International Organization* 55, no. 3 (2001): 553–88.

Chubais, Igor B. "New Russian Identity and the Geopolitics of the Post-Soviet Space." Paper presented at the Nation-Building and State-Building in the Post-Socialist Space: Territorial Identities, Ethno-Cultural Revival and Political Developments, Institute of Geography, RAN, with the Center for Geopolitical Studies and the Open Society Institute, Moscow, May 14–16, 1998.

———. *Ot Russkoi Idei—k Idee Novoi Rossii*. Moscow: Izdatel'skii dom "Sotsial'naia zashchita," 1997.

Citrin, Jack, Ernst B. Haas, Christopher Muste, and Beth Reingold. "Is American Nationalism Changing? Implications for Foreign Policy." *International Studies Quarterly* 38, no. 1 (1994): 1–31.

Citrin, Jack, David O. Sears, Christopher Muste, and Cara Wong. "Multiculturalism in American Public Opinion." *British Journal of Political Science* 31, no. 2 (2001): 247–75.

Citrin, Jack, Cara Wong, and Brian Duff. "The Meaning of American National Identity: Patterns of Ethnic Conflict and Consensus." *Social Identity, Intergroup Conflict, and Conflict Reduction,* edited by Richard D. Ashmore, Lee J. Jussim, and David Wilder, 71–100. Oxford: Oxford University Press, 2001.

Clayton, Jonathan. "Rodionov: NATO Growth Will Upset Arms Control." *Moscow Times,* December 17 1996.

Clunan, Anne L. "Identity and the Emergence of National Interests in Post-Soviet Russia." Ph.D. dissertation, University of California, Berkeley, California, 2001.

Coalson, Robert. "Analysis: Running against Washington." *RFE/RL,* March 7, 2005.

Collier, Ruth Berins, and David Collier. *Shaping the Political Arena: Critical Junctures, the Labor Movement, and Regime Dynamics in Latin America*. Princeton: Princeton University Press, 1991.

Copeland, Dale. "Trade Expectations and the Outbreak of Peace: Détente 1970–1974 and the End of the Cold War, 1985–1991." *Security Studies* 9, no. 1–2 (1999/2000): 15–58.

Council on Foreign and Defense Policy. "Russia and NATO. Theses of the Council on Foreign and Defense Policy." Edited by Sergei Karaganov. English-language translation of Russian version. Moscow, 1995.

———. "Strategiia dlia Rossii." Edited by Sergei Karaganov. Moscow, 1992.

Crow, Suzanne. "Competing Blueprints for Russian Foreign Policy." *RFE/RL Research Report,* December 18, 1992, 45–50.

———. "Russia Debates Its National Interests." *RFE/RL Research Report,* July 10, 1992, 43–46.

Danilov, Dmitry. "Russia and European Security." In *What Russia Sees,* edited by Dov Lynch, 79–97. Paris: European Union Institute for Security Studies, 2005.

Davydov, Iurii. "Russian Security and East-Central Europe." In *Russia and Europe. The Emerging Security Agenda,* edited by Vladimir Baranovsky, 368–84. London: Oxford University Press for SIPRI, 1997.

"Defend the New Yugoslavia—Appeal to the Seventh Congress of Russian Federation People's Deputies." *Pravda,* December 2, 1992, 1, 3.

Demo, David H. "The Self-Concept over Time: Research Issue and Directions." *Annual Review of Sociology* 18 (1992): 303–26.

Dhanapala, Jayantha. *Prospects for Arms Control and Disarmament.* Speech of the Under-Secretary General for Disarmament Affairs, United Nations at the International Politics Association, University of St. Andrews. March 22, 2001. Available at http://disarmament.un.org/speech/22mar2001.htm, accessed August 19, 2008.

Dobson, Richard B. "Is Russia Turning the Corner? Changing Russian Public Opinion, 1991–1996." Washington, D.C.: Russia, Ukraine, and Commonwealth Branch, Office of Research and Media Reaction, U.S. Information Agency, 1996.

Douglas, Mary. *How Institutions Think.* Syracuse, NY: Syracuse University Press, 1986.

Dube, Lise, Mathieu Jodoin, and Sylvia Kairouz. "On the Cognitive Basis of Subjective Well-Being Analysis: What Do Individuals Have to Say About It?" *Canadian Journal of Behavioural Science* 30, no. 2 (1998): 1–14.

Dvorkin, Vladimir. "An Outlook for Joint Countering of Security Threats." *Russia in Global Affairs,* no. 4 (2005).

Eckstein, Harold. "Case Study and Theory in Political Science." In *Handbook of Political Science,* edited by Fred I. Greenstein and Nelson W. Polsby. Reading, MA: Addison-Wesley, 1975.

Eggert, Konstantin. "Rossiia v Roli 'Evraziiskogo Zhandarma'?" *Izvestiia,* August 7, 1992.

Ellemers, Naomi. "Individual Upward Mobility and the Perceived Legitimacy of Intergroup Relations." In *The Psychology of Legitimacy: Emerging Perspectives on Ideology, Justice, and Intergroup Relations,* edited by John T. Jost and Brenda Major, 205–22. Cambridge: Cambridge University Press, 2001.

———. "The Influence of Socio-Structural Variables on Identity Management Strategies." In *European Review of Social Psychology,* edited by Wolfgang Stroebe and Miles Hewstone, 27–58. London: Wiley, 1993.

Ellemers, Naomi, and Ad van Knippenberg. "Stereotyping in Social Context." In *The Social Psychology of Stereotyping and Group Life,* edited by Russell

Spears, Penelope J. Oakes, Naomi Ellemers, and S. Alexander Haslam, 208–35. Cambridge, MA: Blackwell Publishing, 1997.

Elliott, Gregory C. "Self-Esteem and Self-Consistency: A Theoretical and Empirical Link between Two Primary Motivations." *Social Psychology Quarterly* 49, no. 3 (1986): 207–18.

Emelin, P. "Moscow Also Betrays Them." *Literaturnaia Rossiia,* February 8, 1991, 3.

Emerson, Rupert. *From Empire to Nation: The Rise to Self-Assertion of Asian and African People*. Cambridge, MA: Harvard University Press, 1960.

Federal News Service. "Press Conference with State Duma Vice Chairman Aleksei Arbatov on Vladimir Putin's Foreign Policy." March 5, 2001.

Federiakov, Sergei. "Strategic Defence and Political Realities." *International Affairs* (Moscow), no. 3 (1992): 25–31.

Felgengauer, Pavel. "Kremlin Delivers Another Rebuff to Imperialists." *Moskovskie Novosti,* February 13–19, 2001, 12.

Finnemore, Martha. *National Interests in International Society*. Ithaca: Cornell University Press, 1996.

———. "Norms, Culture, and World Politics: Insights from Sociology's Institutionalism." *International Organization* 50, no. 2 (1996): 325–47.

Finnemore, Martha, and Kathryn Sikkink. "International Norm Dynamics and Political Change." *International Organization* 52, no. 4 (1998): 887–917.

"Five Questions Put to Well-Known Persons." *Moskovskii Komsomolets,* August 8, 2000.

Fond "Obshchestvennoe Mnenie" (FOM). "Dynamics of Russian Attitudes on the USSR's Collapse," December 6, 2001. Available at http://bd.english.fom.ru/report/cat/societas/rus_im/collapse_FSU/eof014603, accessed November 8, 2007.

———. "Referendum on the Fate of the USSR: Ten Years Later," March 14, 2001. Available at http://bd.english.fom.ru/report/map/ed010926, accessed November 8, 2007.

———. "The Treaty of Belovezhsk: Ten Years Later," December 6, 2001. Available at http://bd.english.fom.ru/report/cat/societas/rus_im/collapse_FSU/edo14623, accessed November 8, 2007.

Freeland, Chrystia. *Sale of the Century: Russia's Wild Ride from Communism to Capitalism*. New York: Crown Business, 2000.

"From Eastern Europe into a United Europe." *International Affairs* (Moscow), no. 2 (1992): 132–41.

Fuller, William C., Jr. *Strategy and Power in Russia, 1600–1914*. New York: Free Press, 1992.

Furman, Dmitry. " 'Dinner Jacket' and 'Camouflage Suit.' " *Moscow News*, September 10, 1993.

Gaidukov, Iurii. "The Concepts of Strategy and Military Doctrine in a Changing World." *International Affairs* (Moscow), no. 10 (1992): 60–69.

Galeotti, Mark. "Russia's Emerging Security Doctrine." *Jane's Intelligence Review*, November 1, 2004.

Gecas, Viktor. "The Self-Concept." *Annual Review of Sociology* 8 (1982): 1–33.

Gecas, Viktor, and Michael L. Schwalbe. "Beyond the Looking-Glass Self: Social Structure and Efficacy-Based Self-Esteem." *Social Psychology Quarterly* 46, no. 2 (1983): 77–88.

George, Alexander L. "Case Studies and Theory Development: The Method of Structured, Focused Comparison." In *Diplomacy: New Approaches in History, Theory and Policy*, edited by Paul Gordon Lauren, 43–68. New York: Free Press, 1979.

———. *Presidential Decisionmaking in Foreign Policy*. Boulder, CO: Westview Press, 1980.

Gerber, Theodore P., and Michael Hout. "More Shock than Therapy: Market Transition, Employment, and Income in Russia, 1991–1995." *American Journal of Sociology* 104, no. 1 (1998): 1–50.

Gilpin, Robert. *War and Change in World Politics*. Cambridge: Cambridge University Press, 1981.

Goettemoeller, Rose. "Nuclear Necessity in Putin's Russia." *Arms Control Today* 34, no. 3 (2004): 14–19.

———. "Nuclear Weapons in Current Russian Policy." In *The Russian Military*, edited by Steven E. Miller and Dmitri Trenin, 183–216. Cambridge, MA: MIT Press, 2004.

Golan, Galia. "Russia and the Iraq War: Was Putin's Policy a Failure?" *Communist and Post-Communist Studies* 37 (2004): 429–49.

Goldstein, Judith, and Robert O. Keohane, eds. *Ideas and Foreign Policy: Beliefs, Institutions, and Political Change*. Ithaca: Cornell University Press, 1993.

Golts, Alexander. "Let U.S. Have Its NMD—and Modified ABM Pact." *Russia Journal*, May 11, 2001.

Goncharov, Sergei. "Osobye Interesy Rossii—v Chem Oni Zakluchaiutsia?" *Izvestiia*, February 25, 1992.

Gornostaev, Dmitri. "Russian Foreign Minister Formulates Russia's New Strategic Objectives in International Arena." *Nezavisimaia Gazeta*, March 17, 1998.

———. "Security: Strategic Balance in Missile Defense Systems Is Preserved." *Nezavisimaia Gazeta*, October 1, 1997, 4.

Gorshkov, Mikhail. "What Russians Say About the Results of 2000 and Their Hopes for 2001." *Nezavisimaia Gazeta,* January 11, 2001.

Gorshkov, Mikhail K. *Vneshniaia Politika Rossii: Mneniia Ekspertov.* Moscow: RNICiNP po zakazu moskovskovo predstavitel'stva Fonda im. F. Eberta, 2001.

Gray, Colin S. "National Style in Strategy." *International Security* 6, no. 2 (1981): 21–47.

———. *Nuclear Strategy and National Style.* Lanham, MD: Hamilton Press, 1986.

Grazhdanskii soiuz. *Programma Deistvii po Vyvody Ekonomiki Rossii iz Krizisa.* Moscow, 1992.

Grigoriev, Oleg. "START II Has No Analogues." *Nezavisimaia Gazeta,* February 5, 1993, 4.

Guk, Sergei. "It Wouldn't Be Out of Place to Estimate the Expense." *Izvestiia,* January 30, 1992, 5.

Haas, Ernst B. *Nationalism, Liberalism, and Progress.* 2 vols. Ithaca: Cornell University Press, 1997.

———. "Reason and Change in International Life." *Journal of International Affairs* 44 (1990): 209–40.

———. *When Knowledge Is Power: Three Models of Change in International Organizations.* Berkeley: University of California Press, 1990.

———. "Words Can Hurt You: Or Who Said What to Whom about International Regimes." *International Organization* 36, no. 2 (1982): 207–44.

Haslam, S. Alexander, and Michael J. Platow. "The Link between Leadership and Followership: How Affirming a Social Identity Translates Vision into Action." *Personality and Social Psychology Bulletin* 27 (2001): 1469–79.

Hatch, Mary Jo, and Majken Schultz. "Introduction." In *Organizational Identity,* edited by Mary Jo Hatch and Majken Schultz, 1–15. Oxford: Oxford University Press, 2004.

Hesli, Vicki L. *Governments and Politics in Russian and the Post-Soviet Region.* Boston: Houghton Mifflin, 2007.

Hobsbawm, Eric. "Introduction: Inventing Traditions." In *The Invention of Tradition,* edited by Eric Hobsbawm and Terence Ranger, 1–14. Cambridge: Cambridge University Press, 1983.

Hogg, Michael A., and Dominic Abrams. *Social Identifications: A Social Psychology of Intergroup Relations and Group Processes.* London: Routledge, 1988.

Hogg, Michael A., Deborah J. Terry, and Katherine M. White. "A Tale of Two Theories: A Critical Comparison of Identity Theory with Social Identity Theory." *Social Psychology Quarterly* 58, no. 4 (1995): 255–69.

Holden, Gerard. *Russia after the Cold War: History and the Nation in Post-Soviet Security Politics*. Boulder, CO: Westview Press, 1994.

Hopf, Ted. *Social Construction of International Politics: Identities and Foreign Policies, Moscow, 1955 and 1999*. Ithaca: Cornell University Press, 2002.

Howard, Judith A., and Jocelyn A. Hollander. "Marking Time." *Sociological Inquiry* 63, no. 4 (1993): 425–43.

Huddy, Leonie. "Context and Meaning in Social Identity Theory: A Response to Oakes." *Political Psychology* 23, no. 4 (2002): 825–38.

———. "From Social to Political Identity: A Critical Examination of Social Identity Theory." *Political Psychology* 22, no. 1 (2001): 127–56.

Huntington, Samuel. *The Clash of Civilizations and the Remaking of World Order*. New York: Simon and Schuster, 1998.

Ignatow, Assen. *Das Russische Europa-Bild Heute: Ambivalenz der Politischen und Kulturellen Perzeptionen*. Cologne: Bundesinstitut für ostwissenschaftliche und internationale Studien, 1997.

Igrunov, Viacheslav. "Russia after the 2000 Presidential Elections—The Yeltsin Succession and What Comes Next." Paper presented at the Center for Slavic Studies and the Berkeley Program in Post-Soviet Studies, University of California, Berkeley, California, April 5, 2000.

International Affairs (Moscow), no. 11 (1992): 1.

Ivanenko, Vlad. "The Importance of Being Normal." *Russia in Global Affairs*, no. 4 (2005).

Ivanov, Sergei. "As NATO Grows, So Do Russia's Worries." *New York Times*, April 7, 2004, A19.

Jakobson, Max. "Is Kosovo a Turning Point for International Relations?" *International Herald Tribune*, August 31, 1999.

———. "Russia Heads Off toward a Solution of Its Own." *International Herald Tribune*, November 12, 1999, 10.

James, William. *The Principles of Psychology*. Vols. 1–2. New York: Henry Holt, 1890.

Jepperson, Ronald L., Alexander Wendt, and Peter J. Katzenstein. "Norms, Identity, and Culture in National Security." In *The Culture of National Security*, edited by Peter J. Katzenstein. New York: Columbia University Press, 1996.

Jervis, Robert. "The Implications of Prospect Theory for Human Nature and Values." *Political Psychology* 25, no. 2 (2004): 163–76.

———. *The Meaning of the Nuclear Revolution*. Ithaca: Cornell University Press, 1989.

———. *Perception and Misperception in International Politics*. Princeton: Princeton University Press, 1976.

Jervis, Robert, and Seweryn Bialer. *Soviet-American Relations after the Cold War.* Durham: Duke University Press, 1991.

Jervis, Robert, Richard Ned Lebow, and Janice Gross Stein, eds. *Psychology and Deterrence.* Baltimore: Johns Hopkins University Press, 1986.

Jervis, Robert, and Jack Snyder. *Dominoes and Bandwagons: Strategic Beliefs and Great Power Competition in the Eurasian Rimland.* New York: Oxford University Press, 1991.

Johnston, Alastair I. *Cultural Realism: Strategic Culture and Grand Strategy in Chinese History.* Princeton: Princeton University Press, 1995.

Kahneman, Daniel, Paul Slovic, and Amos Tversky. *Judgment under Uncertainty: Heuristics and Biases.* Cambridge: Cambridge University Press, 1982.

Kahneman, Daniel, and Amos Tversky. *Choices, Values, and Frames.* New York and Cambridge: Russell Sage Foundation and Cambridge University Press, 2000.

———. "The Framing of Decisions and the Psychology of Choice." *Science* 211, no. 30 (1981): 452–58.

———. "Prospect Theory: An Analysis of Decision under Risk." *Econometrica: Journal of the Econometric Society* 47, no. 2 (1979): 263–92.

Karaganov, Sergei. "New Contours of the World Order." *Russia in Global Affairs,* no. 4 (2005).

———. "The Problems Facing Primakov." *Nezavisimaia Gazeta,* January 18, 1996, 2.

———. "Russia and the International Order." In *What Russia Sees,* edited by Dov Lynch, 23–44. Paris: European Union Institute for Security Studies, 2005.

———. "Russia Needs a Foreign Policy Consensus." *Moscow News,* March 13, 1993.

Karniol, Rachel, and Michael Ross. "The Motivational Impact of Temporal Focus: Thinking about the Future and the Past." *Annual Review of Psychology* 47 (1996): 593–620.

Karpov, Mikhail. "Smolensk-Sennaia Square Catches Hell Again." *Nezavisimaia Gazeta,* October 3, 1995, 2.

Katz, Mark. "Playing the Angles: Russian Diplomacy before and during the War in Iraq." *Middle East Policy* 10, no. 3 (2003): 43–50.

Katzenstein, Peter J. *Cultural Norms and National Security.* Ithaca: Cornell University Press, 1996.

Katzenstein, Peter J., ed. *The Culture of National Security: Norms and Identity in World Politics.* 1st ed. New York: Columbia University Press, 1996.

Kazantsev, Boris. "Obvious Bias to the Use of Force." *International Affairs* (Moscow), no. 4 (1999): 1–5.

Khong, Yuen Foong. *Analogies at War: Korea, Munich, Dien Bien Phu, and the Vietnam Decisions of 1965*. Princeton: Princeton University Press, 1992.

Kiecolt, K. Jill. "Stress and the Decision to Change Oneself: A Theoretical Model." *Social Psychology Quarterly* 57, no. 1 (1994): 49–63.

Kier, Elizabeth. *Imagining War: French and British Military Doctrine between the Wars*. Princeton: Princeton University Press, 1997.

Kihlstrom, John F., Jennifer S. Beer, and Stanley B. Klein. "Self and Identity as Memory." In *Handbook on Self and Identity,* edited by Mark R. Leary, Geoff MacDonald, and June Price Tangney, 68–90. New York: Guilford Press, 2003.

Klauer, Thomas, Dieter Ferring, and Sigrun-Heide Filipp. " 'Still Stable after All This . . . ?' Temporal Comparison in Coping with Severe and Chronic Disease." *International Journal of Behavioral Development* 22, no. 2 (1998): 339–55.

Kobrinskaia, Irina. "Rossia-Tsentral'naia Evropa-NATO." In *Rossiia: Novye Parametry Bezopasnosti,* 8–40. Moscow: Pedagogicheskii Ob"edinenie "Raduga" for the Moscow Carnegie Center of the Carnegie Endowment for International Peace, 1995.

Kokoshin, Andrei A. "What Is Russia: A Superpower, a Great Power, or a Regional Power." *International Affairs: A Russian Journal,* no. 6 (2002).

Kondrashov, Stanislav. "Tough Choice of the Times—Parliamentary Hearings on START II Treaty Begin." *Izvestiia,* March 5, 1993, 4.

Koretskii, Aleksandr. "START II Hearings: We've Got to Reduce Missiles, because There's No Money for Maintaining Them." *Kommersant-Daily,* July 20, 1995, 4.

Kortunov, Andrei V. President of the Russian Science Foundation. Interview by Anne Clunan. February 23, 1998.

Kortunov, Andrei, and Alexei Iziumov. "What Is Meant by State Interests in Foreign Policy." *Literaturnaia gazeta,* July 11, 1990, 14.

Kortunov, Andrei V., and Andrei Volodin. *Contemporary Russia: National Interests and Emerging Foreign Policy Perceptions*. Cologne: Bundesinstitut für ostwissenschaftliche und internationale Studien, 1996.

Kortunov, Sergei. "Budet' Li Smena Kursa?" *Nezavisimaia Gazeta,* December 10, 1995.

———. "Rossiia: Ne Serdit'sia, a Sosredotochit'sia." *Russia in Global Affairs,* no. 5 (2005).

———. "Russia's National Identity in a New Era." Cambridge: Strengthening Democratic Institutions Project, Belfer Center for Science and International Affairs, September 1998.

———. "Russia's Way: National Identity and Foreign Policy." *International Affairs* (Moscow) 44, no. 4 (1998).

———. "Russia–United States: Way to Partnership." *Mirovaia Ekonomika i Mezhdunarodnaia Otnosheniia,* no. 7 (1996): 70–78.

———. "Toward a New Pattern of Strategic Relationship." *International Affairs* (Moscow), no. 10 (1991): 18–29.

Kovalev, Andrei, and Andrei Sebentsov. "The Shadows of the Past on the Road into the Future." *International Affairs* (Moscow), no. 9 (1991): 39–52.

Kozhokin, Evgenii. "The Russian Parliament and Foreign Policy." *International Affairs* (Moscow), no. 9 (1992): 32–43.

Kozin, Vladimir. "New Dimensions of NATO." *International Affairs* (Moscow), no. 3 (1993): 53–60.

Kozyrev, Andrei. "Russia Looks West." *Moscow News,* September 29–October 6, 1991.

———. "Washington Summit: An End to Nuclear Confrontation." *International Affairs,* no. 8 (1992): 3–9.

Kratochwil, Friedrich V. *Rules, Norms, and Decisions.* Cambridge: Cambridge University Press, 1989.

Krylov, Vladimir. "Dead-End Branch: Memorandum to the Deputy Prior to the Vote on Ratification." *Sovetskaia Rossiia,* January 23, 1999.

Kuchins, Andrew C. "Explaining Mr. Putin: Russia's New Nuclear Diplomacy." *Arms Control Today* 32, no. 8 (2004).

Kullberg, Judith S. *The End of New Thinking? Elite Ideologies and the Future of Russian Foreign Policy.* Columbus: Mershon Center at the Ohio State University, 1993.

Kuzar, Vladimir. "NATO an Instrument of Global U.S. Strategy." *Krasnaia Zvezda,* May 22, 1998.

Lapidus, Gail W. "Putin's War on Terrorism: Lessons from Chechnya." *Post-Soviet Affairs* 18, no. 1 (2002): 41–49.

Larrabee, F. Stephen, and Theodore W. Karasik. *Foreign and Security Policy Decisionmaking under Yeltsin.* Santa Monica, CA: Rand, 1997.

Larson, Deborah Welch. *Anatomy of Mistrust: U.S.-Soviet Relations During the Cold War.* Ithaca: Cornell University Press, 1997.

Larson, Deborah Welch, and Alexei Shevchenko. "Shortcut to Greatness: The New Thinking and the Revolution in Soviet Foreign Policy." *International Organization* 57, no. 1 (2003): 77–109.

Lavrov, Sergei. " 'Seven-Plus-One' Plus UN." *International Affairs* (Moscow), no. 10 (1991): 9–17.

Legro, Jeffrey W. "The Transformation of Policy Ideas." *American Journal of Political Science* 44, no. 3 (2000): 419–32.

Legvold, Robert, Karl Kaiser, and Alexei G. Arbatov. "Introduction." In *Russia and the West: The 21st Century Security Environment,* edited by Alexei G.

Arbatov, Karl Kaiser, and Robert Legvold, 3–18. Armonk, NY, and London: M.E. Sharpe, 1999.

Leontyev, Mikhail. "Restoring Russia's Future." *Russia in Global Affairs*, no. 4 (2005).

Levy, Jack. "Loss Aversion, Framing Effects, and International Conflict: Perspectives from Prospect Theory." In *Handbook of War Studies II,* edited by Manus I. Midlarsky. Ann Arbor: University of Michigan Press, 2000.

Levy, Jack S. "Declining Power and the Preventive Motive for War." *World Politics* 40, no. 1 (1987): 82–107.

———. "Learning and Foreign Policy: Sweeping a Conceptual Minefield." *International Organization* 48, no. 2 (1994): 279–312.

Ligachev, Egor. Former Politburo member. Interview by Anne Clunan. June 24, 1997.

Lipman, Masha, and Michael McFaul. "Putin and the Media." In *Putin's Russia: Past Imperfect, Future Uncertain,* edited by Dale Herspring, 55–74. Lanham, MD: Rowman and Littlefield, 2005.

Litovkin, Viktor. "Playing the 'Security Door.'" *Obshchaia Gazeta,* May 8–16, 2001, 3.

Lukin, Alexander. "Forcing the Pace of Democratization." *Journal of Democracy* 10, no. 2 (1999): 35–40.

———. "Russia between East and West." Paper presented at the Joint Session of the European Consortium for Political Research, Edinburgh, March 28–April 2, 2003.

Lukin, Vladimir P., and Aleksandr I. Utkin. *Rossiia i Zapad: Obshchnost ili Otchuzhdenie?* Moscow: Sampo, 1995.

Lustick, Ian S. "Hegemony and the Riddle of Nationalism: The Dialectics of Political Identity in the Middle East." Philadelphia: University of Pennsylvania Browne Center for International Politics (1997), 1–23.

Lynch, Dov, ed. *Russia Faces Europe, Chaillot Paper No. 60.* Paris: European Union Institute for Security Studies, 2003.

Mahoney, James. "Uses of Path Dependency in Historical Sociology." Paper presented at the American Political Science Association Annual Meeting, Atlanta, Georgia, September 2–5, 1999.

Main, Steven J. "Russia's Military Doctrine." *Conflict Studies Research Center Analytical Papers,* April 2000.

Malashenko, Aleksei. "Rossiia i Islam." *Nezavisimaia Gazeta,* 1992.

Malashenko, Igor. "Soviet-American Relations after Totalitarianism and the Cold War." *International Affairs* (Moscow), no. 6 (1991): 3–14.

Malcolm, Neil. "New Thinking and After: Debate in Moscow about Europe." In *Russia and Europe: An End to Confrontation?* edited by Neil Malcolm,

151–81. London and New York: Pinter Publishers for the Royal Institute of International Affairs, 1994.

Malcolm, Neil, and Alex Pravda. "Democratization and Russian Foreign Policy." *International Affairs* 72, no. 3 (1996): 537–52.

Mandelbaum, Michael. "Preserving the New Peace: The Case against NATO Expansion." *Foreign Affairs* 74 (1995): 9–13.

March, James G., and Johan P. Olsen. "The Institutional Dynamics of International Political Orders." *International Organization* 52, no. 4 (1998): 943–69.

Marcussen, Martin, Thomas Risse, Daniela Engelmann-Martin, Hans Joachim Knopf, and Klaus Roscher. "Constructing Europe? The Evolution of French, British, and German Nation State Identities." *Journal of European Public Policy* 6, no. 4 (1999): 614–33.

Marx, Karl. "The Eighteenth Brumaire of Louis Bonaparte." In *The Marx-Engels Reader,* edited by Robert C. Tucker, 594–617. New York: Norton, 1978.

Maslin, Yevgeny, and Ivan Safranchuk. "Nuclear Deadlock: A Way Out." *Disarmament Diplomacy,* no. 46 (2000).

May, Ernest. *"Lessons" of the Past.* Oxford: Oxford University Press, 1973.

McDermott, Rose. "Editor's Introduction." *Political Psychology* 25, no. 2 (2004): 147–62.

———. "Prospect Theory in Political Science: Gains and Losses from the First Decade." *Political Psychology* 25, no. 2, Prospect Theory in Political Science (2004): 289–312.

McFaul, Michael. "Putin's Risky Westward Turn." *Christian Science Monitor,* November 9, 2001, 11.

Mead, George Herbert. *Mind, Self, and Society.* Chicago: University of Chicago Press, 1934.

Mearsheimer, John J. "Back to the Future: Instability in Europe after the Cold War." *International Security* 15, no. 1 (1990): 5–56.

———. "The Case for a Ukrainian Nuclear Deterrent." *Foreign Affairs* 72, no. 3 (1993): 50–66.

Medvedev, Roy. "Russia Again at the Crossroads." *Russian Social Science Review* 39, no. 5 (1998): 77–96.

Medvedev, Sergei. "Rossiia v Kontse Epokhi Moderna: Vneshniaia Politika, Bezopasnost', Identichnost'." In *Rossiia i Zapad v Novom Tysiacheletii: Mezhdu Globalizatsiei i Vnutrennei Politikoi,* edited by Sergei Medvedev, Aleksandr Konovalov, and Sergei Oznobishchev, 41–67. Garmisch-Partenkirchen, Germany: George C. Marshall European Center for Security Studies, 2002.

Mercer, Jonathan. "Anarchy and Identity." *International Organization* 49, no. 2 (1995): 229–52.

———. "Prospect Theory and Political Science." *Annual Review of Political Science* 8, no. 1 (2005): 1–21.

Meyer, John W., John Boli, George M. Thomas, and Francisco O. Ramirez. "World Society and the Nation-State." *American Journal of Sociology* 103, no. 1 (1997): 144–81.

Mezhdunarodnaia Zhizn', No. 5, 1998.

Migranian, Andranik. "Real and Illusory Guidelines in Foreign Policy." *Rossiiskaia Gazeta,* August 4, 1992, 7.

Mikhailenko, Valerii Ivanovich. "Russia in the New World Order: Power and Tolerance in Contemporary International Relations." *Demokratizatsiya* 11, no. 2 (2003): 198.

Mirskii, Georgii I. " 'Obshchnost' Sud'by' i Natsional'noe Samosoznanie." *Mirovaia Ekonomika i Mezhdunarodnoe Otnosheniia* 1998, no. 4 (1998): 5–16.

Mitrofanov, Aleksei. "Russia's New Geopolitics." Cambridge: Strengthening Democratic Institutions Project, Belfer Center for Science and International Affairs, July 1998.

Mummendey, Amelie, Thomas Kessler, Andreas Klink, and Rosemarie Mielke. "Strategies to Cope with Negative Social Identity: Predictions by Social Identity Theory and Relative Deprivation Theory." *Journal of Personality and Social Psychology* 76, no. 2 (1999): 229–45.

Mummendey, Amelie, and Sabine Otten. "Aversive Discrimination." In *Blackwell Handbook of Social Psychology: Intergroup Processes,* edited by Rupert Brown and Samuel L. Gaertner, 112–32. Malden, MA: Blackwell Publishers, 2003.

Nadein, Vladimir. "Our Speaker Finally Puts American Congress in Its Place." *Izvestiia,* April 14, 1993, 2.

Narochnitskaia, Natalia. "Russia and the Worldwide Eastern Question." *International Affairs* (Moscow), no. 3 (1999).

———. "Russia's National Interests." *International Affairs* (Moscow), no. 4–5 (1992): 105–13.

"National Security Concept of the Russian Federation." Approved by Presidential Decree No. 1300 of December 17, 1999; given in wording of Presidential Decree No. 24 of January 10, 2000. *Rossiiskaia Gazeta,* January 18, 2000.

Nazarkin, Iurii. "A Treaty the World Needs." *International Affairs* (Moscow), no. 2 (1992): 23–29.

Nekrasova, Marina. "Together and Apart." *Obshchaia Gazeta,* April 6–12, 1995, 5.

Neumann, Iver B. *Russia and the Idea of Europe: A Study in Identity and International Relations.* 1st ed. London: Routledge, 1996.

Nuclear Threat Initiative. *5/14/2003: Duma Ratifies Moscow Treaty after Delays.*

Available at www.nti.org/db/nisprofs/russia/treaties/start3.htm, accessed February 10, 2006.

Nye, Joseph S., Jr. "Nuclear Learning and U.S.-Soviet Security Regimes." *International Organization* 41, no. 3 (1987): 371–402.

Oakes, Penelope J. "Psychological Groups and Political Psychology: A Response to Huddy's 'Critical Examination of Social Identity Theory.'" *Political Psychology* 23, no. 4 (2002): 809–24.

Odnokolenko, Oleg. "Star Wars: Episode 2001." *Itogi,* April 2001, 14–19.

———. "To Forget and Give In." *Segodnia,* January 17, 2001, 1, 4.

Official Kremlin International News Broadcast. "Interview Granted by Sergei Prikhodko, Assistant to the RF President for International Affairs." May 21, 1997.

———. "Main Speeches at the International Conference 'New Security.'" April 16, 1998.

———. "On the Alignment of Forces in Parliament and Possible Scenarios of Developments at the 6th Congress of People's Deputies of the Russian Federation. A Memorandum for the Government." April 1, 1992.

———. "Press Conference with Foreign Minister Igor Ivanov." July 10, 2000.

———. "Remarks by Foreign Minister Evgenii Primakov at the Duma Committee for International Affairs." February 8, 1996.

———. "Round-Table Regarding Russia/NATO Founding Act." May 22, 1997.

O'Loughlin, John, Gearóid Ó Tuathail, and Vladimir Kolossov. "A 'Risky Westward Turn'? Putin's 9-11 Script and Ordinary Russians." *Europe-Asia Studies* 56, no. 1 (2004): 3–34.

Onuf, Nicholas Greenwood. *World of Our Making: Rules and Rule in Social Theory and International Relations.* Columbia: University of South Carolina Press, 1989.

"Osnovnye polozheniia voennoi doktriny Rossiiskoi Federatsii." *Rossiiskaia gazeta,* November 18, 1993, 1, 4.

Ostapchuk, Anna, and Evgenii Krasnikov. "Kremlin Tries to Promote People's Capitalism." *Moscow News,* September 25, 1997.

Ovcharenko, Aleksey. "A Russian Naval Perspective." Paper presented at the Meeting on the Future of Russia-U.S. Strategic Arms Reductions: START III and Beyond, Cambridge, Massachusetts, February 2–6, 1998.

Pankov, Iurii. "Europe Is Closer to Russia." *Krasnaia Zvezda,* April 7, 2001.

Parrish, Scott. "Chaos in Foreign Policy Decision-Making." *Transition,* May 17, 1996.

Parrish, Scott D. "The USSR and the Security Dilemma: Explaining Soviet Self-Encirclement, 1945–1985." Ph.D. dissertation, Columbia University, 1993.

Paul, T. V. "Soft Balancing in the Age of U.S. Primacy." *International Security* 30, no. 1 (2005): 46–71.

"Perestroika, Sixth Winter." *International Affairs* (Moscow), no. 2 (1991): 97–109.

Petrovskaia, Iulia. "Ivanov Perestal byt Pokladistym." *Nezavisimaia Gazeta,* March 27, 2003.

Piadyshev, Boris. "We Need a National Security Concept." *International Affairs* (Moscow) 1991, no. 4 (1991): 173–75.

Pierson, Paul. *Politics in Time: History, Institutions, and Social Analysis*. Princeton: Princeton University Press, 2004.

Pikayev, Alexander A. "The Rise and Fall of START II: The Russian View." *Carnegie Endowment Working Paper,* 1999.

Piontkovskii, Andrei, and Vitalii Tsygichko. "Tango s Rossiei." *Segodnia*, February 14, 2001, 4.

Pipes, Richard. *Russia under the Old Regime*. New York: Charles Scribner and Sons, 1974.

Podberezkin, Aleksei. "Russia's New Path." Cambridge: Strengthening Democratic Institutions Project, Belfer Center for Science and International Affairs, July 1998.

Podvig, Pavel. "A History of the ABM Treaty in Russia." *PONARS Policy Memo Series* 109 (February 2000).

———. Interview by Anne Clunan. March 9, 2005.

———. "Putin's Boost Phase Defense: the Offer that Wasn't." *PONARS Policy Memo Series* 180 (November 2000).

———. *Russian Strategic Forces in the Next Decade.* Russian Strategic Nuclear Forces. Available at http://russianforces.org/podvig/eng/publications/forces/20050100asp.shtml, accessed February 10, 2006.

———. "U.S.-Russian Cooperation in Missile Defense. Is It Really Possible?" *PONARS Policy Memo Series* 316 (November 2003).

———. "Who Is In Charge? Russia Handles Arms Control Negotiations." *PONARS Policy Memo Series* 277 (November 2002).

Podvig, Pavel L. "Protivoraketnaia Oborona kak Faktor Strategicheskikh Vsaimootnoshenii SSSR/Rossii i SShA v 1945–2003 gg." Ph.D. dissertation, Institute of World Economics and International Relations, Russian Academy of Sciences, 2004.

Popov, Nikolai. "Vneshniaia Politika Rossii (Analiz Politikov i Ekspertov)." Part 1 of 2. *Mirovaia Ekonomika i Mezhdunarodnoe Otnosheniia,* no. 3 (1994): 52–59.

———. "Vneshniaia Politika Rossii (Analiz Politikov i Ekspertov)." Part 2 of 2. *Mirovaia Ekonomika i Mezhdunarodnoe Otnosheniia*, no. 4 (1994): 5–15.

Pozdniakov, Elgiz. "The Geopolitical Collapse and Russia." *International Affairs* (Moscow), no. 9 (1992): 3–11.
———. "Russia Is a Great Power." *International Affairs* (Moscow), no. 3–13 (1993): 129–36.
———. "Russia Today and Tomorrow." *International Affairs* (Moscow), no. 2 (1993): 22–31.
———. "We Must Rebuild What We Have Destroyed with Our Own Hands." *International Affairs* (Moscow), nos. 4–5 (1992): 129–36.
Prikhodko, Oleg. "Global Protection System: New Challenges." *International Affairs* (Moscow), no. 11 (1992): 82–87.
Primakov, Evgenii. "Mnogopoliarnii Mir i OON." *Mezhdunarodnaia Zhizn'*, no. 10 (1997): 3–8.
———. "Rossiia Byla i Ostaetsia Velikoi Derzhavoi." *Panorama* (1996), 1–2.
Prizel, Ilya. *National Identity and Foreign Policy: Nationalism and Leadership in Poland, Russia, and Ukraine.* 1st ed. Cambridge: Cambridge University Press, 1998.
Prokhanov, Aleksandr. "Tragediia Tsentralizma." *Literaturnaia Rossiia,* January 5, 1990, 4–5.
Pushkov, Aleksei. "Novyi Evropeiskii Poriadok." *Nezavisimaia Gazeta,* May 16, 1998, 1, 4.
———. "Russia Confirms Great Power Status." *Moscow News,* February 25, 1994.
———. "Tame Foreign Minister Seeks New Image." *Moscow News,* December 16, 1994.
"Putin Pays Yeltsin's Debts." *Segodnia,* December 28, 2000.
Putin, Vladimir. "Address to the Nation." Moscow, Russia, 2004.
———. "Annual Address to the Federal Assembly." Moscow, Russia, 2002.
———. "Annual Address to the Federal Assembly." Moscow: President of Russia Official Web Portal, 2005.
———. "Russia at the Turn of the Millennium." *Irish Times,* December 31, 1999.
Rahr, Alexander. "'Atlanticists' Versus 'Eurasians' in Russian Foreign Policy." *RFE/RL Research Report,* May 29, 1992, 17–22.
Rasputin, Valentin. "After Events, on the Eve of Events." *Sovetskaia Rossiia,* January 23, 1992, 4.
Razuvaev, Vladimir. "Russia and Europe: A Rapprochement." *International Affairs* (Moscow) 1991, no. 7 (1991): 40–49.
Reddaway, Peter, and Vladimir Glinski. *The Tragedy of Russia's Reforms: Market Bolshevism against Democracy.* Washington, D.C.: United States Institute of Peace Press, 2001.

Reicher, Stephen D., and Nick Hopkins. *Self and Nation: Categorization, Contestation, and Mobilization*. London: SAGE Publications, 2001.

Reus-Smit, Christian. "The Constitutional Structure of International Society and the Nature of Fundamental Institutions." *International Organization* 51, no. 4 (1997): 555–89.

Reuters. "Breakdown of Voting in Russia Duma on START-2." April 14, 2000.

RIA Novosti. "NATO Enlargement and Russia's National Security." *Russian Executive and Legislative Newsletter,* February 24, 1997.

Risse, Thomas. " 'Let's Argue!': Communicative Action in World Politics." *International Organization* 54, no. 1 (2000): 1–39.

Rivkin, David B., and Lee A. Casey. "Six Reasons why Arms Control Advocates are Wrong: The ABM Treaty Is Not in Force." *The Heritage Foundation Backgrounder,* 2000.

Rogov, Sergei. "Ne Stoit Vpadat' v Isteriku." *Nezavisimaia Gazeta EV,* May 16, 2001.

———. "Rossiia i NATO." *SShA: Ekonomika, Politika, Ideologiia,* no. 10 (1996): 3–9.

———. "Soglasovannyi Primakovym i Solanoi Dokument Po-Raznomu Traktuiut v Moskve i Vashingtone." *Nezavisimaia Gazeta,* May 16, 1997, 1, 4.

Romashkin, Petr. "Objectives of Future Reductions." Paper presented at the Meeting on the Future of Russia-U.S. Strategic Arms Reductions: START III and Beyond, Cambridge, Massachusetts, February 2–6, 1998.

ROMIR. *Chto Ugrozhaet Bezopastnosti Rossii?* Available at www.romir.ru/socpolit/vvps/11_2000/russia-security.htm, accessed July 22, 2001.

———. "Tseli Vneshnei Politiki Rossii." (September 2000). Available at www.romir.ru/socpolit/vvps/11_2000/foreign-policy.htm, accessed July 22, 2001.

Rose, Richard, Neil Munro, and William Mishle. "Resigned Acceptance of an Incomplete Democracy: Russia's Political Equilibrium." *Post-Soviet Affairs* 20, no. 3 (2004): 195–218.

Rosenberg, Morris, Carmi Schooler, Carrie Schoenbach, and Florence Rosenberg. "Global Self-Esteem and Specific Self-Esteem: Different Concepts, Different Outcomes." *American Sociological Review* 60, no. 1 (1995): 141–56.

"Rossiia Predopredeleno Igrat' v Mire Vazhnuiu i Samostoiatel'nuiu Rol'." *Mezhdunarodnaia Zhizn'* 3 (1998): 80–88.

Ruggie, John Gerard. "Continuity and Transformation in the World Polity: Toward a Neorealist Synthesis." *World Politics* 35 (1983): 261–85.

———. "International Regimes, Transactions, and Change: Embedded Liberalism in the Postwar Economic Order." *International Organization* 36, no. 2 (1982): 379–415.

———. "International Structure and International Transformation: Space, Time, and Method." In *Global Changes and Theoretical Challenges: Approaches to World Politics for the 1990s*, edited by Ernst-Otto Czempiel and James Rosenau. Lexington, MA: Lexington Books, 1989.

———. "Territoriality and Beyond: Problematizing Modernity in International Relations." *International Organization* 47, no. 1 (1993): 139–74.

———. "What Makes the World Hang Together? Neo-Utilitarianism and the Social Constructivist Challenge." *International Organization* 52, no. 4 (1998): 855–85.

"Russian Foreign Minister Participates in TV Review of Foreign Relations in 2002." *BBC Monitoring*, December 22, 2002.

"Russian Political Elite Analysing Russia's Place in Today's World." *Izvestiia*, February 6, 2001.

"Russian Reaction to NATO's Summit in Prague." *BBC Monitoring*, November 25, 2002.

"Russian START II Vote Nears." *Disarmament Diplomacy*, no. 32 (1998).

"Russian TV Studio Discussion Divided on NATO." *Foreign Broadcast Information Service*, April 3, 2003.

"Russia's National Interests." *International Affairs* (Moscow), no. 8 (1992): 134–43.

"Russkaia Ideia: Mify i Real'nost'." *Kommersant Vlast'*, no. 1 (1997): 6–16.

Ryan, Michael. *Social Trends in Contemporary Russia*. London: St. Martin's Press, 1993.

Ryzhkov, Vladimir. "More of the Andropov Approach, Less Security." *Novaya Gazeta*, September 9, 2004, 4–5.

———. "Real'nosti Chetvertoi Rossiikoi Respubliki." *Mezhdunarodnaia Zhizn'*, no. 4 (1999): 3–13.

Sagan, Scott D. "Why Do States Build Nuclear Weapons? Three Models in Search of a Bomb." *International Security* 21, no. 3 (1996): 54–86.

Satarov, Georgii, ed. *Rossiia v Poiskakh Idei: Analiz Pressy: Sbornik 1*. Moscow: Upravelenie delami Prezidenta, 1997.

Schulze, Peter W., ed. *Die Außen- und Sicherheitspolitik im Neuen Russland: Eine Elitestudie*. Bonn: Russian Independent Institute of Social and National Problems (RNISiNP) and the Friedrich Ebert Stiftung Moscow, 2001.

Searle, John. *The Construction of Social Reality*. New York: Free Press, 1995.

"Sergei Karaganov Divides the World into Three Parts." strana.ru, February 6, 2001. Available at www.cdi.org/russia/johnson/5078.html, accessed September 22, 2008.

Sergounin, Alexander A. "Post-Communist Security Thinking in Russia: Changing Paradigms." *Columbia International Affairs Online Working Papers,* 2000, 1–69.

Sestanovich, Stephen, ed. *Rethinking Russia's National Interests.* Washington, D.C.: Center for Strategic and International Studies, 1994.

Sewell, William H., Jr. "Historical Events as Transformations of Structures: Inventing Revolution at the Bastille." *Theory and Society* 25, no. 6 (1996): 841–81.

Shaburkin, Aleksandr. "Russian Generals Testing Europeans' Nerves." *Vremia MN,* March 1, 2001, 2.

Sherif, Muzafer. *Group Conflict and Cooperation: Their Social Psychology.* London: Routledge and Kegan Paul, 1966.

Sherif, Muzafer, and Carolyn Sherif. *Groups in Harmony and Tension.* New York: Harper, 1953.

Shevtsova, Lilia. "Vybornoe Samoderzhavie pri Putine: Perspektivy i Problemy Evoliutsii Politicheskogo Rezhima." *Brifing Moskovskogo Tsentra Karnegi,* January 2001.

Shevtsova, Lilia, ed. *Rossiia: Desat' Voprosov o Samom Vazhnom.* Moscow: Moscow Carnegie Center, 1997.

Shlapentokh, Vladimir. "'Old', 'New' and 'Post' Liberal Attitudes toward the West: From Love to Hate." *Communist and Post-Communist Studies* 31, no. 3 (1998): 199–215.

Shmelev, Nikolai. "Russia: The Emerging Consensus on National Reconstruction." *Politik und Gesellschaft Online,* no. 1 (2000).

Simoniia, Nodar. "Sever-Iug: Konflikt Neizbezhen?" *Moskovskie Novosti,* March 22, 1992.

SIPRI. *Military Expenditure Database.* Available at www.sipri.org/contents/milap/milex/mex_database1.html, accessed December 4, 2007.

Smelser, Neil J. "Self-Esteem and Social Problems: An Introduction." In *The Social Importance of Self-Esteem,* edited by Andrew M. Mecca, Neil J. Smelser, and John Vasconcellos, 1–23. Berkeley: University of California Press, 1989.

Smirniagin, Leonid. Member of the Presidential Commission on the National Idea. Interview by Anne Clunan. June 4, 1998.

Smith, Anthony D. *The Ethnic Origins of Nations.* Oxford: B. Blackwell, 1986.

———. *National Identity.* Reno: University of Nevada Press, 1991.

———. *Nationalism and Modernism: A Critical Survey of Recent Theories of Nations and Nationalism.* London: Routledge, 2001.

Snyder, Jack. *Myths of Empire: Domestic Politics and International Ambition.* Ithaca: Cornell University Press, 1991.

Socor, Vladimir. "Kremlin Redefining Policy in 'Post-Soviet Space.'" *Eurasia Daily Monitor,* February 8, 2005.

———. "Kremlin Redefining Policy in the 'Post-Soviet Space.'" *Jamestown Foundation Eurasia Daily Monitor* 2, no. 27 (2005).

Sokolov, Oleg, and Iurii Kliukin. "Starting Off for a Secure Future." *International Affairs,* no. 3 (1993): 3–14.

Sokov, Nikolai. "An Assessment of the Draft Russian Military Doctrine." Monterey, CA: Center for Nonproliferation Studies, 1999.

———. "'Denuclearization' of Russia's Defense Policy?" Monterey, CA: Center for Nonproliferation Studies. Available at http://cns.miis.edu/pubs/reports/denuke.htm, accessed July 25, 2001.

———. "The Duma Ratifies the Moscow Treaty." Monterey, CA: Center for Nonproliferation Studies, 2003.

———. "The Fate of Russian Nuclear Weapons: An Anticlimax on August 11." Center for Nonproliferation Studies. Available at http://cns.miis.edu/pubs/reports/denuke2.htm, accessed July 25, 2001.

———. "'Kosovo Syndrome' and the Great Nuclear Debate of 2000." *PONARS Policy Memo,* no. 181 (2000): 1–5.

———. "Russia's New National Security Concept: The Nuclear Angle." Monterey, CA: Center for Nonproliferation Studies, 2000.

Solodovnik, Sergei. "Yabloko Favors Pragmatism in Foreign Policy." *Moscow News,* December 1, 1995.

Solov'ev, Aleksandr I. "Integrativnaia Ideologiia: Panatseia? Lovushka? Mistifikatsiia?" *Kommersant Vlast',* no. 2 (1997): 22–26.

Spinner-Halev, Jeff, and Elizabeth Theiss-Morse. "National Identity and Self-Esteem." *Perspectives on Politics* 1, no. 3 (2003): 515–32.

Stankevich, Sergei. "Derzhava v Poiskakh Sebia." *Nezavisimaia Gazeta,* March 28, 1992, 4.

"START II Resolution on Ratification." *Arms Control Today,* May 2000.

Steele, Jonathan. "The Bear's Necessities." *The Guardian,* January 4, 1993, 19.

Stein, Janice Gross. "Political Learning by Doing: Gorbachev as Uncommitted Thinker and Motivated Learner." *International Organization* 48, no. 2 (1994): 155–83.

Stepanov, Georgii, and Maksim Iusin. "Pragmatizm v Monopolarnom Mire." *Izvestiia,* July 11, 2000, 2.

Stets, Jan E., and Peter J. Burke. "Identity Theory and Social Identity Theory." *Social Psychology Quarterly* 63 (2000): 224–37.

Stets, Jan E., and Michael M. Harrod. "Verification across Multiple Identities: The Role of Status." *Social Psychology Quarterly* 67, no. 2 (2004): 155–71.

Stryker, Sheldon. "Developments in 'Two Social Psychologies': Toward an Appreciation of Mutual Relevance." *Sociometry* 40, no. 2 (1977): 145–60.

———. "Identity Salience and Role Performance: The Relevance of Symbolic Interaction Theory for Family Research." *Journal of Marriage and the Family* 30, no. 4 (1968): 558–64.

———. *Symbolic Interactionism: A Social Structural Version*. Menlo Park, CA: Benjamin/Cummings, 1980.

Stryker, Sheldon, and Peter J. Burke. "The Past, Present, and Future of an Identity Theory." *Social Psychology Quarterly* 63, no. 4 (2000): 284–97.

Swidler, Ann. "Culture in Action: Symbols and Strategies." *American Sociological Review* 51, no. 2 (1986): 273–86.

Tajfel, Henri. *Differentiation between Social Groups: Studies in the Social Psychology of Intergroup Relations*. New York: Academic Press, 1978.

Tajfel, Henri, ed. *Social Identity and Intergroup Relations*. Cambridge: Cambridge University Press, 1982.

Tajfel, Henri, and John Turner. "An Integrative Theory of Intergroup Conflict." In *The Social Psychology of Intergroup Relations*, edited by W. G. Austin and S. Worchel, 33–47. Monterey, CA: Brooks/Cole, 1979.

———. "An Integrative Theory of Intergroup Conflict." In *Organizational Identity*, edited by Mary Jo Hatch and Majken Schultz, 56–65. Oxford: Oxford University Press, 2004.

Tajfel, Henri, and John C. Turner. "The Social Identity Theory of Intergroup Behavior." In *Psychology of Intergroup Relations*, edited by S. Worchel and W. G. Austin, 7–24. Chicago: Nelson-Hall, 1986.

Tarasov, Stanislav. "Lovushki Globalizatsii." *Obshchaia gazeta*, March 8–14, 2001, 1, 4.

Telen, Liudmila. "Controversy at Congress." *Moscow News*, April 12, 1992.

Thelen, Kathleen. *How Institutions Evolve: The Political Economy of Skills in Germany, Britain, the United States, and Japan*. Cambridge: Cambridge University Press, 2004.

Tishkov, Valery. *Ethnicity, Nationalism, and Conflict in and after the Soviet Union: The Mind Aflame*. London: Sage Publications, 1997.

Titscher, Stephan, Michael Meyer, Ruth Wodak, and Eva Vetter. *Methods of Text and Discourse Analysis*. Thousand Oaks, CA: SAGE Publications, 2000.

Tolz, Vera. "Forging the Nation: National Identity and Nation Building in Post-Communist Russia." *Europe-Asia Studies* 50, no. 6 (1998): 993–1022.

———. "Russia: Westernizers Continue to Challenge National Patriots." *RFE/RL Research Report*, December 11, 1991, 1–9.

Tolz, Vera, and Elizabeth Teague. "Russian Intellectuals Adjust to the Loss of Empire." *RFE/RL Research Report* 1, no. 8 (1992).

Tompson, William. "The Russian Economy under Vladimir Putin." In *Russian Politics under Putin*, edited by Cameron Ross, 114–32. Manchester: Manchester University Press, 2004.

Torbakov, Igor. "The 'Statists' and the Ideology of Russian Imperial Nationalism." *RFE/RL Research Report,* December 11, 1992, 10–16.

"A Transformed Russia in a New World." *International Affairs* (Moscow), no. 4–5 (1992): 81–104.

Treisman, Daniel. "Blaming Russia First." *Foreign Affairs* (November–December 2000).

———. "Russia Renewed?" *Foreign Affairs* 81, no. 6 (November–December 2002): 58–72.

Trenin, Dmitri. "'Novyi Kurs' Putina: Povorot Zakreplen. Shto Dal'she?" *Carnegie Endowment for International Peace Moscow Center Briefing Center* 4, no. 6 (2002): 1–6.

———. "Reading Russia Right." *Carnegie Endowment for International Peace Policy Brief,* no. 42 (2005): 1–12.

———. "Russia and Anti-Terrorism." In *What Russia Sees,* edited by Dov Lynch, 99–114. Paris: European Union Institute for Security Studies, 2005.

———. "Russian Foreign Policy after Ukraine." Paper presented at Stanford University, Palo Alto, California, February 17, 2005.

———. "Russia's Nuclear Policy in the 21st Century Environment." *Proliferation Papers* (Autumn 2005): 5–28.

———. *Russia's Security Relations with the West after Kosovo and Chechnya, Les Notes de Ifri No. 19 Sèrie Transatlantique.* Paris: Institut français des relations internationales, 2000.

———. "Traditionalism Makes a Comeback." *Russia Profile* (2004).

———. "What You See Is What You Get." *The World Today,* April 2004, 13–16.

Trenin, Dmitri, and Bobo Lo. *The Landscape of Russian Foreign Policy Decision-Making.* Washington, D.C., and Moscow: Carnegie Endowment for International Peace, 2005.

Trenin, Dmitrii. "Rossiia i Amerika: Vremia ne Ochen' Vysokie Ozhidane." *Mirovaia Ekonomika i Mezhdunarodnaia Otnosheniia,* no. 1 (1999): 53–57.

———. "Rossiia i Novaia Evropeiskaia Sistema." *Rubezhi* 1, no. 16 (1997): 109–21.

———. "Russia's French Accent." *Moscow Times,* March 13, 1998.

Trofimenko, Genrikh. "What Military Doctrine Do We Need?" *International Affairs* (Moscow), no. 3 (1991): 70–78.

Tsygankov, Andrei P. "Finding a Civilizational Idea: 'West,' 'Eurasia,' and 'Euro-East' in Russia's Foreign Policy." *Geopolitics* 12 (2005): 375–99.

———. *Pathways after Empire: National Identity and Foreign Economic Policy in the Post-Soviet World.* Lanham, MD: Rowman and Littlefield, 2001.

———. *Russia's Foreign Policy: Change and Continuity in National Identity.* Lanham, MD: Rowman and Littlefield, 2006.

———. "Vladimir Putin's Vision of Russia as a Normal Great Power." *Post-Soviet Affairs* 21, no. 2 (2005): 132–58.

———. *Whose World Order: Russia's Perception of American Ideas after the Cold War.* Notre Dame, IN: University of Notre Dame, 2004.

Turner, John C. "Henri Tajfel: An Introduction." In *Social Groups and Identities: Developing the Legacy of Henri Tajfel,* edited by William P. Robinson. Oxford: Butterworth Heinemann, 1996.

———. "Social Comparison and Social Identity: Some Prospects for Intergroup Behavior." *European Journal of Social Psychology* 5 (1975): 5–34.

Turner, John C., Penelope J. Oakes, S. Alexander Haslam, and Craig McGarty. "Self and Collective: Cognition and Social Context." *Personality and Social Psychology Bulletin* 20, no. 5 (1994): 454–63.

Turner, Ralph H. "Role Change." *Annual Review of Sociology* 16 (1990): 87–110.

———. "The Self in Social Interaction." In *The Self in Social Interaction,* edited by Chad Gordon and Kenneth Gergen, 93–106. New York: Wiley, 1968.

Tversky, Amos. "Features of Similarity." *Psychological Review* 84, no. 4 (1977): 327–52.

Tversky, Amos, and Daniel Kahneman. "The Framing of Decisions and the Psychology of Choice." *Science* 211, no. 4481 (1981): 453–58.

———. "Judgment under Uncertainty: Heuristics and Biases." *Science* 185, no. 4157 (1974): 1124–31.

———. "Loss Aversion in Riskless Choice: A Reference-Dependent Model." *Quarterly Journal of Economics* 106, no. 4 (1991): 1039–61.

Tyler, Tom R., and Steven L. Blader. "Autonomous vs. Comparative Status: Must We Be Better Than Others to Feel Good About Ourselves?" *Organizational Behavior and Human Decision Processes* 89, no. 1 (2002): 813–38.

Urban, Michael. "Remythologising the Russian State." *Europe-Asia Studies* 50, no. 6 (1998): 969–92.

Urusov, Mikhail. "How Does the American Missile Shield Threaten Russia?" *Literaturnaia Gazeta,* March 21–27, 2001, 8.

Van Knippenberg, Ad. "Strategies of Identity Management." In *Ethnic Minorities: Social-Psychological Perspectives,* edited by Jan Pieter van Oudenhoven and Tineke M. Willemsen, 59–76. Amsterdam: Sets and Zeitlinger, 1989.

Vasil'ev, Aleksei. "Rossiia i Musul'mansky Mir—Partnery ili Protivniki?" *Izvestiia,* March 19, 1992.

Veenstra, Kristopher, and S. Alexander Haslam. "Willingness to Participate in Industrial Protest: Exploring Social Identification in Context." *British Journal of Social Psychology* 39, no. 2 (2000): 153–72.

Velekhov, Leonid. "Russian Defense Minister Promises 'Appropriate Measures' in Response to NATO Expansion." *Segodnia,* November 16, 1995, 2.

"Vladimir Putin: RF Zainteresovana v Ratifikatsii Dogovora o Sokrashchenii SNP." Strana.ru, April 25, 2003.

Vox Populi. "USIA Survey no. I93060: NATO." Moscow: United States Information Agency, 1993.

Vserossiiskii tsentr izucheniia obshchestvennogo mneniia (VTsIOM). "Analiz Rezultatov Oprosov. Eksperty o Kharaktere Peremen v Rossii." *Ekonomicheskie i Sotsial'nye Peremeny: Monitoring Obshchestvennogo Mneniia* 2 (May 1993): 11–18.

———. *Vneshniaia Politika Rossii—1993: Analiz Politikov i Ekspertov. Sotsiologicheskoe Issledovanie Vzgliadov i Predstavlenii po Problemam Vneshnei Politiki Uchastnikov Vneshnepoliticheskogo Protsessa v Rossii, Iiun 1993 g.* Moscow: VTsIOM and SINUS Moscow, with funding from the Friedrich Ebert Stiftung, 1993.

———. "Vneshnopoliticheskaia Elita i Vneshniaia Politika." *Ekonomicheskie i Sotsial'nye Peremeny: Monitoring Obshchestvennogo Mneniia* 1 (January 1994): 31–34.

Vujacic, Veljko. "Serving Mother Russia: The Communist Left and Nationalist Right in the Struggle for Power, 1991–1998." In *Russia in the New Century,* edited by Victoria E. Bonnell and George W. Breslauer, 290–325. Boulder, CO: Westview Press, 2001.

Vyzhutovich, Valerii. "Liberal Jitters." *Moscow News,* July 16, 1992.

Wallander, Celeste, ed. *The Sources of Russian Foreign Policy after the Cold War.* Boulder, CO: Westview Press, 1996.

Walt, Stephen M. "Alliance Formation and the Balance of World Power." *International Security* 9, no. 4 (Spring 1985): 3–43.

"We and the World: Russia's Foreign Policy: Three Views." *Moskovskie Novosti,* January 3, 1993, 13.

Weber, Max. *Economy and Society.* Translated by E. Frischoff. Edited by Guenther Roth and Claus Wittrich. 1918; repr. New York: Bedminster, 1968.

———. "The Profession and Vocation of Politics." In *Weber: Political Writings,* edited by Peter Lassman and Ronald Speirs, 309–69. Cambridge: Cambridge University Press, 1994.

———. "The Social Psychology of the World's Religions." In *From Max Weber: Essays in Sociology,* edited by H. H. Herth and C. Wright Mills. New York: Oxford University Press, 1958.

Wendt, Alexander. "Anarchy Is What States Make of It." *International Organization* 46, no. 2 (1992): 391–425.

———. "Collective Identity Formation and the International State." *American Political Science Review* 88 (1994): 384–96.

———. *Social Theory of International Politics.* Cambridge: Cambridge University Press, 1999.

"What Foreign Policy Should Russia Pursue. A Forum." *International Affairs* (Moscow), no. 2 (1993): 3–21.

Wohlforth, William C. "Realism and the End of the Cold War." *International Security* 19, no. 3 (1994/95): 91–129.

Woodruff, David. "The End of 'Primitive Capitalist Accumulation'? The New Bankruptcy Law and the Political Assertiveness of Russian Big Business." *PONARS Policy Memo,* no. 274 (2002).

———. "Pension Reform in Russia: From the Politics of Implementation to the Politics of Law-Making." *PONARS Policy Memo,* no. 234 (2001).

Woolf, Amy F. "Nuclear Arms Control: The Strategic Offensive Reductions Treaty." Washington, D.C.: Congressional Research Service, Library of Congress, 2006.

Yasmann, Victor. "Analysis: The Kremlin after Beslan." *RFE/RL,* September 9, 2004.

———. "Kremlin Articulates Its Ideological Platform." *RFE/RL Political Weekly,* October 13, 2004.

———. "Moscow Looks at the World." *RFE/RL Political Weekly,* December 16, 2004.

Yavlinskii, Grigorii. *Uroki Ekonomicheskoi Reformy.* Moscow: Epicenter, 1993.

Yazkova, Alla Alekseyevna. "Where Will the New 'Security Line' in Europe Run?" *Mirovaia Ekonomika i Mezhdunarodnaia Otnosheniia,* no. 4 (1995): 102–10.

" 'Za' i 'Protiv' Razoruzheniia. Kto Seichas Ugrozhaet Rossii." *Argumenty i fakty* 1997, 5.

Zagorski, Andrei. "Russia and European Institutions." In *Russia and Europe. The Emerging Security Agenda,* edited by Vladimir Baranovsky, 519–40. London: Oxford University Press for SIPRI, 1997.

———. "Russia and the Shared Neighbourhood." In *What Russia Sees,* edited by Dov Lynch, 61–78. Paris: European Union Institute for Security Studies, 2005.

Zagorskii, Andrei. "Rossiia i Evropa." *Mezhdunarodnaia Zhizn'* (Moscow), 1993, no. 1 (1993).

———. "Rossiia i Rasshirenie NATO—Endshpil'." *Pro et Contra* 1, no. 1 (1996): 78–89.

———. "Russia and Europe." *International Affairs* (Moscow), no. 1 (1993): 43–51.

Zagorskii, Andrei V., Anatolii A. Zlobin, Sergei Solodovnik, and Mark A. Khroustlev. *After the Disintegration of the Soviet Union: Russia in a New*

World, Report of the Center for International Studies, Moscow State Institute of International Affairs, February 1992. Moscow: Center of International Studies, Moscow State Institute of International Studies (MGIMO), 1992.

———. Vice Rector of MGIMO. Interview by Anne Clunan. February 12, 1998.

Zelditch, Morris, Jr. "Theories of Legitimacy." In *The Psychology of Legitimacy: Emerging Perspectives on Ideology, Justice, and Intergroup Relations,* edited by John T. Jost and Brenda Major, 33–53. Cambridge: Cambridge University Press, 2001.

Zevelev, Viktor. "The Redefinition of the Russian Nation, International Security, and Stability." In *Russia in the New Century, Stability or Disorder?* edited by Victoria E. Bonnell and George W. Breslauer, 265–89. Boulder, CO: Westview Press, 2001.

Zhirinovskii, Vladimir. *Vladimir Zhirinovsky Speaks with Russia.* Moscow: Izdatel'sko-informatsionnoe agentsvo "Rait," 1997.

———. Interview by Anne Clunan. June 19, 1997.

Zimmerman, William. *The Russian People and Foreign Policy.* Princeton: Princeton University Press, 2002.

———. "Slavophiles and Westernizers Redux: Contemporary Russian Elite Perspectives." *Post-Soviet Affairs* 21, no. 3 (2005): 183–209.

———. "Survey Research and Russian Perspectives on NATO Expansion." *Post-Soviet Affairs* 17, no. 3 (2001): 235–61.

Ziuganov, Gennadii. "What to Expect from the Moscow Meeting of the Group of Seven Countries: About a 'Special Danger.'" *Sovetskaia Rossiia,* April 18, 1996, 3.

Index

Pages in *italics* indicate figures and tables.